VICTORIAN BIOGRAPHY

A Checklist of
Contemporary Biographies of
British Men & Women
Dying between 1851 and 1901

Compiled by Peter Bell

With an Introduction by
Professor Colin Matthew
St Hugh's College, Oxford
Editor, The New Dictionary of National Biography

Edinburgh - Peter Bell (Bookseller) - 1993

VICTORIAN BIOGRAPHY

A Checklist of
Contemporary Biographies of
British Men & Women
Dying between 1851 and 1901

Compiled by Peter Bell

With an Introduction by
Professor Colin Matthew
St Hugh's College, Oxford
Editor, The New Dictionary of National Biography

Edinburgh - Peter Bell (Bookseller) - 1993

Copyright Peter Bell, 4, Brandon Street, Edinburgh EH3 5DX, Scotland
First impression February 1993
Fifth impression November 1996

ISBN 1 871538 11 4

ERRATA

Page 15. *Under* BOURNE, Hugh *delete* the first entry, which relates to a
   James Bourne
Page 30. *Under* CLARENCE & AVONDALE *read* ... Prince Edward: a memory
Page 60. *Delete* GRANT, William
Page 106. *For* NASMYTH, John *read* NASMYTH, James
Page 162. *For* AYR, Agnes Templeton *read* TEMPLETON, Agnes

Printed by DUPLIQUICK, 28A Great King Street, Edinburgh EH3 6QH

INTRODUCTION

Professor H.C.G. MATTHEW

The second half of the 19th century marked the start of extensive biographical research in Britain in two ways. First, through the availability of accurate information about contemporaries. Guides which had started before 1850 such as *Who's Who* and *Dod's Parliamentary Companion* became fuller and more accurate.

These, with Debrett and other such annual guides, and the annual publication of full guides to the holders of governmental and military positions, meant that details about the national elite became easily available. Kelly's series of Post Office directories offered a national coverage of information in a standard form for addresses and occupations where previously such information had been provided in certain cases by local directories such as Gore for Liverpool (one of the few which survived Kelly's national challenge), but mostly not at all or in a very haphazard format.

Second, biographical information about the British past accompanied the Victorians' greater knowledge about themselves. Genealogical dictionaries such as those of Burke and Lodge linked the present and past histories of the landed class. Given the enthusiasm with which the British business class bought land or married into it, most propertied families were included by 1914 in Burke's *Peerage* or *Gentry* either directly or as collaterals. Particular types of family were dealt with in works such as Gillow's *Biographical Dictionary of English Catholics*.

Allied to this collection of contemporary and historical fact came depth of research linked to opinion and assessment in Leslie Stephen's *Dictionary of National Biography*, of which the first volume appeared in 1885. This included a generous number of those who died in the 19th century (about 12,000 of the 37,000 entries in the first *DNB* died in that century). An interesting half-way house between the DNB and *Who's Who* was Boase's *Modern English Biography*, an incomparable guide to the lives of those who died between 1850 and 1900, and the only British biographical dictionary to have a useful analytical index.

This gathering of contemporary and historical biographical detail was accompanied by a considerable expansion of the writing of biographies. This especially British medium was not of course new in the 19th century. But the expectation of publishers that they could sell adequate numbers of copies of biographies of a myriad of minor figures was new, as was the readiness of authors to write on such persons, and families to make materials available for them. Some of these lives reflect the desire to portray significant figures within particular groups in British society - especially among religious denominations - and many were exemplary lives designed to encourage qualities such as moral probity and entrepreneurial innovation (e.g. the many biographies by Samuel Smiles and his series *The Lives of the Engineers*). But many were less obviously didactic and reflected the Victorian enthusiasm for personality and their rather unquestioning assumption of the importance of individuality and individual action. Victorian liberalism presupposed the capacity of the individual to shape his or her own destiny within the confines of the liberal society permitted by the British constitution, and most of these biographies were accounts of public life at various levels, national or local. The emphasis on the public was accompanied by a corresponding reticence about private foibles: few biographies recorded private torments of the sort revealed in Liddon's *Life of Pusey* (1882-), a book ironically much more revealing than Lytton Strachey's expose of *Eminent Victorians* published at the end of the First World War, the book which blew out of the water the decorum of the Victorian 'Life and Letters' approach.

Late-Victorian biographical research is a complex business and its bibliography is not a simple matter, even for those with access to a copyright library. Peter Bell's extensive work in tracking down and listing British biographies facilitates such research and this latest assemblage of biographical work for the years 1851 - 1901 (the period of Boase's *Modern English Biography*) is warmly to be welcomed.

H.C.G. Matthew

PREFACE

Here is attempted, for the first time, a listing of what H. J. Hanham has called those 'memoirs of the great and the far from great, the innumerable biographies ..., [the] more or less worthless hagiographies ...' of British men and women dying between 1851 and 1901. These are the so-called 'tombstones' which seem to be such a stumbling block to those interested in researching individuals living in the Victorian period.

What comprises a 'biography' is extremely difficult to define, but the intention here has been to complement the work already done by William Matthews for British autobiographies (1), and by John Burnett for working class autobiographies (2); and by Matthews again for printed diaries and correspondence. (3) In other words most autobiographies and diaries including letters, journals and correspondence) are excluded here. Also excluded are funeral sermons (which would constitute a separate bibliography and which on examination rarely contain biographical material), and memoirs prefixing a volume of sermons, verse, plays, novels or essays - another huge category. The idea throughout has been to examine wherever possible all titles, and to include only material which, however minor, will be of some real use to Nineteenth Century scholars.

Only people dying between the year of the Great Exhibition (1851) and the death of Queen Victoria (1901) are included, as this does include the majority of people commonly accepted as being 'Victorian'. The dates also follow those of Frederic Boase, whose magisterial *Modern English Biography* (4) formed one of the main sources for this work; as well being the opening date of H. J. Hanham's definitive *Bibliography* (5), and the terminal date of the main *DNB*. The only people thus excluded would be people already famous before 1851 and dying after 1901, such as Florence Nightingale (1820-1910), or Field-Marshal the Duke of Cambridge (1819-1904).

Most biographies seem to have been published within a short period of the subject's death, so that only books published within these years are considered contemporary.

The 'British' subjects included were English, Scots, Welsh and Irish men and women, together with a limited number of naturalised Britons (Sir Anthony Panizzi or Sir Edward Mallet for example). As the bulk of the work was done in Edinburgh, the Scots are probably more thoroughly treated than might otherwise have been the case; although I feel that the Welsh and Irish could have been better served. British people overseas have been restricted to those with an imperial (especially Indian) or missionary role. People emigrating are usually excluded, as are all biographies (with one or two Indian exceptions) published overseas.

The women's entries are separated because they are loosely based on my existing bibliography *Victorian women: an index to biographies and memoirs* (6), which also included modern titles. A comparison of these two works will show that, when modern books are excluded, the number of contemporary biographies of Victorian women falls dramatically and is restricted almost entirely to religious women.

Photographic illustrations (especially portraits) have been noted where seen or known, because this was originally done in the seven Catalogues of second-hand books which formed the initial inspiration for this bibliography. (7)

Sizes of books are approximate rather than bibliographically precise. A pamphlet implies a slight item, although not all such have necessarily been noted. The abbreviations after a title (where given) indicates the place in which the title has been checked, although in the case of references noted as being in the British Library Catalogue or National Union Catalogue, this has only been done via the printed Catalogues.

An attempt has been made to exclude any obviously juvenile items, together with any which would not warrant an extensive search on the part of the researcher, as well as a rather larger category of titles for which a reference, but no location, is known.

Any corrections or omissions would be gratefully acknowledged with a view to incorporating them into any future revision.

Peter Bell. Edinburgh, 1993

(1) William Matthews. *British autobiographies: a bibliography* ... (1955): Archon Books, 1968. Matthews' definition of an autobiography is often very broad indeed so that some of his titles are excluded here.
(2) John Burnett and others, editors. *The autobiography of the working class: an annotated critical bibliography*. Volume 1: 1790-1900. Brighton: Harvester Press, 1987.
(3) William Matthews. *British diaries: an annotated bibliography of British diaries written between 1442 and 1942*. University of California Press, 1950. Again Matthews' definition of a diary is very broad indeed so that some of the titles he includes are excluded here.
(4) Frederic Boase. *Modern English biography*. Truro, 1892-1921. 6 vols: reprinted: London: Cass, 1965. 6 vols.
(5) H. J. Hanham. *Bibliography of British history, 1851-1914*. Oxford U.P., 1976.
(6) Peter Bell. *Victorian women: an index to biographies and memoirs*. Edinburgh: The author, 1989. (Out-of-print)
(7) Peter Bell & C.R. Johnson, *booksellers. British biography, 1800-1920*. 1980-85. 3 Catalogues + 4 Supplements. (No longer available)

ABBREVIATIONS

b.	born
(B&J)	Bell & Johnson. (Reference 7, above)
(BL)	British Library Catalogue
c.	*circa*
d.	died
(NC)	New College Library, University of Edinburgh
(NLS)	National Library of Scotland
(NUC)	National Union Catalogue
photo.port.	Photographic portrait
(WCA)	Working class autobiographies. (Reference 2, above)

Whenever the word 'clergyman' is used this denotes a member of the Church of England.

PART 1

BIOGRAPHIES OF VICTORIAN MEN

A'BECKETT, Gilbert Abbott, 1811-56, police magistrate and comic writer on 'Punch'
The A'Becketts of 'Punch': memories of father [Gilbert Abbott] and sons [Arthur William & Gilbert Arthur] / by Arthur William A'Beckett. Westminster: A. Constable, 1903.

A'BECKETT, Gilbert Arthur, 1837-91 <u>see</u> **A'BECKETT, Gilbert Abbott**

ABERDEEN, George Hamilton Gordon, <u>4th Earl of</u>, 1784-1860, Prime Minister
The Earl of Aberdeen / by Arthur Gordon. London: Sampson Low, Marston, 1893. (The Prime Ministers of Queen Victoria series)

ABERDEEN, George John James Hamilton-Gordon, <u>5th Earl of</u>, 1816-64 <u>see</u> **HADDO, Lord**

ABERNETHY, James, 1814-96, civil & dock engineer
The life and work of James Abernethy, C.E., F.R.S.E., Past President of the Institution of Civil Engineers / by his son James Scott Abernethy. London: T. Brettell, 1897.

ABINGTON, Leonard James, 1785-1857, editor of the 'Pottery Mercury'; Baptist
Personal recollections of the late Leonard James Abington, of Hanley, Staffordshire. With memoir and extracts from his correspondence ... Hanley: Albutt & Daniel, 1868. photo.port.(B&J)

ACLAND, <u>Sir</u> Henry Wentworth, <u>1st Bart</u>. 1815-1900, Oxford medical professor
Sir Henry Wentworth Acland, Bart., K.C.B., F.R.S., Regius Professor of Medicine in the University of Oxford: a memoir / by James Beresford Atley. London: Smith, Elder, 1903. (NC)

ACLAND, <u>Sir</u> Thomas Dyke, <u>10th Bart</u>., 1787-1871, 'head of the religious party in the House of Commons'
Some few personal recollections of Sir Thomas Dyke Acland. [By John Taylor Coleridge]. Printed for private circulation. Exeter: printed by Townsend, [1872]. 12mo.

ACLAND, <u>Sir</u> Thomas Dyke, <u>11th Bart</u>., 1809-98, M.P.; educational reformer
Memoir and letters of the Right Hon. Sir Thomas Dyke Acland. Edited by his son Arthur Herbert Dyke Acland. Printed for private circulation. London, 1902.

ADAMS, Thomas, 1807-73, religious Nottingham lace manufacturer
Religion and business: memorials of Thomas Adams, J.P., of Nottingham, lace manufacturer / by William Milton. London: Hamilton Adams, 1874. (NUC)

ADAMSON, John, 1787-1855, Newcastle solicitor & antiquarian; Portugese scholar
Obituary notice of the late John Adamson, Esq., [etc.]. Newcastle-upon-Tyne: printed by Thomas & James Pigg, 1856. Pamphlet. (Reprinted from the 'Gentleman's Magazine')

ADENEY, William, n.d, religious biography
Wearing not rusting, or labour for God: a memoir of Mr William Adeney ... / by [his son] W. Adeney. London: W.H. Dalton, 1860. (BL)

AIKMAN, John Logan, 1820-85, United Presbyterian Minister
In memoriam: J. Logan Aikman, D.D., United Presbyterian Church, Anderston, Glasgow. Edinburgh: A. Elliot, 1885.

AINSWORTH, William Harrison, 1805-82, publisher, magazine proprietor; 'the novelist of Manchester'
William Harrison Ainsworth and his friends / by Stewart Marsh Ellis. London: Bodley Head, 1910. 2 volumes.

AIRD, Gustavus 1813-98, Free Church Minister
   The life of Gustavus Aird, A.M., D.D., Creich, Moderator of the Free Church of Scotland 1888 / by Alexander MacRae. Stirling: Eneas Mackay, [1908].

AIRLIE, David Stanley William Drummond Ogilvy, <u>9th Earl of</u>, 1856-1900, soldier killed in Boer War
   The happy warrior: a short account of the life of David, 9th Earl of Airlie. Printed for private circulation. Winchester: printed by Jacob & Johnson, 1901. (B&J)

AITKEN, James, 1831-80, Church of Scotland Minister
   Memoir and remains of the Rev. James Aitken, Minister of St Luke's Church, Glasgow. [By R. S. Hutton]. Glasgow: Thomas Murray, 1867. photo. port. (NC)

ALBANY, <u>Prince</u> Leopold George Duncan Albert, <u>Duke of</u> <u>see</u> LEOPOLD, <u>Prince</u>

ALBERT (FRANCIS CHARLES AUGUSTUS EMMANUEL), Prince Consort, 1819-61
   The early years of H.R.H. the Prince Consort / compiled under the direction of ... the Queen by Charles Grey. London: Smith, Elder, 1867.
-------.   The life of H.R.H. the Prince Consort / by Theodore Martin. London: Smith, Elder, 1875-80. 5 volumes; Peoples' Edition. 1882. small folio.
   and very many other funeral sermons and popular titles

ALBERT VICTOR CHRISTIAN EDWARD, <u>Prince</u> <u>see</u> CLARENCE, <u>Duke of</u>

ALBRIGHT, Arthur, 1811-1900, Quaker chemical manufacturer in Birmingham
   Arthur Albright. Born March 12 1811 - Died July 3 1900. Notes of his life. Printed for private circulation. Birmingham: printed at the Guild Press, 1901. Pamphlet.

ALCOCK, John, 1804-86, Irish clergyman
   Walking with God: a memoir of the Venerable John Alcock, late Archdeacon of Waterford / by his daughter [Deborah A. Alcock]. London: Hodder & Stoughton, 1887. photo.port.

ALDIS, <u>Sir</u> Charles, 1776-1863, surgeon
   Biographical memoir of Sir Charles Aldis and Dr [Charles James Berridge] Aldis ... / by Charles Aldis. For private circulation. London, 1852. (BL)

ALDIS, Charles James Berridge, 1808-1872, physician <u>see</u> **ALDIS, <u>Sir</u> Charles**

ALEXANDER, William, 1763-1855, Independent Minister
   Memoirs of the Rev. William Alexander / by his son John Alexander. Norwich: Fletcher & Alexander, 1856.

ALEXANDER, William Henry, 1799-1864, Quaker
   Memorials of William H. Alexander and Sophia Alexander, of Ipswich. London: F. B. Kitto, 1867. (BL)

ALEXANDER, William Lindsay, 1808-84, Scottish Congregational Minister in Liverpool
   Dr Lindsay Alexander / by Elizabeth T. M'Laren. London: Hodder & Stoughton, [1911]. (Little Books on Religion series)
-------.   W. Lindsay Alexander, D.D., LL.D.: his life and work. [By James Ross]. London: J. Nisbet, 1887.

ALFORD, Henry, 1810-71, Dean of Canterbury; editor of the 'Contemporary Review'
   Life, journals and letters of Henry Alford, D.D., late Dean of Canterbury. Edited by his widow [Frances Alford]. London: Rivingtons, 1873. (NC)

ALLAN, Bryce, d.1874, shipowner
   In memoriam: the late Mr Bryce Allan / by Robert Henry Lundie. London: J. Nisbet,

ALLAN, Robert, 1806-63, geologist
A biographical notice of the late Robert Allan, Esq.. With extracts from his journal / by William C. Henry. [London: printed by W. Clowes, 1864]. (NC)

ALLAN, William, d.1893, Scottish designer
In memoriam: William Allan, designer, died twenty-first January 1893. For private circulation among his fellow workers. [1893]. Pamphlet. (B&J)

ALLEN, (Charles) Grant Blairfindie, 1848-99, Scottish-Canadian novelist; popular scientific writer
Grant Allen: a memoir / by Edward Clodd. London: Grant Richard, 1900.

ALLEN, Frederic, 1827-79, Quaker then Swedenborgian; worked for fire and life insurance offices
A short memoir of Frederic Allen. With extracts from his letters. Edited by his sister Charlotte Sturge. For private circulation. Bristol: J. W. Arrowsmith, 1887. (NLS)

ALLEN, John, 1810-86, Archdeacon of Salop, with extensive literary friendships; school inspector
John Allen, Vicar of Prees and Archdeacon of Salop: a memoir/ by his son-in-law Richard Macgregor Grier. London: Rivingtons, 1889.

ALLEN, John, b.1839, Leeds tractarian youth
A little history of John Allen, of Saviour's, Leeds. Leeds: Harrison, [1858]. photo.port. (NLS)

ALLEN, Richard, 1803-86, Irish Quaker; temperance worker; philanthropist
A Christian philanthropist of Dublin: a memoir of Richard Allen / by Hannah Maria Wigham. London: Hodder & Stoughton, 1886. photo.port. (NC)

ALLIN, Thomas, 1784-1866, Minister in the Methodist New Connection
Memoir of the Rev. Thomas Allin ... / by Samuel Hulme. London: Hamilton, Adams, 1881. (NLS)

ALLON, Henry, 1818-92, Congregational leader; editor of 'British Quarterly Review'
Henry Allon, D.D., pastor and teacher: the story of his ministry. With selected sermons and addresses / by William Hardy Harwood. London: Cassell, 1894.

AMHERST, Francis Kerrill, 1819-83, Roman Catholic Bishop of Northampton
Memoirs of Francis Kerrill Amherst, D.D., Lord Bishop of Northampton / by Mary Francis Roskell. Edited by Henry Francis John Vaughan. Leamington: Art & Book Company, 1903. (BL)

ANDERSON, Alexander, 1822-55, young Free Church Minister
Life in the Spirit: a memorial of the Rev. Alexander Anderson, M.A. / by Norman Lockhart Walker ... London: J. Nisbet, 1859. (NC)

ANDERSON, Christopher, 1782-1852, Baptist missionary to the Gaelic-speaking areas of Scotland
The life and letters of Christopher Anderson, author of 'Annals of the English Bible' [etc.] / by his nephew Hugh Anderson. Edinburgh: W. P. Kennedy [etc.], 1854. (NC)

ANDERSON, David William, 1845-73, Scottish Free Presbyterian Minister
Memorials of the Rev. David William Anderson, D.D., of Free St John's Church, Haddington. Edited by John Chalmers. Edinburgh: Maclaren & Macniven, 1873. photo.port.

ANDERSON, George, 1804-78 <u>see</u> **ANDERSON, Peter**

ANDERSON, James, 1840-94, Scottish Presbyterian missionary in China
A missionary Minister: memorials of the Rev. James Anderson, Minister of the Old Kirk Parish, Edinburgh. With a selection from his sermons.[Edited by] Archibald Scott ... Edinburgh: R. & R. Clark, 1895. (NC)

ANDERSON, John, 1805-55, Free Church missionary in India
The late Rev. John Anderson of the Free Church Mission, Madras. [A collection of obituary notices. Edited by John Braidwood]. Edinburgh: Johnstone & Hunter, 1855. (NLS)
-------. True yoke-fellows in the mission field: the life and labours of the Rev. John Anderson and the Rev. Robert Johnston, traced in the rise and development of the Madras Free Church Mission / by John Braidwood. London: J. Nisbet, 1862. photographic portraits & illustrations. (NLS)

ANDERSON, Peter, 1804-68, Scottish lawyer; antiquarian writer
An Inverness lawyer [Peter Anderson] and his sons [John, George and Peter Anderson], 1796-1878 / by Isabel Harriet Anderson. Aberdeen University Press, 1900. (NLS)

ANDERSON, William, 1799-1873, United Presbyterian Minister; 'political preacher'
Life of the Rev. William Anderson, LL.D., Glasgow / by George Gilfillan. London: Hodder & Stoughton, 1873. (NC)

ANDERSON, William, 1812-95, United Prebyterian Missionary in West Indies
William & Louisa Anderson: a record of their life and work in Jamaica and Old Calabar / by William Marwick. Edinburgh: A. Elliot, 1897. (NC)

ANNAN, Robert, 1834-67, Scottish life-saver; wood merchant; home missionary
The Christian hero: a sketch of the life of Robert Annan / by John Macpherson. London: Morgan & Chase, 1867. 12mo.

APPELBEE, Robert, 1807-94, Nottingham worthy & Swedenborgian
Robert Appelbee / by Thomas Cochrane Lowe. London: James Speirs, 1895. Pamphlet.(Reprinted from the 'New Church Magazine'). (NLS)

APPLETON, Charles Edward Cutts Birchall, 1841-79, founder of the 'Academy'; man of letters; Fellow of St John's College, Oxford
Dr Appleton: his life and literary relics / by John Hoblyn Appleton & Archibald Henry Sayce. London: Trubner, 1881.

ARCHER, Thomas, 1806-64, Scottish Minister in London
Memoir of Thomas Archer, D.D., Minister of Oxendon Chapel, London / by John Macfarlane. London: J. Nisbet, 1867.

ARMSTRONG, Edmund John, 1841-65, Irish poet; translator from the classics
The life and letters of Edmund J. Armstrong. Edited by George Francis Armstrong. London: Longmans, Green, 1877.

ARMSTRONG, George, 1792-1857, clergyman in Ireland & Bristol
A memoir of the late Rev. George Armstrong, formerly Incumbent of Bangor in the Diocese of Down; and latterly ... of ... Bristol. With extracts from his journals and correspondence / by Robert Henderson. London: Edward T. Whitfield, 1859. (NLS)

ARMSTRONG, John, 1813-56, Anglican Bishop in South Africa
A memoir of John Armstrong, D.D., late Lord Bishop of Grahams Town / by Thomas Thellusson Carter ... Oxford: J.H. & J. Parker, 1857.

ASHWORTH, John, 1813-75, Free Methodist pastor; author of 'Strange Tales from humble life' which sold 3 million copies

Life and labours of John Ashworth, author of 'Strange tales', &c. / by Andrew L. Calman. Manchester: Tubbs & Brook, 1875. 12mo.

ASPINALL, Clarke, 1827-91, Liverpool coroner; temperance worker
Clarke Aspinall: a biography / by Walter Lewin. London: E. Arnold, 1893. (95 copies printed) (NLS)
-------. Missed: a brief but loving memorial of the late Clarke Aspinall. By a lay fellow worker. Liverpool, 1892. (B&J)

ATHERTON, Henry, 1811-89, Lancashire New Connection Methodist
The life of Henry Atherton of Lees / by Charles Shaw. London: Methodist New Connection Book Room, [1890]. (NLS)

ATKIN, Frederick, 1820-99, temperance worker
Frederick Atkin (A.B.M.T.A.), lecturer and preacher: a biography / by J. S. Balmer. London: Ideal Publishing Union, 1901.

ATTWOOD, Thomas, 1783-1856, political radical; M.P.; journalist
Life of Thomas Attwood / by C. M. Wakefield. [Privately printed]. London: Harrison, 1885.

AULD, Walter Ross Taylor, 1859-80, religious Highland boy
Memorials of Walter R. T. Auld, Olrig, Caithness, N.B. / by his mother [C.R.] Auld. (1881 - no location): reprinted Inverness, 1967. Pamphlet.

AUSTEN, Charles John, 1779-1852, naval brother of Jane Austen
Jane Austen's sailor brothers, being the adventures of Sir Francis Austen, G.C.B., Admiral of the Fleet, and Rear-Admiral Charles Austen / by John Henry & Edith Charlotte Hubback. London: John Lane, 1906.

AUSTEN, Sir Francis William, 1774-1865 <u>see</u> **AUSTEN, Charles John**

AYTOUN, William Edmondstoune, 1813-65, Scottish poet & academic
Memoir of William Edmondstoune Aytoun, D.C.L., author of 'Lays of the Scottish Cavaliers', etc., etc. / by Theodore Martin. Edinburgh: W. Blackwood, 1867.

BABINGTON, Charles Cardale, 1808-95, Professor of Botany, Cambridge University
Charles Cardale Babington: [an obituary] / by John Eyton Bickersteth Mayor. Private issue. Cambridge, 1895. (Reprinted from the 'Eagle') (NLS)

BACHE, Francis Edward, 1833-58, musician, composer
Brother musicians: reminiscences of Edward and Walter Bache / by Constance Bache. London: Methuen, 1901.

BACHE, Walter, 1842-88, pianist <u>see</u> **BACHE, Francis Edward**

BACKHOUSE, James, 1794-1869, Quaker missionary in Australia & Africa; made tour of penal settlements; botanist
Memoir of James Backhouse / by his sister [Sarah Backhouse]. York: William Sessions, 1870; 2nd edition. 1877.

BACON, Francis Gray, d. c.1892, child
Francis Gray Bacon: recollections of his short life / by J.E.W.. Printed for private circulation. Ardrossan: printed by A. Guthrie, [1892]. 4to. (B&J)

BACON, William, d.1869 aged 53 years, Quaker
    A brief account of the closing days of William Bacon, who died at Maldon, twentieth of 5th Month 1869, aged 53 years. Sudbury: J. Wright, 1869. 32mo. Pamphlet. (B&J)

BAGEHOT, Walter, 1826-77, barrister; journalist; editor of 'The Economist'
    Life of Walter Bagehot / by his sister-in-law Emilie Isabel Barrington. London: Longmans, Green, 1914.
    -------. Walter Bagehot: in memoriam. Printed for private circulation only. London, 1878. photo.port. (B&J)

BAGGE, Philip Salisbury, 1817-90, clergyman in Norfolk
    Philip Salisbury Bagge, M.A., priest, 37 years Rector of Walpole St. Peter, Norfolk: a memoir / by H. E. Beale ... Wisbech: Leach, [1890]. Pamphlet. (NLS)

BAGNALL, John Nock, 1826-84, Birmingham ironmaster; lay deacon
    John Nock Bagnall: a memoir / by his daughter Mary Willett. London: J. Masters, 1885.

BAILLIE, George, d.1873, Glasgow lawyer; benefactor of schools & a library
    Memoir of Mr George Baillie, the founder of Baillie's Institution. By a member of the Faculty of Procurators [i.e. Hugh Barclay]. Glasgow: J. Maclehose, 1873.

BAINBRIDGE, Edwin Armstrong, 1866-86, Wesleyan missionary in Australia & New Zealand
    Edwin Bainbridge: a memoir / by his old schoolfellow Thomas Darlington. London: Morgan & Scott, [1888]. (NLS)

BAINBRIDGE, Emerson Muschamp, 1817-92, Newcastle religious businessman and worthy
    Memoir of Emerson Muschamp Bainbridge, of Newcastle-upon-Tyne. Edited by Thomas Darlington. Privately printed. Edinburgh: printed by R. & R. Clark, 1893. (NLS)

BAIRD, John, 1799-1861, Church of Scotland Minister; work with gypsies
    Memoir of the late Rev. John Baird, Minister of Yetholm, Roxburghshire. With an account of his labours in reforming the gypsy population of that parish / by William Baird. London: J. Nisbet, 1862. (NC)

BAKER, Samuel, 1856-99, Irish Quaker missionary in India
    Samuel Baker, of Hoshangabad: a sketch of Friends' Missions in India / by Caroline W. Pumphrey. London: Headley, 1900. (NC)

BAKER, Sir Samuel (White), 1821-93, African explorer; travel writer; sportsman
    Sir Samuel Baker: a memoir / by Thomas Douglas Murray & Arthur Silva White. London: Macmillan, 1895.

BAKER, Thomas, n.d., Somerset Baptist
    Thomas Baker, the apostle of Boroughbridge, Somerset. [By Samuel Newnam]. Bridgwater: John Whitby, [1890]. (NLS)

BAKER, William, 1787-1853, currier and alderman in Bridgwater
    A brief memoir of the life and character of William Baker ... prepared principally from his diary and correspondence. Edited by John Bowen. Taunton: Frederick May, 1854.

BAKER, William Richard, 1798-1861, Independent Minister; temperance worker
    The life and memorials of the late Rev. W. R. Baker, author ... Edited by his sister Eliza L. Edmunds. London: W. Tweedie, 1865.

BALFE, Michael William, 1808-70, Irish composer & singer
    Balfe, his life and work / by William Alexander Barrett. London: Remington, 1882.

-------. A memoir of Michael William Balfe / by Charles Lamb Kenney. London: Tinsley, 1875. (NLS)

BALFOUR, Alexander, 1824/5-86, Liverpool shipowner & co-founder of Y.M.C.A.
Alexander Balfour: a memoir / by Robert Henry Lundie. 2nd edition. Liverpool: Philips, Son & Nephew, 1889. (BL)

BALFOUR, Andrew Howden, 1818-86, Scottish surgeon
In memoriam: Andrew Howden Balfour, surgeon, Portobello. Born 5th December 1818 - Died 17th November 1886. Printed for private circulation. Edinburgh, 1887. (B&J)

BALFOUR, Ernest Roxburgh, 1874-97, rower & rugby player in Edinburgh & Oxford
Ernest R. Balfour. [By Robert J. Mackenzie]. [Privately printed]. Edinburgh: T. Nelson, [1898]. (NC)

BAMFORD, John, n.d., Methodist
The disciple among the poor: memorials of Mr John Bamford, of Shadlow / by his son John M. Bamford. London: for the author by the Wesleyan Conference Office, 1873. photo.port. (B&J)

BAMFORD, Samuel, 1788-1872, Lancashire radical, poet & handloom weaver
Incidents and anecdotes of the late Samuel Bamford / by James Dronsfield. Oldham: Hirst & Rennie, 1872. (B&J)

BANNATYNE, Archibald, 1810-63, Free Church Minister
Truth in love: a few memorials of Rev. Archibald Bannatyne ... [With a funeral sermon / by Macintosh Mackay. Edited with an introductory memoir by his widow]. Glasgow: T. Mackay, 1864. (BL)

BARCLAY, Hugh, 1799-1884, Sheriff-Substitute for Perthshire & local worthy
Sheriff Barclay: narrative of his public life. Edinburgh: J. Menzies, 1884. 12mo. (Reprinted from the 'Perthshire Advertiser') (NLS)

BARCLAY, Joseph, 1831-81, Anglican Bishop of Jerusalem
Joseph Barclay, D.D., LL.D., third Anglican Bishop of Jerusalem: a missionary biography. [By J. B. Courtenay] London: S. W. Partridge, 1883. (NC)

BARHAM, Francis Foster, 1808-71, 'The Alist'; newspaper editor; writer
A memorial of Francis Barham: a selection of autobiographical and other compositions ... Edited by Isaac Pitman. London: Fred. Pitman, 1873.

BARING, Charles, 1807-79, Bishop of Gloucester and Bristol, then of Durham
Biographical sketch of the late Bishop of Durham, the Right Rev. Charles Baring, D.D.. Newcastle-upon-Tyne, 1879. (Reprinted from the 'Newcastle Daily Journal')

BARKER, Peter, 1808-73, blind joiner & bellringer
A memoir of the life of Peter Barker, blind joiner of Hampsthwaite. Pateley Bridge: Thomas Thorpe, 1873; 2nd edition. 1876. Pamphlet. (B&J)

BARLOW, Henry, 1783-1858, of Newington Butts
Henry Barlow, of Newington Butts: a memoir in memoriam. [By Henry Clark Barlow]. Privately printed. London, 1859. (NUC)

BARLOW, Henry Clark, 1806-76, Dante scholar and writer
A brief memoir of Henry Clark Barlow. Privately printed. London, 1868.

BARLOW, John, 1815-56, Professor of Anatomy and Physiology in the Veterinary College, Edinburgh; Quaker
A memoir of John Barlow. London: Tract Association of the Society of Friends, [1858].

BARNE, Henry, 1813-86, evangelical clergyman
Henry Barne: a memoir / by his widow [Emily Barne]. London: John Kensit, 1887. (NLS)

BARNES, William, 1801-86, Dorset dialect poet; philologist, clergyman
The life of William Barnes, poet and philologist / by his daughter Lucy Baxter. London: Macmillan, 1887. photo. port.

BARR, Hugh, 1825-73, United Presbyterian Minister in Fife
Too late for martyrdom: memorials of the Rev. Hugh Barr, Kingskettle: memoir / by Thomas Dunlop. Edinburgh: Andrew Elliot, 1875. photo. port.

BARRY, Sir Charles, 1795-1860, architect; designed & built the Houses of Parliament 1840-60
The life and works of the late Sir Charles Barry, R.A., F.R.S., architect / by Alfred Barry. 1867; 2nd edition. London: John Murray, 1870 as 'Memoir of ...'; reprinted New York: Benjamin Blom, 1970.

BARTER, Richard, 1802-70, Irish doctor and sanitary reformer
Recollections of the late Dr. Barter. Dublin: William McGee, 1875. (NLS)

BARTHOLOMEW, Francis Medley, d.1894, schoolmaster; traveller in India
Francis Medley Batholomew: his last journey, as gathered from his letters and those of his friends. [With a prefatory note by William H. Bartholomew]. Printed for private circulation. London: Rivington, Percival, 1895. photo.port. (NLS)

BARTLETT, William Henry, 1809-54, illustrator especially of Middle Eastern scenes
A brief biography of William Henry Bartlett, topographical artist ... / by John Britton. London: Bradbury & Evans, 1885. 16mo. (100 copies) (Reprinted from the 'Art Journal')
-------. Brief memoir of the late William Henry Bartlett, author of 'Walks about Jerusalem' [etc.] and other works / by William Beattie. Published by subscription. London: M. S. Rickerby, 1855. 4to.

BARTTELOT, Edmund Musgrave, 1859-88, soldier especially in Africa
The life of Edmund Musgrave Barttelot, Captain and Brevet-Major, Royal Fusiliers, Commander of the Rear Column of the Emin Pasha Relief Expedition ... from his letters and diary / by Walter George Barttelot. 2nd edition. London: R. Bentley, 1890. photo. port. (B&J)

BASSETT, E. see BASSETT, R.

BASSETT, R., 1777-1852, Welsh clergyman
Home light, or brief memoir and letters of the Rev. R. Bassett, Vicar of Colwinstone; and [of] E. Bassett, Esq., Glamorganshire / by E. Morgan. Carnarvon: printed by H. Humphreys, 1860. 12mo. (B&J)

BASTARD, Abraham, n.d., Cornish Bible Christian & wrestler
The converted wrestler, or the life of Abraham Bastard / by Samuel L. Thorne. London: Elliot Stock, 1877. 16mo; 3rd edition as: 'The Cornish wrestler, or the life of ...' Launceston: Bible Christian Book Room, [1880] (BL)

BATE, William Thornton, 1820-57, naval officer in China; nautical surveyor
A memoir of Captain W. Thornton Bate, R.N. / by John Baillie. London: Longman [etc.], 1859. (NC)

BAXTER, Robert Dudley, 1827-75, parliamentary lawyer; political writer
In memoriam: R. Dudley Baxter, M.A.. [By his widow Mary D. Baxter]. Printed for

private circulation. London: printed by Harrison, [1878]. photo. port. (NC)

BAYLISS, Daniel, 1837-77?, religious shepherd; in New Zealand
   The path of the just: a memoir of Daniel Bayliss, late of Chorley, Staffordshire / by George Poole. London: Hodder & Stoughton, 1879. (NLS)

BAZELY, Henry Casson Barnes, 1842-83, Anglican then Presbyterian
   Henry Bazely, the Oxford evangelist: a memoir / by Edward Lee Hicks. London: Macmillan, 1886.

BEACONSFIELD, Benjamin Disraeli, 1st Earl of see **DISRAELI, Benjamin**

BEADON, Frederick, 1777-1879 aged 101 years, Chancellor of Wells Cathedral
   Memoir on the life of the Rev. Frederick Beadon ... / by George William Norman. Privately printed. Bromley: Strong, 1879. Pamphlet.

BEAUMONT, Joseph, 1794-1855, doctor and Wesleyan Methodist
   A biographical and critical sketch of Dr Beaumont, the eloquent orator / by Richard Wrench. London: Partridge, 1859.
-------. A brief sketch of the life, character, labours and death of the late Rev. Dr. Beaumont, who died in Waltham Street Chapel, Hull, on Sunday January 21st 1855. [1855]. Pamphlet. (B&J)
-------. The life of the Rev. Joseph Beaumont, M.D.. [By his son] Joseph Beaumont. London: Hamilton, Adams, 1856.
-------. Sketch of the late Dr. Beaumont ... supplied from the family of the deceased ... London: Houlston & Stoneman, [1855]. 12mo. (Reprinted from 'The Watchman') (NLS)

BECKWITH, John Charles, 1789-1862, Major-General; established Protestant schools in
      Piedmont
   General Beckwith: his life and labours among the Waldenses of Piedmont ... / by Jean Pierre Meille ... London: T. Nelson, 1873. (NC)

BEECH, Hugh, 1787-1856, Wesleyan Minister
   The good soldier: outlines of the life, labours and character of the Rev. Hugh Beech, Wesleyan Minister / by John Hugh Beech. London: A. Heylin, 1856. (NLS)

BEECH, John Hugh, 1816-84, Methodist Minister
   Outer life of a Methodist preacher; and sermons. Burslem: James Dean, 1884. photo.port. (NLS)

BEGG, James, 1808-83, leading Free Church Minister; Moderator
   Memoirs of James Begg, D.D., Minister of Newington Free Church, Edinburgh / by Thomas Smith. Including an autobiographical chapter. Edinburgh: James Gemmell, 1885-88. 2 volumes. (NLS)

BELL, Henry Glassford, 1805-74, Scottish advocate; man of letters
   Henry Glassford Bell: a biographical sketch / by Anna Macgregor Stoddart. Edinburgh: printed by R. & R. Clark, 1892. (Note: DNB gives incorrect date of birth)

BELLASIS, Edward, 1800-73, Catholic; lawyer employed in Parliamentary practice
   Memorials of Mr Sergeant Bellasis (1800-1873) / by Edward Bellasis. London: Burns & Oates, 1893.

BELLETT, George, 1797-1886, clergyman in Bridgnorth; antiquarian
   Memoir of the Rev. George Bellett ...: autobiography, and continuation / by his daughter. With an introduction by Samuel Bentley. Printed for private circulation. London: J. Masters, 1889. (NUC)

BELLETT, John Gifford, 1795-1864, Irish barrister; one of the founders of the Plymouth

Brethren sect
Recollections of John Gifford Bellett / by his daughter [L. M. Bennett]. London: A. S. Rowse, 1895. (NUC)

BELLHAM, William Green, n.d., Primitive Methodist
The spiritual hero, or the life of Mr William Green Bellham, one of the pioneers or early Ministers of the Primitive Methodist Connection / by Oliver Jackson. London: Thomas King, 1858. 12mo. (B&J)

BENNET, Alexander, 1832-67, Church of Scotland Minister
Memorials of the late Rev. Alexander Bennet. Edited by William Peters. Kinross: David Brown, [1869]. photo.port.

BENNETT, James, 1774-1862, Congregational Minister; theological writer
Memorials of the late Rev. James Bennett, D.D., comprising a brief biographical sketch. [With] the funeral oration[s] / by J. Jefferson, and by Samuel McAll. London: Hamilton, Adams, 1863. (NC)

BENNETT, John Hughes, 1812-75, Professor of Medicine at Edinburgh University
John Hughes Bennett / by John Gray McKendrick. [Edinburgh: printed by Oliver & Boyd, c.1875]. Pamphlet.

BENNETT, William James Early, 1804-86, Anglo-Catholic priest
The story of W. J. E. Bennett, founder of S. Barnabas' Pimlico, and Vicar of Frome-Selwood ... / by Frederick Bennett. London: Longmans, Green, 1909.

BENNETT, Sir William Sterndale, 1816-75, composer; Professor of Music at Cambridge University
The life of William Sterndale Bennett / by his son James Robert Bennett. Cambridge: University Press, 1907.

BENSON, Edward White, 1829-96, Archbishop of Canterbury
The life of Edward White Benson, sometime Archbishop of Canterbury [1883-96] / by his son Arthur Christopher Benson. London: Macmillan, 1889. 2 volumes; abridged edition. 1901.
-------. The life-work of Edward White Benson, D.D., sometime Archbishop of Canterbury / by James Anderson Carr. London: Elliot, Stock, 1898.
-------. Popular life of Archbishop Benson. London: 'Church Bells' Office, [1896].

BENSON, John, 1817-66, Newcastle worthy & Methodist; temperance
A memoir of the late Councillor John Benson ... / by Richard Chew. Newcastle-upon-Tyne: William Reid, 1866. Pamphlet. (BL)

BENTLEY, John, 1786-1858, religious working-man
The Christian workman, being a memoir of John Bentley / by Samuel Allen Windle. Derby: printed by Rowbottom, [1858]. Pamphlet. (NLS)

BERESFORD, Lord William Leslie de la Poer, V.C., 1847-1900, soldier; sportsman
Lord William Beresford, V.C.: some memories of a famous sportsman, soldier and wit / by Amy Charlotte Menzies ... London: Herbert Jenkins, 1917.

BERNAL OSBORNE (born BERNAL), Ralph, 1808-82, Liberal M.P.; connoisseur
The life of Ralph Bernal Osborne, M.P. / by Philip Henry Dudley Bagenal. For private circulation. London: R. Bentley, 1884.

BERRY, Charles Albert, 1852-99, Congregational leader; traveller
Charles A. Berry, D.D.: a memoir / by James Siddall Drummond. London: Cassell, 1899. (NC)

BERRY, Cornelius, 1788-1864, Independent Minister near Harlow

Biographical sketch of the Rev. Cornelius Berry. To which is subjoined the sermon preached on occasion of his death / by John Hayden. London: Jackson, Walford & Hodder, [1865].

BEST, Robert, d.1887 aged 65, Lancashire Congregationalist Minister

Memoir of the Rev. Robert Best / by his son-in-law James Johnston. Bolton: Alfred Blackshaw, 1888. photo. port. (B&J)

BETTS, Robert Wye, d.1868 aged c.44, Congregational Minister in Surrey

Christian excellence illustrated in a biographical sketch of the Rev. Robert Wye Betts, late Minister of Hanover Chapel, Peckham ... / by Thomas Ray. London: Hodder & Stoughton, 1869. 12mo. (NLS)

BETTY, William Henry West, 'Young Roscius', 1791-1874, child actor from the Regency period

An authentic biographical sketch of the life of W. H. W. Betty, the celebrated Young Roscius / by George Davies Harley. London: R. Phillips, 1804. (BL)

-------. The life of William Henry West Betty, the celebrated and wonderful Young Roscius ... London: John Fairburn, 1804. (BL)

-------. Memoirs of Mr. W. H. W. Betty, the English Roscius. To which is affixed a sketch of the theatrical career of his son Mr Henry Betty. London: B.D. Cousins, [1846]. (BL)

-------. Memoirs of the life of William Henry West Betty, known by the name of Young Roscius ... [By John Merritt]. Liverpool: J. Wright, 1804. (BL)

-------. Roscius in London ... : biographical memoir of William Henry West Betty, from the earliest period of his infancy ... London: B. Crosby, 1805. (BL)

BEWICK, William, 1795-1866, portrait painter; copyist especially of Rembrant

Life and labours of William Bewick, artist. Edited by Thomas Landseer. London: Hurst & Blackett, 1871. 2 volumes; reprinted East Ardsley: E. P. Publishing, 1978.

BIANCONI, Charles (Carlo), 1786-1875, coach & carriage operator throughout Ireland

Charles Bianconi: a biography, 1786-1875 / by his daughter Mary Anne O'Connell. London: Chapman & Hall, 1878. photo.port. (NLS)

BICKERSTETH, Edward, 1850-97, Anglican Bishop in Japan

Life and letters of Edward Bickersteth, Bishop of South Tokyo / by Samuel Bickersteth. London: Sampson Low, Marston, 1899.

BICKERSTETH, Henry see **LANGDALE, Baron**

BICKERSTETH, Robert, 1816-84, Bishop of Ripon from 1856

A sketch of the life and episcopate of the Right Rev. Robert Bickersteth, D.D., Bishop of Ripon, 1857-1884 / by his son Montagu Cyril Bickersteth. London: Rivingtons, 1877.

BIELBY, Robert, n.d., Yorkshire Baptist

A memoir of Mr Robert Bielby, of Bridlington Quay, Yorkshire. Bridlington: printed by R. Hickson, 1864. Pamphlet. (B&J)

BIGNOLD, Sir Samuel, 1791-1875, M.P.; established Norwich Union Fire (later Life) Insurance Company

A memoir of the late Sir Samuel Bignold, Knt.. Norwich: R. G. Hickling, 1875. photographic illustrations. Pamphlet.

BILBOROUGH, William Hudson, 1816-91, Baptist; educator of the poor

In memoriam: William Hudson Bilborough. Born ... August 4th 1816 - Died ... January 27th 1891. [By John Haslam]. Leeds: Walter & Laycock, [1891]. photo. port. (B&J)

BINNEY, Thomas, 1798-1874, Congregational leader

A memorial of the late Rev. Thomas Binney, LL.D.. Edited by John Stoughton. London: Hodder & Stoughton, 1874.
-------. Thomas Binney, his mind, life and opinions ... / by Edward Paxton Hood. London: James Clark, 1874.

BINNIE, Thomas, 1792-1867, Glasgow builder
Memoir of Thomas Binnie, builder in Glasgow, 1792-1867 / by his son Thomas Binnie. Printed for private circulation. Glasgow, 1882. photo. port.

BIRCH, Samuel, 1813-85, Egyptologist
Biographical notices of Dr Samuel Birch from the British and foreign press; portraits; and a bibliography of his principal works. With an introduction / by Walter de Gray Birch. London: Trubner, 1886. (NC)
-------. Memoir of the late Samuel Birch, LL.D. [etc.], President of the Society of Biblical Archaeology. Part 1: Biographical notice, list of works, &c. / by Ernest Alfred Wallis Budge. Part 2: Remarks on Dr Birch's Chinese labours / by Robert Kennaway Douglas. London: Harrison, 1859. Pamphlet. (Reprinted from the 'Transactions of the Society for Biblical Archaeology')

BIRCHENALL, John, 1800-80, surgeon & Methodist in Macclesfield
The life of John Birchenall, M.R.C.S., F.L.S., of Macclesfield ... / by Alfred J. French ... London: Wesleyan Conference Office, [1881]. photo. port. (NLS)

BIRD, Charles Smith, 1795-1862, Chancellor of Lincoln Cathedral
Sketches of the life of the Rev. Charles Smith Bird, M.A., F.L.S., late Fellow of Trinity College, Cambridge, Vicar of Gainsborough, Lincolnshire, and Chancellor of Lincoln Cathedral / by Claude Smith Bird. London: J. Nisbet, 1864. (NC)

BIRD, Golding, 1814-54, physician
Biographical notice of the late Dr Golding Bird. [By his brother Frederic Bird]. 1855. (Reprinted from the 'Association Medical J.')
-------. Biographical sketch of the late Dr Golding Bird, being an address to students delivered at the request of the Edinburgh Medical Missionary Society / by John Hutton Balfour. Edinburgh: T. Constable, 1855. (NC)

BISHOP, Benjamin, 1780-1855, Quaker
Memoir of Benjamin Bishop. With extracts from his letters. [Edited by R.R.]. Gloucester: John Bellows, 1865. Pamphlet. (NLS)

BLACK, James, 1819-80, United Presbyterian Minister
In memoriam: James Black. Born Feb. 6 1819 - Died Dec. 10 1880. [Edited by J.B.B.]. Privately printed. Edinburgh, 1882. photo. port. (NC)

BLACK, Robert John, n.d., Irish Presbyterian
Robert J. Black: his life and life's work / compiled by Alexander Irwin. Londonderry: 'Derry Standard' Office, 1901. (B&J)

BLACK, William, 1841-98, Scottish novelist
William Black, novelist: a biography / by Thomas Wemyss Reid. London: Cassell, 1902.

BLACKBURN, Richard Stead, n.d., missionary in Africa
Christian manhood, or memorials of a noble life, being biographical sketches of the Rev. R. S. Blackburn, missionary to Fernando Po, West Africa / by Thomas Mitchell. London: John Dickenson [etc.], [188-]. (B&J)

BLACKBURNE, Francis, 1782-1867, Lord Chancellor of Ireland
Life of the Right Hon. Francis Blackburne, late Lord Chancellor of Ireland ..., chiefly in connection with his public and political career / by his son Edward Blackburne. London:

Macmillan, 1874.

BLACKIE, John Stuart, 1809-95, classicist & man of letters; advocate
John Stuart Blackie: a biography / by Anna Macgregor Stoddart. Edinburgh: W. Blackwood, 1895. 2 volumes; one volume 1896.
-------. The life of Professor John Stuart Blackie, the most distinguished Scotsman of his day. By various eminent writers. Edited by John G. Duncan. Glasgow: John J. Rae, [1895].
-------. Professor Blackie, his sayings and doings: a biographical sketch / by his nephew Howard Angus Kennedy. London: James Clarke, 1895.

BLACKWOOD, John, the third, 1818-79, important Edinburgh publisher, including of 'Blackwood's Magazine'
A selection from the obituary notices of the late John Blackwood, editor of 'Blackwood's Magazine'. [Edited by William Blackwood]. Printed for private circulation. Edinburgh, 1880. (BL)

BLACKWOOD, Sir Stevenson Arthur, 1832-93, Clerk to the Treasury; Principal Secretary to Post Office
A few words about the late Sir Arthur Blackwood, Secretary to the Post Office / by Harry Buxton Forman. Printed for friends. London, 1894. (50 copies)
-------. In memoriam: Sir Arthur Blackwood, K.C.B.. [By Catherine M. Marsh]. Edinburgh: Andrew Stevenson, 1894. 16mo. (NLS)
-------. Some records of the life of Stevenson Arthur Blackwood, K.C.B.. Compiled by a friend [Sydney, Duchess of Marlborough] and edited by his widow [Harriet Sydney Blackwood] London: Hodder & Stoughton, 1896; popular edition. 1897.

BLAIR, James Ernest, 1868-77, child of the manse
A short race well run, or recollections of James Ernest Blair / by his father John Blair. Edinburgh: W. Oliphant [etc.], 1880. 12mo.

BLAKE, George Bannerman, 1831-63, Scottish Presbyterian Minister in Sunderland
A memorial sketch of the late Rev. George Bannerman Blake ... With a selection from his sermons. London: J. Nisbet, 1864.

BLAKENEY, John Edward, 1824-95, Archdeacon of Sheffield
'A man greatly beloved': memories of the life and work of John Edward Blakeney, D.D., Vicar and Archdeacon of Sheffield ... / by William Odom ... 2nd edition. London: 'Home Words' Publishing Office, [1895].

BLAMIRE, William, 1790-1862, stock breeder; M.P.; Tithe Commissioner
A biographical sketch of the late William Blamire, Esquire, of The Oaks and Thackwood Nook, formerly M.P. for the County of Cumberland / by Henry Lonsdale. London: Routledge, Warne & Routledge, 1862. Pamphlet. (NUC)

BLANCHARD, Edward Litt Laman, 1820-89, journalist; playwright
The life and reminiscences of Edward Laman Blanchard. With notes from the diary of William Blanchard [and a biographical sketch of William Blanchard / by D. Meadows]. Edited by Clement William Scott and Cecil Howard. London: Hutchinson, 1891. 2 volumes.

BLEECK, Charles, d.188-, doctor, probably at Warminster Cottage Hospital
A brief memoir of Charles Bleeck, F.R.C.S., Warminster. Printed for private circulation. Warminster: printed by B. W. Coates, [188-]. 16mo. photo. port. (B&J)

BLOMFIELD, Charles James, 1786-1857, Bishop of London 1828-56
Bishop Blomfield and his times: an historical sketch ... / by George Edward Biber. London: Harrison, 1857. (Reprinted from the 'Churchman's Magazine')
-------. A memoir of Charles James Blomfield, D.D., Bishop of London [1828-56]. With selections from his correspondence. Edited by his son Alfred Blomfield. London: John

Murray, 1863. 2 volumes; one volume 1864. (NC)

BLOOMER, W. Caleb H., 1830-72, ran a ragged school in Midlands; Congregationalist
  layman
  Life consecrated to Christ, or brief memorials of the late W. Caleb H. Bloomer, of
Halesowen / by Henry Newman ... Stourbridge: T. Mark, [1874]. 12mo. (B&J)

BLYTHE, David, 1795-1883, 'King of the Gypsies'
  David Blythe, the Gypsy King: a character sketch / by Charles Stuart. Kelso: J. & J.H.
Rutherfurd, 1883. photo.port.

BLYTHE, John Dean, 1842-69, factory worker; miscellaneous writer
  A sketch of the life, and a selection from the writings, of John Dean Blythe. [Edited by
T.W.]. Manchester: Tubbs & Brook, 1870. 12mo. photo. port. (B&J)

BOAZ, Thomas, 1806-61, Congregational missionary in India
  The mission pastor: memorials of Rev T. Boaz, LL.D., twenty-four years missionary to
Calcutta / by his widow [Eliza Boaz]. Edited by his brother-in-law. London: John Snow,
1862.

BOILEAU, John Theophilus, 1805-86, soldier & mathematician
  Memoir of Major-General J. T. Boileau ... / by Charles Rathbone Low ... London: W.
H. Allen, 1887. (NLS)

BOLDERO, Harry Stuart, 1863-87, Scottish naval cadet
  A young heart of oak: memories of Harry Stuart Boldero, Lieutenant R.N. ... London:
Hodder & Stoughton, 1891. photo. port. (NLS)

BOLTON, Jasper, 1841-71, Irish land agent
  Quickly ripened, or recollections of the late Jasper Bolton. London: J. F. Shaw, [1872].
(BL)

BONAR, Andrew Alexander, 1810-92, Free Church Minister
  The life of the Rev. Dr. Andrew A. Bonar / by Fergus Ferguson ... Glasgow: John J.
Rae, [1893]. (NC)
-------. Reminiscences of Andrew A. Bonar, D.D.. Edited by his daughter Marjory Bonar.
London: Hodder & Stoughton, 1895. (NC)

BONAR, Horatius, 1808-89, Free Church Minister; hymn writer
  Horatius Bonar, D.D.: a memorial. Edinburgh: Andrew Stevenson, 1889. photo.
port.(NC); 2nd edition. London: J. Nisbet, 1890.
-------. Memories of Dr Horatius Bonar: addresses delivered at the Centenary
celebrations. By relatives and public men ... [Edited by] W. E.. Edinburgh: Oliphant,
Anderson & Ferrier, 1909. (NC)

BONAR, John James, 1803-91, Free Church Minister
  Parting memorial of John James Bonar, D.D., first Minister of Saint Andrew's Parish
and Congregation, Greenock, being some record of services in connection with his funeral.
Greenock: James Mackelvie, 1892.

BONER, Charles, 1815-70, tutor; author; in Germany
  Memoirs and letters of Charles Boner. With letters of Mary Russell Mitford to him
during ten years. Edited by R.M. Kettle [i.e. Rosa Mosa Stuart]. London: R. Bentley, 1871.
2 volumes. (NLS); another edition. London: James Weir, 1876. 2 volumes.

BONNAR, Thomas, 1810-73, owner of firm of Bonnar & Carfrae, Edinburgh, interior
  decorators
  In memoriam: Thomas Bonnar / by Adam Lind Simpson. Edinburgh, 1876. (NLS)

BOORNE, James, 1794-1893, Baptist Minister

Memorials of James Boorne, for twenty-one years Pastor of Devonshire Road Baptist Chapel, Greenwich. [Edited by Samuel Boorne]. London: E. Wilmshurst, [1894]. (NLS)

BOOTH, Edwin Thomas, 1833-95 see **BOOTH, Junius Brutus**

BOOTH, Henry, 1788-1869, managing director Liverpool & Manchester Railway; railway engineer

Memoir of the late Henry Booth, of the Liverpool and Manchester Railway and afterwards of the London and North-Western Railway / by Robert Smiles. Printed for private circulation. London: printed by Wyman, 1869. (NUC)

BOOTH, John Clegg, 1819-73, temperance worker

A biographical sketch of John Clegg Booth, late temperance advocate, York / by J. S. Balmer. London: T. Barlow, 1874. 12mo.

BOOTH, Junius Brutus, 1796-1852, actor; later in USA

The Elder [Junius Brutus] and the Younger [Edwin Thomas] Booth / by Asia Frigga Clarke. London: David Bogue, [1882].

-------. Memoirs of Junius Brutus Booth, from his birth to the present time ... London: Chapple, 1817. (NUC)

BORROW, George (Henry), 1803-81, author; agent for British & Foreign Bible Society in Europe; travel writer

George Borrow and his circle ... [Edited] by Clement King Shorter. London: Hodder & Stoughton, 1913.

-------. The life of George Borrow / compiled from unpublished official documents, his works, correspondence, etc. by Herbert George Jenkins. London: John Murray, 1912.

BOUGH, Samuel, 1822-78, landscape painter

Sam Bough, R.S.A.: some account of his life and works / by Sidney Gilpin [i.e. George Coward]. London: G. Bell, 1905.

BOULTBEE, Thomas Pownall, 1818-84, clergyman

Quiet strength: a memorial sketch of the life and works of the late Rev. T. P. Boultbee .../ by Gordon Calthrop. London: W. Hunt, 1884. 12mo.

BOURNE, Hugh, 1772-1852, founded the Primitive Methodist Connection

The life and letters of James Bourne. Edited by his son-in-law William Benson. 2nd revised and enlarged edition. London: Farncombe, [1875].

-------. The life of the venerable Hugh Bourne / by William Antliff. London: George Lamb, 1872. (NUC); new & revised edition. as: 'The life of Henry Bourne, founder of the Primitive Methodist Connection'. Edited by Colin C. McKechnie. London: James B. Knapp, 1892. (NC)

-------. The life of the venerable Hugh Bourne / by Jesse Ashworth. London: Joseph Toulmin, [1888]. (NC)

-------. Memoirs of the life and labours of the venerable Hugh Bourne / by John Walford. Edited by William Antliff. London: T. King, 1855-56. 2 volumes. (NUC)

-------. Recollections and characteristic anecdotes of the late of Rev. Hugh Bourne / by John Simpson. London: John Day, 1859. 12mo. (NLS)

and other popular biographies

BOWEN, Sir Charles Synge Christopher, 1st Baron Bowen, 1835-94, judge; classicist; poet

Lord Bowen: a biographical sketch. With a selection from his poems / by Henry Stewart Cunningham. Privately printed. London: printed by W. Clowes, 1896; 2nd edition. London: John Murray, 1897.

BOWEN, John, 1815-59, Anglican Bishop of Sierra Leone from 1857

Memorials of John Bowen, late Bishop of Sierra Leone / compiled from his letters and journals by his sister. London: J. Nisbet, 1862.

BOWLY, Samuel, 1802-84, Quaker; temperance worker; company chairman; anti-slaver
The life of the late Samuel Bowly, the apostle of temperance/ by Frederick Sessions. London: A. Kingdon, [1884].
-------. Memorials of Samuel Bowly. Born March 23 1802 - Died March 23 1884 / compiled by his daughter Maria Taylor. Printed for private circulation. Gloucester: John Bellows, 1884. photo. port. (B&J)

BOWREY, James John, 1845-97,
In memoriam: James John Bowrey, 1845-1897: [contributions by various authors. Edited by James Watson, of Porus]. Guildford: Billing, [1898].(BL)

[BOYD, Andrew Kennedy Hutchinson], 1825-99, Church of Scotland Minister; writer
Anecdotes and recollections of A.K.H.B. / by D. R. Anderson. Paisley: Alexander Gardner, 1900. Pamphlet. (NLS)

BOYLE, Robert, 1821-78, inventor; missionary lecturer; sanitary reformer
Robert Boyle, inventor and philanthropist: a biographical sketch / by Lawrence Saunders. London: Gilbert Wood, 1885.

BRADLAUGH, Charles, 1833-91, radical M.P.; atheist; public advocate of birth control
The biography of Charles Bradlaugh / by Adolphe Smith Headingley. London: Remington, 1880. photo.port; 2nd revised edition. 1883.
-------. Charles Bradlaugh: a record of his life and work .../ by his daughter Hypatia Bradlaugh Bonner & John Mackinnon Robertson. London: T. Fisher Unwin, 1894. 2 volumes; 2nd edition. 1895.
-------. Life of Charles Bradlaugh, M.P. / by Charles R. Mackay. London: D. J. Gunn, 1888. *Suppressed. (B&J)
-------. Reminiscences of Charles Bradlaugh / by George William Foote. London: Progressive Publishing, 1891. Pamphlet.
and other biographies

BRADLEY, Joshua, 1817-91, manager of a Manchester cotton mill and local benefactor
From little piecer to manager: reminiscences in the life of Joshua Bradley, donor of Hyde Town Hall clock and bells. Oldham: W.E. Clegg, [1906]: reprinted Longden Publications, 1974.

BRADSHAW, Henry, 1831-86, Cambridge University Librarian
A memoir of Henry Bradshaw, Fellow of King's College, Cambridge and University Librarian / by George Walter Prothero. London: Kegan Paul, Trench, 1888.

BRAIDWOOD, James, 1816-84, religious grocer in Leith
Memoir of Mr James Braidwood, Leith / by William Scott, *Balerno*. Edinburgh: A. Elliot, 1885. (NLS)

BRAMWELL, George William Wilshere, 1st Baron, 1808-92, Appeal Court judge
Some account of George William Wilshere, Baron Bramwell of Hever, and his opinions/ by Charles Fairfield. London: Macmillan, 1898.

BRASSEY, Thomas, 1805-70, railway contractor
The life and labours of Mr Brassey, 1805-1870 / by Arthur Helps. London: Bell & Daldy, 1872; reprinted New York: Kelley, 1969.

BRAY, William, 'Billy', 1794-1868, converted miner; Bible Christian
The King's son, or a memoir of Billy Bray / compiled largely from his own memoranda by Frederick William Bourne. London: Bible Christian Book Room. 1871; new illustrated edition. 1883; reprinted London: Epworth Press, 1937.

BRAYLEY, Edward Wedlake, the elder, 1773-1854, antiquarian; librarian
A brief memoir of Edward Wedlake Brayley / by John Britton. Privately printed. London: Nichols, 1855. 16mo. (From the 'Gentlemans Magazine')

BREALEY, George, 1823-88, Plymouth Brethren
'Always abounding', or recollections of the life and labours of the late George Brealey, the evangelist of the Blackdown Hills / by his son Walter John Henry Brealey. [3rd] revised edition. London: W. G. Wheeler, [1897].

BREMNER, Andrew Kennedy, 1865-87, early death of a child of the Manse
A child of faith in an age of doubt: memorials of Andrew Kennedy Bremner / by his brother [Robert Locke Bremner]. London: Hodder & Stoughton, 1890. (NC)

BRETT, Robert, 1808-74, surgeon; founded Guild of St Luke; tractarian
Robert Brett ... : in memoriam. Reprints from the principal Church journals ... Including a sermon preached ... / by Thomas William Belcher. [Edited by T. W. Belcher]. London: J. Masters, 1874; 2nd edition. 1891.
-------. Robert Brett, of Stoke Newington: his life and work / by Thomas William Belcher. London: Farran, [1889].

BRETT, William Henry, 1818-86, missionary in British Guiana
'The Apostle of the Indians of Guiana': a memoir of the life and labours of the Rev. W. H. Brett, D.D., for forty years a missionary in British Guiana / by Fortunato Pietro Luigi Josa. London: Wells Gardner, Darton, 1886. (NC)

BREWSTER, Sir David, 1781-1868, Principal of St Andrews University; scientist; Free Church layman
The home life of Sir David Brewster / by his daughter [Margaret Maria] Gordon. Edinburgh: Edmonston & Douglas, 1869. photo. port. (NC)

BRIERLEY, Morgan, 1820-97, scientific writer
Morgan Brierley: a memoir. With a selection from his writings / by his daughter Helen Brierley. Rochdale: printed by James Clegg, 1900. (B&J)

BRIGGS, John, 1785-1875, Major-General in India; orientalist
Memoir of General John Briggs, of the Madras Army. With comments on some of his words and work / by Evans Bell. London: Chatto & Windus, 1885. (NLS)

BRIGHT, Sir Charles Tilston, 1832-1888, telegraph engineer; laid first Atlantic Cable in 1858
The life story of the late Sir Charles Tilston Bright, civil engineer ... / by Edward Brailsford Bright & Charles Bright. London: A. Constable, [1899]. 2 volumes; revised and abridged edition by Charles Bright. 1908.

BRIGHT, John, 1811-89, radical Quaker M.P. and businessman; anti Corn Law leader; orator
John Bright / by Charles Anthony Vince. London: Blackie, 1898. (Victorian Era Series)
-------. John Bright: a monograph / by Richard Barry O'Brien ... London: Smith, Elder, 1910.
-------. John Bright: a non-political sketch of a good man's life / by Charles Bullock. London: 'Home Words' Publishing Office, [1889?].
-------. The life and speeches of the Right Hon. John Bright, M.P. / by George Barnett Smith. London: Hodder & Stoughton, 1881. 2 volumes; abridged edition. 1889 as 'The life of ...'
-------. The life and times of the Right Hon. John Bright, M.P. / by William Robertson. London: Cassell, [1877]. 2 volumes. 4to. photographically illustrated. [Probably incorporated into:]
-------. The life and times of the Right Hon. John Bright / by William Robertson. Published for the author. Rochdale: 'Observer' Steam Printing Works, [1877].

photographic portraits & illustrations; new edition as: 'Life and times of ...' London: Cassell, 1883.

-------. The life of John Bright / by Lewis Apjohn. Newcastle-upon-Tyne: Walter Scott Publishing, [188-]. photo. port.

-------. The life of John Bright / by George Macaulay Trevelyan. London: Constable, 1913; 2nd edition. 1925.

BRIGHTWELL, Thomas, 1787-1868, lawyer; microscopist; Mayor of Norwich
Memorials of the life of Mr Brightwell of Norwich / by his daughter [Cecilia Lucy Brightwell]. Printed for private circulation. Norwich: Fletcher, 1869. photo. port.

BRISCOMBE, Walter, b.1836, Methodist Minister; temperance worker
Life sketch of the Rev. Walter Briscombe / by W. Pilkington. Preston: W. Pilkington, 1891. (B&J)

BROADBENT, Arnold Edward, d.189-, domestic biography
A memorial of Arnold Edward Broadbent, son of the late Butterworth Broadbent, Snow Lea, Longwood. [By S.A. Broadbent]. [For private circulation]. Huddersfield: printed by Preston, [1898]. (B&J)

BROCK, William, 1807-75, Baptist Minister; anti-slaver
The life of William Brock, D.D., first Minister of Bloomsbury Chapel, London / by Charles Morton Birrell. London: J. Nisbet, 1878. photo.port.

-------. William Brock, D.D., first Pastor of Bloomsbury Chapel: a biography / by George Wilson M'Cree. London: James Clarke, 1876. photo. port. (NLS)

BROCKY, Charles, 1807-55, artist
Sketch of the life of Charles Brocky, the artist / by Norman Wilkinson. London, 1870. (BL)

BRODIE, Sir Benjamin Collins, 1st Bart., 1783-1862, Royal surgeon
Biographical sketch of Sir Benjamin Brodie, late Sergeant-Surgeon to the Queen, and President of the Royal Society / by Henry Wentworth Acland. London: Longman [etc.], 1864. (From 'Proceedings of the Royal Society')

-------. Sir Benjamin Collins Brodie / by Timothy Holmes. Edited by Ernest Abraham Hart. London: T. F. Unwin, 1897. (Masters of Medicine series)

BRONTE (born PRUNTY), Patrick, 1777-1861, father of the Bronte girls; poet; clergyman
The father of the Brontes, his life and work at Dewsbury and Hartshead. With a chapter on 'Currer Bell' [i.e. Charlotte Bronte] / by William W. Yates. Leeds: Fred. R. Spark, 1897.

BROOKE, Edward, b.1799, Yorkshire squire & mineowner
Squire Brooke: a memorial of Edward Brooke, of Fieldhouse, near Huddersfield. With extracts from his diary and correspondence / by John Holt Lord. London: T. Woolmer, [1873]. (BL)

BROOKE, Gustavus Vaughan, 1818-66, Irish-born tragedian and theatre manager
The life of Gustavus Vaughan Brooke, tragedian / by William John Lawrence. Belfast: W. & G. Baird, 1892. (500 copies)

BROOKE, Sir Victor Alexander, 3rd Bart., 1843-91, sportsman, naturalist; golfer
Sir Victor Brooke, sportsman and naturalist: a memoir of his life, and extracts from his letters and journals. Edited by Oscar Leslie Stephens ... London: John Murray, 1894.

BROOKES, Warwick, 1806-82, Manchester book illustrator
In memoriam: Warwick Brookes. [By Thomas Letherbrow]. [Manchester, 1882]. photographic portrait & illustrations. (Reprinted from the 'Manchester City News') (B&J)

BROOKS, Charles William Shirley, 1816-74, editor of 'Punch'
A great 'Punch' editor, being the life, letters and diaries of Shirley Brooks / by George Somes Layard. London: Sir Isaac Pitman, 1907. (BL)

BROUGH, Peter, 1797-1883, banker; philanthropist; Paisley worthy
Peter Brough, a Paisley philanthropist / by James B. Sturrock. Paisley: Alexander Gardner, 1890. (NLS)

BROUGHAM, Henry Peter, 1st Baron Brougham & Vaux, 1778-1868, Lord Chancellor; reformer
Henry, Lord Brougham and Vaux: a critical biography / by George Henry Francis. London, 1858. (Reprinted in part from 'Fraser's Mag.')
-------. Lives of Lord Lyndhurst and Lord Brougham, Lords Chancellor and Keepers of the Great Seal of England / by John Campbell. Edited by Mary Scarlett Campbell. London: John Murray, 1869. [But note]: 'Misrepresentations in Campbell's "Lives of Lyndhurst and Brougham" corrected' / by Edward Burtenshaw Sugden, Lord St. Leonards. London: John Murray, 1869.
-------. Lord Brougham / by Francis Adams. Birmingham: Cornish, 1869. Pamphlet. (NLS)
-------. Memoir of Lord Brougham / by George Harris. London: Butterworths, 1868. Pamphlet. (NLS)
-------. Memoirs of the Right Hon. Henry Lord Brougham / by J. Harwood. London: Altman, 1850. 16mo. (NLS)

BROUGHTON, Henry Vivian, 1818-93, Canon of Peterborough Cathedral
Biographical sketch of the Rev. Henry Vivian Broughton, Hon. Canon of Peterborough Cathedral / by H. E. S.. With sermon preached at the Parish Church, Wellingborough / by R. W. Wynter. Printed for private circulation. Wellingborough: Dennes, [1893]. 12mo. (B&J)

BROWN, Alexander, d.1860 aged 21, in Bengal Civil Service
Crushed hopes crowned in death, particularly the last days of Alexander Brown, Bengal Civil Service, who died at sea on his way home, Jan. 3 1860, aged 21 / by his father David Brown, *of Aberdeen.* 2nd edition. London: J. Nisbet, 1862.

BROWN, David, 1803-97, Free Church Minister & theologian
David Brown, D.D., LL.D., Professor and Principal of the Free Church College, Aberdeen: a memoir / by William Garden Blaikie. London: Hodder & Stoughton, 1898. (NC)

BROWN, Ford Madox, 1821-93, decorative artist, especially of frescoes
Ford Madox Brown: a record of his life and work ... / by [his grandson] Ford Maddox Heuffer. London: Longmans, 1896.
-------. Ford Madox Brown / by Helen Maria Madox Rossetti. London: De La More Press, 1901.

BROWN, James Baldwin, 1820-84, liberal Congregational Minister; writer; biographer
In memoriam: James Baldwin Brown, B.A., Minister of Brixton Independent Church. Born August 19 1820 - Died June 23 1884. Edited by Elizabeth Baldwin Brown. London: James Clarke, 1884. (NLS)

BROWN, John, 1784-1858, Secession then United Presbyterian Minister
Memoir of John Brown, D.D., Senior Minister of the United Presbyterian Congregation, Broughton Place, Edinburgh, and Professor of Exegetical Theology to the United Presbyterian Church / by John Cairns. Edinburgh: T. Constable, 1860. [&] 'Supplementary Chapter to the life of Rev. John Brown, D.D.: a letter to the Rev. John Cairns, D.D.' / by John Brown, M.D.. 2nd edition. Edinburgh: Edmonston & Douglas, 1861. Pamphlet. (NC)

BROWN, John, 1810-82, Scottish essayist & doctor

Dr John Brown: a biography and a criticism / by John Taylor Brown. Edited with a short sketch of the biographer / by W. B. Dunlop. London: A. & C. Black, 1903. (NC)

-------. Dr John Brown and his sister Isabella: outlines / by Elizabeth T. M'Laren. 1889; 4th (illustrated) edition. Edinburgh: D. Douglas, 1890; many editions.

BROWN, John, 1826-83, personal attendant to Queen Victoria

Life and biography of John Brown ..., for 30 years personal attendant of ... the Queen ... / by Henry Llewellyn Williams. London: E. Smith, [1883]. Pamphlet. (NLS)

BROWN, John Taylor see **BROWN, John**, 1810-82

BROWN, Oliver Madox, 1855-74, novelist; water-colourist

Oliver Madox Brown: a biographical sketch, 1855-1874 / by John H. Ingram. London: Elliot Stock, 1883. (NLS)

BROWN, Robert, 1822-63, religious businessman in India & Ceylon

Passages in the life of an India merchant, being memorials of Robert Brown, late of Bombay / compiled by his sister Helen Colvin. 3rd edition. London: J. Nisbet, 1868.

BROWN, Thomas Edward, 1830-97, Manx poet & clergyman; headmaster

Thomas Edward Brown, the Manx poet: an appreciation / by Selwyn George Simpson ... London: Walter Scott Publishing, 1906.

BROWNE, Charles Alfred, 1801?-66, Adjutant-General in India

A brief sketch of the life of General Charles A. Browne, formerly Military Secretary to the Government of Madras; afterwards [for 5 months] Honorary Secretary to the Church Missionary Society ... By a general officer. Dublin: George Herbert, 1881. photo.port. (NLS)

BROWNE, Edward Harold, 1811-91, Bishop of Ely then Winchester

Edward Harold Browne, D.D., Lord Bishop of Winchester, and Prelate of the Most Noble Order of the Garter: a memoir / by George William Kitchen. London: John Murray, 1895. (NC)

BROWNE, Hablot Knight ('Phiz'), 1815-82, illustrator, especially of Dickens, Lever and Ainsworth

Life and labours of Hablot K. Browne, 'Phiz' ... / by David Croal Thomson. London: Chapman and Hall, 1884.

-------. 'Phiz' (Hablot Knight Browne): a memoir. Including a selection from his correspondence and notes on his principal works / by Frederick George Kitton. London: George Redway, 1882. Pamphlet.

BROWNE, Sir James, 1839-96, General in India; railway engineer

The life and times of General Sir James Browne, R.E., K.C.B., K.C.S.I. (Buster Browne) / by James John McLeod Innes. London: John Murray, 1905.

BROWNHILL, Thomas Robson see **ROBSON (Thomas) Frederick**

BROWNING, Robert, 1812-89, major poet

The life and letters of Robert Browning / by Alexandra Leighton Orr. London: Smith, Elder, 1891. 2 volumes; revised edition in part rewritten by Frederic George Kenyon. London: Smith, Elder, 1908.

-------. Life of Robert Browning / by William Sharp. London: Walter Scott, 1890. (Great Writers series)

-------. Robert Browning / by Gilbert Keith Chesterton. London: Macmillan, 1903. (English Men of Letters series)

-------. Robert Browning - personalia / by Edmund Gosse. London: T. Fisher Unwin, 1890. 12mo.

BROWNLOW, William Robert, 1830-1901, Roman Catholic Bishop
Bishop Brownlow (1830-1901) / by Vincent Macnabb. London: Catholic Truth Society, 1901. Pamphlet. (NLS)

BRUCE, John, 1794-1880, Free Church Minister
In memoriam: the Rev. John Bruce, D.D., St Andrew's Free Church, Edinburgh. Edinburgh: John Maclaren, 1881. 12mo. photo. port. (NC)

BRUCE, John Collingwood, 1805-92, Newcastle schoolmaster & antiquary
The life and letters of John Collingwood Bruce, LL.D., D.C.L., F.S.A., of Newcastle-upon-Tyne / by his son Gainsford Bruce. Edinburgh: W. Blackwood, 1905. (NC)

BRUNEL, Isambard Kingdom, 1806-59, the foremost engineer of his day
The life of Isambard Kingdom Brunel, civil engineer / by [his son] Isambard Brunel. London: Longmans, Green, 1870.

BUCHANAN, Robert, 1802-75, leading Free Church Minister; Church historian
Robert Buchanan, D.D.: an ecclesiastical biography / by Norman Lockhart Walker. London: T. Nelson, 1877. (NC)

BUCHANAN, Robert Williams, 1841-1901, poet; novelist; dramatist
Robert Buchanan: some account of his life, work and his literary friendships / by Harriet Jay. London: T. Fisher Unwin, 1903.

BUCKINGHAM, James Silk, 1786-1855, traveller; prolific author; M.P.
Outline sketch of the voyages, travels, writings and public labours of James Silk Buckingham, Esq. / compiled from authentic sources. London: Peter Jackson, [184-?]. (B&J)

BUCKLAND, Francis Trevelyan, 1826-80, army surgeon; eccentric; zoologist
The life of Frank Buckland / by his brother-in-law George Cox Bompas. London: Smith, Elder, 1885.

BUCKLAND, William, 1784-1856, Dean of Westminster; geologist
The life and correspondence of William Buckland, D.D. F.R.S., sometime Dean of Westminster, twice President of the Geological Society and first President of the British Association / by his daughter [Anna B. Gordon]. London: John Murray, 1894.

BUCKLE, Henry Thomas, 1821-62, 'historian of civilization'; linguist
The life and writings of Henry Thomas Buckle / by Alfred Henry Huth. London: Sampson Low [etc.], 1880. 2 volumes.

BUCKLEY, Joseph, 1804-68, Manchester cotton spinner; Quaker
Memoirs of Joseph Buckley. Edited by his daughter [H. Buckley]. Glasgow: Robert Smeale, 1874. (NLS)

BUDGETT, Samuel, 1794-1851, wholesale provision merchant near Bristol
The successful merchant: sketches of the life of Mr Samuel Budgett, late of Kingswood Hill / by William Arthur. London: Hamilton, Adams, 1852; many other editions.

BUIST, George, 1805-60, newspaper editor in Scotland & Bombay
Memoir with testimonials of George Buist, LL.D. ... Addressed to his friends. Cupar: G.S. Tullis, 1846.

BULLAR, Joseph, 1808-?69, Southampton doctor
The beloved physician: a memoir of the late Dr. Joseph Bullar / by Henry Dayman. Southampton: W. Sharland, [1869]. Pamphlet. (NLS)

BULWER LYTTON see LYTTON

BUNBURY, Sir Charles James Fox, 8th Bart., 1809-86, Sheriff of Suffolk; botanist; in South Africa
Life, letters and journals of Sir Charles James Fox Bunbury. Edited by his wife Frances Joanna Bunbury. [Printed for private circulation] London, [1894]. 3 volumes; abridged edition as: 'The life of Sir Charles James Fox Bunbury, Bt. ...' Edited by his sister-in-law Katharine M. Lyell. London: John Murray, 1906. 2 volumes.

BUNTING, Jabez, 1779-1858, Wesleyan Minister leader; doctor
The life of Jabez Bunting, D.D.. With notices of contemporary persons and events / by Thomas Percival Bunting. London: Longman [etc.], 1859-87. 2 volumes. (Volume 2 completed by George Stringer Rowe) (NC)

BURFIELD, Henry John, 1827-81, clergyman in Leicester
Memoir of the late Rev. H. J. Burfield, M.A., Vicar of St. Mark's, Leicester and Hon. Canon of Ripon. With a selection of his sermons. Edited by his sister [E. Burfield]. Leicester: J. & T. Spencer, [1883]. photo. port. (NLS)

BURGESS, John, 1813-76, water colourist
The late John Burgess, Esq.: a sketch / by Rosario Aspa. [1877] (Reprinted from the 'Leamington Spa Chronicle')

BURGON, John William, 1813-88, Dean of Chichester; religious biographer
John William Burgon, late Dean of Chichester: a biography, with extracts from his letters and early journals / by Edward Meyrick Goulburn. London: John Murray, 1892. 2 volumes. (NC)

BURGOYNE, Sir John Fox, 1st Bart., 1782-1871, Irish Field Marshal; Royal Engineer; Chairman of Board of Public Works in Ireland
The life and correspondence of Field Marshal Sir John Burgoyne, Bart./ by his son-in-law George Wrottesley. London: R. Bentley, 1873. 2 volumes.
-------. A sketch of the life and death of the late Field-Marshal Sir John Burgoyne, Bart .../ by Francis Head. London: John Murray, 1872. Pamphlet. (NLS)

BURKE, Thomas Nicholas (Anthony), 1830-83, Irish Dominican
The life of the Very Rev. Thomas N. Burke, O.P. / by William John Fitzpatrick. London: Kegan Paul, Trench, Trubner, 1885. 2 volumes; revised edition. 1894.

BURN, James, d.1895 aged 36, spiritual biography
A trophy of invincible grace in the conversion of James Burn, who died June 17th 1895, aged 36 years / by his father [J. Burn]. London: F. Kirby, [1895?].

BURNABY, Frederick Gustavus, 1842-85, soldier; traveller; military balloonist
The life, adventures and political opinions of Frederick Gustavus Burnaby (Colonel Commanding Royal Horse Guards, Blue)/ by R. K. Mann. London: F. V. White, 1882. Pamphlet. (NLS)
-------. The life and times of Colonel Fred. Burnaby, late Colonel-Commanding Royal Horse Guards - Blues / by James Redding Ware and R. K. Mann. London: Field and Tuer [etc.] , [1885].
-------. The life of Colonel Fred. Burnaby / by Thomas Wright. London: Everett, 1908.
-------. Life, speeches and adventures of Col. Fred. Burnaby. [By R. K. Mann]. London: Diprose and Bateman, 1885. Pamphlet.

BURNE-JONES, Sir Edward Coley, 1st Bart., 1833-98, pre-Raphaelite artist
Edward Burne-Jones: a record and a review / by Malcolm Bell. London: G. Bell, 1892. 4to.; 4th edition 1899.
-------. Memorials of Edward Burne-Jones / by G.B.J. [i.e. Georgiana, Lady Burne-Jones]. London: Macmillan, 1904. 2 volumes.

BURNES, James, 1801-62, Physician-General of India

Memoir of James Burnes, K.H., F.R.S., &c., Physician-General, Bombay Army. Compiled from the recent Indian periodicals. [By W.A. Laurie]. Edinburgh, 1850. 12mo. (B&J)

BURNS, Sir George, 1st Bart., 1795-1890, Glasgow shipowner; founded the Cunard Line
Sir George Burns, Bart.: his times and friends / by Edwin Hodder. London: Hodder & Stoughton, 1890.

BURNS, James Drummond, 1823-64, Free Church Minister in Scotland, then Hampstead
Memoir and remains of the Rev. James D. Burns, M.A., of Hampstead / by James Hamilton. London: J. Nisbet, 1869. (NC)
-------. Reminiscences of the late Rev. James D. Burns ... [1864]. (From the 'Weekly Review' etc.)

BURNS, William Chalmers, 1815-68, Presbyterian missionary in China
Memoir of the Rev. William C. Burns, M.A., missionary to China from the English Presbyterian Church / by the late Islay Burns. London: J. Nisbet, 1870; new edition. 1885.

BURNS, William Hamilton, 1779-1859, Free Church Minister
The Pastor of Kilsyth, or memorials of the life and times of the Rev. W. H. Burns, D.D./ by Islay Burns. London: T. Nelson, 1860. (NC)

BURROWS, Henry William, 1816-92, clergyman
Henry William Burrows: memorials / by Elizabeth Wordsworth. London: Kegan Paul [etc.], 1894. (NLS)

BURTON, Sir Richard Francis, 1821-90, traveller; writer; linguist
The life of Captain Sir Richard F. Burton, K.C.M.G., F.R.G.S. [etc.] / by his wife Isabel Burton. London: Chapman & Hall, 1893. 2 volumes; edited in one volume by William Henry Wilkins. London: Duckworth, 1898.
-------. The life of Sir Richard Burton / by Thomas Wright. London: Everett, 1906. 2 volumes. (BL)
-------. The real Sir Richard Burton / by Walter Phelps Dodge. 2nd edition. London: T. Fisher Unwin, 1907.
-------. Richard F. Burton, K.C.M.G.: his early, private and public life. With an account of his travels and explorations / by Francis Hitchman. London: Sampson Low, 1887. 2 volumes. (NLS)
-------. A sketch of the career of Richard F. Burton ... By Alfred Bates Richards up to 1876. By Andrew Wilson up to 1879. By St. Clair Baddeley up to the present date 1886. London: Waterlow, 1886. (BL)
-------. The true life of Capt. Sir Richard F. Burton, K.C.M.G., F.R.G.S., etc. / written by his niece Georgiana M. Stisted ... London: H. S. Nichols, 1896.

BUTCHER, Henry William, d. c.1878, clergyman
In memoriam: Rev. H. W. Butcher ... 1: Obituary notice. 11: The funeral ... 111: Funeral services ... Margate: R. Robinson, [1878]. (BL)

BUTLER, George, 1819-90, Principal of Liverpool College; clergyman
Recollections of George Butler / by [his wife] Josephine Elizabeth Butler. Bristol: J. W. Arrowsmith, [1892]. (NC)

BUTLER, William John, 1818-94, Dean of Lincoln
Life and letters of William John Butler, late Dean of Lincoln, and sometime Vicar of Wantage. [By Arthur John Butler]. London: Macmillan, 1897.

BUTTERWORTH, Henry, 1786-1860, London law publisher
Memoir of the late Henry Butterworth, F.S.A. [1861]. Pamphlet. (Reprinted with additions from the 'Gentleman's Magazine') (NLS)

BUXTON, Fowell Arthur, n.d., Quaker

Memorials of Fowell Arthur Buxton. For private circulation only. London: printed by Samuel Harris, 1886. (B&J)

C., Henry, 1833-51, dead Eton pupil

A brief record of an Eton boy [Henry C.]. 2nd edition. London: R.B. & G. Seeley, 1851. 32mo. Pamphlet. (NLS)

CADBURY, Richard, 1835-99, Birmingham Quaker & cocoa manufacturer & philanthropist

Richard Cadbury of Birmingham / by his daughter Helen Cadbury Alexander. London: Hodder & Stoughton, 1906.

CADMAN, William, 1815-91, leading evangelical clergyman

A memorial of the late Rev. William Cadman, Canon of Canterbury and Chaplain to the Archbishop, Rector of Holy Trinity, St. Marylebone. Edited by Leonard Edmund Shelford. For private circulation. London: Wells Gardner, Darton, 1899. (BL)

CAIRNS, Sir Hugh McCalmont Cairns, 1st Earl, 1819-85, M.P.; Lord Chancellor

Brief memories of Hugh McCalmont, first Earl Cairns. [By Catherine M. Marsh]. London: J. Nisbet, 1885.(NC)

CAIRNS, John, 1818-92, United Presbyterian Minister; academic

Life and letters of John Cairns, D.D., LL.D. / by Alexander Robertson MacEwen. London: Hodder & Stoughton, 1895; and later editions.
-------. Principal Cairns / by John Cairns. Edinburgh: Oliphant, Anderson & Ferrier, [1897]. (Famous Scots Series)

CALDECOTT, Randolph, 1846-86, book illustrator

Randolph Caldecott: a personal memoir of his early art career / by Henry Blackburn. London: Sampson Low [etc.], 1886. photo. port.

CALDERWOOD, Henry, 1830-97, United Presbyterian Minister; philosopher

The life of Henry Calderwood, LL.D., F.R.S.E. / by his son [William Leadbeter Calderwood] and David Woodside ... London: Hodder & Stoughton, 1900. (NC)

CALLAWAY, Henry, 1817-90, Anglican Bishop of Kaffraria

Henry Callaway, M.D., D.D., first Bishop for Kaffraria, his life history and work: a memoir / by Marian S. Benham. Edited by William Benham. London: Macmillan, 1896.

CALLAWAY, William Fleetwood, 1834-86, printer in Ceylon and compiler of Cingalese dictionary

The life of W. F. Callaway / by Eric A. Lawrence. With recollections / by Robert William Dale and John Spencer Curwen. Printed for private circulation. [London: printed by Unwin Bros], 1890. photo. port. (NLS)

CALLIS, John Samuel, 1870-97, missionary in Uganda

In Uganda for Christ: the life story of the Rev. John Samuel Callis, B.A., of the Church Missionary Society / by Richard Deare Pierpont. London: Hodder & Stoughton, 1898.

CALTHROP, Gordon, 1823-94, clergyman

Found faithful: a memory of the late Reverend Gordon Calthrop, Vicar of St. Augustine's, Highbury, and Prebendary of St. Paul's / by Charles Bullock. London: 'Home Words', [1894]. (NLS)

CALTHROP, Richard, d.188- , sailor killed in the bombardment of Algiers
Richard Calthrop, his life, letters and death / by Louisa Calthrop. London: Knight, 1889. photo. port.

CALVERT, Edward, 1799-1883, artist
A memoir of Edward Calvert, artist / by his third son (Samuel Calvert) ... London: Sampson Low, 1893. 4to.

CALVERT, James, 1813-92, Wesleyan missionary to Fiji
James Calvert of Fiji / by George Stringer Rowe. London: Charles H. Kelly, 1893.
-------. James Calvert, or from dark to dawn in Fiji / by R. Vernon. London: S. W. Partridge, [1890]. (NLS)

CAMPBELL, Duncan, 1796-1873, West Highland Free Church Minister
Campbell of Kiltearn / by Duncan Macgregor. Edinburgh: Maclaren & MacNiven, 1874. 12mo.

CAMPBELL, Hugh, 1801-60, Primitive Methodist Minister
The standard bearer fallen, being a brief sketch of the life and labours of the Rev. Hugh Campbell / by ... Thomas Greenbury. London: R. Davies, 1862. 12mo. (NC)

CAMPBELL, Hugh, 1803-55, Presbyterian Minister in England
In memoriam: a sketch of the life and labours of the late Rev. Hugh Campbell, Professor of Theology and Church History in the Theological College of the Presbyterian Church in England / by ... Peter Lorimer. London: J. Nisbet, 1855. (NC)

[CAMPBELL, James Ure], n.d., navvy who went blind
The story of a working man's blindness / by George Alexander Johnston Ross. Glasgow: printed by 'Springburn Express' Office, 1894; 9th edition 1898.

CAMPBELL, John, 1794-1867, Congregational Minister; miscellaneous writer; editor
Life and labours of John Campbell, D.D. / by Robert Ferguson & Andrew Morton Brown. London: R. Bentley, 1867.

CAMPBELL, John ('Will Harrow'), 1808-92, agricultural labourer; poet
A village poet / by Robert Menzies Fergusson. Paisley: Alexander Gardner, 1897.

CANDLISH, Robert Smith, 1806-73, Free Presbyterian leader
Life of Robert Smith Candlish, D.D., Minister of St George's Free Church and Principal of the New College, Edinburgh / by Jean L. Watson. Edinburgh: James Gemmell, 1882. 12mo.
-------. Memorials of Robert Smith Candlish, D.D., Minister of St George's Free Church and Principal of the New College, Edinburgh / by William Wilson & Robert Rainy. Edinburgh: A. & C. Black, 1880. photo. port. (NC)

CANNING, Charles John Canning, 1st Earl, 1812-62, M.P.; Governor-General of India 1856-62
Earl Canning / by Henry Stuart Cunningham. Oxford: Clarendon Press, 1891. (Rulers of India series)

CAPERN, Edward, 1819-94, 'The rural postman of Bideford' & poet
Recollections of Edward Capern / by William Ormond. Bristol, [1860?]. (BL)

CAPPER, Samuel, 1782-1852, Quaker Minister & temperance worker
Memoir of Samuel Capper. [By Katherine Backhouse]. London: William & Frederick G. Cash, 1855.

CAREY, Eustace, 1791-1855, Baptist missionary in Calcutta
Evans Carey, a missionary in India: a memoir / by Esther Carey. London: Pewtress,

1857. (NLS)

CARLETON, William, 1794-1869, Irish realist novelist
The life of William Carleton, being his autobiography and letters, and an account of his life and writings from the point at which the autobiography breaks off ... / by David James O'Donoghue ... London: Downey, 1896. 2 volumes.

CARLILE, Warrand, 1796-1881, Scottish Presbyterian missionary in Jamaica
Thirty-eight years mission life in Jamaica: a brief sketch of the Rev. Warrand Carlile, missionary at Brownsville. By one of his sons [i.e. Gavin Carlile]. London: J. Nisbet, 1884. (NLS)

CARLISLE, Thomas, 1838-70, Irish Methodist New Connection Minister
The earnest Minister: a memoir of the Rev. Thomas Carlisle / by William Cooke ... London: Hodder & Stoughton, 1871. (NLS)

CARLYLE, Thomas, 1795-1881, thinker, writer, biographer, essayist
Life of Thomas Carlyle / by Richard Garnett. London: Walter Scott Publishing, 1887. (Great Writers series)
-------. Some personal reminiscences of Thomas Carlyle / by Andrew James Symington. Paisley: Alexander Gardner, 1886.
-------. Thomas Carlyle / by Hector Copland Macpherson. Edinburgh: Oliphant, Anderson & Ferrier, [1897]. (Famous Scots Series)
-------. Thomas Carlyle / by James Anthony Froude. [Part 1] A history of the first forty years of his life, 1795-1835. London: Longmans, Green, 1882. 2 volumes. [Part 2] A history of his life in London, 1834-1881. London: Longmans, Green, 1884. 2 volumes.
and many other titles

CARMENT, David, 1772-1856 <u>see</u> **CARMENT, James**

CARMENT, James, 1816-80, Free Church Minister
Memoir of the Rev. James Carment, of Comrie / by Samuel Carment ... Dalkeith: John Carment [etc.], 1886. photo.port.
*Includes a biography of Rev. David Carment. (NC)

CARMICHAEL, James Drummond, 1849-81, Highland laird
Memorials of James Drummond Carmichael, Arthurstone. Edited by Alexander Monfries. For private circulation. Dundee: printed by John Leng, [1885]. photo.port. (NC)

CARPENTER, Philip Pearsall, 1819-77, Unitarian Minister; shell collector
Memoirs of the life and work of Philip Pearsall Carpenter ..., chiefly derived from his letters. Edited by his brother Russell Lant Carpenter. 2nd edition. London: C. Kegan Paul, 1880.

CARRODUS, John Tiplady, 1836-95, violinist
J. T. Carrodus, violonist: a life story, 1836-1895 / by Ada Carrodus. With an account of his student days / by Clara Molique. London: A. J. Bowden, 1897. (NLS)

'CARROLL, Lewis' <u>see</u> **DODGSON, Charles**

CARTER, Thomas Thellusson, 1808-1901, tractarian clergyman; work with 'female penitents'
The beautiful life of an ideal priest, or reminiscences of Thomas Thellusson Carter, Hon. Canon of Christ Church, Oxford, and Warden of the House of Mercy, Clewer / by Henry Mortimer Luckock. Lichfield: 'Johnson's Head', 1902. Pamphlet. (NLS)
-------. Life and letters of Thomas Thellusson Carter, Warden of the House of Mercy, Clewer ... Edited by William Henry Hutchings. London: Longmans, Green, 1903.

-------. Life and work of the Rev. T. T. Carter, Hon. Canon of Christ Church, Oxford, and Warden of the House of Mercy, Clewer / by Jane Francis Mary Carter. London: Longmans, Green, 1911.

CARTHEW, Thomas Henry, 1856-96, Bible Christian then United Methodist Free Church missionary to East Africa
Life of Thomas H. Carthew, missionary to East Africa / by Joseph Kirsop. London: Crombie, 1897. (NUC)

CARUS, William, 1804-91, distinguished evangelical clergyman
'Speaking years': a memory of the Rev. William Carus, M.A., formerly Canon of Winchester. With extracts from his writings/ by Charles Bullock. London: 'Home Words', [1891]. (NLS)

CARVOSSO, Benjamin, 1789-1854, Cornish Wesleyan missionary in Australia
The faithful pastor: a memoir of Rev. Benjamin Carvosso, forty years a Wesleyan Minister, and one of the first Wesleyan missionaries to Australia and Van Diemen's Land/ by George Blencowe. London: J. Gladding, 1857. 12mo. (NLS)

CASSELL, John, 1817-65, publisher
John Cassell / by Geoffrey Holden Pike. London: Cassell, 1894. (The World's Workers series)
-------. John Cassell, his life and work ... / by John William Kirton. London: Cassell, 1891. Pamphlet. (NLS)

CASSON, Hodgson, 1788-1851, Methodist Minister
Christianity in earnest as exemplified in the life and labours of the Rev. Hodgson Casson / by Allen Steele. London: Charles H. Kelley, 1853; and other editions. (NLS)

CAVAGNARI, Sir Pierre Louis Napoleon, 1841-79, British Resident in Kabul
The life and career of Major Sir Louis Cavagnari, C.S.I., K.C.B., British Envoy at Cabul ... / by Kally Prosono Dey. Calcutta: Ghose, 1881. (BL)

CAVAN, Frederick John William Lambart, 8th Earl of, 1815-87, Irish peer
Frederick John William, eighth Earl of Cavan: a life sketch. To which is added a selection of the late Earl's addresses. [By C. A. C.]. Printed for private circulation only. [c.1888]. photo.ports. (NC)

CHADS, Sir Henry Ducie, 1788-1868, Admiral
Memoir of Admiral Sir Henry Ducie Chads. By an old follower [i.e. Montagu Burrows]. Portsea: Griffin, 1869.

CHALMERS, Frederick Skene Courtenay, 1804-85, soldier in India
Frederick Chalmers: a sketch. [By Catherine M. Marsh]. London: J. Nisbet, 1896. (NLS)

CHALMERS, George Paul, 1833-78, painter
George Paul Chalmers, R.S.A. / by Alexander Gibson. Edinburgh: David Douglas, 1879. 4to. (BL)
-------. George Paul Chalmers, R.S.A., and the art of his time / by Edward Pinnington. Glasgow: T. R. Annan, 1896. Folio. (100 copies)

CHALMERS, James, 1841-1901, missionary explorer in South Pacific
James Chalmers, missionary and explorer of Rarotonga and New Guinea / by William Robson. [1887]; new edition.London: S. W. Partridge, 1903.
-------. James Chalmers of New Guinea: missionary, pioneer, martyr / by Cuthbert Lennox. London: Andrew Melrose, 1902.

CHALMERS, Thomas, 1821-83, schoolmaster, then paper mill owner

In memoriam: Thomas Chalmers, Longcroft. Born August 18 1821 - Died November 30 1883. Privately printed. Edinburgh: printed by T. & A. Constable, 1884. photo.port. (NLS)

CHAMBERS, Robert, 1802-71, important Edinburgh publisher and author
   Memoir of Robert Chambers. With autobiographic reminiscences of William Chambers. Edinburgh: W. & R. Chambers, 1872; 13th edition with supplementary chapter, 1884.

CHAMBERS, William, 1800-83 <u>see</u> **CHAMBERS, Robert**

CHAPMAN, Daniel, 1799-1857, Methodist Minister
   Memorials of the Rev. David Chapman / by James Grose ... Boston [Lincs]: printed by R. Roberts, 1857. (NLS)

CHAPMAN, George, 1846-91, Anglo-Catholic clergyman
   George Chapman: a narrative of a devoted life. [By R.S.] ... London: Swan Sonnenschein, 1893. (NLS)
-------. Some brief recollections of the late Rev. George Chapman, M.A., first Vicar of the Annunciation, Brighton. (By one of his people). With an introduction by John Bagot-de la Bere. Oxford: printed by Mowbray, [1892]. photo.port. (NLS)

CHAPMAN, James, 1799-1879, Anglican Bishop of Colombo
   Memorials of James Chapman, D.D., first Bishop of Colombo. With a prefatory letter from Richard Durnford. London: Skeffington, 1892. photo. port. Pamphlet. (NLS)

CHAPMAN, John, 1846-91, Secretary of the Church Missionary Society
   Memorials of the Rev. John Chapman, late Secretary of the Church Missionary Society ... Together with memoirs of his life and character. London: Seeley, Jackson & Halliday, 1863.

CHARLESWORTH, John, 1782-1864, clergyman
   A quiet worker for good: a familiar sketch of the late John Charlesworth, B.D. ..., Rector of St. Mildred's, Bread Street, London ... / by John Purcell Fitzgerald. London: Dalton & Lucy, 1865. 12mo. (NLS)

CHARLETON, Robert, 1809-72, Quaker pin manufacturer, pacifist & teetotaller
   Memoir of Robert Charleton, compiled chiefly from his letters. Edited by his sister-in-law Anna F. Fox. London: Samuel Harris, 1873; 2nd edition with considerable additions. 1876. (NLS)

CHEEK, Arthur Marcus Hill, 1840-57, young religious soldier killed in India
   The martyr of Allahabad: memorials of Ensign Arthur Marcus Hill Cheek, of the Sixth Native Bengal Infantry, murdered by Sepoys at Allahabad / by Robert Meek. [2nd edition with additions]. London: J. Nisbet, 1858. (NLS)

CHESNEY, Francis Rawdon, 1789-1872, General; explorer in Middle East
   The life of the late General F. R. Chesney, Colonel Commandant Royal Artilley, D.C.L., F.R.S. [etc.]. / by his wife [Louisa Chesney] and daughter [Mrs. Jane O'Donnell]. Edited by Stanley Lane-Poole. London: Remington, 1885; 2nd edition 1893. (NLS)

CHESTER, William Bennett, 1820-93, Anglican Bishop of Killaloe [&c.]
   'A bishop beloved': a memoir of the late Right Rev. William Bennett Chester, D.D. .../ by Charles Bullock. London: 'Home Words', [1894]. (NLS)

CHEW, Richard, 1827-95, founder of United Methodist Free Church
   Memoir of the Rev. Richard Chew / by Edward Boaden. London: Andrew Crombie, 1896.

CHICHESTER, Henry Thomas Pelham, 3rd Earl of, 1804-86, religious peer

'The cedar is fallen': a tribute of respect to the late Earl of Chichester / by John Benjamin Figgis. Brighton: D. B. Friend, 1886. 32mo. Pamphlet. (NLS)

CHILDERS, Hugh Culling Eardley, 1827-96, Liberal Chancellor & Home Secretary; in Australia
The life and correspondence of the Right Hon. Hugh C. E. Childers, 1827-1896 / by his son Spencer Edmund Childers. London: John Murray, 1901. 2 volumes.

CHILDREN, John George, 1777-1852, zoologist, entomologist
Memoir of J. G. Children ... / by A[nna] A[tkins]. [Privately printed. 1853]. (BL)

CHRISTIAN, Ewan, 1814-95, Church architect
Ewan Christian - architect. [Edited by Elisabeth Rundle Charles]. Printed for private circulation. Cambridge: University Press, 1896.

CHRISTIE, Albany James, 1817-91, Jesuit priest
In memoriam: a short sketch of Father Albany James Christie, of the Society of Jesus / by Richard Frederick Clarke. London: Burns & Oates, 1891. Pamphlet. (Reprinted from 'The Month') (NLS)

CHRISTIE, William Dougal, 1816-74, M.P., diplomat; author; defender of J.S. Mill
W. D. Christie, C.B.. 'Confidential at present'. [1876]. Pamphlet.(B&J)

CHRISTISON, Sir Robert, 1st Bart., 1797-1882, toxicologist; medical adviser to the Crown
The life of Sir Robert Christison, Bart., M.D. [etc.], Professor of Materia Medica in the University of Edinburgh, Physician to the Queen in Scotland, etc.. Edited by his sons. Edinburgh: W. Blackwood, 1885-86. 2 volumes.

CHURCH, Sir Richard, 1785-1873, liberator of Greece; generalissimo of the Greek army
Chapters in an adventurous life: Sir Richard Church in Italy and Greece / by E. M. Church. Edinburgh: W. Blackwood, 1895. (NLS)
-------. Sir Richard Church, C.B., G.C.H., Commander-in-Chief of the Greeks in the War of Independence / by Stanley Lane-Poole. London: Longmans, Green, 1890. (NLS)

CHURCH, Richard William, 1815-90, Dean of St Paul's Cathedral
Life and letters of Dean Church. Edited by his daughter Mary Caroline Church. London: Macmillan, 1894.
-------. Richard William Church / by Augustus Blair Donaldson. London: Rivingtons, 1905.

CHURCHILL, Lord Randolph Henry Spencer-, 1849-95, Conservative statesman father of Sir Winston Churchill
The life and speeches of Lord Randolph Henry Spencer-Churchill, M.P. for Woodstock ... Edited by Frank Banfield. London: J. & R. Maxwell, [1884]. (NLS)
-------. Lord Randolph Churchill / by Winston Churchill. London: Macmillan, 1906. 2 volumes; in one volume 1907; revised edition [with new correspondence]. London: Odhams, 1952.
-------. Lord Randolph Churchill / by Archibald, Earl of Rosebery. London: Arthur L. Humphreys, 1906.
-------. Randolph Spencer-Churchill as a product of his age, being a personal and political monograph / by Thomas Hay Sweet Escott. London: Hutchinson, 1895.

CHURCHILL, Robert Ernest Houghton, b.1851, Methodist schoolboy
The praying school-boy: a brief memoir of Robert Ernest Houghton Churchill / by his stepmother [Mrs Charles Churchill]. London: Elliot Stock, 1869. 12mo. (B&J)

CLARE, Henry, d.1894, a converted, formerly violent cripple
A debtor to mercy alone: a brief record of the power of Divine Grace in the life and death of Henry Clare, of West Kington, Wilts.. London: William Wileman, [1897].

Pamphlet. (NLS)

CLARE, John, 1793-1864, native poet; in an asylum 1837-64
   The life of John Clare / by Frederick Martin. London: Macmillan, 1865.
   -------. Life and remains of John Clare, the Northamptonshire peasant poet / by John Law Cherry. London: Warne, 1873. (BL)

CLARENCE & AVONDALE, Prince Albert Victor Christian Edward, Duke of, 1864-92, heir to the British throne who died prematurely
   His Royal Highness Duke of Clarence and Avondale: a memoir ... / by James Edmund Vincent. London: John Murray, 1893.
   -------. Ich dien! I serve! Prince Albert Victor: a memory / by Charles Bullock. London: 'Home Words' Publishing Office, [1892?]; 2nd edition as '... Prince Albert Victor ...'

CLARENDON, George William Frederick Villiers, 4th Earl of, 1800-70, diplomat & statesman
   The life and letters of George William Frederick, fourth Earl of Clarendon, K.G., G.C.B. / by Herbert Maxwell. London: Edward Arnold, 1913. 2 volumes.

CLARK, Joseph, d.1866 aged 66, Quaker schoolmaster
   A brief memoir of Joseph Clark, for nearly twenty years Superintendent of Severn Street First-Day School, Birmingham. Birmingham, 1867.

CLARK, (Josiah) Latimer, 1822-98, Irish electrical engineer
   Mr Latimer Clark, C.E.: a sketch of his life and work / by H. T. Humphreys. London: W. Poole. [1882]. (Reprinted from 'Celebrities of the Day') (NLS)

CLARK Robert, 1850-1900, Anglican missionary in India
   Robert Clark, of the Panjab, pioneer missionary and statesman / by Henry Martyn Clark. London: Andrew Melrose, 1907. (NLS)

CLARK, Stewart, 1814-97, Postmaster-General, North West Territories, India
   Stewart Clark, one of nature's noblemen / by Sophy Emily Stewart Clark. London: Balliere, 1898. (BL)

CLARKE, William Fairlie, 1833-84, doctor; medical writer
   William Fairlie Clarke, M.D., F.R.C.S., author of 'Diseases of the tongue', etc.: his life and letters, hospital sketches and addresses / by E. A. W. [Eliza Ann Walker]. London: William Hunt, 1885. (NLS)

CLAY, John, 1796-1858, chaplain to Preston Gaol & penal reformer
   The prison chaplain: a memoir of the Rev. John Clay, B.D., late Chaplain of the Preston Gaol ... / by his son Walter Lowe Clay. Cambridge: Macmillan, 1861: reprinted Montclaire, N.J.: Patterson Smith, 1969.

CLEGG, Alfred Henry, 1858-86, Methodist missionary in the Gambia
   Fallen on the field, being memorials of the Rev. Alfred Henry Clegg, missionary to the Gambia / by John S. Pawlyn. London: T. Woolmer, 1889. (NLS)

CLEGHORN, Thomas, 1818-74, advocate & founder of the Wellington School for young offenders
   Memorial sketch of Thomas Cleghorn. [By D.M.]. Printed for private circulation. [Edinburgh: printed by Frank Murray], 1881.

CLEMINSON, Frederick, n.d., Methodist
   Freddie Cleminson: the brief story of a blessed life / by Thomas M'Cullagh. London: Wesleyan Conference Office, [1899]. 16mo.

CLERK-MAXWELL, James see MAXWELL, James Clerk

CLONCURRY, Valentine Browne Lawless, 2nd Baron, 1773-1853, radical Irish peer
The life, times and contemporaries of Lord Cloncurry / by William John Fitzpatrick. Dublin: James Duffy, 1855. (BL)

CLOSE, Francis, 1797-1882, evangelical Dean of Carlisle
Memorials of Dean Close. Edited by one who knew him. Carlisle: B. Stewart, 1885. (NLS)

CLOUGH, Arthur Hugh, 1819-61, Oxford academic; poet
Arthur Hugh Clough: a monograph / by Samuel Waddington. London: G. Bell, 1883.

CLOUGH, Robert, 1830-94, temperance worker
Life of Robert Clough, temperance advocate (of Rochdale) / written by his daughter Lily Clough. Sheffield: Parker, 1898.

CLOWES, William, 1780-1851, co-founder of Primitive Methodism
The life of the Reverend and venerable William Clowes, one of the patriarchs of the Primitive Methodist Connection / by William Garner. New edition. London: William Lister, 1868.
-------. The life of the venerable William Clowes, one of the founders of the Primitive Methodist Connection / by John Davison. London: Thomas King, 1854. (BL)
-------. The venerable William Clowes: a sketch / by Thomas Guttery. London: Joseph Toulson, [1888]. (NC)

CLYDE, Sir Colin Campbell, 1st Baron, 1792-1863, Field-Marshal; suppressed the Indian Mutiny
Clyde and Strathnairn / by Owen Tudor Burne. Oxford: Clarendon Press, 1891. (Rulers of India Series)
-------. Colin Campbell, Lord Clyde / by Archibald Forbes. London: Macmillan, 1895. (English Men of Action series)
-------. The life of Colin Campbell, Lord Clyde, illustrated by extracts from his diary and correspondence ... / by Lawrence Shadwell. Edinburgh: W. Blackwood, 1881. 2 volumes.

COBDEN, Richard, 1804-1865, calico printer; statesman; Anti Corn Law League leader
In memoriam: the life and labours of Richard Cobden / by A. T. Scott. London: William Tweedie, 1865. Pamphlet. (NLS)
-------. The life of Richard Cobden / by John Morley. London: Chapman & Hall, 1881. 2 volumes; in one volume 1883; revised edition 1903; and many later editions.
-------. Richard Cobden, the apostle of free trade, his political career and public services: a biography / by John McGilchrist. London: Lockwood, 1865. photographic portrait & illustrations. (NLS)
and other biographies

CODRINGTON, Sir Edward, 1770-1851, Admiral
Memoir of the life of Admiral Sir Edward Codrington. With selections from his public and private correspondence. Edited by his daughter Jane Bourchier. London: Longmans, Green, 1873. 2 volumes; abridged edition as: 'Memorial of ...'. 1875.

COGAN, Eliezer, 1762-1855, Presbyterian then Congregational Minister; headmaster
Memoir of the late Rev. Eliezer Cogan. London: Charles Green, 1855. (Reprinted from 'The Christian Reformer')

COLBECK, James Alfred, 185? -88, missionary in Burma
A short memoir of James Alfred Colbeck, mission priest (S.P.G.) and Chaplain of Mandalay, Burma, who entered into rest, March 2 1888 / by his brother [George H. Colbeck]. London: S.P.C.K., 1902. Pamphlet. (Mission Heroes series) (NLS)

COLBORNE, John, 1st Baron Seaton, 1778-1863, Field-Marshal; Governor of Upper Canada 1830-8, and of the Ionian Islands 1843-9

The life of John Colborne, Field-Marshal Lord Seaton, G.C.B. [etc.] / compiled from his letters, records of his conversations, and other sources by George Charles Moore Smith. London: John Murray, 1903. (BL)

COLBY, Thomas Frederick, 1784-1852, General; Director of the Ordnance Survey
Memoir of the life of Major-General Colby, R.E. ... / by Joseph Ellison Portlock. London: Seeley, Jackson & Halliday, 1869.

COLDSTREAM, John, 1806-63, doctor
Biography of the late John Coldstream, M.D., F.R.C.P.E., being an address ... / by John Hutton Balfour. Edinburgh: printed by T. Constable, 1864. (NLS)
-------. Sketch of the life of John Coldstream. [By John Phillips Coldstream]. Edinburgh: Maclaren & Macniven, 1877. (BL)

COLE, George Vicat, 1833-93, 'the most popular landscape painter of his time'
The life and paintings of Vicat Cole, R.A. / by Robert Chignell London: Cassell, 1898. 3 volumes. 4to. (BL)

COLENSO, John William, 1814-83, heretical Anglican Bishop in South Africa
The life of John William Colenso, D.D., Bishop of Natal / by George William Cox. London: W. Ridgway, 1888. 2 volumes.

COLERIDGE, Sir John Duke, 1st Baron, 1820-94, Lord Chief Justice
Life and correspondence of John Duke, Lord Coleridge, Lord Chief Justice of England. Written and edited by Ernest Hartley Coleridge. London: W. Heinemann, 1904. 2 volumes.

COLLEY, Sir George Pomeroy- see **POMEROY-COLLEY, Sir George**

COLLIER, Charles, c.1785-1870, army doctor
Deputy Inspector General of Army Hospitals, Charles Collier ...: a life sketch / by his daughter M.A.E.L.. For private circulation. London, 1870. photo. port. 16mo. (BL)

COLLIER, John Payne, 1789-1883, Shakespeare critic
Notes on the life of John Payne Collier ... / by Henry Benjamin Wheatley. London: Elliot Stock, 1884. 12mo. (NLS)

COLLINS, (Edward James) Mortimer, 1827-76, novelist
Mortimer Collins, his letters and friendships. With some account of his life. Edited by Frances Collins. London: Sampson Low [etc.], 1877. 2 volumes. photo.port.

COLLINS, Thomas, 1810-64, Methodist Minister
The life of the Rev. Thomas Collins / by Samuel Coley. 2nd edition. London: Elliot Stock, 1869; abridged by Simpson Johnston. 1896. (NLS)
-------. Thomas Collins, a typical evangelist / by Simpson Johnson. London: Robert Culley, [1906]. 12mo. (Library of Methodist Biography) (NLS)

COLLINS, Sir William, 11, 1819-95, publisher, bookseller; temperance worker
A souvenir: Sir William Collins. [Glasgow: Collins, 189-].

COLMAN, Alan Cozens-Hardy, d.1876, director of Norwich engineering firm; on Norfolk County Council
In memoriam: Alan Cozens-Hardy Colman / by his sister Laura Elizabeth Stuart. Printed for private circulation. Norwich: Fletcher, 1898. (B&J)

COLMAN, Jeremiah James, 1830-98, mustard, starch and blue manufacturer; M.P.
Jeremiah James Colman: a memoir / by one of his daughters Helen Caroline Colman. Privately printed. London: Chiswick Press, 1905.

COLQUHOUN, Sir James, of Luss, 11th Bart., 1804-73, laird; M.P.; drowned
Memorials of James, eleventh Baronet of Colquhoun and Luss. Helensburgh: Macneur & Bryden, 1876. 12mo. photo. port. (NC)

COLVILLE, John, 1827-66, evangelist
James Colville, Yr, of Burnside, Campbeltown, evangelist: a memoir of his life and work / by his widow [Mary A. Colville]. Edinburgh: A. Elliot, 1888. (NC)

COLVIN, Andrew, n.d., Blyth Methodist
Saint Andrew of Blyth, or memorials of the life of Andrew Colvin of that town. Compiled and edited by R. W. G. Hunter. Rochdale: Joyful News Depot, 1897.

COLVIN, John Russell, 1807-57, Lieut.-Governor North Western Provinces, India 1853-7
John Russell Colvin, the last Lieut-Governor of the North-West under the [East India] Company / by Auckland Colvin. Oxford: Clarendon Press, 1895. (Rulers of India Series) (NC)

COMBE, George, 1788-1858, phrenologist
The life of George Combe, author of 'The Constitution of man' / by Charles Gibbon. London: Macmillan, 1878. 2 volumes. (NLS)

COMBER, Thomas James, 1852-87, missionary in Africa
Thomas J. Comber, missionary pioneer to the Congo / by John Brown Meyers. London: S. W. Partridge, [1888].

COMBERMERE, Sir Stapleton Cotton, 1st Viscount, 1773-1865, M.P.; Governor of Barbados; Commander-in-Chief India
Memoirs and correspondence of Field-Marshal Viscount Combermere, G.C.B., from his family papers / by Mary, Viscountess Combermere & William Wallingford Knollys. London: Hurst & Blackett, 1866. 2 volumes. (NLS)

COMPTON, Henry [i.e. Charles MACKENZIE], 1805-77, comedian
Memoir of Henry Compton. Edited by Charles & Edward Compton. London: Tinsley, 1879.

CONDER, Josiah, 1789-1855, bookseller; writer; editor of 'Eclectic Review'
Josiah Conder: a memoir / by Eustace Rogers Conder. London: John Snow, 1857. (NUC)

CONGELTON, John Vesey Parnell, 2nd Baron, 1805-83, traveller; Plymouth Brethren
'Not of the world': memoir of Lord Congleton / by Henry Groves. London: J. F. Shaw, 1884. (NLS)

CONOLLY, John, 1794-1866, mental health reformer
A memoir of John Conolly, M.D., D.C.L., comprising a sketch of treatment of the insane in Europe and America / by James Clark. London: John Murray, 1869. (NLS)

COODE, Athelstan, 1858-97, clergyman in Cornwall
Athelstan Coode. [By James Truron]. London: Skeffington, 1898. (B&J)

COOK, Archibald, 1789-1865, Free Church Minister see **COOK, Finlay**

COOK, Finlay, 1778-1858, Free Church Minister
Memoir and letters of Rev. Finlay Cook and of Rev. Archibald Cook. Edited by John Kennedy. Inverness: Northern Counties Newspaper & Printing & Publishing Company, 1895. (NC)

COOK, John Aubone, 1811-53, clergyman
Memoir of the Rev. John Aubone Cook, M.A., Vicar of South Benfleet and Rural

Dean / by W. E. Heygate. London: Joseph Masters, 1860. Pamphlet. (NLS)

COOKE, Henry, 1788-1868, Irish Presbyterian leader
The life and times of Henry Cooke, D.D., LL.D., President of Assembly's College, Belfast / by his son-in-law Josias Leslie Porter. Belfast: William Mullan, 1871; People's Edition, 1875.

COOKE, William, 1806-84, New Connection Methodist Minister
Memoir of the Rev. William Cooke, D.D. ... / by Samuel Hulme. London: C. D. Ward, 1886. (NLS)

COOKE, Sir William Bryan, 8th Bart., 1782-1851, Yorkshire banker & M.P.
In memoriam: Sir W. Bryan Cooke, Esq., of Wheatley. Doncaster: Brooke, White & Hatfield, 1852. 12mo. Pamphlet. (B&J)

COOP, Timothy, d.1887 aged 69, Lancashire businessman, Methodist and temperance worker
The life of Timothy Coop, or the story of a consecrated business career ... / by William Thomas Moore. London: Christian Commonwealth Publishing, [1889]. photo. port.

COOPER, Daniel, n.d., work with destitute women and girls
A brief memoir of the late Daniel Cooper. With some account of his life-work / by John Matthias Weylland ... London: Morgan & Scott, [18--]. 12mo. photo.port. (B&J)

CORBETT, John, 1817-1901, salt manufacturer; canal and railway director; M.P.
John Corbett, Esq., of Impney, Worcestershire: a sketch. Stourbridge: Mark & Moody, [c.1901]. Pamphlet. (Reprinted from the 'County Express') (NLS)

CORRIE, George Elwes, 1793-1885, Master of Jesus College, Cambridge
Memorials of the life of George Elwes Corrie, D.D., Master of Jesus College, Cambridge ... sometime Norrisian Professor on the University of Cambridge, drawn principally from his diary and correspondence. Edited by Michael Holroyd. Cambridge: University Press, 1890.

COTTON, Sir Arthur Thomas, 1803-1899, general & irrigation engineer in India; philanthropist
General Sir Arthur Cotton, R.E., K.C.S.I.: his life and work ... / by his daughter [Elizabeth Reid, Lady Hope] ... London: Hodder & Stoughton, 1900.
-------. Sir Arthur Cotton, philanthropist and engineer / by Henry Morris. London: Christian Literature Society for India, 1901.

COTTON, George Edward Lynch, 1813-66, Anglican Bishop of Calcutta
Memoir of George Edward Lynch Cotton, D.D., Bishop of Calcutta and Metropolitan. With selections from his journals and correspondence. Edited by Sophia Anne Cotton. London: Longmans, Green, 1871. (NC)

COTTON, James Henry, 1781-1862, Dean of Bangor
The life and speeches of the Very Rev. J. H. Cotton, B.C.L., Dean of Bangor and Rector of Llanllechyd ... Edited by William Hughes, *Curate of Glasynfryn, Bangor.* Bangor: Nixon and Jarvis, 1874. (B&J)

COUCH, Jonathan, 1789-1870, 'the Cornish ichthyologist'
Life of Jonathan Couch, F.L.S., of Polperro, the Cornish ichthyologist / by Bertha Couch. Liskeard: John Philp, [1891]. (BL)

COULTHART, John Ross, 1807-87, Scottish bank manager and sanitary reformer
Memoir of John Ross Coulthart, of Aston-under-Lyne in the County of Lancaster, forty years manager of the Ashton, Stalybridge, Hyde and Glossop Bank / by William Kingo Armstrong. Edinburgh: printed for the author by M'Farlane & Erskine, 1876.

COUSINS, Samuel, 1801-87, mezzotint engraver
Memoirs of Samuel Cousins / by George Pycroft. Printed for private circulation. Exeter, [1887]. (BL)
-------. Samuel Cousins / by Alfred Whitman. London: G. Bell, 1904. [A catalogue with memoir]

COVELL, Francis, 1808-79, Pastor
A brief account of the Lord's dealing with the late Mr. F. Covell, Minister of Providence Chapel, Croydon ... [By George Covell]. London: W. H. Guest, 1880.
-------. Gathered fragments in the life of Francis Covell, Minister of the Gospel and Pastor of Providence Chapel, Croydon. [By Ebenezer Wilmshurst]. London: E. Wilmshurst, [1896].

COWAN, Alexander, 1775-1859, Edinburgh religious philanthropist
Alexander Cowan. [By Thomas Constable]. Woodhill, 1876. Pamphlet. (Extracted from 'Archibald Constable and his literary correspondents') (NLS)

COWEN, Joseph, junior, 1831-1900, radical M.P. & reformer; journalist; temperance advocate
The life and speeches of Joseph Cowen, M.P. / by Evan Rowland Jones. London: Sampson Low [etc.], [1886]. (NLS)
-------. Life of Joseph Cowan, M.P. for Newcastle, 1874-86. With letters from his speeches and verbatim report of his last speech / by William Duncan. London: Walter Scott Publishing, 1904.

COX, David, 1783-1859, landscape painter in water-colours
A biography of David Cox. With remarks on his works and genius / by William Hall. Edited with additions by John Thackeray Bunce. London: Cassell, Petter, Galpin, 1881.
-------. Memoir of the life of David Cox, Member of the Society of Painters in Water Colours. With selections from his correspondence and some account of his works ... / by Nathaniel Neal Solly. London: Chapman & Hall, 1873. photographically illustrated. (BL)

COX, Edward Townsend, 1769-1863, doctor, accoucheur
Edward Townsend Cox, Birmingham. Privately printed. [London, 1870]. photo. port.

COX, William Spiller, 1870-97, missionary in Sierra Leone
Early promoted: a memoir of the Rev. William Spiller Cox, M.A., of Queen's College, and Wycliffe Hall, Oxford, missionary to Sierra Leone / compiled by his father [Edward Webster Cox] ... London: Sampson Low, Marston, 1897.

CRABB, James, 1774-1851, Wesleyan Minister; 'The gypsy's friend'
A memoir of the Rev. James Crabbe, late of Southampton / by John Rudall. London: Walton & Maberly, 1854.

CRABBE, William Thomson, 1844-99, medical missionary in Birmingham
W. Thomson Crabbe, F.R.C.S.E., medical missionary / by Annie Robina Butler. London: S.W. Partridge, 1899. (NLS)

CRAIG, James, b.1818, English Presbyterian missionary in Europe
The Gospel on the Continent: incidents in the life of James Craig. Edited by his daughter. London: Hodder & Stoughton, 1895. (NC)

CRAIG, Robert, 1792-1860, Free Church Minister
Memorials of the life and labours of the Rev. Robert Craig / by Robert Clark Craig. Glasgow: D. Bryce, 1862.

CRAIGIE, Henry, 1807-67, Writer to the Signet
Christian stewardship: reminiscences of the life and labours of the late Henry Craigie, W.S., Edinburgh / by William Watson. Edinburgh: John Menzie, 1871. 12mo. (NC)

[CRAIK, James], b.1801, Church of Scotland Minister; educationalist
    Memorials [of James Craik / by his wife Margaret Craik]. Only for my family.
[London: printed by R. Clays], 1871. (NLS)

CRAN, James, 1811-92, Deputy Chief Constable of Aberdeenshire
    In memoriam: James Cran. Printed for private circulation. [Aberdeen], 1892.

CRICHTON, Andrew, 1837-67, Free Church Minister
    Memorials of the late Rev. Andrew Crichton, B.A., of Edinburgh and Dundee. Edited
by William Garden Blaikie. London: J. Nisbet, 1868. photo. port.

CRICHTON, David Maitland Makgill, 1801-51, advocate; Free Churchman
    Memoir of the late David Maitland Makgill Crighton, of Nether Rankeilour / by James
Taylor. 2nd edition. Edinburgh: T. Constable, 1853. (NC)

CROLY, George, 1780-1860, clergyman; prolific writer & critic
    A few personal recollections of the late Rev. George Croly ... With extracts from his
speeches and writings / by Richard Herring. London: Longman [etc.], 1861. (NLS)

CROOM, David M., d.1882, Scottish Congregational Minister
    A remembrance of David M. Croom, Sept. 9 1882. [Edited by D. B. Croom]. Privately
printed. Edinburgh: T. & A. Constable, [1882]. (B&J)

[CROPPER, John], d.1874, philanthropst
    The blessed life, past and future: two commemorative discourses [in memory of John
Cropper] / by Charles Morton Burrell. Printed for private circulaton. London:
Spottiswoode, 1874.

CROSFIELD, George, 1848-64, child
    Memoir of George Crosfield. Born 1848 - Died 1864. [By Henry and Elizabeth
Crosfield]. Printed for private circulation. London: printed by William Potter, 1866.

CROSS, William Henry, 1856-92, barrister; M.P.
    Memoir of William Henry Cross, 1856-1892. [Edited by James Grey and Alexander
Pearson]. Printed for private circulation. London: Spottiswoode, 1893.

CROSSKEY, Henry William, 1826-93, Unitarian; educationalist
    Henry William Crosskey, LL.D., F.G.S., his life and work / by Richard Acland
Armstrong ... Birmingham: Cornish, 1895.

CROSSLEY, Francis William, b.1839, Irish mechanical engineer & 'saint'
    The life of Francis William Crossley. Edited by James Rendel Harris. London: J.
Nisbet, 1899. (NC)

CRUICKSHANK, John, 1787-1875, mathematician at Aberdeen University
    John Cruickshank, Professor in the Marischal College and University of Aberdeen: a
memoir / by Joseph Ogilvie. Aberdeen: D. Wylie, 1896. (250 copies)

CRUIKSHANK, George, 1792-1878, comic illustrator; temperance advocate
    George Cruikshank the artist, the humorist and the man. With some account of his
brother Robert. A critico-bibliographical essay / by William Bates. Birmingham:
Houghton & Hammons, 1878. (NLS)
-------. The life of George Cruikshank in two epochs / by Blanche Jerrold. London: Chatto
& Windus, 1882. 2 volumes; reprinted London: Ward Lock, 1970.
-------. A memoir of George Cruikshank, artist and humourist ... / by Walter Hamilton.
London: Elliot Stock, 1878. (NLS)

CRUIKSHANK, (Isaac), Robert, 1789-1856 see CRUIKSHANK, George

CUFF, William, 1841-77, East End Baptist slum Minister
   The Rev. William Cuff in Shoreditch: realistic sketches of East London life and work. By a travelling correspondent. London: James Clarke, 1879. photo. port. (NLS)

CUMMING, John, 1807-81, Church of Scotland Minister in London; 'a prominent Conservative'
   In memoriam: the Rev. John Cumming, D.D. F.R.S.E., Minister of the Scottish National Church, Crown Court, London (1832-79). Printed for private distribution. [London, 1881]. (NC)

CUNNINGHAM, Robert Tennant, 1852-88, Free Church Minister
   Memorials of Robert T. Cunningham, M.A.. Edited by David Miller. Edinburgh: A. Elliot, 1890.

CUNNINGHAM, William, 1805-61, Free Church Principal
   Life of William Cunningham, D.D., 1805-61, Principal and Professor of Theology and Church History, New College, Edinburgh / by Robert Rainy and James Mackenzie. London: T. Nelson, 1871. (NC)

CURRIE, Bertram Wodehouse, 1827-96, banker; Roman Catholic convert
   Bertram Wodehouse Currie: a memorial [of his death] / by Caroline Louisa Currie. For private circulation. Roehampton: Manresa Press, 1897. (NLS)
   -------. Bertram Wodehouse Currie, 1827-1896: recollections, letters and journals. Edited by Caroline Louisa Currie. Privately printed. Roehampton: Manresa Press, 1901. 2 volumes.

CURTIS, John, 1794-1855, Irish Jesuit priest
   Life of Father John Curtis, of the Society of Jesus. [By Fanny M. Taylor]. Revised by Edward Purbrick. Dublin: M.H. Gill, [1891]. (BL)

CURWEN, John, 1816-80, Independent Minister; invented the Tonic Sol-fa method of singing
   Memorials of John Curwen / compiled by his son John Spencer Curwen. With a chapter on his home life / by his daughter [Isabella Banks]. London: John Curwen, 1882. photo. port.

DALE, Robert William, 1829-95, Congregational leader; radical M.P.
   The life of R. W. Dale, of Birmingham / by his son Alfred William Winterslow Dale. London: Hodder & Stoughton, 1898.

DALE, Thomas Pelham, 1821-92, imprisoned ritualist priest
   The life and times of Thomas Pelham Dale, sometime Rector of St. Vedast's, Foster Lane, City, London. Edited by his daughter Helen Pelham Dale ... London: G. Allen, 1894. 2 volumes.

DALHOUSIE, Sir James Andrew Broun Ramsay, 10th Earl & 1st Marquis of, 1812-60, Governor General of India 1847-56
   Life of the Marquis of Dalhousie / by Lionel James Trotter. London: W. H. Allen, 1889. (Statesmen Series)
   -------. The life of the Marquis of Dalhousie, K.T. / by William Lee-Warner. London: Macmillan, 1904. 2 volumes; reprinted Shannon: Irish U.P., 1972.
   -------. The Marquis of Dalhousie / by William Wilson Hunter. Oxford: Clarendon Press, 1890. (Rulers of India series)

DALHOUSIE, John William Ramsay, 13th Earl of, 1847-87, Liberal M.P.: died, with his wife, of food poisoning on board ship

Biographical sketch of the life of the Earl and Countess of Dalhousie. With an account of the funeral, tributes to their memory, etc. / by Samuel Hay. Dunoon: S. Martin, 1888. photo.port. (NC)

DALLAS, Alexander Robert Charles, 1791-1869, clergyman; Secretary of the Society for Irish Church Missions to Roman Catholics
Incidents in the life and ministry of the Rev. Alex. R. C. Dallas, A.M., Rector of Wonston and Honorary Secretary to the Society for Irish Church Missions to Roman Catholics / by his widow [Anne Briscoe Dallas]. London: J. Nisbet, 1871.

DALY, Sir Henry Dermot, 1821-95, General in India; Governor-General of Central India
Memoirs of General Sir Henry Dermot Daly, G.C.B., C.I.E., sometime Commander of the Central Indian Horse, Political Assistant for Western Malwa, etc., etc. / by Hugh Daly. London: John Murray, 1905.

DALY, Robert, 1783-1872, Church of Ireland Bishop of Cashel, Emly, Waterford and Limerick from 1843; biographer
Memoir of the late Right Rev. Robert Daly, D.D., Lord Bishop of Cashel / by Mrs Hamilton Madden. London: J. Nisbet, 1875. (NC)

DANIELS, William, 1812-80, minor Liverpool artist
W. Daniels, artist / by William [Edwards] Tirebuck. Liverpool, 1879. Pamphlet. (B&J)

DARBY, John Nelson, 1800-82, founder of the Darbyite Congregation of the Plymouth Brethren
John Nelson Darby: a memorial. 2nd edition. London: Alfred Holness, [188-]. Pamphlet. (B&J)

DARLING, James, d.1890 aged 71, temperance hotel owner in Edinburgh
James Darling: a memorial sketch / by Andrew Thomson. With sermon / by John Smith, *M.A., Edinburgh*. Edinburgh: A. Elliot, 1891. photo. port. (NC)

DARWIN, Charles Robert, 1809-82, naturalist; evolutionist
The life and letters of Charles Darwin, including an autobiographical chapter. Edited by his son Francis Darwin. London: John Murray, 1887. 3 volumes; and later editions including an abridgement as: 'Charles Darwin: his life told in an autobiographical chapter, and in a selected series of his published letters'. Edited by his son Francis Darwin. London: John Murray, 1892. *The autobiography has subsequently been reprinted alone, and with that of T. H. Huxley.
-------. Life of Darwin / by George Thomas Bettany. London: Walter Scott, 1887. (Great Writers series)

DAUNT, Achilles, 1832-78, Church of Ireland Dean of Cork
Spent in the service: a memoir of the Very Rev. Achilles Daunt, D.D., Dean of Cork. With selections from his letters, diary and sermons / by Frederick Richards Wynne. 2nd edition. London: Hodder & Stoughton, 1879. photo. port.

DAVIDSON, George, 1791-1873, Free Church Minister
Life and times of the late Rev. George Davidson, Latheron ... / by Alexander Mackay. Edinburgh: MacLaren & MacNiven, 1875. (NC)

DAVIDSON, George Dutch, 1879-1901, painter
George Dutch Davidson: a memorial volume / by David Foggie & John Duncan. Dundee: Graphic Arts Association, 1902. 4to. (NLS)

DAVIDSON, Thomas, 1838-78, United Presbyterian probationer Minister; poet
The life of a Scotch Probationer, being a memoir of Thomas Davidson. With his poems and extracts from his letters / by the late James Brown. 1877; 2nd revised and enlarged edition. Glasgow: J. Maclehose, 1878. photo. port. (NC)

DAVIDSON, Thomas, 1840-1900, writer; utopian; in USA; 'one of the twelve most learned men in the world'
Memorials of Thomas Davidson, the wandering scholar. Collected and edited by William Angus Knight. London: T. Fisher Unwin, 1907.

DAVIES, Arthur Henry, 1864-95, invalid Primitive Methodist
Discipline and service, or memorials of Arthur Henry Davies / by Thomas Davies. London: S.W. Partridge, [1897].

DAVIES, John, b.1788, clergyman working with canalmen and watermen
Memoir of the Rev. John Davies, M.A., Rector of St Clement's, Worcester / by George Lea. London: Seeley, Jackson & Halliday, 1859.

DAVIS, Lewis, 1829-88, Welsh coal & ironmaster; Wesleyan
A noble life: incidents in the career of Lewis Davis, of Ferndale / by David Young. London: Charles H. Kelly, 1899. (NLS)

DAVIS, Richard, 1790-1863, Dorset missionary in New Zealand
A memoir of the Rev. Richard Davis, for thirty-nine years a missionary in New Zealand / by John Noble Coleman. London: J.Nisbet, 1865. (NC)

DAVY, Edward, 1806-85, doctor; inventor; telegraph engineer; in Australia from 1839
Memoir of Edward Davy ... / by his nephew Henry Davy. London: James Gray, [1883]. (Reprinted from the 'Electrician') (BL)

DAWES, Richard, 1793-1867, Dean of Hereford; restored the Cathedral
A biographical notice of the late Very Rev. Richard Dawes, M.A., Dean of Hereford / by William Charles Henry. For private circulation. London: W. Clowes, 1867. (Reprinted from the 'Hereford Times') (NUC)

DAWSON, George, 1821-76, Baptist; journalist; newspaper editor
George Dawson: a sketch reprinted from the 'Birmingham Daily Post', December 1st 1876 ... Birmingham: printed by A. Pumphrey, [1876]. Pamphlet.
-------. The life of George Dawson, M.A., being an account of his parentage, and his career as a preacher lecturer, municipal and social reformer, politician and journalist / by William Wright Wilson. Birmingham: Percival Jones, 1905.
-------. Memory of George Dawson: a discourse .. / by Henry William Crosskey. Birmingham: H. C. Osborne, 1876. 12mo.
-------. Recollections of George Dawson and his lectures in Manchester in 1846-7 / by Alexander Ireland. [Manchester], 1882. Pamphlet. (B&J)

DAWSON, Henry, 1811-78, landscape painter
The life of Henry Dawson, landscape painter, 1811-1878 ... / compiled and illustrated by Alfred Dawson. London: Seeley, 1891. folio.

DELANE, John Thaddeus, 1817-79, editor of 'The Times' 1841-77
John Thaddeus Delane, editor of 'The Times': his life and correspondence / by Arthur Irwin Dasent. London: John Murray, 1908. 2 volumes.

DELEPIERRE, Joseph Octave, 1802-79, bibliophile; Belgian consul in London 1849-75
Joseph Octave Delepierre: in memoriam ... / by J[ohann] N[icolaus] T[rubner]. [1880]. 4to. (BL)

DE LISLE, Ambrose Lisle March Phillipps, 1809-78, leading Catholic layman
Life and letters of Ambrose Phillipps de Lisle ... / by Edmund Sheridan Purcell. Edited and finished by Edwin de Lisle. London: Macmillan, 1900. 2 volumes.

DE LISLE, Rudolph Edward Lisle March Phillipps, 1853-85, naval officer
Memoir of Lieutenant Rudolph de Lisle, R.N., of the Royal Naval Brigade on the

Upper Nile / by Henry N. Oxenham. London: Chapman & Hall, 1887.

DE MORGAN, Augustus, 1806-71, mathematician; astronomer
Memoir of Augustus de Morgan / by his wife Sophia Elizabeth de Morgan. With selections from his letters. London: Longmans, Green, 1882.

DEMPSTER, George, 1802-89, advocate
George Dempster (of Skibo): in memoriam. Privately printed. 1889. 12mo. Pamphlet. (NLS)

DENISON, Edward, 1840-70, barrister; M.P.; philanthropist
A brief record, being selections from letters and other writings of the late Edward Denison, M.P. for Newark. Edited by Baldwin Leighton. Privately printed. London: printed by R. Barrett, 1871. photo.port. (B&J)
-------. Edward Denison: a voice from the past for the present need / by Elizabeth Boyd Bayly. London: Kegan Paul, Trench, Trubner, 1884. Pamphlet. (NLS)

DENMAN, Thomas, 1st Baron Denman, 1779-1854, M.P.; Lord Chief Justice 1832-50
Memoir of Thomas Denman, first Lord Denman, formerly Lord Chief Justice of England / by Joseph Arnould. London: Longmans, Green, 1873. 2 volumes.

DENNY, William, 1847-87, Scottish shipbuilder and naval architect
The life of William Denny, ship-builder, Dumbarton / by Alexander Balmain Bruce. London: Hodder & Stoughton, 1888.

DENT, Digby Henry, d.1875 aged 31 years, Superintendent of Prisons, Straits Settlements; killed on duty there
Two commissions: a brief record of Digby Henry Dent / by his sister-in-law. London: Marshall Brothers, 1899. Pamphlet. (NLS)

DE QUINCEY, Thomas, 1785-1859, laudanum addict; miscellaneous writer, critic & journalist
De Quincey and his friends: personal recollections, souvenirs and anecdotes. Written and collected by James Hogg. London: Sampson Low [etc.], 1895.
-------. Personal recollections of Thomas de Quincey / by John Ritchie Findlay. London: A. & C. Black, 1886. 12mo.

DERBY, Edward George Geoffrey Smith Stanley, 14th Earl of, 1799-1869, Prime Minister; race horse owner; classicist
The Earl of Derby / by George Saintsbury. London: Sampson Low, Marston, 1892, (Prime Ministers of Queen Victoria Series)
-------. The life of the Earl of Derby / by Thomas Edward Kebbel. London: W. H. Allen, 1890. (The Statesman Series)

DERING, Edward Heneage, 1827-92, 'a Tory of the most old-fashioned type'
A brief sketch of the life, family and labours of Edward Heneage Dering, of Beddesley Clinton. London: Art & Book Company, [189-].

DICK, Robert, 1811-66, Scottish baker, botanist & geologist
Robert Dick, baker, of Thurso, geologist and botanist / by Samuel Smiles. London: John Murray, 1878.

DICKENS, Charles (John Huffam), 1812-70, major novelist
Charles Dickens: the story of his life. [By John Camden Hotten]. 2nd edition. London: J. C. Hotten, [c.1860]. photo. port.
-------. The life of Charles Dickens / by John Forster. London: Chapman & Hall, 1872-4. 3 volumes; and many later editions.
-------. The life of Charles Dickens as revealed in his writings. [By Percy Fitzgerald]. London: Chatto & Windus, 1905. 2 volumes.

-------. Life of Dickens / by Frank Thomas Marzials. London: Walter Scott Publishing, 1887. (Great Writers series)
   and many popular titles

DICKIE, Matthew, 1815-71, United Presbyterian Minister in Bristol
   Memoir of the Rev. Matthew Dickie, Minister of the United Presbyterian Church, Bristol / by William Mackergo Taylor ... Edited by James Davis. Bristol: W. Mack [etc.], [1872]. photo. port. (NC)

DICKINSON, Sebastian Stewart, 1815-78, barrister; M.P.; 'a quiet life of unostentatious usefulness'
   Memorials of S.S. Dickinson. Gloucester: John Bellows, 1882. (B&J)

DICKSON, William Purdie, 1823-1901, Professor of Divinity & Librarian, Glasgow University
   The Curator of Glasgow University Library / by James Lachlan Galbraith. Glasgow: J. Maclehose, 1909. (NC)

DISRAELI, Benjamin, 1st Earl of Beaconsfield, 1804-81, novelist; Tory Prime Minister
   An appreciative life of the Right Hon. the Earl of Beaconsfield ... Edited by Cornelius Brown ... London: A. W. Cowan, 1881. 2 volumes. 26 photo.ports. (originally published in parts)
-------. Benjamin Disraeli: an unconventional biography / by Wilfred Meynell. 2nd edition. London: Hutchinson, 1904. 2 volumes.
-------. Disraeli and his day / by William Fraser. London: Kegan Paul, 1891.
-------. The Earl of Beaconsfield / by Harold Edward Gorst. London: Blackie, 1900. (Victorian Era series)
-------. The Earl of Beaconsfield, his life and work / by Lewis Apjohn. London: Walter Scott Publishing, 1881. photo.port.
-------. The life of Benjamin Disraeli, Earl of Beaconsfield by William Flavelle Monypenny & George Earl Buckle. London: John Murray, 1910-20. 6 volumes; new edition revised by G. E. Buckle. 1929. 2 volumes.
-------. Lord Beaconsfield / by John Anthony Froude. London: Sampson, Low, Marston, 1890. (Prime Ministers of Queen Victoria series)
-------. Lord Beaconsfield: a biography / by Thomas Power O'Connor. Belfast: William Mullan, 1879.
-------. Lord Beaconsfield: a study / by George Brandes. London: R. Bentley, 1880.
-------. A memoir of the Earl of Beaconsfield. London: Longmans, Green, 1881. (Reprinted from 'The Times') (NLS)
-------. Memorials of Lord Beaconsfield. Reprinted from 'The Standard'. London: Macmillan, 1881. (B&J)
-------. The public life of the Right Hon. Earl of Beaconsfield, K.C. / by Francis Hitchman. London: Chapman & Hall, 1879. 2 volumes; revised edition. London: Sampson, Low, 1891.
-------. The Right Hon. Benjamin Disraeli, Earl of Beaconsfield, K.G., and his times / by Alexander Charles Ewald. London: William Mackenzie, 1881-2. 2 volumes (5 Divisions)
-------. The Right Hon. Benjamin Disraeli, M.P.: a literary and political biography, addressed to the new generation. [By Thomas MacKnight]. London: R. Bentley, 1858.
-------. A sketch of the public career of the late Right Hon. the Earl of Beaconsfield, K.G./ by Frederick Arthur Hyndman. London: W. H. Allen, 1881. Pamphlet. (NLS)
-------. Some personal recollections of the later years of the Earl of Beaconsfield, K.G.. Edinburgh: W.Blackwood, 1881. (Reprinted with addtions from 'The Times')
   and many other titles

DITCHER Joseph, d.1875 aged 83, clergyman; ecclesiastical lawyer
   Brief memorial of the Rev. Joseph Ditcher, addressed to his late parishioners, South Brent, Somerset / by Selina Ditcher. London: Nisbet, [1876]. (NLS)

DIXON, Henry Hall, 'The Druid', 1822-70, sporting writer

Life and times of 'The Druid' (Henry Hall Dixon) / by Francis Charles Lawley. London: Vinton, 1895.

DIXON, James, 1788-1871, Wesleyan Minister; 'a great preacher and orator'; in USA
The life of James Dixon, D.D., Wesleyan Minister / written by his son Richard Watson Dixon. London: Wesleyan Conference Office, 1874. (NLS)

DIXON, Joseph, 1806-66, Catholic Archbishop of Armagh 1852-66
The life of the Most Rev. Joseph Dixon, D.D., Primate of All Ireland. [By Mary Frances Cusack]. London: Burns, [1878].

DIXON, Thomas, n.d., Methodist
The earnest Methodist: a memoir of the late Mr Thomas Dixon, of Trantham / by his nephew Joseph Dixon. London: Wesleyan Conference Office, 1871. 12mo. (NLS)

DIXON, William Henry, 1783-1854, clergyman; Yorkshire antiquary
Memoir of the Rev. W. H. Dixon / by Charles Best Norcliffe (formerly Robinson). Printed for private distribution. York, 1860. Pamphlet. (BL)

DOBBIN, William, n.d., Irish Minister
The Rev. William Dobbin, Minister of Annaghlone: a memoir / by Robert Moore. Belfast: 'The Witness' Printing Works, 1901. (B&J)

DOBELL, Sydney Thompson, 1824-74, wine merchant; poet & critic
The life and letters of Sydney Dobell. Edited by E.J. [i.e. Emily Jolly]. London: Smith, Elder, 1878. 2 volumes. photographic illustrations. (NC)

DOBSON, John, 1787-1865, architect in Newcastle; the real author of the modern gothic revival
Memoir of John Dobson of Newcastle-upon-Tyne, Member of the Royal Institute of British Architects ... With a list of his works / by his daughter Margaret Jane Dobson. London: Hamilton, Adams, 1885. (BL)

DOCKER, Mark, n.d., Sheffield Cemetery chaplain
Memoir of the Rev. Mark Docker, late chaplain of Sheffield Cemetery. With selections from his papers and hymns / by R. Pritchett. Sheffield: J.A. Greaves, 1853. 12mo. (B&J)

DODDS, George Theophilus, 1850-82, with the McAll Mission in Paris
The life and work of the Rev. G. Theophilus Dodds, missionary, in connection with the McAll Mission, France / by Horatius Bonar. London: J. Nisbet, 1884. (NC)

DODGSON, Charles Lutwidge, 'Lewis Carroll', 1832-98, children's humourous writer; Oxford mathematician
The life and letters of Lewis Carroll (Rev. C. L. Dodgson) / by Stuart Dodgson Collingwood. London: T. Fisher Unwin, 1898. 2 volumes; in one volume 1899.

DOKE, William Henry, 1859-83, African missionary
A memoir of William Henry Doke, late missionary to the Congo, Central Africa / by his father [William Doke]. London: Alexander & Shepheard, 1884. photo.port. (NLS)

DOMBRAIN, Robert Furley, n.d., missionary in Japan
Youthfulness devotedness: a memoir of Robert Furley Dombrain, T.C.D., engaged missionary under the Loochoo Naval Committee / by William James Ball. Dublin: Samuel B. Oldham, 1854. 12mo. (B&J)

DONNE, William Bodham, 1807-82, Librarian of London Library; Examiner of Stage Plays 1849-74
William Bodham Donne and his friends ... / by Catharine Badham Johnson. London:

Methuen, 1905.

DORMER, Hon. Henry Edward, 1844-66, Catholic soldier
    Biographical memoir of the late the Hon. Henry Edward Dormer, late of the 60th Rifles. [By Frances Raphael Drane]. London: Burns & Oates, 1868. 12mo. (B&J)

DOUDNEY, David Alfred, 1811-94, Church of Ireland clergyman; religious newspaper editor; prolific religious writer; educational pioneer
    Memoir of the Rev. D.A. Doudney, D.D. ... / by David Alfred Doudney [Jun.] and Emily Adams. 2nd edition. London: W.H. & L. Collingridge, 1894. (B&J)
-------. Try and try again, being the lives of two youths [D. A. Doudney & John Doudney Lane] who became clergymen in the Church of England. By Old Jonathan [i.e. D. A. Doudney] London: Mackintosh, 1866. photo.port. (NLS - which says that Part 1 of this title was first issued separately as 'Try'. By Old Jonathan. [n.d.])

DOUGLAS, Carstairs, fl.1865, Presbyterian missionary in China; orientalist
    Memorials of the Rev. Carstairs Douglas, M.A., LL.D., missionary of the Presbyterian Church of England at Amoy, China. [By John Monteath Douglas]. Printed for private circulation. London: printed by Waterlow, 1878. photo. port. (NC)

DOUGLAS, Francis Brown, 1814-84, advocate
    Francis Brown Douglas. [By John Stalker]. Printed for private circulation. Edinburgh: T. Nelson, 1886. 16mo. photo. port. (NC)

DOUGLAS, Henry Marder, 1832-66, Free Church Minister
    Memorials of the late Rev. Henry M. Douglas, Minister of the Free Church, Kirkcaldy. Edited by James Macgregor. Edinburgh: A. Elliot [etc.], 1867. photo. port. (NC)

DOUGLAS, Sir Howard, 3rd Bart., 1776-1861, General in India; Governor of New Brunswick; M.P.
    The life of General Sir Howard Douglas, Bart., G.C.B. [etc.], from his notes, conversations and correspondence / by Stephen Watson Fullom. London: John Murray, 1863. (NLS)

DOUGLASS, Sir James Nicholas, 1826-98, Chief Engineer to Trinity House
    Life of Sir James Nicholas Douglass, F.R.S., &c. (formerly Engineer-in-Chief to the Trinity House) / by Thomas Williams. London: Longmans, Green, 1900.

DOWDLE, James, 1840-1900, Salvationist
    Commissioner Dowdle, the saved railway guard, and first Commissioner of the Salvation Army promoted to glory / by George Scott Railton. With a short sketch of Mrs Commissioner Dowdle. London: Salvation Army, 1912. (Red-Hot Library)

DRANSFIELD, Robert, b.1821, chartist; temperance worker
    Trial and triumph: a life and its lessons, being a biographical sketch of Robert Dransfield ... / by John Alexander Hammerton. Glasgow: Scottish Permissive Bill & Temperance Association, 1892. (NLS)

DRUMMOND, Henry, 1851-97, Free Presbyterian; revivalist;
    Henry Drummond / by James Young Simpson. Edinburgh: Oliphant, Anderson & Ferrier, 1901. (Famous Scots series)
-------. Henry Drummond: a biographical sketch (with bibliography) / by Cuthbert Lennox. London: Andrew Melrose, 1901.
-------. The life of Henry Drummond / by George Adam Smith. London: Hodder & Stoughton, 1899; and later editions.
-------. Memoirs of Professor Henry Drummond. With a wreath of tributes. By leading writers of the day. Edited by T. Cannan Newall. Glasgow: John J. Rae, [190-]. (NC)

DRUMMOND-HAY, <u>Sir</u> John Hay, 1816-93, British Minster to Morocco 1847-86
   A memoir of Sir John Drummond-Hay, P.C., K.C.B., G.C.M.B., sometime Minister to the Court of Morocco, based on his journals and correspondence. Edited by Louisa Annette Edla Brooks & Alice Elda Drummond-Hay. London: John Murray, 1902.

DUFF, Alexander, 1806-78, leading Free Church missionary to India &scholar of India
   Alexander Duff, D.D., LL.D. / by Thomas Smith. London: Hodder & Stoughton, 1883. (Men Worth Remembering series)
-------. The life of Alexander Duff, D.D., LL.D. / by George Smith. London: Hodder & Stoughton, 1879. 2 volumes; one volume edition 1881.
-------. Memorials of Alexander Duff, D.D. / by his son W. Pirie Duff. London: J. Nisbet, [1890]. (NC)
-------. Recollections of Alexander Duff, D.D., LL.D., and of the Mission College which he founded in Calcutta / by Lal Behari Day. Edinburgh: T. Nelson, 1879.

DUKINFIELD, <u>Sir</u> Henry Robert, <u>7th Bart.</u>, 1791-1858, clergyman
   A memoir of Rev. Sir Henry Robert Dukinfield, Bart. ... [By Jane Chowne Dukinfield]. Printed for private circulation. London: W. H. Dalton, 1861. (NUC)

DUNBAR, David, 1828-73, Dumfries schoolmaster; poet
   In memoriam: David Dunbar, Dumfries. Born 3rd April 1828 - Died 23rd June 1873. Printed for private circulation. [Glasgow: printed by Robert Anderson, 1873]. photo.port. (NC)

DUNCAN, Francis, 1836-88, soldier; M.P.; St John's Ambulance Brigade director
   The life of Francis Duncan, C.B., R.A., M.P., late Director of the Ambulance Department of the Order of St. John of Jerusalem in England / by Henry Birdwood Blogg ... London: Kegan Paul, Trench, Trubner, 1892. (B&J)

DUNCAN, James Matthews, 1826-90, physician and co-inventor of chloroform
   James Matthews Duncan: a sketch for his family / by Isabella Newlands (nee Duncan). Privately printed. [1891]. (NLS)

DUNCAN, John, 1794-1881, botanist; weaver
   The life of John Duncan, Scotch weaver and botanist. With sketches of his friends and notices of his times / by William Jolly. London: Kegan Paul, Trench, 1883.

DUNCAN, John, 1796-1870, Free Church Professor of Hebrew & Oriental Languages; 'The Rabbi'
   Life of the late John Duncan, LL.D., Professor of Hebrew and Oriental Languages, New College, Edinburgh / by David Brown, *D.D.*. Edinburgh: Edmonston & Douglas, 1872; 2nd revised edition. 1872. photo. port. (NC)
-------. Recollections of the late John Duncan ... / by Alexander Moody Stuart. Edinburgh: Edmonston & Douglas, 1872.

DUNCOMBE, Augustus, 1814-80, Dean of York 1862-80
   A memorial of Augustus Duncombe, Dean of York. London: Simpkin, Marshall, 1880.

DUNCOMBE, Thomas Slingsby, 1796-1861, Chartist; M.P.; 'the best dressed man in the House of Commons'
   The life and correspondence of Thomas Slingsby Duncombe, late M.P. for Finsbury. Edited by his son Thomas H. Duncombe. London: Hurst & Blackett, 1868. 2 volumes.

DUNDAS, <u>Hon.</u> John Charles, 1845-92, barrister; M.P.; first Chairman of North Riding County Council
   John C. Dundas: a memoir. By M. W.. Privately printed. Leeds: printed by Richard Jackson, 1893. (B&J)

DUNDONALD, Thomas Cochrane, 10th Earl of, 1775-1860, M.P.; admiral; court
martialled; commander of Chilean and Brazilian navies
Dundonald / by John William Fortescue. London: Macmillan, 1895. (English Men of
Action series)
-------. The life and daring exploits of Lord Dundonald. [By John McGilchrist]. London:
James Blackwood, 1861.
-------. Life of the Earl of Dundonald, Rear-Admiral of the United Kingdom and Admiral
of the Red / by Joseph Allen. London: Routledge, Warne and Routledge, 1861.
-------. The life of Thomas, Lord Cochrane, tenth Earl of Dundonald ... completing 'The
autobigraphy of a seaman ...' / by Thomas Barnes Cochrane, 11th Earl of Dundonald and
Henry Richard Fox Bourne. London: R. Bentley, 1869. 2 volumes.

DUNN, William, 1811-85, Church of Scotland Minister
In memoriam: Rev William Dunn, Minister of Cardross, died 8th December 1885.
Helensburgh: Macneur & Bryden, [1886?] photo. port. (NC)

DUNSTONE, John, 1787-1856, blind Cornish Wesleyan
Memoir of John Dunstone, of Camborne, Cornwall, who was blind for forty-four years
till his death in 1856 / by J.B.. 2nd revised edition. London: W. & F.G. Cash, 1857. 12mo.
Pamphlet. (NLS)

DURAND, Sir Henry Marion, 1812-71, soldier & administrator in India; Governor of
Punjab
The life of Major-General Sir Henry Marion Durand, K.C.S.I., C.B., of the Royal
Engineers / by Henry Mortimer Durand. London: W. H. Allen, 1883. 2 volumes.

DURNFORD, Anthony William, 1830-79, Irish soldier killed by Zulus
A soldier's life and work in South Africa, 1872 to 1879: a memoir of the late Colonel A.
W. Durnford. Edited by his brother Edward Durnford. London: Sampson Low, 1882. (BL)

DURNFORD, Richard, 1802-95, Bishop of Chichester
A memoir of Richard Durnford, D.D., sometime Bishop of Chichester. With selections
from his correspondence. Edited by William Richard Wood Stephens. London: John
Murray, 1899.

DURRANT, Billy, d.1890 aged 73, Primitive Methodist; bookseller; poet; temperance
worker
A memoir of Billy Durrant, local preacher, bookseller and poet ... / by Richard Blair.
London: Ralph Fenwick, 1884. (B&J)

DYKES, John Bacchus, 1823-76, Precentor of Durham Cathedral 1849-62
Life and letters of John Bacchus Dykes, M.A., Mus.Doc., Vicar of St Oswald's,
Durham. Edited by Joseph Thomas Fowler. London: John Murray, 1897.

DYSON, John, 1813-95, millowner; Methodist
Memorials of John Dyson, Esq., J.P., late of Green Bank, Thurgoland. With copious
extracts from his letters / by his brother Joseph Dyson. London: Charles H. Kelly, 1896.
(B&J)

EADIE, John, 1810-76, United Presbyterian theologian and writer
Life of John Eadie, D.D., LL.D. / by James Brown. London: Macmillan, 1878. photo.
port. (NC)

EATON, Henry William, 1816-91, Conservative M.P.
Henry William Eaton, M.P. for Coventry for twenty-one years: 1865-1888, 1881-
1887: a sketch. Coventry: W. W. Curtos, [1887]. Pamphlet. (NLS)

EDGAR, John, 1798-1866, Irish Presbyterian; temperance advocate

Memoir of John Edgar, D.D., LL.D., Professor of Systematic Theology for the General Assembly of the Presbyterian Church in Ireland / by William Dool Killen. Belfast: C. Aitchison, 1867. (BL)

EDMUNDS, Richard, n.d., Mayor of Banbury

Memorials of Richard Edmunds, of Banbury. Edited by Thomas Champness. London: Thomas Champness, [1895]. (B&J)

EDWARD, Thomas, 1814-86, 'The Banff naturalist'; shoemaker

Life of a Scotch naturalist, Thomas Edward, Associate of the Linnean Society / by Samuel Smiles. London: John Murray, 1872; new edition. 1882.

EDWARDES, Sir Herbert Benjamin, 1819-68, Major-General in India

Memorials of the life and letters of Major-General Sir Herbert B. Edwardes, K.C.B., K.C.S.I.. [etc.] / by his wife [Emma Edwardes]. London: Kegan Paul, Trench, 1886. 2 volumes.

EDWARDS, Edward, 1812-86, pioneering librarian in British Library, then at Manchester Free Library

Edward Edwards / by Charles W. Sutton. Aberdeen: University Press, 1912. Pamphlet. (Reprinted from the 'Library Association Record')

-------. Edward Edwards, chief pioneer of municipal public libraries / by Thomas Greenwood. London: Scott, Greenwood, 1902.

EGGLESTON, Frederick, 1785-1872, Newark worthy and Wesleyan

Memorials of Mr Frederick Eggleston, Newark-on-Trent / by William Henry Thompson. Leeds: H. W. Walker, 1874. (NLS)

ELDER, John, 1824-69, Glasgow shipbuilder and marine engineer

A memoir of John Elder, engineer and shipbuilder, Glasgow / by William John Macquorn Rankine. Edinburgh: W. Blackwood, 1871; 2nd edition. 1883. (NC)

ELDER, John Robson, 1840-97, Free Church Minister

Memorials of the late Rev. J. R. and Mrs Elder of Arrochar: [biographical sketches] / by Patrick Wood Minto [and others]. Edinburgh: Oliphant, Anderson & Ferrier, 1900. (NC)

ELGIN, James Bruce, 8th Earl of, 1811-63, M.P.; Governor-General of Canada; Viceroy of India

The Earl of Elgin / by George Mackinnon Wrong. London: Methuen, 1905.

ELLERTHORPE, John, 1806-68, life-saver in Hull

The hero of the Humber, or the history of the late Mr John Ellerthorpe (foreman of the Humber Dock Gates, Hull) ... / by Henry Woodcock. London: Elliot Stock, 1868. 12mo; 2nd edition. London: S. W. Partridge, 1880.

ELLETSON, Daniel Hope, d.1878, religious young soldier

Memoir of Daniel Hope Elletson, Second Lieutenant, Forty-Seventh (Lancashire) Regiment, who fell asleep in Jesus, October 29th 1878 / by his mother [Sara C.B. Elletson]. 2nd edition. Lancaster: Thomas Bell, 1878.

ELLIOTT, Henry Venn, 1792-1865, clergyman in Brighton

The life of the Rev. Henry Venn Elliott, M.A., Perpetual Curate of St Mary's, Brighton, and late Fellow of Trinity College, Cambridge / by Josiah Bateman. London: Macmillan, 1868.

ELLIS, Samuel, 1804-76, Sheffield Congrgational deacon

In memoriam of the late Samuel Ellis, of Sheffield. Edited by Samuel Clarkson.

Sheffield: printed by Leader, 1877. (B&J)

ELLIS, William, 1794-1872, Congregational Minister in Pacific
Life of William Ellis, missionary to the South Seas and to Madagascar / by his son John Eimbo Ellis. With a supplementary chapter containing an estimate of his character and work / by H. Allen. London: John Murray, 1873. (NUC)

ELLIS, William, 1800-81, underwriter; educationalist; utilitarian economist
Life of William Ellis, founder of Birkbeck Schools. With some account of his writings and of his labours for the improvement and extension of education / by Edmund Kell Blyth. London: Kegan Paul, Trench, 1889.
-------. Memoir of William Ellis, and an account of his conduct-teaching ... / by Ethel E. Ellis. London: Longmans, Green, 1888. (NLS)

ELLISON, Henry John, 1813-98, clergyman; founder of the Church of England Temperance Society
Henry John Ellison, sometime Vicar of Windsor, founder of the Church of England Temperance Society / by Frederick Sherlock. London: Wells, Gardner, Darton, 1910. 16mo. Pamphlet. (NLS)

ELMSLIE, William Gray, 1848-89, Hebrew scholar; reader for Hodder & Stoughton
Professor Elmslie: a memoir / by William Robertson Nicoll. London: Hodder & Stoughton, [1911]. (NC)
-------. Professor W. G. Elmslie, D.D.: memoir and sermons. Edited by William Robertson Nicoll & A. N. MacNicoll. London: Hodder & Stoughton, 1890. photo. port. (NC)

ELMSLIE, William Jackson, 1832-72, medical missionary in India from 1864
Seedtime in Kashmir: a memoir of William Jackson Elmslie, M.A., M.D. [etc.], late medical missionary, C.M.S., Kashmir / by his widow and his friend William Burns Thomson. London: J. Nisbet, 1875; 3rd edition as: 'A memoir of William Jackson Elmslie, M.A., M.D. [etc.], late medical missionary, C.M.S., Kashmir' / by William Burns Thomson. London: J. Nisbet, 1881. (NC)

ELPHINSTONE, Hon. Mountstuart, 1779-1859, Governor of Bombay
Life of the Honourable Mountstuart Elphinstone / by Thomas Edward Colebrooke. London: John Murray, 1884. 2 volumes. (NLS)
-------. Memoir of the Honourable Mountstuart Elphinstone / by Thomas Edward Colebrooke. London: Bernard Quaritch, 1861. (NLS)
-------. Mountstuart Elphinstone / by James Sutherland Cotton. Oxford U.P., 1892. (Rulers of India series)

ELVEY, Sir George Job, 1816-93, organist, composer
Life and reminiscences of George J. Elvey, Knt, Mus.Doc. [etc.], late Organist to H.M. Queen Victoria, and forty-seven years organist of St George's Chapel, Windsor / by Mary, Lady Elvey. London: Sampson Low, Marston, 1894.

ELWYN, Richard, 1827-97, Headmaster of Charterhouse
Richard Elwyn, Headmaster of Charterhouse, 1885-1897: a brief record of his life / by Robert Patterson. London: Wells Gardner, Darton, 1900.

ERSKINE, Thomas, of Linlathen, 1788-1870, liberal theological writer; advocate
Erskine of Linlathen: selections and biography / by Henry Frank Hornby Henderson. Edinburgh: Oliphant, Anderson & Ferrier, 1899.

ESTLIN, John Bishop, 1785-1855, Bristol eye surgeon
Memoir of John Bishop Estlin ... / by William James, *Unitarian Minister, Bristol.* London, 1855. (From the 'Christian Reformer')

ETHERIDGE, John Wesley, 1804-66, Cornish Wesleyan Minister
Memoirs of the Rev. John Wesley Etheridge, M.A., Ph.D.. Including extracts from his writings and correspondence / by Thornley Smith. London: Hodder & Stoughton, 1871. (NLS)
-------. A tear and a flowerlet, on the Rev. J. W. Etheridge, M.A., Ph.D./ by Josias Harris. Mevagissy, Cornwall: F.S.F. Harris, 1871. (B&J)

EVANS, Evan Herber, 1836-96, Welsh Congregational Minister; 'the most eloquent Welsh preacher of his day'
The life of E. Herber Evans, D.D., from his letters and journals / by Howell Elvet Lewis. London: Hodder & Stoughton, 1900.

EVANS, George, 1802-81, 'humble poet and chainmaker'
George Evans: a sketch / by Edward J. Shaw. Walsall: printed by J. & W. Griffin, 1894. 12mo. Pamphlet. (Reprinted from the 'Walsall Observer') (B&J)

EVANS, John, 'Eglysbach', 1840-97, shepherd; Welsh Methodist Minister; 'The Welsh Spurgeon'
John Evans, 'Eglwys bach', the most popular preacher of Welsh Wesleyan Methodism/ by John Humphreys. London: Charles H. Kelly, 1913.

EVANS, Thomas Rhys, 1852-92, Welsh Congregationalist Minister in London
The life and letters of T. Rhys Evans, Minister of Queen Square Congregational Church, Brighton. With selections from his sermons and addresses / by Richard Lovett. London: James Clarke, 1893.

EVERETT, James, 1784-1872, Wesleyan Methodist Minister; founded the United Methodist Free Church
James Everett: a biography / by Richard Chew. London: Hodder & Stoughton, 1875. photo.port.

EWING, Alexander, 1814-73, liberal Episcopal Bishop of Argyll
Memoir of Alexander Ewing, D.C.L., Bishop of Argyll and the Isles / by Alexander Johnstone Ross. London: Daldy, Isbister, 1877. photo.port.

EWING, James, 1775-1853, radical M.P. for Glasgow; banker & merchant
Memoir of James Ewing, Esq., of Strathleven, formerly Lord Provost of Glasgow, and M.P. for that City. With a series of letters written while on a tour of Italy. [Edited] by Mackintosh Mackay. Glasgow: J. Maclehose, 1866.

EYRE, Edward John, 1815-1901, in Australia & New Zealand; Governor of Jamaica 1862-6
The life of Edward John Eyre, late Governor of Jamaica / by Hamilton Hume. London: R. Bentley, 1867. (NC)

FABER, Frederick William, 1814-63, Catholic priest; poet
A brief sketch of the early life of ... F. W. Faber / by his only surviving brother [Francis Atkinson Faber]. London: Thomas Richardson, 1869. (NLS)
-------. The life and letters of Frederick William Faber, D.D., Priest of the Oratory of St Philip Neri / by John Edward Bowden. London: Thomas Richardson, 1869. (NC)

FAIRBAIRN, Sir William, 1st Bart., 1789-1874, manufacturing engineer in Manchester

The life of Sir William Fairbairn, Bart., F.R.S., LL.D. ... Partly written by himself. Edited and completed by William Pole. London: Longmans, Green, 1877; abridged edition. 1878; reprinted with introduction by Albert Edward Musson. Newton Abbot: David & Charles, 1970.

FAIRLEY, John, 1838-85, Church of Scotland Minister
In memoriam: Rev. John Fairley, B.D., first Minister of Bluevale Parish Church, Glasgow. Ordained 19th September 1872 - Died 18th April 1885, aged 47 years. [Glasgow: printed by Kennedy & Spowart, 1885]. Pamphlet.

FALLOON, William Marcus, d.1891, clergyman
Memoir of William Marcus Falloon, M.A., Rector of Ackworth, and Honorary Canon of Chester. With selections from letters, sermons and papers ... / by Hugh Falloon. Liverpool: J. A. Thompson, 1892. (B&J)

FALSHAW, Sir James, 1st Bart., 1810-89, railway contractor; Lord Provost of Edinburgh
Sir James Falshaw, Bart., J.P. [etc.], Lord Provost of the City of Edinburgh, 1874-1877 / by James Ballantine. Edinburgh: Otto Schultze, 1910. 4to. (75 copies printed)

FANE, Julian Henry Charles, 1827-70, diplomat; poet
Julian Fane: a memoir / by Robert, Earl of Lytton. London: John Murray, 1871.

FARADAY, Michael, 1791-1867, major scientist; Sandemanian
The life and letters of Michael Faraday / by (Henry) Bence Jones. London: Longmans, Green, 1870. 2 volumes.
-------. Michael Faraday: [a biography] / by John Hall Gladstone. London: Macmillan, 1872; 2nd edition with a portrait. 1873.

FARR, William, 1807-83, doctor, then statistician
William Farr, F.S.S., M.D., F.R.S. [etc.] / by F. A. C. Hare. [Privately printed for the author]. London, [1884]. Pamphlet. (NLS)

FARRAR, Cyril Lytton, 1869-91, in Imperial Chinese Customs Service
Memorials of Cyril Lytton Farrar: letters. [Edited by Frederick William Farrar]. Printed for private circulation. Edinburgh: printed by R. & R. Clark, 1891. (B&J)

FAUSSETT, Thomas Godfrey Godfrey-, 1829-77, barrister; antiquarian
Memorials of T. G. Godfrey-Faussett. Edited by William John Loftie. Privately printed. London: James Parker, 1878. (150 copies); 2nd revised edition. London: James Parker, 1878. (NLS)

FAWCETT, Henry, 1833-84, blind M.P.; economist
Life of Henry Fawcett / by Leslie Stephen. London: Smith, Elder, 1885.

FAWCETT, William, n.d., Sheffield magistrate
Memorial sketch of the late William Fawcett, Esq., Justice of the Peace / by William H. Tindell. London: H. J. Tresidder, 1865. (B&J)

FECKMAN, William, 1777-1867, Irish Methodist Minister
Memoir of William Feckman, an earnest and successful evangelist / by George Vance. London: for the author by T. Woolmer, 1885. 12mo. (NLS)

FEILD, Edward, 1801-76, Anglican Bishop of Newfoundland
Memoir of the life and episcopate of Edward Feild, D.D. Bishop of Newfoundland, 1844-76 / by Henry William Tucker. London: Wells Gardner, [1876]. photo. port. (BL)

FERGUS, Robert Walter, 1853-63, religious boy
Nearer to Jesus: memorials of Robert Walter Fergus / by his mother [M. Fergus] ... Edinburgh: T. Nelson, 1870; new edition with postscript. Glasgow: J. N. Mackinlay, 1886.

FERGUSON, Fergus, 1824-97, Evangelical Minister
The life of the Rev. Fergus Ferguson, M.A., D.D., Minister of Montrose Street Evangelical Union Church / by William Adamson. London: Simpkin, Marshall, Hamilton, Kent, 1900.
-------. Memoirs of Professor Fergus Fergusson, D.D., late Montrose Street E.U. Church/ by T. Cannan Newall. Glasgow: John J. Rae, [190-]

FERGUSON, Sir Samuel, 1810-86, Deputy Keeeper of the Public Records of Ireland; Irish poet and Celtic scholar
Sir Samuel Ferguson in the Ireland of his day / by Mary Catherine, Lady Ferguson. Edinburgh: W. Blackwood, 1896. 2 volumes.

FERGUSSON, Donald, 1811-97, Free Church Minister
A student of nature: memorials of the late Rev. D. Fergusson, Minister of the Parish of Inverkeithing, Fifeshire. [Edited with a memoir] by Robert Menzies Fergusson. Paisley: Alexander Gardner, 1898. (NC)

FERGUSSON, Sir William, 1st Bart., 1808-77, Professor of Surgery, King's College London; 'the greatest operative surgeon in Great Britain or probably in Europe'
Sir William Fergusson, Bart.: a biographical sketch / by Henry Smith, F.R.C.S.. London: J. & A. Churchill, 1877. (NLS)

FERNLEY, John, d.187-, Southport Wesleyan
A memoir of John Fernley, Esq., J.P., late of Clairville, Southport / by William John Pope. London: Wesleyan Conference Office, 1874. (B&J)

FERRIER, James Frederick, 1808-64, Scottish philosopher
James Frederick Ferrier / by Elizabeth Sanderson Haldane. Edinburgh: Oliphant, Anderson & Ferrier, 1899. (Famous Scots Series)

FERRIS, William, n.d., Portsmouth Pastor
Memoir, notes of sermons and letters of William Ferris, Pastor of Salem Chapel, Landport, Portsmouth. [By J.W.G.]. London: John Gadsby, 1888. photo. port. (B&J)

FIELD, Edwin Wilkins, 1804-71, 'a great law reformer, also amateur artist'
Edwin Wilkins Field: a memorial sketch / by Thomas Sadler. London: Macmillan, 1872. photo.port.

FIELD, Sir John, 1821-99, Judge Advocate-General in Bombay Army
Sir John Field, K.C.B., soldier and evangelist: a brief memoir / by one of his sons Claud Field. London: Religious Tract Society, 1908.

FILLANS, James, 1808-52, sculptor, mainly in London
Memoir of the late James Fillans, sculptor / by James Paterson. Paisley: Robert Stewart, 1854. 4to. (NLS)

FINCH, Francis Oliver, 1802-62, water-colour painter
Memorials of the late Francis Oliver Finch, Member of the Society of Painters in Water-Colours. With selections from his writings. [By his widow E. Finch]. London: Longman [etc.], 1865. (NLS)

FINLAYSON, Thomas, 1809-72, United Presbyterian Minister; Moderator 1867
Memorials of the Rev. Thomas Finlayson, D.D., Minister of the United Presbyterian Congregation, Rose Street, Edinburgh. [By Alexander MacEwan]. Edinburgh: William Oliphant, 1873. photo.port. (NC)

FINLEY, John, 1776-1853, Minister in Countess of Huntingdon's Connection
A short memoir of the Rev. John Finley, late ministerial trustee of the Countess of Huntingdon's Connection, and for forty-one years Minister of Her Ladyship's Chapel at

Tunbridge Wells. With a brief account of two of his sons [Alfred Hide & Edward Hide Finley] who died before him ... / by his widow [Harriet Finley]. ... London: J. Nisbet, 1856. (NLS)

FIRBANK, Joseph, 1819-86, railway contractor
The life and work of Joseph Fairbank, J.P., D.L., railway contractor / by Frederick MacDermott. London: Longmans, 1887. (BL)

FIRTH, James Henry, d.189- , temperance worker
Life of James Henry Firth, temperance worker / by Daniel Frederick Edward Sykes. Huddersfield: Advertiser Press, 1897. (B&J)

FISK, George, d.1872, clergyman in Malvern
In memoriam: a review of the life and ministry of the late Rev. George Fisk, LL.B., Vicar of Malvern .., being the substance of two sermons preached / by Francis William Davenport. Malvern: printed by H. Cross, 1872. 12mo. (B&J)

FITZGERALD, Edward, 1809-83, letter writer; translator, especially of Omar Khayyam
The life of Edward Fitzgerald / by John Glyde ... London: C. Arthur Pearson, 1900.
-------. The life of Edward Fitzgerald / by Thomas Wright. London: Grant Richards, 1904. 2 volumes.
  see also **GROOME, Robert Hindes**

FITZGIBBON, James, 1780-1863, Adjutant-General in Canada
A veteran of 1812: the life of James Fitzgibbon / by Mary Agnes Fitzgibbon. London: R. Bentley, 1894.

FLEMING, Archibald, 1856-1900, Church of Scotland Minister
In memoriam: Rev. Archibald Fleming, B.A., Minister of St. Paul's Parish, Perth, 1856-1900 ... [Edinburgh: W. Blackwood, 1900]. Pamphlet. (NLS)

FLEMING, John Park, 1790-1869, Glasgow lawyer; property developer
John Park Fleming, 1790-1869. [By J. B. Fleming]. For private circulation. Glasgow: J. Maclehose, 1885. photo.port.

FLETCHER, Alexander, 1787-1860, Secession Minister until 1824 in Perthshire & London
The prince of preachers, being a memorial of the late Rev. Alexander Fletcher / by William Blair. London: Arthur Hall, 1860.

FLETCHER, John William, 1834-82, clairvoyant
John William Fletcher, clairvoyant: a biographical sketch ... / by Susan Elizabeth Gay. London: E. W. Allen, 1883. photo.port.

FLOWER, Sir William Henry, 1831-99, surgeon; zoologist
Sir William Flower / by Richard Lydekker. London: Dent, 1906. (NLS)
-------. Sir William Henry Flower, K.C.B., F.R.S., [etc.], late Director of the Natural History Museum and President of the Royal Zoological Society: a personal memoir / by Charles John Cornish. London: Macmillan, 1904.

FONBLANQUE, Albany (William), 1793-1872, radical journalist; Head of the Statistical Department of the Board of Trade; 'a brilliant talker, a finished scholar, and a student of music and art'
The life and labours of Albany Fonblanque. Edited by his nephew Edward Barrington de Fonblanque. London: R. Bentley, 1874.

FORBES, Alexander Penrose, 1817-75, Episcopal Bishop of Brechin from 1847; leading Scottish tractarian
Bishop Forbes: a memoir / by Donald John Mackey. London: Kegan Paul, Trench,

1888.

-------. A memoir of Alexander, Bishop of Brechin. With a brief notice of his brother the Rev. George Hay Forbes. [By Felicia Skene]. London: J. Masters, 1876. (NC)

FORBES, Edward, 1815-54, Manx botanist
   Memoir of Edward Forbes, F.R.S., D.C.L., LL.D., late Regius Professor of Natural History in the University of Edinburgh / by George Wilson and Archibald Geikie. Cambridge: Macmillan, 1861.
   -------. Memoir of the late Professor Edward Forbes / by John Hughes Bennett. Edinburgh: Simpkin, Marshall, 1855. Pamphlet.

FORBES, George Hay, 1821-75 <u>see</u> **FORBES, Alexander Penrose**

FORBES, James David, 1809-68, alpinist; scientist; Principal of St Andrews University 1859-68
   Life and letters of James David Forbes, F.R.S., D.C.L., LL.D., sometime Professor of Natural Philosophy in the University of Edinburgh, late Principal of the United College in the University of St Andrews ... / by John Campbell Shairp [and others]. London: Macmillan, 1873. photographic illustrations. (NC)
   -------. Principal Forbes and his biographers / by John Tyndall. London: Longmans, Green, 1873. Pamphlet. (NLS)

FORBES, Sir John, 1787-1861, surgeon founder of 'British & Foreign Medical Review' (1836)
   Memoir of Sir John Forbes, Kt., M.D., D.C.L., F.R.S., etc. / by Edmund Alexander Parkes. [Edited by Alexander C. Forbes]. For private circulation. London: printed by Savill & Edwards, 1862. photo.port. (Reprinted from the 'British and Foreign Medico-Chirurgical Review')

FORD, John, 1801-75, York Quaker schoolmaster
   Memorials of John Ford. Edited by Silvanus Thompson. York: William Sessions, 1877. photo.port.

FORDHAM, John Hampden, 1826-85, Vice-President of British & Foreign Bible Society
   Loving memories of John Hampden Fordham: a home sketch ... [Edited by his wife]. Printed for private circulation. [London, 1886]. photo.port. (NLS)

FORSTER, John, 1812-76, barrister; critic; editor; biographer of Dickens
   John Forster. By one of his friends [i.e. Percy Hetherington Fitzgerald] London: Chapman & Hall, 1903.
   -------. John Forster and his friendships / by Richard Renton. London: Chapman & Hall, 1912.

FORSTER, William, 1784-1854, Quaker Minister
   Memoirs of William Forster. Edited by Benjamin Seebohm. London: Alfred W. Bennett, 1865. 2 volumes.
   -------. A tribute to the memory of ... William Forster. By one who honoured and loved him. London, 1857. (BL)

FORSTER, William Edward, 1818-86, statesman; educational reformer; woollen manufacturer
   Life of the Right Hon. William Edward Forster / by Thomas Wemyss Reid. London: Chapman & Hall, 1889. 2 volumes; in one volume 1889; reprinted with introduction by Valerie E. Chancellor. Bath: Adams & Dart, 1970. in one volume.

FORTESCUE (later FORTESCUE-KNOTTESFORD), Edward Bowles Knottesford, 1816-77, clergyman, then Roman Catholic teacher
   In memory of the Very Rev. E. B. K. Fortescue [in his last illness] / by Edward Francis Knottesford Fortescue. Privately printed. [London, 1877]. (50 copies) (BL)

FOWLER, Sir John, 1st Bart., 1817-98, railway & contracting civil engineer
The life of Sir John Fowler, engineer, Bart. [etc.] / by Thomas Mackay. London: John Murray, 1900.

FOWLER, Sir Robert Nicholas, 1st Bart., 1828-91, banker; Conservative M.P.; writer on China, Japan and India; Lord Mayor of London
Sir Robert N. Fowler, Bart., M.P.: a memoir / by John Stephen Flynn. London: Hodder & Stoughton, 1893. (NC)

FOX, Albert, 1836-67, Congregationalist businessman
Albert Fox, the devout merchant: a memoir / by John Jones. Liverpool: Edward Howell, 1867. photo. port. (NLS)

FOX, Charles Armstrong, 1836-1900, clergyman; poet
Charles Armstrong Fox: memorials / gathered by Sophia M. Nugent. London: Marshall, [1901].

FRANCIS, John, 1811-82, manager and publisher of 'The Athanaeum' from 1831
John Francis, publisher of 'The Athenaeum': a literary chronicle of half a century / by John Collins Francis ... London: R. Bentley, 1888. 2 volumes.

FRASER, James, 1818-85, Bishop of Manchester from 1870
James Fraser, second Bishop of Manchester: a memoir, 1818-1885 / by Thomas Hughes. London: Macmillan, 1887.
-------. The Lancashire life of Bishop Fraser / by John Wilson Diggle. London: Sampson Low [etc.], 1889. photographic portrait & illustrations.

FRASER, James Stuart, 1783-1869, General in the Madras Army
Memoir and correspondence of General James Stuart Fraser, of the Madras Army / by his son Hastings Fraser. London: Whiting, 1885.

FRASER, John, 1794-1879, model educator in Scotland; temperance worker; radical
Memoir of John Fraser, Newfield, Johnstone / by his oldest son James Roy Fraser. Paisley: printed by J. & J. Cook, 1879. photo. port. (NLS)

FRASER, John Hutchinson, 1823-84, Free Church Minister
Memoir and remains of the Rev. John H. Fraser, M.A., Rosskeen / by Alexander Cameron. Inverness: Gavin Tait, 1885. (NC)

FREEMAN, Edward Augustus, 1823-92, historian; writer
The life and letters of Edward Augustus Freeman, D.C.L., LL.D. / by William Richard Wood Stephens. London: Macmillan, 1895. 2 volumes.

FREEMAN, Robert, 1841-53, religious boy at Merchant Taylors' School
A slight sketch of the short life and early death of Robert Freeman and his two sisters [M-.A-., d.1848, and Alice 1844-54]. By the Vicar of West Ham [Abel John Ram] ... London: Wertheim, Macintosh & Hunt, [1860]. (NLS)

FREEMAN, Thomas Arthur, n.d., soldier in India
Lieut-Colonel Thomas Arthur Freeman: a memoir. Edinburgh: W. Blackwood, 1901. 4to. (BL)

FRENCH, Thomas Valpy, 1825-91, Anglican Bishop of Lahore, India
An heroic bishop: the life-story of French of Lahore / by Eugene Stock. London: Hodder & Stoughton, [1913].
-------. The life and correspondence of Thomas Valpy French, first Bishop of Lahore / by Herbert Birks. London: John Murray, 1895. 2 volumes.

FRERE, Sir (Henry) Bartle Edward, 1st Bart., 1815-84, Governor of Bombay; first High Commissioner of South Africa

The life and correspondence of the Right Hon. Sir Bartle Frere, Bart., G.C.B., F.R.S., etc. / by John Martineau. London: John Murray, 1895. 2 volumes.

FRISWELL, James Hain, 1825-78, miscellaneous writer

James Hain Friswell: a memoir / by his daughter Laura Hain Friswell. London: George Redway, 1898.

FROUDE, James Anthony, 1818-94, biographer of Carlyle; historian

The life of Froude / by Herbert Paul. London: I. Pitman, 1905.

FRY, Francis, 1803-86, Quaker cocoa and chocolate manufacturer in Bristol

A brief memoir of Francis Fry, F.S.A., of Bristol / by his son Theodore Fry. Not published. London: printed by Barclay & Fry, 1887. photographic portraits & illustrations.

FYFE, James Eckford, 1833-98, United Presbyterian Minister

In memoriam: Rev. James E. Fyfe, Kilmalcolm / by John Thomas Burton. Glasgow: J. T. Smith, 1898. (NLS)

GARDINER, Allen Francis, 1794-1851, naval officer; founded the Patagonian Missionary Society 1844

Captain Allen Gardiner, sailor and saint: Africa - Brazil - Patagonia / by Jesse Page. London: S. W. Partridge, [1897]. (NLS)
-------. The corn of wheat dying and bringing forth much fruit: a sketch of the life of Capt. Allen Gardiner, R.N. / by Charles Bullock. London: William Hunt, [1870].
-------. A memoir of Allen F. Gardiner, Commander R.N. / by John William Marsh. London: J. Nisbet, 1857. 12mo.; 10th edition. 1874.
-------. The story of Commander Allen Gardiner, R.N.. With sketches of missionary work in South America / by John William Marsh and Waite Hockin Stirling. London: J. Nisbet, 1867. (NLS)

GARDINER, Thomas, 1825-77, Free Church missionary to India

The sunlit valley and the path that led to it: a memorial sketch of the Rev. Thomas Gardiner, Old Aberdeen / by Andrew Inglis. Aberdeen: A. & R. Milne, 1878. 12mo. photo.port. (NC)

GARDNER, Alexander Haughton, 1785-1877, mercenary soldier & traveller in India

Soldier and traveller: memoirs of Alexander Gardner, Colonel of Artillery in the service of Maharajah Ranjit Singh. Edited by Hugh Fraser ... Edinburgh: W. Blackwood, 1897.

GARDNER, James, 1861-86, United Presbyterian student Minister

Brief service and early reward, or memorials of James Gardner, B.D., licentiate of the United Presbyterian Church / by Benjamin Martin. Printed for private circulation. [Edinburgh: Ballantyne, Hanson], 1887. (NC)

GARNETT, Robert, d.187-, Lancashire domestic biography

Cherished remembrances of our beloved father, Robert Garnett, late of Vine House, Penketh, Warrington: a family memorial. Warrington: Guardian Office, 1878. photo.port. (B&J)

GARNIER, Thomas, 1809-63, Dean of Lincoln

Some account of the life and character of the late Very Rev. Thomas Garnier, B.C.L., Dean of Lincoln ... Winchester, [1863]. (NLS)

GARRARD, William, n.d., Leicester Minister
Reminiscences of the late William Garrard ('The Watchman on the walls'), Minister of the Gospel at Providence Chapel, Newark Street, Leicester. [Compiled by R. A. Barbour]. London: Robert Banks, 1874. (B&J)

GATE, Robert, 1780-1866, Penrith Methodist
The Christian patriarch: the life of Mr Robert Gate ... / by George G. S. Thomas. London: Elliot Stock, 1869. photo.port. (NUC)

GAUSSEN, William Frederick Armytage, 1863-93, translator from the Russian; technician
Memorials of a short life: a biographical sketch of W.F.A. Gaussen .... Edited by George Forrest Browne. London: T. Fisher Unwin, 1895. (BL)

GAWLER, George, 1796-1869, Governor and Commander-in-Chief South Australia
George Gawler, K.H., 52nd Light Infantry: a life sketch / compiled under the directions of his daughter Jane Cox Gawler, from original documents, letters and other interesting papers in her posseession by C.W.N.. Derby: Bemrose, 1900. Pamphlet. (NLS)

GEERAN (or GUERIN), Thomas, d.1871 claiming to be 105, 'made a living by relating his military adventures and dilating upon his great age'
The life of Thomas Geeran, a centenarian ... / by Henry Herbert Copleston. [Edited by R.H. Williams]. London: Robert Hardwicke, [1870]. photo.port. (NLS)

GELDART, William, d.1863, religious boy
Strength in weakness, or early chastened - early blessed: a brief memoir of William Geldart / by Hannah Ramsome Geldart. 2nd edition. London: Seeley, Jackson & Halliday, 1860. (BL)

GIBSON, David Cooke, 1827-56, young Scottish artist 'with an angel's heart in a human body'
The struggles of a young artist, being a memoir of David C. Gibson. By a brother artist [i.e. W. Macduff]. London: J. Nisbet, 1858.

GIBSON, John, 1790-1866, sculptor
The biography of John Gibson, R.A., sculptor, Rome. Edited by Thomas Matthews. London: W. Heinemann, 1911.
-------. Life of John Gibson, R.A., sculptor. [Edited] by Elizabeth Eastlake. London: Longmans, Green, 1870.

GIFFORD, John, 1821-95, religious leather manufacturer
John Gifford, memories and letters. Edited by his sister Mary Raleigh. Edinburgh: Oliphant, Anderson & Ferrier, 1896. (NC)

GILBERT, Daniel, 1827-95, Roman Catholic priest
Monsignor Gilbert: a memoir / compiled by his nephew John William Gilbert. London: Catholic Truth Society, 1897. (NLS)

GILBERT, Sir John Thomas, 1829-98, Irish historian & archivist
Life of Sir John T. Gilbert, LL.D., F.S.A., Irish historian and archivist, Vice-President of the Royal Irish Academy, Secretary of the Public Record Office of Ireland / by his wife Rosa Mulholland Gilbert. London: Longmans, Green, 1905.

GILBERT, Joseph, 1779-1852, Congregational Minister in Nottingham
Biographical sketch of the Rev. Joseph Gilbert / by his widow [Ann Gilbert]. With recollections of the discourses of his closing years, from notes at the time. By one of his sons [Josiah Gilbert]. London: Jackson & Walford, 1853. 12mo. (NLS)

GILBEY, Alfred, 1833-79, largest wine & spirit merchant in Britain

In memoriam: Alfred Gilbey, November 28 1879. [1879]. (B&J)

GILFILLAN, George, 1813-78, United Presbyterian Minister, lecturer & author in Dundee
George Gilfillan: anecdotes and reminiscences / by David Macrae. 1891; new edition. Glasgow: Morison, 1900.
-------. In memoriam: the Rev. George Gilfillan. 1878. 12mo. (Reprinted from 'The Dundee Advertiser') (NC)

GILL, Thomas Howard, 1797-94, clergyman
Thomas Howard Gill, his life and work ... / by Eliza Fanny Pollard. London: Partridge, [1895]. (NLS)

GILL, William, 1802-79, clergyman
Memoir of the late Rev. William Gill, Vicar of Stannington in the Parish of Ecclesfield. Edited by Alfred Gatty. Sheffield: printed by Clark & Greenup, 1880. Pamphlet. (B&J)

GILL, William, d.1871, Vicar of Malow, Isle of Man
The Reverend William Gill: a sketch. By one of his sons (Thomas Howard Gill). Castletown, IoM: M.J. Blackwell, 1871. (NLS)

GILLOW, George, d.1894, Catholic priest
The life of Father George Gillow. Preston: H.E. Thomson, [1896]. Pamphlet. (NLS)

GILMOUR, James, 1843-91, Scottish missionary in Mongolia
James Gilmour and his boys / by Richard Lovett. London: Religious Tract Society, 1894. (NC)

GILPIN, Bernard, 1803-71, clergyman, then Independent Minister
Memorials of the life and ministry of Bernard Gilpin. With a biography of his first wife [Henrietta Gilpin] ... Edited by ... R.B. Benson. London: Pembrey & Houlston, 1874. photo.port.

GISBORNE, John, 1770-1851, poet; diarist
A brief memoir of the life of John Gisborne, Esq. To which are added extracts from his diary. [Edited by his daughter Emma Nixon]. Derby: W. Bemrose, 1852. (NLS)

GLADSTONE, William Ewart, 1809-98, Liberal Prime Minister; tractarian; reformer of prostitutes
Anecdotes of the Right Hon. W.E. Gladstone. By an Oxford man. London: Joseph Toulmin, [188-].
-------. Gladstone the man: a non-political biography / by David Williamson. 2nd illustrated edition. London: James Bowden, 1898.
-------. Gladstone, 1809-1898: a character sketch / by William Thomas Stead. London: 'Review of Reviews', [1898].
-------. The life of Mr Gladstone told by himself in speeches and public letters / compiled by H.J. Leech. London: C. Kegan Paul, 1893.
-------. The life of the Right Hon. William Ewart Gladstone, M.P. / by George Barnett Smith. Popular edition. London: Cassell, Petter Galpin, [188-].
-------. Life of the Right Hon. William E. Gladstone, M.P.. By a London journalist. London: Haughton, [1880]. (NLS)
-------. The life of William Ewart Gladstone / by John Morley. London: Macmillan, 1903. 3 volumes; and many later editions.
-------. The life of William Ewart Gladstone / by Herbert Woodfield Paul. London: Smith, Elder, 1901.
-------. The life of William Ewart Gladstone. Edited by Thomas Wemyss Reid. London: Cassell, 1899. (BL)
-------. Mr Gladstone: a monograph / by Edward Walter Hamilton. London: John Murray,

1898.

-------. The people's life of the Right Hon. W. E. Gladstone by George Potter. London: G. Potter, [1884].

-------. The Right Hon. W. E. Gladstone / by George William Erskine Russell. London: Sampson Low, Marston, 1891. (Prime Ministers of Queen Victoria series)

-------. Talks with Mr Gladstone / Lionel Arthur Tollemache. London: Edward Arnold, 1898; 3rd revised edition. 1903: reprinted as: 'Gladstone's Boswell: late Victorian conversations ...' Introduced and edited by Asa Briggs. Brighton: Harvester, 1984.

-------. William Ewart Gladstone: a political and literary biography / by George Rose Emerson. London: Ward Lock, 1881. photo.port. (B&J)

-------. William Ewart Gladstone, his life and times / by Lewis Apjohn. London: Walter Scott Publishing, 1888. photo.port.

-------. William Ewart Gladstone, statesman and scholar. Edited by David Williamson. London: Ward Lock, 1898.

and many other contemporary books and pamphlets

GLOVER, Sir John Hawley, 1829-85, naval officer; colonial governor in West Africa, Canada & West Indies
Life of Sir John Hawley Glover, R.N., G.C.M.G. / by [Elizabeth Rosetta] Glover. Edited by Richard Temple. London: Smith, Elder, 1897.

GLOVER, Percy Clabon, 1856-88, tutor
Self-discipline: a memoir of Percy Clabon Glover / by Richard Glover. London: J. Nisbet, 1889. (BL)

GOBAT, Samuel, 1799-1879, German-born Bishop of Jerusalem
Samuel Gobat, Bishop of Jerusalem: his life and work: a biographical sketch, drawn chiefly from his own journals ... London: J. Nisbet, 1884. (NLS)

GOLDSMID, Sir Francis Henry, 2nd Bart., 1808-78, Jewish M.P. & philanthropist
Memoir of Sir Francis Henry Goldsmid, Bart., Q.C., M.P. / by David Woolf Marks and Albert Lowry. London: C.Kegan Paul, 1879; 2nd revised & enlarged edition. 1882. (NLS)

GOLIGHTLY, Charles Pourtales, 1807-85, anti-ritualist clergyman
Reminiscences of Charles Pourtales Golightly: a letter reprinted with additions and a preface from 'The Guardian' newspaper ... / by Edward Meyrick Goulburn. Oxford: Parker, [1886]. (NLS)

GOLLMER, Charles Andrew, 1812-86, missionary in West Africa
Charles Andrew Gollmer, his life and missionary labours in West Africa / compiled from his journals and the Church Missionary Society's publications by his eldest son [Charles Henry Vidal Gollmer] ... London: Hodder & Stoughton, 1899. photo.port.

GOOD, Adolphus Clemens, d. 1894, missionary in Africa
A life for Africa: a biography of the Rev. A. C. Good, Ph.D., missionary in Equatorial Central Africa / by Helen C. Parsons. Edinburgh: Oliphant, Anderson & Ferrier, 1897. (BL)

GOODENOUGH, James Graham, 1830-75, naval attache; Commodore of the Australasian Station
The Christian hero of Santa Cruz, or the last hours of Commodore Goodenough: a tale from real life. London: S.W. Partridge, [1875]. Pamphlet. (NLS)

-------. Commander J. G. Goodenough: a brief memoir / by Clement Robert Markham. Portsmouth: J. Griffin, 1876. (BL)

-------. A life of love and duty, being a memoir of Commodore Goodenough, R.N., C.B., C.M.G.. Edited [i.e. written] by his widow [Victoria H. Goodenough]. [New edition]. London: S.P.C.K., [1891].

GOODSIR, John, 1814-67, Professor of Anatomy, University of Edinburgh

The anatomical memoirs of John Goodsir ... Edited by William Turner ... With a biographical memoir / by Henry Lonsdale. Edinburgh: A. & C. Black, 1868. 2 volumes. (NLS)

-------. Obituary notice of Professor John Goodsir / by John Hutton Balfour. Edinburgh: Neill, 1867. Pamphlet. (NLS)

GOODWIN, Harvey, 1818-91, Bishop of Carlisle from 1869
Harvey Goodwin, Bishop of Carlisle: a biographical memoir / by Hardwicke Drummond Rawnsley. Printed for private circulation only. Cambridge, 1880; new edition. London: John Murray, 1896.

GORDON, Charles, 1772-1855, Scottish Roman Catholic priest
Priest Gordon of Aberdeen / by James Stark. Aberdeen: D. Wyllie, 1909. (B&J)

GORDON, Charles George, 1833-85, General in China and Africa; reformatory work with young boys
Charles George Gordon / by William Francis Butler. London: Macmillan, 1889. (English Men of Action series)

-------. Charles George Gordon: a sketch / by Reginald Henry Barnes & Charles Edward Brown. London: Macmillan, 1885. (NC)

-------. Chinese Gordon: a memoir / by Charles Cornwallis Chesney. London: Edward Stanford, 1869. Pamphlet. (Reprinted from 'Fraser's Magazine')

-------. Chinese Gordon: a succinct record of his life / by Archibald Forbes. London: G. Routledge, 1884. photo.port.; and later editions.

-------. Events in the life of Charles George Gordon, from its beginning to its end / by Henry William Gordon. London: Kegan, Paul, 1886. (BL)

-------. General Gordon, saint and soldier / by J. Wardle, a personal friend. Nottingham: Henry B. Saxton, 1904. (B&J)

-------. General Gordon, soldier, adminstrator and Christian hero: a biographical and historical sketch of his career in China and Soudan / by George Rose Emerson. London: Ward, Lock, [1884].

-------. Gordon anecdotes: a sketch of the career. With illustrations of the character of, Charles George Gordon, R.E. / by James Macaulay. London: Religious Tract Society, [1885].

-------. The life and work of General Gordon at Gravesend / by W. E. Lilly. London: Abraham Kingdom, 1885.

-------. Life of General Gordon. London: Walter Scott Publishing, 1884. photo. port.

-------. The life of Gordon, Major-General, R.E., C.B., [etc.] / by Demetrius Charles Bougler. 1896. 2 volumes; 4th edition. London: T. Fisher Unwin, [189-].

-------. More about Gordon. By one who knew him well [i.e. Octavia Freese]. London: R. Bentley, 1894. 12mo. (B&J) 'Apparently withdrawn after publication'
and many other popular books

GORDON, George Maxwell, 1839-80, missionary in Punjab
George Maxwell Gordon, M.A., F.R.G.S., the pilgrim missionary of the Punjab: a history of his life and work, 1839-1880 / by Arthur Lewis. London: Seeley, 1889. (NC)

GORDON, George William, c.1820-65, politician in Jamaica executed for high treason
A sketch of the life of the late Mr G. W. Gordon, Jamaica / by David King. Edinburgh: W. Oliphant, 1866. Pamphlet. (Reprinted from the 'United Presbyterian Magazine') (NLS)

GORDON, Hon. James Henry Hamilton, 1845-68 see **HADDO, Lord**

GORDON, John, 1827-82, religious biography
John Gordon, of Pitlurg and Parkhill, or memories of a standard-bearer / by his widow [Margaret Maria Gordon]. London: J. Nisbet, 1885. (NC)

GORDON, Lewis Dunbar Brodie, 1815-76, civil engineer

Memoir of Lewis D. B. Gordon, F.R.S.E., late Regius Professor of Civil Engineering and Mechanics in the University of Glasgow. [By Thomas Constable]. For private circulation. Edinburgh, 1877. (NC)

GORDON, Osborne, 1813-83, Oxford University don; clergyman
Osborne Gordon: a memoir. With a selection of his writings. Edited by George Marshall. Oxford: Parker, 1885.

GOSSE, Philip Henry, 1810-88, zoologist; Plymouth Brethren
The life of Philip Henry Gosse, F.R.S. / by Edmund William Gosse. London: Kegan Paul, 1890.

GOUDY, Alexander Porter, 1809-58, Ulster Presbyterian leader; Moderator 1857
Life of the Rev. A. P. Goudy, D.D. / by Thomas Croskey & Thomas Witherow. Dublin: Humphrey & Armour, 1887. (NC)

GOUGH, Sir Hugh, 1st Viscount Gough, 1779-1869, Field-Marshal; Commander-in-Chief India 1843-49
The life and campaigns of Hugh, 1st Viscount Gough, Field-Marshal / by Robert Sangster Rait. Westminster: A. Constable, 1903. 2 volumes. (NLS)

GOULBURN, Edward Meyrick, 1818-97, Dean of Norwich
Edward Meyrick Goulburn, D.D., D.C.L., Dean of Norwich: a memoir / by Berdmore Compton. London: John Murray, 1899.

GRACEY, David, 1841-93, Baptist Minister & college principal
Greatness in gentleness, being personal recollections of the late Rev. Principal David Gracey, of the Pastor's College, Newington / by Jabez J. Hayman. New Southgate: printed by C. & C. Mobbs, [1893]. Pamphlet. (NLS)

GRAHAM, Alexander, d.1860, Glasgow merchant & Scottish Episcopalian
Records of the late Alexander Graham, Esq., of Lancefield / compiled by his friend Charles B. Gribble. Printed for private circulation. Glasgow: D. Bryce, 1860. (NC)

GRAHAM, Sir Gerald, V.C, 1831-99, Colonel Commandant, Royal Engineers
Life, letters and diaries of Lieut-General Sir Gerald Graham, V.C., G.C.G., R.E.. With portraits, plans and his principal despatches / by Robert Hamilton Vetch. Edinburgh: W. Blackwood, 1901.

GRAHAM, Herbert Reginald Curteis, 1858-80, in Royal Lanark Militia
Herbert Reginald Curteis Graham, second son of Reginald John Graham, of the Elms, Eastbourne, and Ellen Leah Boileau, his wife. Was born at Eastbourne, January 19 1858, and died at Malta, August 27 1880. [188-]. Pamphlet. (B&J)

GRAHAM, Sir James Robert George, 2nd Bart., 1792-1861, Home Secretary 1841-46; Peelite leader on the death of Peel
Life and letters of Sir James Graham, second Baronet of Netherby, P.C., K.C.B., 1792-1861 / by Charles Stuart Parker. London: John Murray, 1907. 2 volumes.
-------. The life and times of the Right Hon. Sir James Graham, Bart. / by William Torrens McCullagh Torrens. London: Saunders, Otley, 1863. 2 volumes. (NUC)
-------. The Right Hon. Sir J. R. G. Graham, Bart., of Netherby / by Henry Lonsdale. London: G. Routledge, 1868. ('The Worthies of Cumberland' series)

GRAHAM, John, 1813-95, Prebendary of Lichfield
A memoir of the Rev. John Graham, M.A., Prebendary of Lichfield Cathedral, and for forty years Rector of the parish of S. Chad, Lichfield / by his daughter C. E. Graham ... London: Bemrose, 1899. photo.port.

GRAHAM, John, 1822-79, Ulster Wesleyan Minister

Memoir of the Rev. John Graham / by his brother Charles Graham. London: John F. Shaw, [1882]. (BL)

GRAHAM, Thomas, 1805-69, chemist; Master of the Mint
The life and works of Thomas Graham. Illustrated by 64 unpublished letters ... / by Robert Angus Smith. Edited by J. J. Coleman. Glasgow: John Smith, 1884. (B&J)

GRAHAM, William, 1823-87, Scottish Presbyterian Minister in Liverpool
In memoriam: Rev. William Graham, D.D.. Born May 8th 1823; Ordained in Mount Pleasant Presbyerian Church, Liverpool, March 4th 1846 ...: Died November 26th 1887 ... Liverpool: George Philip, 1888. photo.port. (NC)

GRANT, Colesworthy, 1813-80, illustrator of Indian life; animal protector
Life of Colesworthy Grant, founder of the Calcutta Society for the Prevention of Cruelty to Animals / by Pyarichanda Mittra. Calcutta: I. C. Bose, 1881. 12mo. (BL)

GRANT, Hay Macdowell, 1806-69, diarist; Church of Scotland layman
Hay Macdowell Grant, of Ardnilly: his life, labours and teaching / by Margaret M. Gordon. London: Seeley, Jackson & Halliday, 1876. photo.port. (NC)

GRANT, Horace, 1799-1859, educationalist & writer of text books
Biographical notice of the late Horace Grant. With a list of his publications ... / by Edwin Chadwick. London: Bell & Daldy, [1861]. 12mo.

GRANT, <u>Sir</u> James Hope, 1808-75, Scottish General in India and China
Life of General Sir Hope Grant. With selections from his correspondence. Edited by Henry Knollys. Edinburgh: W. Blackwood, 1894. 2 volumes.

GRANT, <u>Sir</u> John Peter, 1807-93, Indian civil service; Governor of Jamaica
Grant of Rothiemurchas: a memoir of the services of Sir John Peter Grant, G.C.M.H. / by Walter Scott Seton-Karr. Privately printed. London: John Murray, 1899. (BL)

GRANT, Thomas, 1816-70, Roman Catholic Bishop of Southwark from 1851
Thomas Grant, first Bishop of Southwark / by Kathleen O'Meara. London: W. H. Allen, 1886.
-------. Thomas Grant, first Bishop of Southwark / by Grace Ramsay. London: Smith, Elder, 1874. (BL)

GRANT, William, 1814-76, Presbyterian Minister in Liverpool
In memoriam: Rev. William Grant, D.D.. Born May 8th 1823 ... Died November 26th 1887. Liverpool: George Philip, 1888. photo.port. (NC)

GRANVILLE, Granville George Leveson-Gower, <u>2nd Earl</u>, 1815-91, statesman; Foreign Secretary; close friend of Gladstone
The life of Granville George Leveson Gower, second Earl Granville, K.G., 1815-1891 / by Edmond Fitzmaurice. London: Longmans, Green, 1905. 2 volumes.

GRAY, John Miller, 1850-94, literary & art critic; Curator of the Scottish Portrait Gallery
John Miller Gray: memoir and remains. [Edited by James Balfour Paul & William Rae Macdonald]. Edinburgh: David Douglas, 1895. 2 volumes (225 copies printed)

GRAY, Robert, 1809-72, first Anglican Bishop of Capetown
Life of Robert Gray, Bishop of Capetown and Metropolitan of Africa. [By Henrietta Louisa Farrer]. Edited by his son Charles Gray. London: Rivingtons, 1876. 2 volumes; abridged edition. 1883.
-------. A pioneer and founder: reminiscences of some who knew Robert Gray, D.D., first Bishop of Cape Town and Metropolitan of South Africa / by Anne Elizabeth Mary Anderson-Morshead ... London: Skeffington, 1905.

GREATHEAD, Sir Edward Harris, 1812-81, General in India
Memorials of Sir Edward Harris Greathead, K.C.B. ... / by Alexander Cuningham Robertson. Printed for private circulation. London: Harrison, 1885. (BL)

GREATHEAD, William Wilberforce Harris, 1826-78, military engineer in India
A memoir of the life and services of Major-General W. H. H. Greathead, C.B. ... / compiled by a friend and brother officer H[enry] Y[ule]. 1879. (BL)

GREEN, Thomas Hill, 1836-82, Professor of Moral Philosophy, Oxford University from 1877
Memoir of Thomas Hill Green, late Fellow of Balliol College, Oxford, and Whyte's Professor of Moral Philosophy in the University of Oxford / by Richard Lewis Nettleship ... London: Longmans, Green, 1906.

GREGG, John, 1798-1878, evangelical Church of Ireland Bishop of Cork, Cloyne & Ross from 1862
'Faithful unto death': memorials of the life of John Gregg, D.D., Bishop of Cork, Cloyne and Ross ... / by his son Robert Samuel Gregg. Dublin: George Herbert, 1879.

GREGORY, Benjamin Alfred, 1850-76, religious biography
Consecrated culture: memorials of Benjamin Alfred Gregory, M.A. / by Benjamin Gregory. 1885; 2nd edition. London: T. Woolmer, 1888. (NLS)

GREGSON, William, 1822-90, temperance worker
Life of William Gregson, temperance advocate / by John George Shaw. Blackburn: J. & G. Toulmin, 1891. photo.port.

GRELLET, Stephen, d.1855, Quaker missionary in Europe
Memoirs of the life and Gospel labours of Stephen Grellet. Edited by Benjamin Seebohm. 2nd edition. London: A. W. Bennett, 1861. 2 volumes; 3rd abridged edition. London: E. Marsh, 1870.
-------. A missionary life: Stephen Grellet / by Frances Anne Budge. London: J. Nisbet, 1888. (Reprinted from 'The Friends' Quarterly Examiner')
-------. Stephen Grellet / by William Guest. London: Hodder & Stoughton, 1884. (Men Worth Remembering series)

GREY, Sir George, 2nd Bart., 1799-1882, Liberal Home Secretary; statesman
Memoir of Sir George Grey, Bart., G.C.B. / by Mandell Creighton. Privately printed. Newcastle-upon-Tyne: Collingwood Press, 1884. 4to; new edition. London: Longmans, Green, 1901.

GREY, Sir George, 1812-98, colonial governor in Cape Province & in Australasia
Sir George Grey, pioneer of Empire in Southern Lands / by George C. Henderson. London: J. M. Dent, 1907.
-------. The life and times of Sir George Grey, K.C.B. / by William Lee & L. Rees, 1892. 2 volumes; 3rd edition. [1893].
-------. The romance of a pro-consul, being the personal life and memoirs of the Right Hon. Sir George Grey, K.C.B. / by James Milne. London: Chatto & Windus, 1899.

GREY, Henry, 1778-1859, Free Church Minister; Moderator 1844
Thoughts in the evening of life: a sketch of the life of Rev. Henry Grey, D.D.. And passages from the diary of Mrs Grey. Edited by Charles Morton Birrell. London: Religious Tract Society, [1871]. 12mo. (NC)

GREY, John, 1785-1868, agricultural improver; father of Josephine Butler
Memoir of John Grey, of Dilston / by his daughter Josephine Elizabeth Butler. Edinburgh: Edmonston & Douglas, 1869; revised edition. London: Henry S. King, 1874.

GRIERSON, James, 1791-1875, Free Church Minister

In memoriam: notices of the Rev. James Grierson, D.D., given in Errol Free Church, 31st January 1875 / by Robert Cowan & Kenneth Moody-Stuart. Glasgow: D. Bryce, 1875. 12mo. photo. port. (NC)

GRIMOND, Joseph, d.1894, Dundee jute & flax manufacturer
In memory of Joseph Grimond. [By his daughter Nellie Josephine Grimond?]. Privately printed. 2nd November 1894.

GRIMSTON, Hon. Robert, 1816-84, cricketer; barrister
The life of the Hon. Robert Grimston / by Frederick Gale. London: Longmans, Green, 1885. photo.port.

GROOME, Robert Hindes, 1810-89, Archdeacon of Suffolk; friend of Edward Fitzgerald
Two Suffolk friends [being recollections of R. H. Groome and Edward Fitzgerald] / by Frances Hindes Groome. Edinburgh: W. Blackwood, 1895.

GROTE, George, 1794-1871, radical M.P.; a founder of London University
The life and writings of George Grote: an essay / by William McIlwraith. Wolverhampton: printed by Barford & Newitt, [1885]. Pamphlet. (NLS)
-------. The personal life of George Grote / compiled from family documents, private memoranda and original letters to and from various friends by Harriet Grote. London: John Murray, 1873.

GROVE, Sir George, 1820-1900, musical writer
The life and letters of Sir George Grove, C.B. ..., formerly Director of the Royal College of Music / by Charles Larcom Graves. London: Macmillan, 1903.

GROVES, Anthony Norris, 1795-1853, dentist; founder of Plymouth Brethren; missionary in India
Memoir of the late Anthony Norris Groves, containing extracts from his letters and journals / compiled by his widow [Harriet Groves]. London: J. Nisbet, 1856. (BL)

GUEST, John, 1799-1880, Rotherham brass founder & worthy; antiquarian
Sketch of the life and labours of Mr Alderman John Guest, F.S.A., of Rotherham. With selections from his poems and letters / by Thomas Beggs. Worksop: Robert White, 1881.

GULL, Sir William Withey, 1st Bart., 1815-90, Royal Physician
William Withey Gull: a biographical sketch / by Thomas Dyke Acland. 1896. (BL) (Possibly extracted from his 'A collection of the published writings ...', 1894-6. 2 volumes)

GUNN, John, 1801-90, clergyman in East Anglia; geologist
Memorials of John Gunn, M.A., F.G.S., formerly Rector of Irstead and Vicar of Barton Turf [etc.]. With a memoir of the author. Edited by Horace Bolingbroke Woodward [&] Edwin Tully Newton. Norwich: W. A. Nudd, 1891. (B&J)

GURNEY, Samuel, 1786-1856, Quaker banker with Overend, Gurney & Co.; philanthropist
Memorials of Samuel Gurney. [By Hannah Ransome] Geldart. London: W. & F. G. Cash, 1857.

GUTHRIE, Thomas, 1803-73, important Free Church leader and 'apostle of the ragged school movement'
Life of the Rev. Thomas Guthrie, D.D.; compiled mostly from his own lips. [By Jessie L. Watson]. Glasgow: John S. Marr, [1873?]. 12mo.
-------. Thomas Guthrie / by Oliphant Smeaton. Edinburgh; Oliphant, Anderson & Ferrier, [1897]. (Famous Scots Series)
-------. Thomas Guthrie: a tribute and a memorial / by Arthur Marshall. London: E. Curtice, [1873]. (NLS)
-------. Thomas Guthrie, preacher and philanthropist / by Charles John Guthrie.

Edinburgh: A. Elliot, 1899. (NLS)

GUTHRIE, William, b.1839, Montrose revivalist
A brief but bright wilderness journey: a memoir of William Guthrie / by William Mitchell. Montrose: George Walker, 1860. (NC)

HADDO, George John James Hamilton-Gordon, _Lord_, later _5th Earl of_ _Aberdeen_, 1816-64, M.P., religious peer
Memoir of Lord Haddo, in his later years fifth Earl of Aberdeen. Edited by Edward Bishop Elliott. 2nd revised edition 1867; 6th revised edition with additions. London: Seeley, Jackson & Halliday, 1873.
-------. Memoranda of the life of Lord Haddo, in his later years fifth Earl of Aberdeen. Edited by Edward Bishop Elliott. Printed for private circulation. London, 1866. photographically illustrated. (NC)
-------. The true nobility: sketches of the life and character of Lord Haddo, later 5th Earl of Aberdeen; and of his son the Hon. J. H. H. Gordon / by Alexander Duff. London: Religious Tract Society, 1868.

HADFIELD, William, d.1868, local worthy in Congleton, Derbyshire
A jubilee memorial of the late William Hadfield, J.P. / by Thomas Shaw. Manchester: A. Ireland, 1869.

HAIG, Felix Thackeray, 1827-1901, general then missionary in India & Arabia
Memoirs of the life of General F. T. Haig / by his wife [C. A. Haig] ... London: Marshall, 1902. (NLS)

HAKE, William, d.1890 aged 95, religious author from Barnstaple
Seventy years of pilgrimage, being a memorial of William Hake, author of 'How shall we order the child?' / by Robert Cleaver Chapman. Glasgow: Henry Pickering, [1890?]. 12mo. (NLS)

HALDANE, Alexander, 1800-82, barrister
A biographical sketch of Alexander Haldane of the Inner Temple, barrister-at-law, J.P., communicated to the 'Record' of July 28 1882. With extracts and additions. London: printed by Spottiswoode, [1882].

HALL, James, b.1826, Newcastle shipowner and philanthropist on a large scale
James Hall of Tynemouth: a beneficent life of a busy man of business / by William Hayward. For private circulation only. London: Hazell, Watson & Viney, 1896. 2 volumes. (NLS)

HALL, _Sir_ John, 1795-1866, military surgeon in Africa & the Crimea
The life and letters of Sir John Hall, M.D., K.C.B., F.R.C.S. / by Siddhi Mohan Mitra ... London: Longmans, Green, 1911.

HALL, Marshall, 1790-1857, physiologist specialising in nervous diseases
Memoirs of Marshall Hall, M.D., F.R.S. / by his widow [Charlotte Hall]. London: R. Bentley, 1861.

HALL, Robert Constable, 1836-88, Irish Justice of the Peace
A brother beloved: a brief memoir of the late Robert Constable Hall, J.P., of Rockliffe, Blackrock, Cork. Born Feb. 10 1836 - Died Oct. 19 1888 / by his brother Frederick Hall. For private circulation. Cork: printed by Guy, 1909. (B&J)

HALL, Samuel Romilly, 1812-76, Wesleyan Methodist leader
Life of the Rev. Samuel Romilly Hall. With copious extracts from his diaries and

letters / by Thomas Nightingale. London: Welseyan Conference Office, [1879]. (NLS)

HALLE, Sir Charles Friedrich, 1819-95, German-born musician; founder & conductor of the Halle Orchestra, Manchester
Life and letters of Sir Charles Halle, being an autobiography (1819-1860). With correspondence and diaries. Edited by his son Charles Emile Halle and his daughter Marie Halle. London: Smith, Elder, 1896.

HALLEY, Robert, 1796-1876, Congregationalist Minister and theologian
A short biography of the Rev. Robert Halley, D.D., late Principal of New College, London ... Edited by Robert Halley. London: Hodder & Stoughton, 1879.

HAMILTON, Arthur, 1806-58, Chaplain with East India Company
Memoirs of Arthur Hamilton, B.A., of Trinity College, Cambridge, extracted from his letters and diaries. With reminiscences of his conversation / by his friend Christopher Carr. London: Kegan Paul, Trench, 1886.

HAMILTON, David, 1805-60, Ulster Presbyterian Minister
'Faithful unto death': a biographical sketch of the Rev. David Hamilton, Belfast / by his son Thomas Hamilton. Belfast: William Mullan, 1875. 12mo.

HAMILTON, James, 1814-67, Church of Scotland Minister in London
In memory of James Hamilton, D.D., the beloved Minister of the Presbyterian Church, Regent Square [London], died Nov. 24th 1867. [London: printed by Ranken & Wilson, 1867].
-------. Life of James Hamilton, D.D., F.L.S. / by William Arnot. London: J. Nisbet, 1870. (NC)
-------. Memoir of Rev. James Hamilton, D.D., Regent Square, London ... by Robert Naismith. London: J. Nisbet, [1896].

HAMILTON, John, 1830-78, Free Church Minister
Memorials of the late Rev. John Hamilton, Free West Church, Glasgow. With a biographical sketch / by John Laidlaw. Glasgow: D. Bryce, 1881. photo.port.

HAMILTON, Walter Kerr, 1808-69, tractarian Bishop of Salisbury from 1854
Walter Kerr Hamilton, Bishop of Salisbury: a sketch / by Henry Parry Liddon. London: Rivington, 1869. (Reprinted with additions and corrections from 'The Guardian') (NC)

HAMILTON, Sir William, 3rd Bart., 1788-1856, philosopher
Memoir of Sir William Hamilton, Bart., Professor of Logic and Metaphysics in the University of Edinburgh / by John Veitch. Edinburgh: W. Blackwood, 1869. (NC)

HAMILTON, Sir William Rowan, 1805-65, Astronomer-Royal for Ireland
Life of Sir William Rowan Hamilton ... Including selections from his poems, correspondence and miscellaneous writings / by Robert Perceval Graves. Dublin: Hodges Figgis, 1882-91. 3 volumes. [Volume 3 is a pamphlet 'Addendum'] (NLS)

HAMLEY, Sir Edward Bruce, 1824-93, General; M.P.; military historian
The life of General Sir Edward Bruce Hamley, K.C.B., K.C.M.G. / by Alexander Innes Shand. Edinburgh: W. Blackwood, 1895. 2 volumes.

HAMMOND, Maximilian Montague, 1824-55, religious soldier killed at Sebastapol
Memoir of Captain M. M. Hammond, Rifle Brigade. [By his brother Egerton Douglas Hammond]. London: J. Nisbet, 1858.

HAMPDEN, Renn Dickson, 1793-1868, Oxford theologian; controversial & liberal Bishop of Hereford from 1847
Some memorials of Renn Dickson Hampden, Bishop of Hereford. Edited by his daughter Henrietta Hampden. London: Longmans, Green, 1871.

HANBURY, Robert Culling, 1823-67, brewer; M.P.; reformer
Robert Culling Hanbury: a sketch of his life and work. London: George Hunt, [1867]. (B&J)

HANBY, Richard, d.188-, worked at Chetham's Hospital [School] Manchester
Memoir of Richard [Hanby], for more than thirty years a scholar, teacher and superintendent in Saint John's Sunday School; and subsequently for upwards of twelve years house governor of Chetham's Hospital, Manchester / by John Henn. Manchester: John Heywood, 1886. (B&J)

HANNAH, John, 1818-88, Rector of Edinburgh Academy, then Glenalmond College; Vicar of Brighton
John Hannah: a clerical study / by John Henry Overton. London: Rivingtons, 1890.

HANNINGTON, James, 1847-85, martyred Anglican Bishop in Uganda
James Hannington, D.D., F.L.S., F.R.G.S., first Bishop of Eastern Equatorial Africa: a history of his life and work, 1847-1885 / by Edwin Collas Dawson. London: Seeley, 1887. (NC)

HARBOTTLE, Joseph, 1798-1864, poet, Lancashire Baptist Minister
A memoir of Mr Joseph Harbottle, Baptist Minister, Accrington. With selections from his literary remains / by Thomas Taylor ... Ulverston: printed by D. Harbottle, 1866. 12mo. photo. port. (B&J)

HARDING, George, 1809-92, Hampshire Strict Baptist Minister
Outlines of the life of George Harding, nearly sixty years Minister of the Gospel at Swanwick, near Southampton, Hants. [Edited by A.D.]. Fareham: S. & M.A. Harding, 1900. (NLS)

HARDINGE, Sir Henry Hardinge, 1st Viscount, 1785-1856, Field-Marshal; Governor-General in India 1844-47
Viscount Hardinge: [a biography] / by his son Charles Stewart, 2nd Viscount Hardinge. Oxford: Clarendon Press, 1891. (Rulers of India series)

HARDWICKE, Charles Philip Yorke, 4th Earl of, 1799-1873, Admiral; M.P.; statesman
Charles Philip Yorke, fourth Earl of Hardwicke, Vice-Admiral, R.N. / by his daughter Elizabeth Philippa Biddulph. London: Smith, Elder, 1910.

HARE, David, n.d., in India
A biographical sketch of David Hare / by Pyarichanda Mitra. Calcutta: W. Newman, 1877. 12mo. (BL)

HARE, John, 1865-95, comedian
John Hare, comedian, 1865-1895: a biography / by Thomas Edgar Pemberton. London: G. Routledge, 1895.

HARE, Robert Henry, 1816-73, Wesleyan Methodist Minister
The Ministry and character of Robert Henry Hare / by John Middleton Hare. London: for the author by Wesleyan Conference Office, 1874. (NUC)

HARFORD-BATTERSBY, Thomas Dundas, 1822-83, evangelical clergyman; founded the Keswick Conventions
Memoir of T. D. Harford-Battersby, late Vicar of St. John's, Keswick ... By two of his sons. London: Seeley 1890. (NC)

HARKER, Thomas, n.d., Methodist miner
Thomas Harker, coal-winner and soul-winner / by Hopper Joplin. Jarrow: 'Guardian', 1900. Pamphlet. (B&J)

HARKOM, Joseph, 1807-91, Edinburgh gunmaker
In memoriam: Joseph Harkom, died 8th February, 1891. [1891?]. Pamphlet. (NLS)

HARLEY, George, 1829-96, doctor practising in London
George Harley, F.R.S.: the life of a London physician. Edited by his daughter [Ethel Brilliana Tweedie]. London: The Scientific Press, 1899.

HARNESS, Sir Henry Drury, 1804-83, versatile Royal Engineer
General Sir Henry Drury Harness, K.C.B., Colonel Commandant Royal Engineers .../ by Thomas Barnard Collinson. Edited by Charles Edmund Webber. London: Royal Engineers Institute Committee, 1903. (NUC)

HARPER, Hugo Daniel, 1821-95, Headmaster of Sherborne School 1850-77; Principal of Jesus College Oxford
A memoir of Hugo Daniel Harper, D.D., late Principal of Jesus College, Oxford, and for many years Head-Master of Sherborne School, Dorset / by Lester Vallis Lester. London: Longmans, Green, 1896.

HARPER, James, 1795-1879, United Prebyterian theologian; Moderator 1860
The life of Principal Harper, D.D. / by Andrew Thomson. Edinburgh: Andrew Elliot, 1881.

HARPER, John Dick, 1839-62, United Presbyterian theological student
John Dick Harper, student in theology: in memoriam. [Edited by J.J.]. Printed for private circulation. Edinburgh: Andrew Elliot, 1863. 12mo. photo. port. (NC)

HARRIS, James, 1824-83, Jesuit priest
Memoir of Father James Harris, S.J. / by Thomas Harper. Roehampton: Manresa Press, 1884. Pamphlet. (NLS)

HARRIS, John, 1820-84, Cornish mine worker; Wesleyan local preacher; poet
John Harris, the Cornish poet: a lecture on his life and works / by John Gill. Falmouth: Alfred Harris, [1884?] Pamphlet. (NLS)
-------. John Harris, the Cornish poet: the story of his life / by his son John Howard Harris. London: S. W. Partridge, [1893].

HARRIS, Richard, 1777-1854, manufacturer; 'Liberal Whig' M.P. for Leicester 1848-52
Character and its conquests: a memoir of the late Richard Harris, Esq., formerly M.P. for Leicester / by Thomas Lomas. London: B. L. Green, [1855]. (BL)

HARRIS, Sir Thomas Noel, 1785-1860, soldier at Waterloo, in Canada & Gibraltar
Brief memoir of the late Lt.-Col. Sir Thomas Noel Harris, K.H. [etc.] / by his grandson Clement Bettesworth Harris. Printed for private circulation. Revised and corrected edition. London, 1893. (BL)

HARRISON, Henry Bowers, 1830-95, Salford worthy, Sunday School teacher and philanthropist
The life of Henry Bowers Harrison / by his daughter [E. Harrison] ... London: Charles H. Kelly, 1896. (BL)

HARRISON, Joshua Clarkson, 1813-94, Congregationalist leader
Joshua Clarkson Harrison: a memoir. By one who knew him [i.e. F. W. Sauer] ... London: Hodder & Stoughton, 1900. (BL)

HARVEY, James, 1816-83, woollen merchant
From Suffolk lad to London merchant ... : a sketch of the life of James Harvey / by Alfred James Harvey ... Bristol: T. W. Arrowsmith, 1900. (BL)

HARVEY, William Henry, 1811-66, Irish botanist; in South Africa , 1836-42

Memoir of William Henry Harvey, M.D., F.R.S., etc., late Professor of Botany, Trinity College, Dublin. With selections from his journal and correspondence. London: Bell & Daldy, 1869. (NUC)

HASSALL, Arthur Hill, 1817-94, doctor; medical writer, especially on food adulteration
Arthur Hill Hassall, physician and sanitary reformer: a short history of his work in public hygiene ... / by Edwy Godwin Clayton. London: Bailliere, 1908. (BL)

HASWELL, Thomas, 1807-89; composer; Tyneside headmaster
'The maister': a century of Tyneside life, being some account of the life, work and times of Thomas Haswell, who for close on fifty years was Master of the Royal Jubilee Schools at North Shields ... / by George H. Haswell. London: Walter Scott Publishing, 1895.

HATCH, Edwin, 1835-89, Anglican academic; Bampton Lecturer
Memorials of Edwin Hatch, D.D., sometime Reader in Ecclesiastical History in the University of Oxford, and Rector of Purleigh. Edited by his brother [Samuel C. Hatch]. London: Hodder & Stoughton, 1890. photo. port.

HATHERLEY, William Page Wood, 1st Baron, 1801-81, Lord Chancellor 1868-72
A memoir of the Right Hon. William Page Wood, Baron Hatherley. With selections from his correspondence. Edited by his nephew William Richard Wood Stephens. London: R. Bentley, 1883. 2 volumes.

HATTON, Joseph, n.d., Pastor
Memories and sermons of Joseph Hatton, late Pastor of the churches at Smallfields and Shaw's Corner, Red Hill. [By M.B.] ... London: J. Gadsby [1885?]. (B&J)

HAUGHTON, James, 1795-1873, Irish corn & flour merchant; temperance reformer; Unitarian
Memoir of James Haughton. With extracts from his private and published letters / by his son Samuel Haughton. Dublin: E. Ponsonby, 1877. photo.port.

HAUGHTON, John, 1852-98, Indian army
Lieutenant Colonel John Haughton, Commandant of the 36th Sikhs, a hero of Tirah: a memoir / by Arthur Campbell Yate. London: John Murray, 1900. (NLS)

HAVELOCK, Sir Henry, 1st Bart., 1795-1857, Major-General; relieved Lucknow after the Siege
A biographical sketch of Sir Henry Havelock, K.C.B. / by William Brock. 6th edition. London: J. Nisbet, 1858.
-------. General Havelock, or the Christian soldier. Translated from the Italian ... / by Balcarres Dalrymple Wardlaw Ramsay. London: Hatchards, 1871. Pamphlet. (NLS)
-------. Havelock / by Archibald Forbes. London: Macmillan, 1891. (English Men of Action series)
-------. Memoirs of Major-General Sir Henry Havelock, K.C.B. / by John Clark Marshman. London: Longman [etc.], 1860; and other editions.
-------. The story of Sir Henry Havelock, the Hero of Lucknow / by Lucy Taylor. London: T. Nelson, 1902. (Noble Lives series)

HAVERGAL, William Henry, 1793-1870, clergyman; composer of church music
The pastor remembered: a memorial of the Rev. W. H. Havergal, Vicar of Shareshill ... / by Charles Bullock. 2nd edition. London: 'Home Words' Publishing Office, [1870].
-------. Records of the life of the Rev. William H. Havergal, M.A., formerly Rector of St. Nicholas', Worcester ... / by his daughter Jane Miriam Crane. London: 'Home Words' Publishing Office, [1882].

HAWELL, Joseph, 1854-90, Lake District shepherd and Conservative Party speaker
A Skiddaw shepherd's life: in memoriam Joseph Howell / by Hardwicke Drummond

Rawnsley. Keswick: printed by T. Bakewell, 1891. 12mo. Pamphlet. (NLS)

HAWKER, Robert Stephen, 1803-75, Cornish clergyman and poet converted to Catholicism on his deathbed
The life and letters of R. S. Hawker (sometime Vicar of Morwenstow) / by his son-in-law Charles Edward Byles ... London: John Lane, 1905. (NLS)
-------. Memorials of the late Rev. Stephen Hawker, M.A., sometime Vicar of Morwenstow in the Diocese of Exeter. Collected, arranged and edited by Frederick George Lee. London: Chatto & Windus, 1876. (NLS)
-------. Some remarks upon two recent memoirs of R. S. Hawker / by William Maskell. Printed for private circulation. 1876. (30 copies printed)
-------. The Vicar of Morwenstow: a life of Robert Stephen Hawker, M.A. / by Sabine Baring-Gould. (1876); 3rd revised edition. London: Henry S. King, 1899. photo. port. (NLS)

HAWKINS, Charles Vickery, 1872-94, undergraduate at Cambridge University
Charles Vickery Hawkins: memorials of his life. Edited by W. E. Waddington & J. T. Inskip ... London: Hodder & Stoughton, 1896.

HAWTREY, Edward Craven, 1789-1862, Headmaster of Eton 1834-53, then Provost; a great linguist
Memoir of Edward Craven Hawtrey, D.D., Headmaster and afterwards Provost of Eton / by Francis St John Thackeray. London: G. Bell, 1896.

HAZLETON, John, n.d., Baptist
John Hazleton: a memoir / by William Jeyes Styles. London: Robert Banks, 1888. photo.port. (B&J)

HEALY, James, 1824-94, 'the most popular Roman Catholic priest in Ireland'
Memoirs of Father Healy, of Little Bray. [By William John Fitzpatrick]. London: R. Bentley, 1896.

HEATH, Douglas Denon, 1881-97, classicist & mathematician; County Clerk of Middlesex
D. D. Heath. [By H. E. Malden]. [1899]. Pamphlet. (B&J)

HEATHCOTE, Sir William, 1st Bart., 1801-81, M.P. for Oxford University
A country gentleman of the Nineteenth Century, being a short memoir of the Right Hon. Sir William Heathcote, Bart., of Hursley, 1801-1881 / by Francis Awdry. Winchester: Warren, 1906.

HEATON, John Deakin, 1817-80, doctor in Leeds Infirmary from 1850
A memoir of John Deakin Heaton, M.D., of Leeds / by Thomas Wemyss Reid. London: Longmans, Green, 1883.

HELLIER, Benjamin, 1825-88, Yorkshire religious biography
Benjamin Hellier, his life and teaching: a biographical sketch ... Edited by his children [Anna M. & John Benjamin Hellier]. London: Hodder & Stoughton, 1889.

HELMORE, Thomas, 1811-90, clergyman, pioneer of Gregorian music in Church of England
Memoir of the Rev. Thomas Helmore, M.A., late Priest in Ordinary and Master of the Children of Her Majesty's Chapels Royal [etc.] / by Frederick Helmore. London: J. Masters, 1891. (NLS)

HENDERSON, Ebenezer, the elder, 1784-1858, Independent missionary in Europe; Bible printer
Memoir of the Rev. E. Henderson, D.D., Ph.D., including his labours in Denmark, Iceland, Russia, etc. / by Thulia Henderson. London: Knight, [1859].

HENDERSON, Ebenezer, the younger, 1809-79, astronomer; antiquary in Dunfermline
A memoir of the late Ebenezer Henderson ..., Freeman of the City of Dunfermline, astronomer and antiquary / by his niece [Thulia Henderson]. Dunfermline: Journal Printing Works, 1909. (NLS)

HENDERSON, James, 1797-1874, Free Church Minister
In memoriam: notices of the Rev. James Henderson, D.D., given in Free St Enoch's Church, Glasgow ... / by Andrew Melville [and others]. Glasgow: D. Bryce, 1874. 12mo. photo.port. (NC)

HENDERSON, James, 1829-65, farm labourer; medical missionary in China
Memorials of James Henderson, M.D. ..., medical missionary in China. London: J. Nisbet, 1867; 5th edition with 'Appendix ...' 1869. Pamphlet.(NC)

HENSLOW, John Stevens, 1796-1861, botanist; clergyman
Memoir of the Rev. John Stevens Henslow, M.A., F.L.S., F.C.P.S., late Rector of Hitcham, and Professor of Botany in the University of Cambridge / by Leonard Jenyns. London: John van Voorst, 1862. photo. port. (NLS)

HERAUD, John Abraham, 1799-1887, man of letters
Memoirs of John A. Heraud / by his daughter Edith Heraud. London: George Redway, 1898. (NLS)

HERBERT, John Maurice, 1808-82, Welsh judge
John Maurice Herbert, late judge of the County Courts of Cardiff and Glamorganshire / by Thomas Henry Ensor. Cardiff: Daniel Owen, 1883. Pamphlet. (B&J)

HERBERT OF LEA, Sidney Herbert, 1st Baron, 1810-61, statesman; army & sanitary reformer; friend of Florence Nightingale
Sidney Herbert, Lord Herbert of Lea: a memoir / by Arthur Hamilton Gordon, Lord Stanmore. London: John Murray, 1906. 2 volumes.

HERCOCK, Henry, b.1811, Leeds Minister
Memoir of Henry Hercock, late Minister of the Gospel, Leeds, etc. ... [By M. H. Baxter]. London: J. Gadsby, 1882. photo. port.

HERRIES, John Charles, 1778-1855, radical civil servant then M.P.
Memoir of the public life of the Right Hon. John Charles Herries in the reigns of George 111, George 1V, William 1V and Victoria / by his son Edward Herries ... London: John Murray, 1880. 2 volumes.

HERRING, John Frederick, 1795-1865, coach driver, jockey, sporting painter
Memoir of John Frederick Herring, Esq.. Sheffield, 1848. (BL)

HERVEY, Lord Arthur Charles, 1808-94, Bishop of Bath & Wells
A memoir of Lord Arthur Hervey, D.D., Bishop of Bath and Wells / by his son John Frederick Arthur Hervey. Printed for private circulation. Shotley, 1896.

HERVEY, Hubert John Antony, 1859-96, with the British South Africa Company; killed in Second Matabele War
Hubert Hervey, student and imperialist: a memoir / by Albert Henry George, Earl Grey. London: E. Arnold, 1899.

HEWETSON, Robert, n.d., artist; poet
The life and work of Robert Hewetson, boy painter and poet ... / by Henry Bendelack Hewetson. London: Swan Sonnenschein & Allen, 1881. 4to. photographic illustrations.

HEWITSON, William Hepburn, 1812-52, Free Church Minister
Memoir of the Rev. W. H. Hewitson, late Minister of the Free Church of Scotland at

Dirleton / by John Baillie. London: J. Nisbet, 1851.

HEYWOOD, Sir Benjamin, 1st Bart., 1793-1865, Manchester banker; M.P.
A memoir of Sir Benjamin Heywood ... / by his brother Thomas Heywood. [Completed by G. H. Sumner]. With two chapters of domestic life and letters, 1840-65. Printed for private circulation. [1888]. (BL)

HEYWOOD, Sir Thomas Percival, 2nd Bart., 1823-97, Manchester banker
In memoriam: Thomas Percival Heywood. Born March 15th 1825 - Entered into rest October 26th 1897. Manchester: Thomas Fargie, [1897]. (B&J)

HICKINGBOTHAM, William, 1789-1873, Derbyshire Primitive Methodist preacher
A diamond in the rough, or Christian heroism in humble life, being jottings concerning that remarkable peasant preacher William Hickingbotham, of Belper, Derbyshire / by John Barfoot. London: James Clarke, 1874. 12mo. (NLS)

HILL, David, 1804-96, Methodist missionary in China
David Hill, an apostle to the Chinese / by William Theodore Aquila Barber. London: Robert Culley, 1906. 12mo. (Library of Methodist Biography)
-------. David Hill, missionary and saint / by William Theodore Aquila Barber. London: Charles H. Kelly, 1898. photo.port.
-------. How David Hill followed Christ: a biography / by Jane Elizabeth Hellier. London: Charles H. Kelly, [1903]; revised edition as: 'Life of David Hill ...' London: Morgan & Scott, [1906]. (BL)

HILL, Joseph Sidney, 1851-94, Anglican Bishop of Western Equatorial Africa
Joseph Sidney Hill, first Bishop in Western Equatorial Africa ... / by Rose E. Faulkner. London: H. R. Allenson, 1895. (NUC)

HILL, Matthew Davenport, 1792-1872, judge; criminal law reformer
Matthew Davenport Hill. [By his son Alfred Hill]. London, 1872. Pamphlet. (Reprinted from the 'Law Magazine')
-------. The Recorder of Birmingham: a memoir of Matthew Davenport Hill. With selections from his correspondence / by his daughters Rosamond & Florence Davenport-Hill. London: Macmillan, 1878.

HILL, Sir Rowland, 1795-1879, postal reformer
The life of Sir Rowland Hill, K.C.B., D.C.L. [etc.] and the history of the Penny Postage/ by Rowland Hill and his nephew George Birkbeck Norman Hill. London: Thomas de La Rue, 1880. 2 volumes.
-------. Sir Rowland Hill, K.C.B.: a biographical and historical sketch. With records of the family to which he belonged / by Eliezer Edwards. London: F. Warne, 1879. (BL)

HINTON, James, 1822-75, surgeon & philosophical writer
Life and letters of James Hinton. Edited by Ellice Hopkins ... 2nd edition. London: C. Kegan Paul, 1878.

HISLOP, Stephen, 1817-63, drowned Free Church missionary and naturalist in India
Stephen Hislop, pioneer, missionary and naturalist in Central India from 1844 to 1863/ by George Smith ... London: John Murray, 1888.

HOARE, Edward, 1812-94, evangelical leader in Church of England
Edward Hoare, M.A.: a record of his life based upon a brief autobiography. Edited by John Hume Townsend. London: Hodder & Stoughton, 1896.

HOARE, Henry, 1807-65, banker and active Church of England layman
A memoir of the late Henry Hoare, Esq., M.A. ... / by James Braly Sweet. London: Rivingtons, 1869. (NC)

HODGSON, Brian Houghton, 1800-94, zoologist; Indian scholar and diplomat in India, Tibet and Nepal
Life of Brian Houghton Hodgson, British Resident at the Court of Nepal ... / by William Wilson Hunter. London: John Murray, 1896.

HODGSON, Christopher, 1817-98, temperance advocate
Temperance shots at random, or incidents in the life of Mr Christopher Hodgson / by Frederick Atkin. Manchester: printed by Darrah, 1887. photo.port.

HODGSON, Francis, 1781-1852, clergyman; Provost of Eton 1840-52
Memoir of Rev. Francis Hodgson, B.D., scholar, poet and divine. With numerous letters from Lord Byron and others / by his son James Thomas Hodgson. London: Macmillan, 1878. 2 volumes. (NLS)

HODGSON, William Ballantyne, 1815-80, Professor of Commercial Law
Life and letters of William Ballantyne Hodgson, LL.D., late Professor of Economic Science in the University of Edinburgh. Edited by John Miller Dow Meiklejohn. Edinburgh: David Douglas, 1883.

HODSON, William Stephen Raikes, 1821-58, Commander of 'Hodson's Horse', an irregular cavalry regiment in India
A leader of light horse: life of Hodson of Hodson's Horse / by Lionel James Trotter. Edinburgh: W. Blackwood, 1901.
-------. Remarks on Captain Trotter's biography of Major W. S. R. Hodson / by Crawford Trotter Chamberlain. Edinburgh: printed by R. & R. Clark, 1901. Pamphlet.

HOFFMAN, Cadwallader Colden, 1819-65, missionary in West Africa
A memoir of the Rev. C. Colden Hoffman, missionary to Cape Palmas, West Africa / by George Townshend Fox ... London: Seeley [etc.], 1868. (NUC)

HOG, James Maitland, 1799-1858, barrister; anti-slaver; Sabbatarian
Memorial of the late James Maitland Hog, Esq., of Newliston/ by James C. Burns. Edinburgh: John Maclaren, 1858. (NC)

HOGARTH, David, n.d., clergyman in Portland, Dorset
'He rests from his labours': memorials of the Reverend David Hogarth, M.A., for thirty-three years Rector of Portland, Dorset. Edited by Arthur Hill. Edinburgh: Andrew Elliot, 1873. photo. port. (B&J)

HOLDEN, Robert, d.1872, commanded the South Notts Yeomanry officer; Church layman
'A book of remembrance', being recollections of the late Colonel Holden, of Nuttall Temple, Nottingham. By one who knew him well [i.e. F.M.C.W.] ... London: J. Nisbet, [1872]. photo. port.

HOLLAND, John, 1794-1872, Sheffield newspaper editor; poet
The life of John Holland, of Sheffield Park, from numerous letters and other documents furnished by his nephew and executor John Holland Brammall / by William Hudson. London: Longmans, Green, 1874.

HOLME, John, b.1802, clergyman in Cheshire
Life of the Rev. John Holme, for many years Vicar of Lower Peover and Chaplain to ... Lord de Tabley ... / by C. K. Dean. Macclesfield: Swinnerton & Brown, 1875. (B&J)

HOLMES, James, 1777-1860, artist, dandy, friend of Byron & George 1V
James Holmes and John Varley / by Alfred T. Story. London. R. Bentley, 1894.

HOME (born MILNE), David Milne, 1804-90, advocate; social reformer
Biographical sketch of David Milne Home, LL.D., F.R.S.E. [etc.] / by his daughter G. M[ilne] H[ome]. Edinburgh: D. Douglas, 1891.

HOOD, Edwin Paxton, 1820-85, Congregationalist Minister; reformer
Edwin Paxton Hood, poet and preacher: a memorial / by George Henry Giddins. London: James Clarke, 1886. photo.port.

HOOD, Robert, 1837-94, evangelical pastor
Robert Hood, the Bridgeton Pastor: the story of his bright and useful life / by David Hobbs. Edinburgh: John B. Fairgrieve, 1894. (NLS)

HOOK, George, c.1772-1856, Fife sea captain
The thrilling narrative of Captain Hook / by George Beveridge. [Privately published]. Newburgh, Fife. 1901. (B&J)

HOOK, Walter Farquhar, 1798-1875, Anglo-Catholic leader; Dean of Chichester
Dean Hook: an address delivered at Hawarden / by William Ewart Gladstone. London: R. Bentley, 1879. Pamphlet. (NLS)
-------. The life and letters of Walter Farquhar Hook, D.D., F.R.S. / by his son-in-law William Richard Wood Stephens. London: R. Bentley, 1878. 2 volumes. photo. ports; in one volume. 1880.

HOPE, George, 1811-76, model farmer
George Hope, of Fenton Barns: a sketch of his life / compiled by his daughter [Charlotte Hope]. Edinburgh: David Douglas, 1881.

HOPE, John, 1807-93, founder of the Hope Trust; anti-Catholic; anti-smoker; anti-drinking; Writer to the Signet
John Hope, philanthropist and reformer / by David Jamie. Edinburgh: Andrew Elliot, 1900; abridged edition. Edinburgh: Hope Trust, 1907.

HOPE, Peter, 1815-78, Free Church Minister
Memoir of the Rev. Peter Hope, B.D., for twenty-six years Minister of the Free Church of Johnstone and Wamphray ... / by James Dodds. Edinburgh: John Maclaren, 1879. photo.port. (NC)

HOPE-SCOTT (born HOPE), James Robert, 1812-73, Parliamentary lawyer; Catholic
Memoirs of James Robert Hope-Scott of Abbotsford, D.C.L., Q.C., late Fellow of Merton College, Oxford. With selections from his correspondence / by Robert Ornsby. London: John Murray, 1884. 2 volumes.

HOPKINSON, John, 1849-1901, consulting civil & electrical engineer
Memories of John Hopkinson / by his sister [Mary Hopkinson]. For private circulation only. Manchester: Sherratt & Hughes, [1902]. (BL)

HORDEN, John, 1828-93, missionary Bishop of Moosonee in Canada
Forty two years among the indians and eskimos: pictures from the life of the Right Rev. John Horden, first Bishop of Moosonee / by Beatrice Batty. London: Religious Tract Society, 1897. (NC)

HORNBY, Sir Geoffrey Thomas Phipps, 1823-95, Admiral-of-the-Fleet
Admiral of the Fleet Sir Geoffrey Thomas Phipps Hornby, G.C.B.: a biography / by Mary Egerton. Edinburgh: W. Blackwood, 1896. (NLS)

HORNE, Thomas Hartwell, 1780-1862, clergyman; a librarian at British Museum Library 1824-60
Reminiscences, personal and bibliographical, of Thomas Hartwell Horne, B.D., F.S.A. ... With notes / by his daughter Sarah Anne Cheyne. London: Longman [etc.], 1862. (NC)
-------. The Rev. Thomas Hartwell Horne: a memoir / by George Mark Turpin. London, [1862]. (Reprinted from the 'Evangelical Magazine') (BL)

HORROCKS, Thomas, 1835-89, temperance worker

The life story of Thomas Horrocks / by W. Mark Noble. London: National Temperance Publication Depot, [1890]. Pamphlet. (NLS)

HORT, Fenton John Anthony, 1828-92, Church of England theologian
Life and letters of Fenton John Anthony Hort, D.D., [etc.] Hulsean Professor and Lady Margaret Reader in Divinity in the University of Cambridge / by his son Arthur Fenton Hort. London: Macmillan, 1896. 2 volumes.

HOUGHTON, John, 1858-86, Methodist Free Church missionary in East Africa
The martyrs of Golbanti, or missionary heroism illustrated in the lives of Rev. John and Mrs Houghton, of East Africa / by Robert Brewin. London: Andrew Crombie, [1886]. (B&J)

HOUGHTON, Richard Monckton Milnes, 1st Baron, 1809-85, M.P.; statesman; literary associations; pornographer
The life, letters and friendships of Richard Monckton Milnes, first Lord Houghton / by Thomas Wemyss Reid. London: Cassell, 1890. 2 volumes.

HOW, William Walsham, 1823-97, Bishop of Bedford, later of Wakefield
Bishop Walsham How: a memoir / by Frederick Douglas How. London: Isbister, 1898.

HOWELL, David, 1797-1873, Welsh Calvinist Methodist Minister
David Howell, of Swansea: a brief memoir / by Hugh Joshua Hughes. Newport, Mon: for the author by W. Jones, 1885.

HOWELL, Hinds, 1808-99, clergyman
Hinds Howell: a memoir / by [his daughter] Agnes Rous Howell ... Norwich: Agas H. Goose, 1899. (NLS)

HOWORTH, Franklin, 1805-82, Unitarian, then evangelical; temperance reformer
The conquest of gentleness ... : a new estimate of the life of the Rev. Franklin Howorth / by Thomas H. Hayhurst. Bury: 'Times' Office, 1910. (B&J)
-------. The triumph of Christ: memorials of Franklin Howarth / by Thomas Hornblower Gill. London: Hodder & Stoughton, 1883. photo.port. (NLS)

HUDSON, Sir James 'Hurry', 1810-85, diplomat in Italy
Lecture ... in commemoration of Sir James Hudson, British Minister to Victor Emmanuel ... / by Gustavo Dalgas. For private circulation. London, 1887. (BL)

HUGHES, Edward John Rees, 1825-53, clergyman
Four years of pastoral work, being a sketch of the ministerial labours of the Rev. Edward John Rees Hughes, late curate of Lythe, Yorkshire, and Runcton Holme, Norfolk / by Cecil Wray. London: John Masters, 1854. (NLS)

HUGHES, George Edward, 1821-72, ecclesiastical lawyer; sportsman
Memoir of a brother [George Edward Hughes] / by Thomas Hughes. London: Macmillan, 1873.

HUGHES, John 'Ceiriog', 1832-87, Welsh stationmaster & lyric poet
Memoirs of John Ceiriog Hughes. [By Isaac Ffoulkes]. Liverpool, [1887?]

HULLAH, John Pyke, 1812-84, composer, organist, singer
Life of John Hullah, LL.D. / by his wife [Frances R. Hullah]. London: Longmans,

HUNTER, Joseph, 1783-1861, antiquary; English Presbyterian Minister
A brief memoir of the late Joseph Hunter ... [By Sylvester Joseph Hunter]. Privately printed. London, 1861. (BL)

HUNTER, Sir William Wilson, 1840-1900, Indian 'civilian, historian & publicist'
Life of Sir William Wilson Hunter, K.C.S.I. [etc.], a Vice-President of the Royal Asiatic Society, etc. / by Francis Henry Skrine. London: Longmans, Green, 1901.

HURNARD, James, 1808-81, brewer; poet; Quaker
James Hurnard: a memoir, chiefly autobiographical. With selections from his poems. Edited by his widow [Louisa B. Hurnard]. London: Samuel Harris, 1883. photo.port. (NLS)

HUSSEY, James McConnell, 1819-91, Canon of Rochester
Memorials of the Rev. Canon Hussey, D.D., Vicar of Christ Church, North Brixton [etc.]. Edited by Walter Horne. London: W. Wayre, 1891. photo.port.

HUTCHINSON, John, 1793-1865, Precentor of Lichfield Cathedral
In memoriam: John Hutchinson, M.A., Trinity College, Cambridge. [By E.J.E.]. [Newcastle, c.1865].

HUTTON, Richard Holt, 1826-97, editor of the 'Spectator' and other journals
Richard Holt Hutton of 'The Spectator': a monograph / by John Hogben. Edinburgh: Oliver & Boyd, 1899.

HUTTON, Peter, 1811-80, Benedictine; classicist
Brief memoir of Father Hutton / by J. Hirst. Market Weighton: St William's Press, 1886.

HUXLEY, Thomas Henry, 1825-95, leading evolutionist & biologist
Life and letters of Thomas Henry Huxley / by his son Leonard Huxley. London: Macmillan, 1900. 2 vols; 2nd edition. 1903. 3 volumes.
-------. Thomas Henry Huxley: a sketch of his life and work / by Peter Chalmers Mitchell. London: G. P. Putnam, 1901. (Leaders in Science series & Methuen Shilling Library)

IDDESLEIGH, Sir Stafford Henry Northcote, 1st Earl of, 1818-87, Conservative statesman
Life, letters and diaries of Sir Stafford Northcote, first Earl of Iddesleigh / by Andrew Lang. Edinburgh: W. Blackwood, 1890. 2 volumes; in one volume 1891.
-------. The life of the late Right Hon. the Earl of Iddesleigh, G.C.B., Secretary of State for the Foreign Department, Lord Lieutenant of the County of Devon ... / by Charles Worthy. Exeter: H. S. Eland, 1887. Pamphlet. (NLS)

INGLIS, Andrew, 1824-92, Free Church Minister
Beloved for their work's sake: memorials of the Rev. Andrew Inglis and of Mrs [Christina A.] Inglis / by their son [William B. Inglis] ... Dundee: William Kidd, 1893.

INGLIS, John, Hon. Lord Glencorse, 1810-91, Lord Justice-General of Scotland
John Inglis, Lord Justice-General of Scotland: a memoir / by James Crabb Watt. Edinburgh: William Green, 1893. (B&J)

INGRAM, William Clavell, 1834-1901, Dean of Peterborough
A memoir of William Clavell Ingram, D.D., Dean of Peterborough. [Edited by J. H. H. and others] ... Leicester: printed by W. H. Lead, 1903. (B&J)

INNES, Cosmo Nelson, 1798-1874, advocate; historian
Memoir of Cosmo Innes. [By his daughter Mrs John Hill Burton]. Edinburgh: William Patterson, 1874. 4to.

INWARDS, Jabez, 1813-80, phrenologist; Baptist lay preacher; temperance worker
Life and labours of Jabez Inwards ... London: Horsell & Caudwell, [1860]. 12mo. (BL)

IRONS, Joseph, 1785-1852, Independent Minister in London 1818-52
A memoir of the Rev. Joseph Irons, for thirty-three years the faithful and affectionate Pastor of the Independent Church assembling at Grove Chapel, Camberwell, Surrey ... / by Gabriel Bayfield. London: printed by W. H. Collingridge, 1852.

IRVINE, William Stewart, d.1893, doctor
Recollections of William Stewart Irvine, M.D., F.R.C.S.E. / by E. Molyneux. Edinburgh: D. Douglas, 1896. (Reprinted with additions from 'Life and Work'). (NLS)

JACK, Andrew, n.d., religious biography
Healthy religion exemplified in the life of the late Mr Andrew Jack / by Peter Lorimer. Edinburgh, 1852. (BL)

JACK, Archibald, 1788-1870, Congregational Minister in England
A good and faithful servant: memoir of the late Rev. Archibald Jack, of North Shield / by Peter Lorimer. Edinburgh: Thomas C. Jack, 1871. photo. port. (NLS)

JACOB, John, 1812-58, Brigadier-General in India; military writer
General John Jacob, Commandant of Sinde Irregular Horse, and founder of Jacob-abad / by Alexander Innes Shand. London: Seeley, 1900.

JACQUE, George, 1804-92, Minister in the Relief Presbytery; author
Memoir of the Rev. George Jacque, author of 'The Clouds' [etc.] / by William Blair. Auchterarder: Tovani, 1892. 16mo. (NLS)

JAMES, Henry, b.1799, Royal Navy officer
Life of Commander Henry James, R.N.. [Edited from his diaries and letters by E. G. Festing]. London: Spottiswoode, 1899. (BL)

JAMES, John Angell, 1785-1859, Congregational leader
The faithful servant: his life and its lessons. A tribute to the memory of John Angell James / by William Landels. London: J. Nisbet, 1859. (NLS)
-------. John Angell James: a review of his history, character, eloquence and literary labours ... / by John Campbell. London: John Snow, 1860. (NLS)
-------. The life and letters of John Angell James; including an unfinished autobiography. Edited by Robert William Dale. London: J. Nisbet, 1861. photo. port. (NLS)
-------. A tribute of grateful love to the memory of the late Rev. John Angell James. With an estimate of his character and influence / by William Guest. Leeds: W. Slade, 1859. (NLS)
-------. True greatness: a brief memoir of John Angell James, of Birmingham / by George Redford. London, 1860. 16mo. (Reprinted from the 'Evangelical Magazine' with additions) (NLS)

JAMESON, Robert, 1774-1854, mineralogist
Biographical memoir of the late Professor Jameson, Regius Professor of Natural History & Lecturer in Mineralogy and Keeper of the Museum of the University of Edinburgh, &c. / by Laurence Jameson. Edinburgh: printed by Neill, 1864. Pamphlet. (NLS)

JARVIE, Alexander Milne, 1826-86, United Presbyterian Minister
Memorials of a ministry in Dunfermline and Sydney: biographical sketch of the Rev. Alexander Milne Jarvie ... Edinburgh: Andrew Elliot, 1888. (NLS)

JARVIE, John Milne, 1821-99, Scottish Congregational Minister
The life of Rev. J. M. Jarvie, of Greenock / by Alexander Roy Henderson. Edinburgh: Oliver & Boyd, 1901. (NLS)

JEBB, John Beveridge Gladwyn, 1841-93, adventurer, especially in South America
A strange career: life and adventures of John Gladwyn Jebb / by his widow [Bertha Jebb] ... Edinburgh: W. Blackwood, 1894.

JEFFCOCK, Parkin, 1829-66, mining engineer
Parkin Jeffcock, civil and mining engineer: a memoir / by [his brother] John Thomas Jeffcock. Derby: Bemrose, 1867. (NLS)

JEFFERIES, Richard, 1848-87, naturalist and novelist
The eulogy of Richard Jefferies / by Walter Besant. London: Chatto & Windus, 1888. (NLS)
-------. Richard Jefferies: a study / by Henry Stephen Salt. London: Swan Sonnenschein, 1894. (NLS)

JEFFREYS, Julius, 1801-77, surgeon in India; medical writer; inventor of the respirator
A confutative biographical notice of Julius Jeffreys / by Edmund Jeffreys. London, 1855. (BL)

JENKIN, Henry Charles Fleeming, 1833-85, electrical engineer
Memoir of Fleeming Jenkin / by Robert Louis Stevenson. [New edition]. London: Longmans, Green, 1912. (Originally published in his 'Papers, literary, scientific, etc.,' of 1887).

JENKINS, John Horner, d.1887, clergyman
Memorials of the Rev. J. Horner Jenkins, B.A., first Vicar of Hazlewood ... Edited by William Bland. London: Bemrose, [1889].

JENKINS, Stephen, 1815-92, Welsh local preacher and humourist
Humour sanctified: the memoir of Stephen Jenkins, the quaint preacher of Pembrokeshire / by J. R. Hughes, *Abercynon*. Tonypandy: printed for the author by R. Davies, Maddock, 1902. (B&J)

JERRAM, Charles, 1770-1853, evangelical clergyman
The memoirs and a selection from the letters of the late Rev. Charles Jerram, M.A., late Rector of Witney, Oxfordshire. Edited by James Jerram. London: Wertheim & Macintosh, 1855. (NLS)

JERROLD, Douglas (William), 1803-57, comic writer and dramatist
Douglas Jerrold, dramatist and wit / by Walter Copeland Jerrold. London: Hodder & Stoughton, 1914. 2 volumes.
-------. The life and remains of Douglas Jerrold / by his son Blanchard Jerrold. London: W. Kent, 1859.

JERVIS, Thomas Best, 1796-1857, soldier in India
Thomas Best Jervis, Lieutenant-Colonel H.E.I.C.'s Bombay Engineers [etc.], as Christian, soldier, geographer and friend of India, 1796-1857: a centenary tribute / by his son William Paget Jervis. London: Elliot Stock, 1898.

JERVOIS, Sir William Francis Drummond, 1821-97, Lieutenant-General & Governor of South Australia & New Zealand
Lieut-General Sir William F. D. Jervois, G.C.M.G., C.B., F.R.S.. [1898]. (Reprinted from 'The Royal Engineers' Journal')

JESSEL, Sir George, 1824-83, barrister; legal reformer; M.P.; Master of the Rolls
Sir George Jessel: a lecture delivered at the Jewish Working Mens' Club, Whitechapel,

on March 2nd 1884 / by William Willis. London: E. Marlborough, 1893. Pamphlet. (NLS)

JEWITT, Llewellynn Frederick William, 1816-86, illustrator specialising in Gothick architecture
The life and death of Llewellynn Jewitt, F.S.A., etc.. With fragmentary memoirs of some of his famous literary and artistic friends, especially Samuel Carter Hall ... / by William Henry Goss. London: Henry Gray, 1889. (NLS)

JOBSON, Frederick James, 1812-81, Wesleyan Minister
The life of Frederick James Jobson, D.D. / by Benjamin Gregory. With the funeral memorials of [i.e. by] [G.] Osborn and [W.B.] Pope ... Edited by his widow Elizabeth Jobson. London: T. Woolmer, 1884. (NLS)

JOHNSON, William, 1842-95, martyred missionaries in Madagascar
Faithful unto death: a story of the missionary life in Madagascar of William and Lucy S. Johnson. Edited by Phebe Doncaster. London: Headley, 1896. (NLS)

JOHNSTON, Alexander Keith, the elder, 1804-71, Geographer to the Queen for Scotland
In memoriam of the late A. Keith Johnston, LL.D., Geographer to the Queen for Scotland [etc.]. [Edited by his brother T. B. Johnson]. Edinburgh, 1873. 4to.

JOHNSTON, Robert, 1807-53, Scottish Free Church missionary in India
True yoke-fellows in the mission field: the life and labours of the Rev. John Anderson and the Rev. Robert Johnston, traced in the rise and development of the Madras Free Church Mission / by John Braidwood. London: J. Nisbet, 1862. photographic portraits & illustrations.

JOHNSTON, William, 1818-93, Irish Presbyterian Minister
Life and labours of the Rev. William Johnston, D.D., Belfast / by Samuel Prenter. Belfast: Sabbath-School Society of the Presbyterian Church, 1893. (NLS)

JOLLY, James, 1845-86, Free Church Minister
James Jolly, Minister of Chalmers' Territorial Church, Edinburgh: memorials of an earnest life and faithful ministry / by Hector Maiben Adams. Edinburgh: Macniven & Wallace, 1888. photo.port. (NC)

JONES, David, 1808-54, Welsh Baptist Minister & editor
Life and times of the Rev. David Jones, Baptist Minister, Tabernacle, Cardiff ... / by R. Evans. Llanelly: printed at the 'South Wales Press' Office, 1885. (B&J)

JONES, Ebenezer, 1820-60, poet
Ebenezer Jones, the neglected poet, 1820-1860 / by Thomas Mardy Rees. London, 1909. (BL)

JONES, Ernest Charles, 1819-69, Chartist; poet
Life and labours of Ernest Jones, Esq., poet, politician and patriot. By the author of 'The life of Lord Palmerston'. London: F. Farrah, 1869. Pamphlet. (B&J)
-------. The life of Ernest Jones / by Frederick Leary. London: Democrat Publishing Office, 1887. (BL)
Other titles are to found in Manchester Central Library.

JONES, James, n.d., Baptist Minister
A brief memoir of James Jones, 45 years Pastor of the Strict Baptist Church, Shovers Green, Wadhurst, Sussex ... Wadhurst: Miss Betts, [1889?]. (B&J)

JONES, James Rhys, 'Kilsby', 1813-89, Welsh Congregationalist Minister
The life and sayings of the late Kilsby Jones, Congregational Minister, Llandridod / by Vyrnwy Morgan. London: Elliot Stock, 1896.

JONES, Robert, d.1875, religious private solider

The life of a Christian soldier in a barrack room: Private Robert Jones, H.M.'s 65th Regiment / by J. Gelson Gregson. Portsmouth: The Soldiers' Institute, [1894]. (NLS)

JONES, Thomas Wharton, 1808-91, opthalmologist

In memoriam: Thomas Wharton Jones, F.R.S. [By John Tweedy]. [1891]. (Reprinted from 'The Lancet') (B&J)

JORDAN, Joseph, 1787-1873, Manchester surgeon

Life of Joseph Jordan, surgeon ... With some particulars of the life of Dr Edward Stephens / by Frederick William Jordan. Manchester: Sherratt & Hughes, 1904.

JOULE, James Prescott, 1818-89, physicist

Memoir of James Prescott Joule / by Osborne Reynolds. Manchester: Literary & Philosophical Society, 1892 [being a whole issue of 'The Manchester Literary & Philosophical Society Transactions'. Fourth Series. Volume 6)

JOWETT, Benjamin, 1817-93, classicist; Master of Balliol College, Oxford

Benjamin Jowett, Master of Balliol / by Lionel Arthur Tollemache. London: E. Arnold, [1895].
-------. The life and letters of Benjamin Jowett, M.A., Master of Balliol College, Oxford / by Evelyn Abbott & Lewis Campbell. London: John Murray, 1879. 2 volumes.

JOWITT, John, 1811-88, Leeds woollen manufacturer; Quaker

Reminiscences of John Jowitt / by his children [R. B. Jowitt and others]. Printed for private circulation. Gloucester: John Bellows, [1889?] . 4to. photo. port.

JOWITT, John Henry, 1832-82, clergyman

In memoriam: the victory of faith, being some memorials of the late Rev. John Henry Jowitt, M.A., Vicar of Alford with Rigsby ... Alford: printed by Brittan Wakelin, 1882. photo.port. (NLS)

JUKES, Richard, n.d., Primitive Methodist Minister; poet

The poet of the million, or memorials of the life and labours of the late Rev. Richard Jukes of West Bromwich, forty-two years a Primitive Methodist and forty-one a preacher/ by J. Pritchard. London: Wesleyan Conference Office, 1867. 12mo. (B&J)

KAVANAGH, Arthur MacMurrough, 1831-89, Irish M.P. and sportsman without arms or legs

The Right Hon. Arthur MacMurrough Kavanagh: a biography, from papers chiefly unpublished / compiled by his cousin Sarah Louisa Steele. London: Macmillan, 1891.

KEAN, Charles (John), 1811-68, actor-manager

The life and theatrical times of Charles Kean, F.S.A., including a summary of the English stage for the last fifty years ... / by John William Cole. London: R. Bentley, 1859. 2 volumes; in one volume. 1860.

KEBLE, John, 1792-1866, Tractarian leader; author of the 'Christian Year' (109 editions)

The birth-place, churches and other places connected with the author of 'The Christian Year'. With notes by John Frewen Moor. Illustrated with 32 photographs by William Savage. Winchester: William Savage, 1866. 4to.
-------. John Keble / by Edward Frederick Lindley Wood. London: A. R. Mowbray, 1909. (Leaders of the Church 1800-1900 series)
-------. John Keble: a biography / by Walter Lock. London: Methuen, 1893. (English Leaders of Religion series)

-------. John Keble: an essay on the author of 'The Christian Year'/ by John Campbell Shairp. Edinburgh: Edmonston & Douglas, 1866. 12mo.

-------. Kebleland: Keble's home of Hursley, incidents in his life, extracts from his poetical works, [etc.]. Edited by William Thorn Warren. Winchester: Warren, 1900.

-------. A memoir of the Rev. John Keble, late Vicar of Hursley, M.A. / by John Taylor Coleridge. 2nd corrected edition. Oxford: James Parker, 1869. 2 volumes; and later editions.

KEEBLE, George, 1826-98, Minister
Life, letters and last days of George Keeble, Minister of the Gospel ... London: F. Kirby, 1899.

KEENE, Charles Samuel, 1823-91, humourous artist, especially for 'Punch' 1851-90
The life and letters of Charles Samuel Keene / by George Somes Layard. London: Sampson Low [etc.], 1892.

KEIGHLEY, George, 1831-1901, Mayor of Burnley
Alderman George Keighley, being a short account of a strenuous life / by John Allen. Burnley: 'Express' Printing Works, [1905]. Pamphlet. (B&J)

KEITH-FALCONER, Hon. Ion Grant Neville, 1856-87, academic Arabist; cyclist; Free Church missionary
Memorials of the Hon. Ion Keith-Falconer, M.A., late Lord Almoner's Professor of Arabic in the University of Cambridge, and missionary to the Mohammedans of Southern Arabia / by Robert Sinker. Cambridge: Deighton Bell, 1888; new edition. With subsequent history of the Mission, 1903. photo.port.

KELL, Edmund, 1779-1874, Unitarian Minister and schoolmaster
Memorials of the Rev. Edward Kell ... and Mrs [Elizabeth] Kell, of Southampton / by J. D. [i.e. Joanna Dunkin]. London: Williams & Norgate, 1875. (BL)

KELLY, John, 1801-76, Congregational Minister in Liverpool
The Rev. John Kelly: a memorial. [By Edward Hassan]. Liverpool: Philip, Son & Nephew, [1876]. (NLS)

KELLY, Thomas, 1772-1855, publisher; Alderman and Lord Mayor of London
The life of Alderman Kelly, Lord Mayor of London, 1836-7. With extracts from his correspondence / by Richard Crampton Fell. 3rd edition. London: Partridge, 1858. 12mo. (B&J) Possibly a version of: 'Passages from the private and official life of the late Alderman Kelly. With extracts from his correspondence' / by Richard Crampton Fell. London: Groombridge, 1856. (NLS)

KENDALL, Henry, n.d., Primitive Methodist Minister
Short sketch of the life of Rev. Henry Kendall / by his daughter Ada Dixon. London: F. H. Hurd, 1901.

KENEALY, Edward Vaughan Hyde, 1819-80, barrister; defended the Tichborne Claimant and other unsavoury characters
The life and forensic career of Edward Vaugham Kenealy ... With selections from his speeches delivered during celebrated trials... / by Henry Galloway Gill. London: W. H. Ell[?], [1874]. Pamphlet. (NUC)

--------. Memoirs of Edward Vaughan Kenealy, LL.D. / by his daughter Arabella Kenealy. London: John Long, 1908.

KENNEDY, David, 1825-86, Scots tenor singer
David Kennedy, the Scottish singer: reminiscences of his life and work / by Marjorie Kennedy. [With] Singing round the world: a narrative of his Colonial and Indian tours / by David Kennedy, Jun.. Paisley: Alex. Gardner, 1887.

KENNEDY, James, 1815-90, Congregational Minister, Aberfeldy; missionary in India
Memoir of the Rev. James Kennedy, of Aberfeldy and Inverness / by his son John Kennedy, *D.D., Stepney*. London: Daldy, Isbister, 1873. 12mo. (NLS)

KENNEDY, John, 1819-84, Free Church Minister & leader in the Highlands; 'The Second Apostle of the North'
In memoriam: Rev. John Kennedy, D.D., Dingwall. [Inverness, 1884]. photo. port. (NC)
-------. Life of John Kennedy, D.D. / by Alexander Auld. London: T. Nelson, 1887. (NC)

KENT, John, n.d., Norfolk agricultural labourer
True to principal: the story of John Kent, an agricultural labourer in the County of Norfolk / by D. Newton. 3rd edition. London: J. Dickmouth, [187-]. 12mo. (B&J)

KENTISH, John, 1768-1853, Birmingham Independent Minister
Memoir of the Rev. John Kentish / by John Kenrick. Birmingham: William Grew, 1854. (NC)

KERR, Henry Schomberg, 1838-95, aristocrat; in Royal Navy, then a Jesuit priest
Henry Schomberg Kerr, sailor and Jesuit / by Mary Monica Constable Maxwell-Scott. London: Longmans, Green, 1901.

KERSHAW, James, n.d., Macclesfield worthy
James Kershaw: a sketch / by Robert Brown. For private circulation only. Macclesfield: Claye, Brown & Claye, 1899. (B&J)

KEY, Sir Astley Cooper, 1821-88, Admiral
Memoirs of Admiral the Right Hon. Sir Astley Cooper Key, G.C.B., D.C.L. F.R.S., &c. / by Philip Howard Colomb. London: Methuen, 1898.

KEY, Bransby Lewis, 1838-1901, Anglican Bishop of St John's, Kaffraria
The shepherd of the Veld: Bransby Lewis Key, Bishop of St John's, Kaffraria / by Godfrey Callaway. London: Wells Gardner, Darton, 1912. (BL)

KEY, Robert, n.d., East Anglian Methodist
The Norfolk Herald of the Cross and Apostle of East Anglia; or memorials of the late Rev. Robert Key, author of 'The Gospel among the masses' / by T. Lowe. London: R. Fenwick, [1881?]. photo.port.

KEYSELL, Thomas Owen, 1814-62, Methodist Minister in Lancashire
The earnest life: memorials of the Rev. Thomas Owen Keysell. With extracts from his correspondence / by Thomas M'Cullagh. London: Hamilton, Adams, 1864. (NLS)

KEYWORTH, James, 1798-1864, Sheffield religious biography
A witness for Jesus: some recollections of the Testimony borne by James Keyworth to the gracious love of Him who said 'Fear not ...' / by G. William Skyring. London: Morgan & Chase, [1865]. 12mo. (NLS)

KIDD, Henry Erskine, 1838-55, religious sailor
Peace in death: a short account of Henry Erskine Kidd, eldest son of the late Rev. G. Balderston Kidd ... London: John Snow, 1858. 16mo. Pamphlet. (NLS)

KILPIN, Samuel Wells, n.d., Minister in Reading
A memory of the Rev. Samuel Wells Kilpin, late Pastor of Trinity Chapel, Reading / by his widow. For private circulation. Reading: printed by T. Barham, [189-?] 16mo. (B&J)

KIMBER, Charles Dixon, 1863-1901, religious soldier in Boer War
'Promoted': the memorials of Charles Dixon Kimber, Lieut., 48th Imperial Yeomanry / by his sister Ada Thomson. London: J. Nisbet, 1902. (BL)

KING, David, n.d., religious controversialist
Memoir of David King. [By J. Collin] ... / compiled by his wife Louisa king. Birmingham: printed by W.E. Harris, [1898]. *Could be the same as below?*

KING, David, 1806-83, Secession, then United Presbyterian Minister
Memoir of the Rev. David King. LL.D. / by his wife [Elizabeth King] and daughter [Elizabeth Thomson King] ... Glasgow: James Maclehose, 1885. (NLS)

KINGLAKE, Alexander William, 1809-91, traveller; writer
A. W. Kinglake: a biographical and literary study / by William Tuckwell. London: G. Bell, 1902.

KINGSLEY, Charles, 1819-75, clergyman; reformer; author
Charles Kingsley: his letters and memories of his life / by his wife [Frances Eliza Kingsley]. London: Kegan Paul, Trench, 1877. 2 volumes; in one volume 1888.

KINNAIRD, George Wiliam Fox, <u>10th Baron</u>, 1807-78, Perthshire reforming landowner
In memoriam: Lord Kinnaird. [Dundee], 1878. 12mo. (Reprinted from the 'Dundee Advertiser') (NLS)

KIRK, John, 1813-86, Evangelical Minister; editor of 'The Christian News'
Memoirs of the Rev. John Kirk, D.D., Professor of Pastoral Theology in the Evangelical Union Theological Hall. [By Helen Kirk]. Edinburgh: John B. Fairgrieve, 1888. (NC)

KIRKHAM, Gawin, 1830-92, open-air evangelist; Secretary of Ragged School Union
Gawin Kirkham, the open-air evangelist: a record and a tribute / by Frank Cockrem. London: Morgan & Scott, [1894]

KIRKWOOD, Alexander, 1777-1853, Baptist Minister
Memoir of the Rev. Alexander Kirkwood, of Berwick-upon-Tweed. By one of his family. With a sketch of his character / by John Cairns. London: J. Heaton, 1856.

KIRTON, John William, 1831-92, temperance worker
Life of John William Kirton, LL.D., author of 'Buy your own cherries' [etc.] / by James Joseph Ellis. 2nd edition. London: Houlston, 1895.

KITTO, John, 1804-54, printer; author; traveller
Dr Kitto, his life and labours: a lecture delivered before ... the Warwick Athanaeum, January 14 1858 / by George Lacy. Warwick: G. Lacy, [1858]. Pamphlet. (NLS)
-------. Life of John Kitto, D.D., F.S.A. / by John Eadie. Edinburgh: William Oliphant, 1857. (NLS)
-------. Memoirs of Dr John Kitto, D.D., F.S.A. ... / compiled chiefly from his letters and journals / by Jonathan Edwards Ryland ... Edinburgh: William Oliphant, 1856. (NLS)

KNIGHT, Charles, 1791-1873, author and publisher for the masses
Charles Knight: a sketch / by his granddaughter Alice Ada Clowes. London: R. Bentley, 1892.

KNILL, Richard, 1787-1857, Independent missionary in India & St Petersburg
The life of the Rev. Richard Knill of St Petersburg; being selections from his reminiscences, journals and correspondence / by Charles Morton Birrell ... 3rd edition. London: J. Nisbet, 1860; Special Edition. Religious Tract Society, [1878].

KNOWLES, James Sheridan, 1784-1862, actor, playwright
The life of James Sheridan Knowles / by Richard Brinsley Knowles. Revised and edited by F. Harvey. Privately printed. London, 1872. (BL - 25 copies)

KNOWLES, Mark, b. c.1833, barrister of humble origins

From the loom to the lawyer's gown, or self help that was not all for self, being incidents in the life of Mr Mark Knowles, barrister-at-law. [By Harriet Carson]. London: S.W. Partridge, [1884].

KNOX, Robert, 1791-1862, anatomist in Edinburgh; bought bodies from Burke & Hare
A sketch of the life and writings of Robert Knox, the anatomist / by Henry Lonsdale. London: Macmillan, 1870.

KRAUSE, William Henry, 1796-1852, soldier; 'moral agent' on the estate of Earl of Farnham; Church of Ireland evangelical clergyman
Memoir of the late Rev. W. H. Krause, A.M., Minister of Bethesda Chapel, Dublin. With selections from his correspondence. Edited by Charles Stuart Stanford. Dublin: George Herbert, 1854. (NLS)

LAING, Alexander, 1787-1857, 'The Brechin Poet'
The poetry of Scottish rural life, or a sketch of the life and writings of Alexander Laing, author of 'Wayside Flowers'. [By J. Longmuir]. Brechin: printed by D. H. Edwards, 1874. (NC)

LAING, David, 1793-1878, Signet Librarian; antiquary
David Laing, LL.D.: a memoir of his life and literary work / by Gilbert Goudie ... Printed for private circulation. Edinburgh: T. & A. Constable, 1913. (250 copies printed) (NC)
-------. Notices of David Laing, LL.D. [etc.], Librarian to the Society of Writers to H. M. Signet in Scotland ... / drawn up by Thomas George Stevenson. Printed for private circulation. Edinburgh, 1878. 4to. photo. port. (100 copies printed)

LAING, James, 1803-72, Free Church missionary in South Africa
Memorials of the missionary career of the Rev. James Laing, missionary of the Free Church of Scotland in Kaffraria ... / by William Govan. Glasgow: D. Bryce, 1875. photo.port. (NC)

LAKE, Edward, 1823-97, Major-General in Royal Engineers
In memoriam: Edward Lake, Major-General Royal Engineers, C.S.I.. [2 reprinted notices, by John Barton & R. Maclagan]. 2nd edition. London: Hatchards, 1878. 12mo. (NC)

LAKE, William Charles, 1817-97, Dean of Durham
Memorials of William Charles Lake, Dean of Durham, 1869-1894. Edited by his widow Katherine Lake ... London: E. Arnold, 1901.

LAMBERT, Charles William, 1856-95, missionary in Upper Burma
The missionary martyr of Thibaw: a brief record of the life and consecrated missionary labours of Charles William Lambert in Upper Burmah. [Edited from his letters and diaries by J. W. Jordan]. London: S. W. Partridge, [1896]. (NLS)

LANDELS, John, 1851-79, Baptist missionary in Genoa
Memorials of a consecrated life: a biographical sketch of John Landels, missionary in Genoa / by William Landels. London: J. Nisbet, 1881. (NUC)

LANDELS, William, 1823-99, Baptist Minister
William Landels, D.D.: a memoir / by his son Thomas Durley Landels ... London: Cassell, 1900. (NC)

LANDOR, Walter Savage, 1775-1864, author of 'Imaginary Conversations'
Walter Savage Landor: a biography / by John Forster. London: Chapman & Hall, 1869.

2 volumes; in one volume 1895.

LANDSEER, Sir Edwin Henry, 1802-73, animal painter
Memoirs of Sir Edwin Landseer: a sketch of the life of the artist ..., being a new [3rd] edition of 'The early works of Sir Edwin Landseer' / by Frederick George Stephens. London: G. Bell, 1874. 4to. With photographic illustrations. (NLS)
-------. Sir Edward Landseer, R.A. ... / by James Alexander Manson. London: Walter Scott Publishing, 1902. (Makers of Modern Art series)

LANE, Edward William, 1801-76, writer on Middle East
Life of Edward William Lane ..., author of 'The modern Egyptians' ... / by Stanley Lane-Poole. London: Williams & Norgate, 1877. (NC)

LANE, John Doudney see **DOUDNEY, David Alfred**

LANGDALE, Henry Bickersteth, 1st Baron, 1783-1851, Master of the Rolls
Memoirs of the Right Hon. Henry [Bickersteth], Lord Langdale/ by Thomas Duffus Hardy. London: R. Bentley, 1852. 2 volumes.

LANGTON, Thomas, b.1836, Yorkshire evangelist
The life story of Thomas Langton, of Malton, the Yorkshire evangelist / by Isaac C. Watson. Rochdale: Thomas Champness, 1895.

LANSDOWNE, Sir Henry Petty-Fitzmaurice, Earl of Shelburne, 3rd Marquis of, 1780-1863, statesman; Chancellor of the Exchequer
Lord Lansdowne: a biographical sketch / by Abraham Hayward. London, 1872. (Reprinted from the 'Saturday Review')

LATTER, Robert James, 1783-1855, General
Memoir of General Latter / by E. C. C. Baillie. London: J. Nisbet, 1870. (BL)

LAURIE, Sir Peter, 1777/8-1861, army contractor; bank governor; Lord Mayor of London 1832-3
Sir Peter Laurie: a family memoir / by Peter George Laurie. Printed for private circulation. Brentwood: Wilson & Whitchurch, 1901. (NLS)

LAW, Augustus Henry, 1833-80, sailor, then Jesuit priest in British Guiana and Africa
Augustus Law, S.J.: notes in remembrance. London: Burns & Oates, 1886. 16mo. (Reprinted from the 'Irish Monthly')
-------. The life of Augustus Henry Law, priest of the Society of Jesus / by Ellis Schreiber. London: Burns & Oates, 1893.
-------. A memoir of the life and death of the Rev. Father Augustus Henry Law, S.J., formerly, from February 1846 to December 1853, an officer in the Royal Navy. [Edited by William Towry Law]. London: Burns & Oates, 1882-83. 3 volumes.

LAW, Ian Rokeby, 1881-1901, ran a prepatory school in Bury St Edmunds
Ian Rokeby Law: in memoriam / by W.C. & G.C.E. Law. [Privately printed. c.1906]. (B&J)

LAWRENCE, Sir Henry Montgomery, 1806-57, Brigadier-General in India, especially on the North-West Frontier
Life of Sir Henry Lawrence / by Herbert Benjamin Edwardes & Herman Merivale. London: Smith, Elder, 1872. 2 volumes; 3rd edition. 1873.
-------. Sir Henry Lawrence, the pacificator / by James John McLeod Innes. Oxford: Clarendon Press, 1898. (Rulers of India series)

LAWRENCE, John Laird Mair, 1st Baron Lawrence, 1811-79, 'one of the chief men in the preservation of India during the Mutiny'; Governor-General 1863-69.
John Lawrence, 'Saviour of India': the story of his life / by Charles Bruce. Edinburgh:

W. P. Nimmo, Hay Mitchell, 1889.

-------. Life of Lord Lawrence / by Reginald Bosworth Smith. London: Smith, Elder, 1883. 2 volumes; 7th edition. 1901.

-------. Lord Lawrence / by Charles Aitchison. Oxford: Clarendon Press, 1892. (Rulers of India series)

-------. Lord Lawrence / by Richard Temple. London: Macmillan, 1889. (English Men of Action series)

LAWSON, Cecil Gordon, 1849-82, Scottish landscape painter

Cecil Lawson: a memoir ... / by Edmund William Gosse. London: Fine Art Society, 1883. 4to. (BL)

LAYCOCK, John, 1809-89, organ builder in Yorkshire

A short memoir of John Laycock, organ builder, of West Closes, Glusburn / by T. H. Haswell. Keighley: Borough Printing Works, [1889]. Pamphlet. (Reprinted from the 'Craven Herald'). (B&J)

LEACOCK, Hamble James, 1795-1856, missionary in Africa

The martyr of the Pongas, being a memoir of the Rev. H. J. Leacock ... / by Henry Caswall. London: Rivingtons, 1857. (BL)

LEAKE, William Martin, 1777-1860, soldier; classical topographer; collector

A brief memoir of the life and writings of ... Lieutenant-Colonel William Martin Leake / by John Howard Marsden. Privately printed. London, 1864. 4to.

LECHMERE, Sir Edmund Anthony Harley, 3rd Bart., 1826-94, M.P.; banker

In memoriam: Sir Edmund A. H. Lechmere, Baronet. Privately printed. [1895]. 12mo. (B&J)

LEE, Robert, 1804-68, Church of Scotland Minister; liturgical innovator

Life and remains of Robert Lee, D.D., F.R.S.E., Minister of the Church and Parish of Old Greyfriars [etc.] / by Robert Herbert Story ... London: Hurst and Blackett, 1870. 2 volumes.

LEE, Samuel, 1783-1852, Professor of Arabic, then of Hebrew, Cambridge University; 'a profound linguist'

A scholar of a past generation: a brief memoir of Samuel Lee, D.D., Professor of Arabic, and afterwards Professor of Hebrew in the University of Cambridge ... / by his daughter [Alice M. Lee]. London: Seeley, 1896.

LEECH, John, 1817-64, chief comic artist on 'Punch' 1842-64

John Leech, artist and humourist: a biographical sketch / by Frederick George Kitton. London: George Redway, 1883; revised edition. 1894. 12mo. Pamphlet.

-------. John Leech: his life and work / by William Powell Frith. London: R. Bentley, 1891. 2 volumes.

LEES, Frederic Richard, 1815-97, 'the ablest temperance and prohibitionist advocate of the late 19th Century'

Dr Frederic Lees, F.S.A. (Edin.): a biography ... / by Frederic Lees ... London: H. J. Osborn, 1904. (B&J)

LEFROY, Edward Cracroft, 1855-91, clergyman; poet

Edward Cracroft Lefroy, his life and poems ... / by Wilfrid Austin Gill. London: John Lane The Bodley Head, 1897.

LEFROY, Thomas Langlois, 1776-1869, Irish judge; M.P.

Memoirs of Chief Justice Lefroy / by his son Thomas Lefroy. Dublin: Hodges, Foster, 1871.

LEGG, William, 1800-71, Independent Minister in Reading

Memoirs of the Rev. William Legg, B.A., thirty-eight years Pastor of Broad Street Chapel, Reading / by George Colborne. Reading: Barcham & Beecroft, 1871. photo.port. (NLS)

LEGGE, James, 1815-97, missionary in Far East, then Professor of Chinese at Oxford University

James Legge, missionary and scholar ... / by Helen Edith Legge. London: Religious Tract Society, 1905.

LEIFCHILD, John, 1780-1862, Independent Minister

John Leifchild, D.D., his public ministry, private usefulness, and personal characteristics. Founded upon an autobiography / by John R. Leifchild. London: Jackson, Walford & Hodder, 1863. (NC)

LEIGH, Samuel, 1785-1852, the first Methodist missionary in Australia (1816); later in New Zealand

The life of the Rev. Samuel Leigh, missionary to the settlers and savages of Australia and New Zealand ... / by Alexander Strachan. New edition. London: Hamilton, Adams, 1863; another edition. London: Wesleyan Mission House, 1870. (NLS)

-------. Remarkable incidents in the life of the Rev. Samuel Leigh, missionary to the settlers and savages of Australia and New Zealand ... / by Alexander Strachan. London: Hamilton, Adams, 1853. (NLS)

-------. What he did for convicts and cannibals: some account of the life and work of the Rev. Samuel Leigh, the first Wesleyan missionary to New South Wales and New Zealand / by Anne E. Keeling. London: Charles H. Kelly, 1896.

LEIGHTON, Frederick, <u>1st Baron Leighton</u>, 1830-96, painter; President of the Royal Academy

Frederick Lord Leighton, late President of the Royal Academy of Arts: an illustrated record of his life and works / by Ernest Rhys. London: G. Bell, 1900.

-------. The life, letters and work of Frederick Leighton / by Emilie Isabel Barrington. London: G. Allen, 1906. 4to. 2 volumes.

LEITCH, William Leighton, 1804-83, 'last of the great English teachers of landscape painting'

W. L. Leitch, landscape painter: a memoir / by Andrew MacGeorge. London: Blackie, 1884. 4to.

LEMAN, George, 1809-80, York solicitor and M.P.

Death, biography and funeral of Mr George Leman, late M.P. for the City of York. York: 'Daily Herald' Office, 1882. Pamphlet. (B&J)

LEMON, Mark, 1809-70, first editor of 'Punch'

With a show in the North: reminiscences of Mark Lemon / by Joseph Hatton. London: W. H. Allen, 1871.

LEOPOLD (GEORGE DUNCAN ALBERT), Prince, <u>Duke of Albany</u>, 1853-84, Queen Victoria's youngest son

Life and speeches of H.R.H. Prince Leopold. [Compiled by J. H. Ware]. London: Diprose & Bateman, 1884. (BL)

LEVER, Charles James, 1806-72, popular Irish novelist

The life of Charles Lever / by William John Fitzpatrick. London: Ward, Lock, 1879. 2 volumes; revised edition. [1884].

LEVINGSTON, Charles, d.1864, clergyman on Isle of Wight

In memoriam: the Rev. Charles Levingston, M.A., Rector of St. Lawrence, Isle of Wight, obiit October 24th 1864. London: J. Nisbet, 1864. photo. port. (B&J)

[LEWIN, William Charles James] see **TERRISS, William**

LEWIS, Samuel Savage, 1836-91, classical lecturer, Cambridge Univeristy Fellow
   Life of the Rev. Samuel Savage Lewis, M.A., F.S.A., Fellow and Librarian of Corpus Christi College, Cambridge / by Agnes Smith Lewis. Cambridge: Macmillan & Bowes, 1892.

LIDDELL, Henry George, 1811-98, Dean of Christ Church, Oxford
   Henry George Liddell, D.D., Dean of Christ Church, Oxford: a memoir / by Henry Lewis Thompson. London: John Murray, 1899. (NC)

LIDDLE, Josiah, 1818-66, Leeds Methodist
   Light and love: memorials of Josiah Liddle of Halifax. Part 1: Biographical sketch. Part 2: Bible-class lessons ... / by James Alexander Macdonald. Leeds: H. W. Walker, 1867. 12mo. photo.port. (NLS)

LIDDON, Henry Parry, 1829-90, Church of England theologian
   Dr Liddon / by George William Erskine Russell. London: A.R. Mowbray, 1905. 12mo. (English Churchman's Library [and] Leaders of the Church, 1800-1900 series)
-------. Life and letters of Henry Parry Liddon, D.D., D.C.L., LL.D., Canon of St Paul's Cathedral, and sometime Ireland Professor of Exegesis in the University of Oxford / by John Octavius Johnston ... London: Longmans, Green, 1904.

LIGHTBOWN, Henry, d.189-., Salford mill owner and local worthy
   Henry Lightbown, J.P.: a memoir and appreciation / by Henry Ernest Radbourne. Manchester: R. S. Chrystal, 1900. photo. port. (B&J)

LIGHTFOOT, Joseph Barber, 1828-89, theologian; Bishop of Durham 1879-89
   Bishop Lightfoot. London: Macmillan, 1894. (Reprinted from the 'Quarterly Review') (NC)

LILFORD, Thomas Littleton Powys, 4th Baron, 1833-96, ornithologist
   Lord Lilford, Thomas Littleton, 4th Baron, F.Z.S., President of the British Ornithological Union: a memoir / by his sister Mrs Dawtrey Drewitt. London: Smith, Elder, 1900.

LINGARD, John, 1771-1851, Roman Catholic priest and important historian
   Life and letters of John Lingard, 1771-1851 / by Martin Haile [*pseud.*] & Edwin Bonney. London: Herbert Daniel, [1911]. (BL)

LINK, Robert, n.d., religious biography
   Goodness and mercy: a memorial of Robert Link, Senior Deacon of Gower Street Chapel, London. Oxford: J. C. Pembrey, 1898.

LINNELL, John, 1792-1882, portrait & landscape painter
   The life of John Linnell / by Alfred Thomas Story. London: R. Bentley, 1892. 2 volumes.

LIVESEY, Joseph, 1794-1884, teetotal leader
   Joseph Livesey, the pioneer of the temperance movement: his life and labours / by William Edward Armytage Axon. Manchester, 1894.
-------. Joseph Livesey, the story of his life (founded principally upon his autobiography) 1794-1884. Edited by James Weston. London: S. W. Partridge, [1884].
-------. Life of the late Joseph Livesey, founder of the temperance movement. Manchester: Abel Heywood, [1885]. Pamphlet. (NLS)

LIVESEY, Thomas, n.d., radical Manchester town councillor

Life and times of the late Alderman T. Livesey / by M. R. Lahee. Manchester: Abel Heywood, [1865]. 12mo; Rochdale, 1874. (B&J)

LIVINGSTONE, David, 1813-73, medical missionary; African explorer

David Livingstone / by T. Banks Maclachlan. Edinburgh: Oliphant, Anderson & Ferrier, [1897]. (Famous Scots series)

-------. David Livingstone / by Thomas Hughes. London: Macmillan, 1889. (English Men of Action series)

-------. The life and explorations of David Livingstone, LL.D., carefully compiled from reliable sources. [By John S. Roberts and others]. London: Adam, [1875]. 4to; and later editions.

-------. The life of David Livingstone, LL.D., the great missionary explorer / by J. S. Robertson. London: Walter Scott, [1882].

-------. 'Nyaka' - the doctor: the story of David Livingstone ... / by William Allan Elliott. London: London Missionary Society, 1908.

-------. The personal life of David Livingstone, LL.D., D.C.L., F.R.S., chiefly from his unpublished journals and correspondence in the possession of his family / by William Garden Blaikie. London: John Murray, 1880; and later editions. (NC)

and other titles

LIVINGSTONE, William, 1819-97, Free Church Minister

In memoriam: the Rev. William Livingstone, South Free Church, Kirriemuir. Edinburgh: Macniven & Wallace, 1898. 12mo. (NC)

LOCKE, Joseph, 1805-60, railway engineer; M.P.

The life of Joseph Locke, civil engineer, M.P., F.R.S. / by Joseph Devey. London: R. Bentley, 1862.

LOCKHART, John Gibson, 1794-1854, biographer; novelist; son-in-law of Scott

The life and letters of John Gibson Lockhart. Edited by Andrew Lang. London: J. C. Nimmo, 1897. 2 volumes. (NLS)

LOCKHART, William Peddie, 1835-93, merchant; temperance worker; cricketer

W. P. Lockhart, merchant and preacher: a life story / compiled by his wife [Mary Jane Lockhart] ... London: Hodder & Stoughton, 1895.

LOCKWOOD, Abraham, b.1792, New Connection Methodist

Little Abe, or the bishop of Berry Brow, being the life of Abraham Lockwood, a quaint and popular Yorkshire local preacher in the Methodist New Connection / by F. Jewell. London: Robert Culley, [1880]. (NLS)

LOCKWOOD, Sir Frank, 1846-97, M.P.; Solicitor-General; noted caricaturist

Sir Frank Lockwood: a biographical sketch / by Augustine Birrell. London: Smith, Elder, 1898.

LONDESBOROUGH, Albert Denison, 1st Baron, 1805-60, M.P.; owned a racing stud .

Obituary notices of the late ..., comprising a brief biographical sketch ... and addresses of condolence ... Printed for private circulation. Tadcaster, 1860. (B&J)

LONG, George, 1800-79, geographer; editor; classicist

In memoriam: George Long / by Henry John Matthews. [Brighton], 1879. (Reprinted from the 'Brighton College Magazine') (BL)

LONSDALE, James Gylby, 1816-92, clergyman; classicist

A memoir of the Rev. James Lonsdale, late Fellow and Tutor of Balliol College, Oxford / by Russell Duckworth ... London: Longmans, Green, 1893.

LONSDALE, John, 1788-1867, Bishop of Lichfield from 1843

The life of John Lonsdale, Bishop of Lichfield. With some of his writings. Edited by his son-in-law Edmund Beckett Denison. London: John Murray, 1868. photo.port.

LOVER, Samuel, 1797-1868, 'painter, etcher, lyric poet, musical-composer, executant, novelist and dramatist'
The life of Samuel Lover, R.A., artistic, literary and musical. With selections from his unpublished papers and correspondence / by Bayle Bernard. London: Henry S. King, 1874. 2 volumes.
-------. Samuel Lover: a biographical sketch. With selections from his writings and correspondence / by Andrew James Symington. Glasgow: Blackie, 1880.

LOW, David, 1768-1855, Scottish Episcopal Bishop
A biographical sketch of the Right Rev. David Low, D.D., LL.D., formerly Bishop of the United Dioceses of Ross, Moray and Argyll ... / by Matthew Forster Conolly. Edinburgh: Robert Grant, 1859. (BL)
-------. A memoir of the Right Rev. David Low, D.D., LL.D., formerly Bishop in the United Diocese of Ross, Moray and Argyle ... / by William Blatch. London: Rivingtons, 1855.

LOWDER, Charles Fuge, 'Father Lowder', 1820-80, ritualist slum priest in London Docks
Charles Lowder: a biography. [By Maria C. Trench]. London: Kegan Paul, Trench, 1881.

LOWE, John, 1835-92, Congregational medical missionary in India
Rev. John Lowe, F.R.C.S.E., Secretary and Superintendent, Edinburgh Medical Missionary Society. Edinburgh: The Society, 1892. Pamphlet.

LOWE, Robert see SHERBROOKE, 1st Viscount

LOWTH, John Jackson, 1804-55, soldier
A short memoir of the life of Colonel John J. Lowth, C.B., of the 38th Regiment, A.D.C. to the Queen. [By G.T.L.]. Winchester: printed by Jacob & Johnson, 1855. 12mo. (B&J)

LUCAS, Frederick, 1812-55, Catholic; founder and editor of the 'Tablet'; M.P.
Frederick Lucas: a biography / by Christopher James Riethmuller. London: Bell & Daldy, 1862.
-------. The life of Frederick Lucas, M.P. / by his brother Edward Lucas. London: Burns & Oates, 1886. 2 volumes.

LUCAS, Jabez, d.1858, consumptive navvy; religious
The Christian navvy's home, or the story of Jabez Lucas, a patient of The Brompton [Consumption] Hospital. London: Wertheim, Macintosh & Hunt, [c.1862]. 12mo. (NLS)

LUCAS, James, 1813-74, 'The Hertfordshire hermit'
An account of Lucas the hermit of Redcoat's Green, near Hitchin, Herts.. Hitchin, 1874. 12mo. (Reprinted from the 'North Herts & South Beds. Journal') (BL)
-------. The history of the hermit of Hertfordshire (J. Lucas). Hitchin, 1874. (Rewritten from the 'Herts Express') (BL)

LUCRAFT, Benjamin, 1809-97, Chartist; temperance advocate; educationalist; trade unionist
Benjamin Lucraft: a biography / by George H. Dyer. London, [1879]. (BL)

LUMSDEN, Sir Harry Burnett, 1821-96, soldier in India; founded the Guides
Lumsden of the Guides: a sketch of the life of Lieut-Gen. Sir H.B. Lumsden, K.C.S.I., C.B.. With selections from his correspondence and occasional papers. London: John Murray, 1899. (BL)

LUMSDEN, James, 1810-75, Principal of Free Church College, Aberdeen

Principal Lumsden: a memorial and estimate / by John Rae. Aberdeen: A. & R. Milne, 1876. 12mo. photo.port.

LUNDIE, Robert Henry, 1824-95, Liverpool Presbyterian Minister

In memoriam: Robert Henry Lundie, M.A., D.D.. London: George Philip, 1895. (B&J)

LYELL, Sir Charles, 1st Bart., 1797-1875, geologist

Life, letters and journals of Sir Charles Lyell, Bart.. Edited by his sister-in-law [Katharine Murray] Lyell. London: John Murray, 1881. 2 volumes.

LYNCH, Thomas Toke, 1818-71, Minister in Manchester; hymn-writer

Memoir of Thomas T. Lynch. Edited by William White. London: Isbister, 1874. photo.port. (B&J)

LYNDHURST, John Singleton Copley, 1st Baron, 1772-1863, Lord Chancellor 1823-30

A brief memoir of Lord Lyndhurst / by William Sidney Gibson. London: Butterworths, 1866. Pamphlet. (NLS)

-------. A life of Lord Lyndhurst, from letters and papers in posession of his family / by Theodore Martin. London: John Murray, 1883.

-------. Lives of Lord Lyndhurst and Lord Brougham, Lords Chancellors and Keepers of the Great Seal of England / by John Campbell. Edited by Mary Scarlett Campbell. London: John Murray, 1869. [But note:] 'Misrepresentations in Campbell's "Lives of Lyndhurst and Brougham"' / corrected by Edward Burtenshaw Sugden, Lord St. Leonards. London: John Murray, 1869.

LYONS, Edmund Lyons, 1st Baron, 1790-1858, Admiral; ambassador; Commander-in-Chief 1855-58

Life of Vice-Admiral Edmund, Lord Lyons ... / by Sydney Marow Eardley-Wilmot. London: Sampson Low, Marston, 1898.

LYONS, Richard Bickerton Pemell, 2nd Baron & 1st Earl Lyons, 1817-87, Ambassador

Lord Lyons: a record of British diplomacy / by Thomas Wodehouse Legh, Baron Newton. London: E. Arnold, 1913. 2 volumes.

LYTTON, Edward (George Earle Lytton) Bulwer-Lytton, 1st Baron, 1803-73, M.P., novelist

Edward Bulwer, first Baron Lytton of Knebworth: a social, personal and political monograph / by Thomas Hay Sweet Escott. London: G. Routledge, 1910.

-------. The life, letters and literary remains of Edward Bulwer, Lord Lytton / by his son [Edward Bulwer, 1st Earl Lytton]. London: Kegan Paul, Trench, 1883. 2 volumes.

-------. The life of Edward Bulwer, first Lord Lytton / by his grandson Victor [Edward], 2nd Earl of Lytton. London: Macmillan, 1913. 2 volumes. [But see:] 'Bulwer Lytton: an exposure of the errors of his biographers' / by William Alfred Frost. London: Lynwood, 1913. (BL)

-------. Lord Lytton, the man & the author: a discourse delivered in Westminster Abbey / by Benjamin Jowett. To which is attached a carefully written biography / by Mansfield Marsdon. London: Farrah, 1873. Pamphlet. (NLS)

McALL, Robert Whitaker, 1821-93, founder of the non-sectarian Protestant McAll Mission in Paris

Robert Whitaker McAll, founder of the McAll Mission, Paris: a fragment. By himself. A souvenir / by his wife [Sarah McAll]. London: Religious Tract Society, 1896. (NLS)

MACARA, William, 1812-89, Free Church Minister

In affectionate remembrance of Rev. William Macara, for forty-five years Minister of the Free Church, Strathmiglo, who died 11th March 1889. Manchester: Palmer & Howes, 1889.

M'ARTHUR, Sir William, 1809-87, Irish; London & Australia merchant; Wesleyan; Lord Mayor of London

Sir William M'Arthur, K.C.M.G.: a biography - religious, parliamentary, municipal, commercial / by Thomas M'Cullagh. London: Hodder & Stoughton, 1891.

McAULAY, Alexander, 1818-90, Wesleyan Minister

Rev. Alexander McAulay (President of the Conference, 1876) as I knew him / by William Sampson. London: Charles H. Kelly, 1893.

MACAULAY, Thomas Babington, 1st Baron Macaulay, 1800-59, statesman; historian

The life and letters of Lord Macaulay / by his nephew George Otto Trevelyan. London: Longmans, Green, 1876. 2 volumes; 2nd edition. with additions and corrections. 1877. 2 volumes; in one volume 1881; many later editions.
-------. A memoir of Lord Macaulay. [By Henry Hart Milman]. London: Longman [etc.], 1862. Pamphlet. (Reprinted from 'Papers of the Royal Society') (NLS)
-------. The public life of Lord Macaulay / by Frederick Arnold. London: Tinsley Brothers, 1862. (BL)
and other biographies

M'CABE, Edward, Cardinal, 1816-85, Roman Catholic Archbishop of Dublin

A memoir of His Grace the Most Rev. Edward McCabe, D.D., Lord Archbishop of Dublin and Primate of Ireland. By a Catholic clergyman. 1878; 2nd revised and enlarged edition. Dublin: James Duffy, 1879. (NLS)

MacCARTHY, Charles Fennell, n.d., Superintendent of the Irish Church Missions Dublin

Patient continuance: a sketch of the life and labours of the late Rev. Doctor MacCarthy of Dublin. By a fellow worker. Dublin: George Herbert, 1878. 16mo. photo.port. (B&J)

McCAUL, Alexander, 1799-1863, Church of England missionary to the Jews; Professor of Hebrew

A memorial sketch of the Rev. Alexander McCaul, D.D. ..., Professor of Hebrew and Old Testament Exegesis, King's College London / by his eldest son Joseph Benjamin MacCaul ... To which are appended two funeral sermons preached ... by ... William Edward Jelf and ... Charles Bradley. London: Rivingtons, 1863. 12mo. (NLS)

McCOSH, James, 1811-94, philosopher; Free Church Minister; later President of Princeton

The life of James McCosh: a record chiefly autobiographical. Edited by William Milligan Sloane. Edinburgh: T. & T. Clark, 1896.

McCREE, George Wilson, 1823-92, temperance advocate; Primitive Methodist

George William McCree, his life and work. With extracts from his journals / by his elder son [Charles Wilson McCree]. London: J. Clarke, 1893. (NLS)

MacDERMOTT, Robert, 1832-59, Irish medical lecturer; Greek scholar

Memoir of the late Dr Robert McDermott, M.R.I.A.. 3rd edition. Dublin: W. B. Kelly, 1860. 12mo. (Reprinted from 'The Irish Quarterly Review') (NLS)

MacDEVITT, James, 1831-79, Irish Roman Catholic Bishop

The Most Rev. James MacDevitt, D.D., Bishop of Raphoe: a memoir / by John MacDevitt. Dublin: M.H. Gill, 1880. photo.port.

MACDONALD, Donald, 1825-1901, Highland Presbyterian Minister, formerly in the Free Church

Memoir and remains of the Rev. Donald Macdonald, Shieldaig, Ross-shire / by Donald Macfarlane. Glasgow: John M'Neilage, 1903; new edition. Glasgow: N.D. Adshead, 1957.

MACDONELL, James, 1842-79, editor of 'Northern Daily Express'; leader writer
James Macdonell, journalist / by William Robertson Nicoll. London: Hodder & Stoughton, 1890; new edition. 1900. (NLS)

McDOUGALL, Francis Thomas, 1817-86, surgeon, then Anglican Bishop of Labuan and Sarawak
Memoirs of Francis Thomas McDougall, D.C.L., F.R.C.S., sometime Bishop of Labuan and Sarawak, and of [Harriette] his wife / by Charles John Bunyon. London: Longmans, Green, 1889.

MACFADYEN, John Allison, 1837-89, Scottish Congregational Minister in Manchester
Life of John Allison MacFadyen, M.A., D.D., first Pastor of Chorlton Road Congregational Church, Manchester / by Alexander Mackennal. London: Hodder & Stoughton, 1891. (BL)

M'FARLAN, James, 1845-89, Church of Scotland Minister; poet
James M'Farlan. [A memorial volume. Edited by Helen M'Farlan]. Privately printed. Edinburgh: T. & A. Constable, 1892. (NLS)

MACFARLANE, John, 1807-74, Free Church Minister
In memoriam: Rev. John Macfarlane, late Minister of Free Church, Dalkeith. Edinburgh: A. Elliot, 1875. 12mo.

MACFARLANE, John, 1807-75, United Presbyterian Minister in London
Memoir of John MacFarlane, LL.D. / by William Graham. Edinburgh: William Oliphant, 1876. photo.port.

MACFARREN, Sir George Alexander, 1813-87, composer, conductor
George Alexander MacFarren, his life, works and influence / by Henry Charles Banister. London: G. Bell, 1891.

MACGILL, Hamilton Montgomerie, 1807-80, United Presbyterian Minister
Memories of Dr Hamilton MacGill / by C. H. Macgill. Edinburgh: A. Elliot, 1880.

MACGREGOR, George Hogarth Carnaby, 1864-1900, Scottish evangelist
George H. C. MacGregor, M.A.: a biography / by Duncan Campbell MacGregor. London: Hodder & Stoughton, 1900; popular edition. 1901.

MACGREGOR, James, 1830-1894, Church of Scotland Minister
Life and letters of the Rev. James Macgregor, D.D., Minister of St. Cuthbert's Parish, Edinburgh ... / by Frances Balfour. London: Hodder & Stoughton, 1912.

MACGREGOR, John ('Rob Roy'), 1825-92, barrister; founded Shoeblacks Brigade in London; traveller by canoe
John Macgregor ('Rob Roy') ... / by Edwin Hodder. London: Hodder Brothers, 1894; popular edition. 1895.

MACGREGOR, William Malcolm, 1854-85, Scottish misisonary to China
Only for Jesus: memorials of the late William M. MacGregor, missionary to China / by Lewis Munro ... Dingwall: Lewis Munro, [1888].

MACINNES, Harry, 1863-84, undergraduate at Cambridge killed rock climbing
Joyfully ready: a sketch of the life of Harry MacInnes / by his mother. 2nd edition. London: Seeley, 1886.

MACINTOSH, Charles Calder, 1806-68, Free Church Minister; revivalist

Memorials of the life and ministry of Charles Calder Macintosh, D.D., of Tain and Dunoon ... Edited by William Taylor ... Edinburgh: Edmondston & Douglas, 1870. photo.port.; 2nd edition. 1871.

MACKARNESS, John Fielder, 1820-89, Bishop of Oxford
Memorials of the episcopate of John Fielder Mackarness, D.D., Bishop of Oxford from 1870 to 1888 ... / by Charles Coleridge Mackarness. Oxford: James Parker, 1892.

[MACKAY, A. F.], n.d., Scottish religious soldier
The sword and the seed basket: passages in the life of a non-commissioned officer. [By C. A. Mackenzie, *D.D*]. 3rd edition. Edinburgh: J. Nisbet, 1895.

MACKAY, Alexander Murdoch, 1849-90, engineer then missionary in Uganda
A. M. Mackay, pioneer missionary of the Church Missionary Society to Uganda / by his sister J. W. H[arrison]. London: Hodder & Stoughton, 1890; new edition. 1970. A later edition perhaps as: 'The story of the life of Mackay of Uganda, pioneer missionary' / by his sister J. W. H[arrison]. 11th edition. London: Hodder & Stoughton, 1902.

MACKAY, John, 1825-57, Baptist missionary martyred in Indian Mutiny
The missionary martyr of Delhi: a memoir of the Rev. John Mackay, Baptist missionary, who was killed at Delhi, May 1857 / by John Culross. London: J. Heaton, 1860.

MACKAY, William Murray, 1828-98, Free Church Minister
In memoriam: Rev. W. Murray Mackay, Minister of Young Street Free Church, Glasgow. Printed for private circulation. Glasgow: J. Maclehose, 1899. (NC)

McKECHNIE, Colin Campbell, 1821-96, Yorkshire Primitive Methodist Minister
Life of Rev. Colin C. McKechnie / by John Atkinson. London: Thomas Mitchell, 1898.

MacKENZIE, Charles see COMPTON, Henry

MACKENZIE, Charles Frederick, 1825-62, Anglican missionary bishop in East Africa
Memoir of Bishop Mackenzie / by Harvey Goodwin. Cambridge: Deighton Bell [etc.], 1864. see also **MACKENZIE, Anne**

MACKENZIE, Francis Lewis, 1833-55, Scot dying while at Cambridge University
Early death not premature, being a memoir of Francis L. Mackenzie, late of Trinity College, Cambridge / by Charles Popham Miles. With notice of Henry Mackenzie, B.A., scholar of Trinity College, Cambridge. London: J. Nisbet, 1856.

MACKENZIE, Henry, d.1853 aged 25 see **MACKENZIE, Francis Lewis**

MACKENZIE, John, 1835-99, Scot with London Missionary Society in South Africa
John Mackenzie, South African missionary and statesman / by William Douglas Mackenzie. London: Hodder & Stoughton, 1902. (NLS)

MACKENZIE, John Kenneth, 1850-88, medical missionary in China
John Kenneth Mackenzie, medical missionary to China / by [Mary Isabella] Bryson. London: Hodder & Stoughton, 1891.

MACKENZIE, Sir Morell, 1837-92, throat specialist held responsible for the death of Kaiser Frederick 111
Sir Morell Mackenzie, physician and operator: a memoir. Compiled and edited from private papers and personal reminiscences by Hugh Reginald Haweis. London: W. H. Allen, 1893.

MACKENZIE, Peter, 1824-95, Wesleyan Methodist Minister
From coal pit to pulpit: anecdotes and incidents from the life of the Rev. Peter

Mackenzie / by James Ashcroft Noble. London: J. Robinson, 1895. (BL)
-------. The people's life of the Rev. Peter Mackenzie: the man and his work / by R. Wilberforce Starr. London: W. H. Smith, 1896.
------ . Peter Mackenzie as I knew him / by Dinsdale Thomas Young. London: Hodder & Stoughton, 1904.
-------. Peter Mackenzie, his life and labours / by Joseph Dawson. London: Charles H. Kelly, 1896. photo.port.; popular edition. 1904.
-------. Scenes from the life of the Rev. Peter Mackenzie .../ by M.H. & Thomas Pearson. Leeds: Pearsons, [1895]. (BL)

MACKENZIE, Richard James, 1821-54, army surgeon
Memoir of the life and writings of the late Richard James Mackenzie ... / by James Warburton Begbie and John Struthers. Edinburgh: Sutherland & Knox, 1855. (Reprinted from the 'Edinburgh Medical and Surgical Journal') (BL)

MACKENZIE, William Bell, 1806-70, clergyman
Memorials of the life and ministry of the Rev. William Bell Mackenzie / by Gordon Calthrop. London, [1872]. (BL)

M'KERCHAR, James, d.1896, Scottish religious banker
An earnest life: memoir of James M'Kerchar, J.P., late banker, Aberfeldy / by R. M'Kerchar. Edinburgh: Oliphant, Anderson & Ferrier, 1902. (NLS)

McKERROW, William, 1803-78, United Presbyterian Minister in Manchester; reformer; educationalist
Memoir of William McKerrow, D.D., Manchester / by his son James Muir McKerrow. London: Hodder & Stoughton, 1881. photo. port. (NC)

MACKINTOSH, John, 1822-51, theological student
The earnest student, being memorials of John Mackintosh / by Norman MacLeod. Edinburgh: T. Constable, 1854.

MACKNESS, James, 1804-51, religious doctor; medical writer
Memorials of James Mackness, Esq., M.D. ... Edited by [Mary M. Howard]. London: John Churchill, 1851. (NLS)

MACKONOCHIE, Alexander Heriot, 1825-87, ritualist priest
Alexander Heriot Mackonochie: a memoir. [By Eleanor A. Towle]. Edited by Edward Francis Russell. London: Kegan Paul, Trench, Trubner, 1890.

MACLAGAN, David, 1785-1865, 'Physician to the Forces and Surgeon in Ordinary to the Queen in Scotland'
Tributes to the memory of Dr David Maclagan. [1865]. Pamphlet. (Reprinted, with the addition of a photograph, from the 'Daily Review', Edinburgh) (NLS)

MACLAGAN, David, d.1883, Manager, Edinburgh Life Insurance Company; actuary
David Maclagan, F.R.S.E. / by Norman Lockhart Walker. London: T. Nelson, 1884. photo. port.

McLAREN, Duncan, 1800-86, draper; radical Edinburgh M.P. & Provost
The life and work of Duncan McLaren / by John Beveridge Mackie. London: T. Nelson, 1888. 2 volumes.

MACLAREN, John, 1826-59, United Presbyterian Minister
Memoir of the Rev. John Maclaren, Minister of the United Presbyterian Mission Church, Cowcaddens. Including selections from his letters and sermons / by Peter Leys. Glasgow: Maurice Ogle, 1861.

McLAUCHLAN, Thomas, 1815-56, Free Church Minister

Dr Thomas McLaughlan / by William Keith Leask ... Edinburgh: Oliphant, Anderson & Ferrier, 1903.

MACLENNAN, Farquhar, *alias* **Fearchair-a-Ghunna,** 1784-1868, Scottish vagrant
Fearchair-a-Ghunna, the Ross-shire wanderer: his life and sayings. By the author of 'The Maid of Fairburn'. 2nd enlarged edition. Inverness: J. Noble, 1887; 3rd revised and enlarged edition. Stirling: Eneas Mackay, 1908. Pamphlet. (NLS)

MACLEOD, Adam Gordon, 1823-92, Free Church Minister
Biography of the Rev. Adam Gordon Macleod, Minister of the Free Church, Croy / by Andrew Gordon MacLeod. Printed for the author. Inverness: N. Macleod, 1898. (B&J)

MACLEOD, Sir Donald Friell, 1810-72, Indian civil servant
Memoir of Sir Donald Friell MacLeod: a record of forty-two years' service in India / by Edward John Lake. London: Religious Tract Society, [1874]. 16mo. (BL)

MACLEOD, Norman, senior, 1783-1862, Church of Scotland Minister; Moderator
Memorials of the Rev. Norman MacLeod (Senr), D.D., Minister of St Columba's Church, Glasgow ... / by his son John N. MacLeod. Edinburgh: Edmonston & Douglas, 1898.

MACLEOD, Norman, junior, 1812-72, Church of Scotland Minister; pioneer religious journalist; editor of 'Good Words'
Memoir of Norman MacLeod, D.D., Minister of Barony Parish, Glasgow ... / by his brother Donald Macleod. London: Daldy, Isbister, 1876. 2 volumes. photo.port.; in one volume, 1877.
-------. Norman MacLeod / by John Wellwood. Edinburgh: Oliphant, Anderson & Ferrier, [1897]. (Famous Scots Series)
-------. Norman MacLeod, D.D.: a slight contribution towards his biography / by Alexander Strahan. London: Henry S. King, 1872. (Reprinted with additions from the 'Contemporary Review')

MACLEOD, Roderick, 1794-1868, Free Church Minister at Snizort, Isle of Skye
Brief memorials of the life, character and ministry of the Rev. Roderick MacLeod / by Mackintosh Mackay. Edinburgh: John Maclaren, 1869. photo.port. (NLS)

MACLISE, Daniel, 1806-70, historical painter
A memoir of Daniel Maclise, R.A. / by William Justin O'Driscoll. London: Longmans, Green, 1871.

MACMILLAN, Alexander, 1818-96, co-publisher with his brother Daniel (below)
Life and letters of Alexander Macmillan / by Charles Larcom Graves. London: Macmillan, 1910.

MACMILLAN, Daniel, 1813-57, founder of the publishing firm of Macmillan & Company
Memoir of Daniel Macmillan / by Thomas Hughes. London: Macmillan, 1882.

MACNAIR, William Watts, 1849-89, surveyor in India
Memoir of William Watts MacNair ..., the first European explorer of Kaffristan / by John Eliot Howard. London: Keymer, [1889]. oblong 4to. (NLS)

MACNEIL, John, 1854-96, missionary in Australia
John MacNeil, late evangelist in Australia, and author of 'The spirit-filled life': a memoir / by his wife [Hannah MacNeil] ... London: Marshall, 1897. (NLS)

McNEILL, Sir John, 1795-1883, surgeon in India; diplomat in Persia
Memoir of the Right Hon. Sir John McNeill, G.C.B., and of his second wife Elizabeth Wilson / by their grand-daughter [Florence MacAlister]. London: John Murray, 1910. (BL)

M'OWAN, Peter, 1795-1870, Scottish Methodist Minister
A man of God, or providence and grace exemplified in a memoir of the Rev. Peter M'Owan / compiled chiefly from his letters and papers by John M'Owan. Edited by G. Osborn. London: Wesleyan Conference Office, 1873. (NLS)

MACREADY, William Charles, 1793-1873, tragedian
William Charles Macready / by William Archer. London: Kegan Paul, Trench, Trubner, 1890. (Eminent Actors Series)
and other biographies

MADDEN, Richard Robert, 1798-1886, Irish surgeon; colonial administrator; traveller; miscellaneous writer
The memoirs, chiefly autobiographical, from 1798 to 1886, of R. R. Madden, M.D., F.R.C.S., formerly Colonial Secretary of Western Australia; H.M. Commissioner of Inquiry into the slave trade [etc.]. Edited by his son Thomas More Madden. London: Ward & Downey, 1891. (NLS)

MADEN, Robert, 1832-88, Lancashire Baptist & social reformer
A memorial of Robert Maden, of Ramsbottom. Born March 1 1832 - Died Ramsbottom, December 3 1888. [By Charles Williams]. London: Baptist Tract & Book Society, 1889. photo.port. (B&J)

MADGE, Thomas, 1786-1870, Unitarian Minister
Memoir of the Rev. Thomas Madge, late Minister of Essex Street Chapel, London / by William James. London: Longman, Green, 1871. photo.port.

MADGE, Travers, 1823-66, itinerant preacher in Manchester
Thomas Madge: a memoir / by Brooke Herford. Manchester: Johnson & Rawson, 1867. 12mo. (NLS)

MAGEE, William Connor, 1821-91, Archbishop of York; 'one of the greatest orators and most briliant controversialists of his day'
The life and correspondence of William Connor Magee, Archbishop of York, Bishop of Peterborough / by John Cotter Macdonnell. London: Isbister, 1896. 2 volumes.

MAIN, Thomas, 1816-81, Free Church Minister
Memorials of the life and Ministry of Thomas Main, D.D. / by his widow [Williamina] Main. Edinburgh: Macniven & Wallace, 1883.

MAINE, Sir Henry James Sumner, 1822-88, legal expert and writer; in India
Sir Henry Maine: a brief memoir of his life ... / by Mountsuart Elphinstone Grant Duff. With some of his Indian speeches and minutes. Selected and edited by Whitley Stokes. London: John Murray, 1892.

MALAN, Solomon Caesar [i.e. Cesar Jean Solomon MALAN], 1812-94, clergyman; orientalist; ornithologist
Solomon Caesar Malan, D.D.: memorials of his life and writings / by his eldest surviving son Arthur Noel Malan. London: John Murray, 1897. (BL)

MALLET, Sir Louis, 1823-90, French-born Secretary to the Board of Audit; later Under-Secretary of State for India
Sir Louis Mallet: a record of public service and political ideals / by Bernard Mallet. London: J. Nisbet, 1905.

MANNING, Henry Edward, Cardinal, 1808-92, Church of England clergyman, later the Roman Catholic Cardinal Archbishop of Westminster
The Cardinal Archbishop of Westminster. With notes / by John Oldcastle [i.e. Wilfrid Meynell]. London: Burns & Oates, [1886?].
-------. Cardinal Manning / by Arthur Wollaston Hutton. London: Methuen, 1892.

(English Leaders of Religion Series) (NC)

-------. Cardinal Manning / by Joseph Raymond, Cardinal Gasquet. London: Catholic Truth Society, 1895.

-------. Cardinal Manning as presented in his own letters and notes / by Stanley Roamer. London: Elliot Stock, 1896. (NC)

-------. Life of Cardinal Manning, Archbishop of Westminster / by Edmund Sheridan Purcell. London: Macmillan, 1895. 2 volumes; 2nd [expurgated] edition. 1896. 2 volumes; 4th edition in one volume. 1896. (NC)

and other biographies

MANTELL, Gideon Algernon, 1790-1852, surgeon; geologist

A reminiscence of Gideon Algernon Mantell, LL.D., F.R.S., F.G.S., &c., &c.. By a member of the Council of the Clapham Athanaeum. To which is appended an obituary / by Benjamin Silliman. London: D. Batten, 1853. Pamphlet. (NLS)

MAPLES, Chauncey, 1852-95, Anglican missionary Bishop of Likoma, East Africa

Chauncey Maples, D.D., F.R.G.S., pioneer missionary in East Central Africa for nineteen years, and Bishop of Likoma, Lake Nyassa, 1895: a sketch of his life. With selections from his letters / by his sister (Ellen Maples). London: Longmans, 1897. (BL)

MARCH, Charles, 1793-1865, naval officer; agent of the Bible Society; shipping agent

Life on the deep: memorials of Charles March, Commander R.N./ by his nephew [Septimus March]. London: Religious Tract Society, [1875].

MARRIOTT, Wharton Booth, 1823-71, schoolmaster at Eton; clergyman

Memorials of Wharton Booth Marriott, B.D., F.S.A., formerly ... Assistant Master at Eton. Edited by Fenton John Anthony Hort. London: J. Mitchell, 1873.

MARSDEN, George William, 1812-93, Camberwell solicitor and Vestry Clerk

G. W. Marsden: a memoir / by Edward Foskett. Privately printed. London, 1896. Pamphlet. (B&J)

MARSDEN, Isaac, 1807-82, Doncaster Methodist

Reminiscences of Isaac Marsden, of Doncaster / by John Taylor. London: T. Woolmer, 1883. (NLS)

MARSDEN, James, 1797-1874, Yorkshire Methodist

Memorials of James Marsden, of Oldham and Dewsbury, who for fifty-seven years served his generation as a missionary collector, Sunday School teacher, prayer leader, class leader, local preacher and visitor of the sick and dying / by George Scott, *Wesleyan Methodist Minister.* Leeds: H.W. Walker, 1874. 12mo. (NLS)

MARSH, John Finch, 1789-1873, Quaker; linen draper

A memoir of John Finch Marsh, of Croydon, who died in the autumn of 1873 / by his daughter [Priscilla Pitt]. Privately printed. Croydon: Hannah Marsh, [1873]. (NC)

MARSH, William, 1775-1864, clergyman; 'Millennial Marsh'

The life of the Rev. William Marsh, D.D. / by his daughter [Catherine M. Marsh]. London: J. Nisbet, 1867.

MARSHALL, Andrew, 1779-1854, United Secession, then Free Church Minister

Memoir of Andrew Marshall ... / by John Dick Marshall. With jubilee speech, sermons, etc.. Glasgow: R. Forrester, 1889. 4to. (100 copies) (BL)

MARSHALL, James, 1796-1855, Presbyterian Minister, then Anglican clergyman

A memoir of the Rev. James Marshall, late Incumbent of Christ Church, Clifton, and formerly a Presbyterian Minister in Scotland / compiled by his son James Marshall. London: Bell & Daldy, 1857.

MARSHALL, Sir James, 1829-89, Chief Justice of Gold Coast; Catholic
Memoir of Sir James Marshall, C.M.G. ... Taken chiefly from his own letters / by William Robert Brownlow. London: Burns & Oates, 1890. (NLS)

MARTIN, Anthony, 1813-78, surgeon; Unitarian; Evesham worthy
Memoir of Anthony Martin, Esq., of Evesham / by Herbert New. [With] Funeral address / by John Gordon. Printed for private distribution. Evesham: W. & H. Smith, 1878. photo.ports. Pamphlet. (NLS)

MARTIN, Gavin, 1838-74, missionary see **MARTIN, William**

MARTIN, Sir James Ronald, 1793-1874, Inspector-General of Army Hospitals
Inspector-General Sir James Ronald Martin, C.B., F.R.S. / by Joseph Fayrer. London: A. D. Innes, 1897. (NLS)

MARTIN, John, 1812-75, 'Young Irelander' in 1848; nationalist M.P.
The life and letters of John Martin. With sketches of ... other 'Young Irelanders'/ by P. A. S[illard]. Dublin: James Duffy, 1893; 2nd edition. 1901.

MARTIN, Samuel, 1802-50, Free Church Minister
Memoir of the late Rev. Samuel Martin, Minister of the Free Church, Bathgate / by John Duns. Edinburgh: W. P. Kennedy, 1854.

MARTIN, William, 1835-85, missionary in India
Martin memorials: life and work of William and Gavin Martin, missionaries in Rajputana, India / by William F. Martin. Edinburgh: Andrew Elliot, 1886. (NLS)

MARTINEAU, James, 1805-1900, Unitarian leader and theologian
James Martineau, D.D., S.T.D.: a biography and study / by Abraham Willard Jackson. London: Longmans, Green, 1900. (NC)
-------. The life and letters of James Martineau / by James Drummond and Charles Barnes Upton. London: J. Nisbet, 1902. 2 volumes. (NC)

MARWOOD, William, 1820-83, common executioner of England
The life of Marwood ... Leeds, 1884. Pamphlet. (Yorkshire Pocket Library, No.4) (NLS)

MASON, Benjamin Burnett, d.189-, wine & spirit merchant in Hull
Memoir of the late Benjamin B. Mason, J.P. / compiled by W.G.B. Page & Samuel B. Mason. Printed for private circulation. Hull: W.G.B. Page, 1892. (B&J)

MASON, Sir Josiah, 1795-1881, Birmingham steel pen maker - 4 million per week; philanthropist
Josiah Mason: a biography / by John Thackray Bunce. Printed for private circulation. Birmingham: 'Journal' Printing Works, 1882. photo.port. (NUC); new edition. London: W. & R. Chambers, 1890.
-------. The story of Sir Josiah Mason, the prince of penmakers / by Lucy Taylor. London: T. Nelson, 1894. Pamphlet.

MASON, Robert Gray, 1797-1867, temperance worker in Scotland; poet
Sketch of the life and labours of Robert Gray Mason, temperance advocate / by William Logan. Glasgow: William Tweedie, 1864. 16mo. (NLS)

MASSY, Godfrey, 1803-52, Church of Ireland clergyman
Foot prints of a faithful shepherd: a memoir of the Rev. Godfrey Massy, Vicar of Bruff, and Honorary Secretary of The Limerick Protestant Orphan Society. With a sketch of his times/ by Dawson Massy. London: Seeley, Jackson & Halliday, 1855.

MATHESON, Duncan, 1779-1852, Scottish evangelist

Life and labours of Duncan Matheson, the Scottish evangelist/ by John Macpherson. London: Morgan & Scott, [1871].

MATHESON, Hugh Mackay, 1821-98, Presbyterian missionary in China
Memorials of Hugh M. Matheson. Edited by his wife [Mary Matheson] ... London: Hodder & Stoughton, 1899.

MATHEW, Theobald, 1790-1856, Irish Catholic priest & temperance leader
Father Mathew: a biography / by John Francis Maguire. Cork, 1863; 2nd edition. London: Longman, 1864; abridged edition re-edited by Rosa Mulholland. Dublin: Eason, [1880].
-------. Father Mathew, his life and times / by Frank James Mathew. London: Cassell, 1890.

MATHEWS, Charles James, 1803-78, architect & builder, then actor
The life of Charles James Mathews, chiefly autobiographical. With selections from his correspondence and speeches. Edited by Charles Dickens [Jun.] London: Macmillan, 1879. 2 volumes.

MAULE, Sir William Henry, 1788-1858, M.P.; judge
Memoir of the early life of the Right Hon. Sir W. H. Maule. Edited by his niece Emma Leathly. London: R. Bentley, 1872.

MAURICE, (John) Frederick Denison, 1805-72, clergyman and liberal theologian
Frederick Denison Maurice / by Charles Frederick Gurney Masterman. London: Mowbray, 1907. (Leaders of the Church, 1800-1900 series)
-------. The life of Frederick Denison Maurice, chiefly told in his own letters. Edited by his son Frederick Maurice. London: Macmillan, 1884. 2 volumes.

MAWE, Thomas Laverach, d.1856, Wesleyan
Memoir of Thomas Laverach Mawe, Melton-Mowbray, who died December 14th 1856. [By W. E.]. London: Simpkin, Marshall [etc.], 1857. 16mo. (NLS)

MAXWELL, Eustace George David, 1876-95, undergraduate from Pembroke College, Cambridge, killed in railway accident
Eustace G. D. Maxwell. [By Mrs Amy Maxwell]. London: Marshall, [1895].

MAXWELL, James Clerk, 1831-79, experimental physicist of international stature
The life of James Clerk Maxwell. With a selection from his correspondence and occasional writings / by Lewis Campbell and William Garnett. London: Macmillan, 1882: new edition abridged and revised. 1884.

MAYDWELL, William Lockwood, d.1865, Northampton solicitor's religious clerk
Memoir of W. L. Maydwell, who died at Hertford June 5th 1865/ by the late Bernard Gilpin. Hertford: Stephen Austin, [186-]. (B&J)

MAYO, Robert Southwell Bourke, 6th Earl of, 1822-72, murdered Viceroy of India
The Earl of Mayo / by William Wilson Hunter. Oxford: Clarendon Press, 1891. (Rulers of India series)
-------. A life of the Earl of Mayo, fourth Viceroy of India by William Wilson Hunter. London: Smith, Elder, 1875. 2 volumes.

MEADE, Sir Richard John, 1821-94, General in India
General Sir Richard Meade and the Feudatory States of Central and Southern India: a record of forty-three years service as a soldier, political officer and administrator / by Thomas Henry Thornton. London: Longmans, 1898.

MELLY, Andre, n.d., Liverpool worthy
Recollections of the late A. Melly. Privately printed. Liverpool: printed by Joseph A.

D. Watts, 1872. (B&J)

MELVIN, James, 1795-1853, Rector of Aberdeen Grammar School; Latinist
James Melvin, Rector of the Grammar School of Aberdeen: a sketch / by David Masson. Aberdeen: Centenary Committee, 1895. (250 copies)

MENDS, Sir William Robert, 1812-97, Admiral, chiefly in China
Life of Admiral Sir William Robert Mends, G.C.B. [etc.], late Director of Transports / by his son Bowen Stilon Mends. London: John Murray, 1899.

MERCER, John, 1791-1866, calico manufacturer & textile chemist
The life and labours of John Mercer, F.R.S., F.C.S., etc., the self-taught chemical philosopher ... / by Edward Andrew Parnell. London: Longmans, Green, 1886. photo. port.

MEWBURN, Francis, 1785-1867, railway solicitor
Memoir of Francis Mewburn, Chief Bailiff of Darlington, and first railway solicitor / by his son Francis Mewburn. Darlington: printed by the 'Times' Office, 1867. (BL)

MIALL, Edward, 1809-81, Independent Minister; radical M.P.; editor of 'The Nonconformist'
Life of Edward Miall, formerly Member of Parliament for Rochdale and Bradford / by his son Arthur Miall. London: Macmillan, 1884. photo.port.

MILL, James, 1808-73, surgeon and magistrate in Wick and Thurso
Memorials of the life of James Mill, F.R.C.S.E., J.P., Chief Magistrate of Thurso, illustrated by extracts from his family letters. Printed for private circulation. Edinburgh, 1885. photo.port.

MILL, John Stuart, 1806-73, philosopher, economist and political thinker
John Stuart Mill: a criticism. With personal reminiscences / by Alexander Bain. London: Longmans, Green, 1882. (B&J)
-------. Life of John Stuart Mill / by William Leonard Courtenay. London: Walter Scott Publishing, 1889. (Great Writers series)
-------. The life of John Stuart Mill, politician and philosopher, critic and metaphysician .../ by Mansfield Marston. London: T. Farrah, [1873]. (NLS)

MILLAIS, Sir John Everett, 1st Bart., 1829-96, painter; President of the Royal Academy
The life and letters of Sir John Everett Millais, President of the Royal Academy / by his son John Guille Millais. London: Methuen, 1899. 2 volumes; abridged edition. 1905.

MILLAR, John, 1804-74, poet; businessman
Memoir of John Millar, of Sheardale. With an appendix / by Andrew Thomson. Printed for private circulation. Edinburgh: A. Elliot, 1876. photographically illustrated. (B&J)

MILLER, Hugh, 1802-56, man of letters; geologist; Free Church layman; editor
Hugh Miller / by William Keith Leask. Edinburgh: Oliphant, Anderson & Ferrier, 1896. (Famous Scots series)
-------. Labour & triumph: the life and times of Hugh Miller / by Thomas Nicholas Brown. London: Richard Griffin, 1858.
-------. The life and letters of Hugh Miller / by Peter Bayne. London: Strahan, 1871. 2 volumes.
-------. Life of Hugh Miller / by Jean L. Watson. Edinburgh: James Gemmell, 1880. 12mo.
-------. The life of Hugh Miller: a sketch for working men. London, 1862. 12mo. (Reprinted from 'The Northern Daily Express')

MILLER, Hugh, 1812-79, doctor in Scotland and India
Life of Hugh Miller, Fellow of the Faculty of Physicians and Surgeons of Glasgow, Bombay and Broomfield / by William W. Peyton. Printed for private circulation.

[Edinburgh], 1883. (NC)

MILLER, Samuel, 1810-81, Free Church Minister
Memorials of the late Rev. Samuel Miller, D.D., Minister of St Matthews Free Church, Glasgow. With a biographical sketch / by Thomas Smith. Glasgow: D. Bryce, 1883. photo.port.

MILLS, George, 1820-65, on Sheffield Town Council
Memorials of Mr Councillor George Mills, of Sheffield / by W.R. Sunman. With addenda / by James Caughey and John Guttridge. Sheffield: printed by J. Morton, 1865. 12mo.

MILLS, John, 1821-96, Manchester banker
From tinder box to the 'larger' light: threads from the life of John Mills, banker (author of 'Vox humanae'), interwoven with early century recollections / by his wife [Isabel Mills]. Manchester: Sherratt & Hughes, 1899.

MILMAN, Henry Hart, 1791-1868, Dean of St Paul's
Henry Hart Milman, D.D., Dean of St Paul's: a biographical sketch / by his son Arthur Milman. London: John Murray, 1900.

MILMAN, Robert, 1816-76, Anglican Bishop of Calcutta from 1867
Memoirs of the Right Rev. Robert Milman, D.D., Lord Bishop of Calcutta and Metropolitan of India. With a selection from his correspondence and letters / by his sister Frances Maria Milman. London: John Murray, 1879.

MILNE, John, 1807-68, Free Church Minister in Calcutta & Perth
Life of the Rev. John Milne, of Perth / by Horatius Bonar. London: J. Nisbet, 1868. (NLS)

MILNES, Richard Monckton, 1st Baron Houghton, 1809-85, M.P.; traveller; man of letters; pornographer
The life, letters and friendships of Richard Monckton Milnes, first Lord Houghton / by Thomas Wemyss Reid ... London: Cassell, 1890. 2 volumes.

MILROY, Andrew, 1801-73, Free Church Minister
Memorials of a quiet Ministry, being the life and letters of Andrew Milroy, Minister of the Free Tron Church, Edinburgh [etc.] / by his son Andrew Wallace Milroy. London: J. Nisbet, 1886.

MILSON, Parkinson, 1825-92, Primitive Methodist Minister
Life of Rev. Parkinson Milson (Primitive Methodist Minister)/ by George Shaw. Hull: William Andrews [etc.], 1893. (NLS)

MIMPRISS, Robert, 1797-1875, Sunday School worker; milleniarian
Robert Mimpriss: a memoir of his life and work. London: The Systematic Bible Teacher Depository, [1876]. (NLS)

MITCHEL, John, 1815-75, Irish republican transported to Australia
Life of John Mitchel / by William Dillon. London: Kegan Paul, Trench, 1888. 2 volumes.
-------. The life of John Mitchel. With an historical sketch of the '48 movement in Ireland/ by P. A. Sillard. Dublin: James Duffy, 1901. 16mo. (NLS)

MITCHELL, David, 1847-96, Free Church Minister
In memory of the Rev. David Mitchell, Kirkurd. [Edited by Mrs M.E. Mitchell]. Edinburgh: Andrew Elliot, 1897.

MITCHELL, Hugh, 1822-94, Free Church Minister; ardent geologist

A brief memorial of the Rev. Hugh Mitchell, M.A., LL.D., Ferryden Free Church, Montrose. Aberdeen: John Avery, 1896. (NC)

MOBERLY, George, 1803-85, Headmaster of Winchester College; Bishop of Salisbury
Dulce Domum: George Moberly, D.C.L., Headmaster of Winchester College, 1835-1866; Bishop of Salisbury, 1869-1885: his family and friends / by his daughter Charlotte Anne Elizabeth Moberly. London: John Murray, 1911.

MOFFAT, Robert, 1795-1883, pioneering missionary in South Africa
Life and labours of Robert Moffat, D.D., missionary in South Africa ... / by William Walters. London: Walter Scott Publishing, [1892].
-------. A life's labours in South Africa: the story of the life-work of Robert Moffat, apostle of the Bechuana Tribe. London: John Snow, 1871. photo.port.
-------. The lives of Robert and Mary Moffat / by their son John Smith Moffat. London: T. Fisher Unwin, 1885. photo.port.; new edition. 1886.
-------. Robert Moffat, African missionary / by Jabez Marrat. London: Charles H. Kelly, [1884].
-------. Robert Moffat, the missionary hero of Kuruman / by David J. Deane. London: S. W. Partridge, [189-].
and other titles

MOGRIDGE, George, 1787-1854, miscellaneous writer
George Mogridge, his life, character and writings / by Charles Williams. London: Ward and Lock, 1856.

MOIR, David, 1817-56, Superintendent of the Edinburgh City Mission
Christian devotedness and ministerial usefulness exemplified: a memoir of the Rev. David Moir, lately Superintendent of the Edinburgh City Mission [etc.] / by Alexander Reid. Edinburgh: Thomas C. Jack, 1856.

MOLESWORTH, Sir William, 8th Bart., 1810-55, radical M.P.; Colonial Secretary
Life of the Right Hon. Sir William Molesworth, Bart., M.P., F.R.S. / by Millicent Garrett Fawcett. London: Macmillan, 1901. (NLS)
-------. Notices of the late Sir William Molesworth, Bart., M.P., Secretary of State for the Colonies. [By T. Wollcombe]. Printed for private circulation. London, 1857. (B&J)
-------. The Philosophical Radicals of 1832, comprising the life of Sir William Molesworth, and some incidents connected with the Reform Movement from 1832 to 1842. [By Harriet Grote]. Printed for private circulation. London: printed by Savill and Edwards, 1866. (B&J)

MONTAGU, John, 1797-1853, soldier; Colonial Secretary at the Cape
Biographical memoir of John Montagu. With a sketch of some of the public affairs connected with the Colony of the Cape of Good Hope during his administration as Colonial Secretary from 1834 to 1853 / by William Abiah Newman. London: Harrison, 1855. (BL)

MONTEFIORE, Sir Moses Haim, 1st Bart., 1784-1885 aged 101, Jewish member of Stock Exchange; philanthropist
Sir Moses Montefiore: a biographical sketch. Reprinted ... from 'The Times' / by Isaac Davis. London: 'Jewish Chronicle' Office, 1883. Pamphlet. (NLS)
-------. Sir Moses Montefiore: a centennial biography. With extracts from letters and journals / by Lucien Wolf. London: John Murray, 1884.
-------. Sir Moses Montefiore: the story of his life / by James Weston [i.e. Edward Step]. London: S. W. Partridge, [1885]. (NLS)

MONTGOMERY, Henry, 1788-1865, Irish Unitarian
Henry Montgomery, LL.D. / by John Armstrong Crozier. Belfast: Ulster Unitarian Christian Association, [1888]. Pamphlet. (BL)
-------. The life of the Rev. Henry Montgomery ... With selections from his speeches and writings / by John Armstrong Crozier. Volume 1 (all published). Belfast: W. H. Greer,

1875. (BL)

MONTGOMERY, James, 1771-1854, poet and journalist
James Montgomery: a lecture delivered in Norfolk Street Chapel, Sheffield / by John Kirk. London: Hamilton, Adams, 1861. (B&J)
-------. James Montgomery: a memoir, political and poetical/ by J.W. King London: Partridge, 1858. (NUC)
-------. James Montgomery, Christian poet and philanthropist/ by Jabez Marrat. London: Wesleyan Conference Office, [1879]. 12mo. (NLS)
-------. The life of James Montgomery / by Helen Cross Knight. Boston: Gould & Lincoln, 1857.
-------. Life, times and character of James Montgomery / by Samuel Ellis. London: Jackson, Walford & Hodder, 1864.
-------. Memoirs of the life and writings of James Montgomery. Including selections from his correspondence [etc.] / by John Holland & James Everett. London: Longman [etc.], 1854-56. 7 volumes.

MOON, William, 1818-94, blind inventor of Moon's embossed type for the blind
William Moon, LL.D., F.R.G.S., F.S.A., and his work for the blind / by John Rutherfurd. London: Hodder & Stoughton, 1898.

MOORE, Albert Joseph, 1841-93, painter
Albert Moore: his life and works / by Alfred Lys Baldry. London: G. Bell, 1894. (BL)

MOORE, George, 1806-76, owned lace factory; philanthropist
George Moore, merchant and philanthropist / by Samuel Smiles. London: G. Routledge, 1878; abridged edition. 1879.

MOORE, George Henry, 1810-70, Irish hunting squire; M.P.; traveller in Middle East
An Irish gentleman - George Henry Moore: his travels, his racing, his politics / by [his son] Maurice George Moore. London: T. Werner Laurie, [1913].

MOORE, Henry, 1831-95, marine painter & watercolourist
Henry Moore, R.A. / by Frank [i.e. Francis John] Maclean. London: Walter Scott Publishing, 1905. (BL)

MOORE, Thomas, 1780-1852, poet; published 'Irish Melodies' 1807-34
Thomas Moore, his life, writings and contemporaries / by Henry R. Montgomery. London: Thomas Cantley Newby, 1860.
-------. Memoirs, journal and correspondence of Thomas Moore. Edited by ... Lord John Russell. London: Longman [etc.], 1853-56. 8 volumes; abridged edition 1860. (BL)
and other biographies

MOORHOUSE, Henry, 1840-80, evangelist
Henry Moorhouse, the English evangelist / by John Macpherson. London: Morgan & Scott, [1881]. (NLS)

MORANT, Alfred William Whitehead, 1828-81, Leeds Borough Engineer
Memoir of Alfred William Whitehead Morant, M.Inst.C.E. [etc.] / by Wyatt Papworth. Printed for printed circulation. [1881]. 12mo. (Reprinted with additions from 'The Builder') (NLS)

MORE, Alexander Goodman, 1830-95, Irish naturalist & ornithologist
Life and letters of Alexander Goodman More, F.R.S.E., F.L.S., M.R.I.A.. With selections from his zoological and botanical writings. Edited by C.B. Moffat. Dublin: Hodges, Figgis, 1898.

MORELL, John Daniel, 1816-91, Congregational Minister; school inspector
Memorials of John Daniel Morehead, M.A., LL.D., Her Majesty's Inspector of

Schools / by Robert Masters Theobald. London: Edward Stewart, 1891. photo.ports.

MORESBY, <u>Sir</u> Fairfax, 1786-1877, Admiral of the Fleet
Two admirals. Admiral of the Fleet Sir Fairfax Moresby, G.C.B., K.M.T., D.C.L. (1786-1877), and his son John Moresby: a record of the life and service in the British navy for a hundred years ... / by John Moresby. London: John Murray, 1909.

MORGAN, <u>Sir</u> Richard Francis, 1821-76, Chief Justice in Ceylon
Forty years of official and unofficial life in an oriental Crown Colony, being the life of Sir Richard F. Morgan, Kt. / by William Digby. London: Longmans, Green, 1879. 2 volumes. (BL)

MORGAN, William, 1818-84, Welsh theologian
Life of the Rev. William Morgan, Professor of Theology at the Presbyterian College, Carmarthen ... / by his son John Lloyd Morgan. With sermons and a portrait. London: Elliot Stock, 1886. photo.port.

MORIER, <u>Sir</u> Robert Burnett David, 1826-93, diplomat
Memoirs and letters of the Right Hon. Sir Robert Morier, G.C.B., from 1820 to 1876 / by his daughter Rosslyn Wemyss. London: E. Arnold, 1911. 2 volumes.

MORISON, James, 1816-93, Scottish founder of the Evangelical Union in 1843
The life of the Rev. James Morison, D.D., Principal of the Evangelical Union Theological Hall, Glasgow / by William Adamson. London: Hodder & Stoughton, 1898.
-------. Principal James Morison, the man and his work: a monograph / by Oliphant Smeaton ... Edinburgh: Oliver & Boyd, 1901.

MORISON, John, 1791-1859, Congregational pastor in London; editor of the 'Evangelical Magazine'
Service and suffering: memoirs of the life of John Morison / by John Kennedy. London, 1860. (BL)

MORLEY, Henry, 1822-94, academic; writer; critic
The life of Henry Morley, LL.D., Professor of English Language and Literature at University College, London / by Henry Shaen Solby. London: E. Arnold, 1898.

MORLEY, Samuel, 1809-86, textile manufacturer employing 8,000 people; radical M.P.; nonconformist
The life of Samuel Morley / by Edwin Hodder. London: Hodder & Stoughton, 1887.
-------. Samuel Morley: personal reminiscences. The address delivered at the funeral. With additions / by Joshua Clarkson Harrison. London: Hodder & Stoughton, 1886. photo.port. 16mo. (NLS)

MORRIS, Francis Orpen, 1810-93, clergyman & ornithological writer
Francis Orpen Morris: a memoir / by his son Marmaduke Charles Frederick Morris. London: John C. Nimmo, 1897.

MORRIS, William, 1834-96, utopian; writer; printer; poet
The life of William Morris / by John William Mackail. London: Longmans, 1899. 2 volumes; and later many editions.

MORRISON-GRANT, Lewis, 1872-93, poet
Lewis Morrison-Grant: his life, letters and last poems. Edited by Jessie Annie Anderson. Paisley: Alexander Gardner, 1894. (NLS)

MORTON, Hugh, 1831-94, religious businessman; temperance advocate
The life-story of Hugh Morton, Newmilns, a worker for Christ / by Robert Gilchrist. Ardrossan: A. Guthrie, [1895]. (NLS) The Preface notes the following unlocated book: 'In memoriam. Hugh Morton, Newmilns' / by John Thomas Burton. Edinburgh: Baillie,

c.1894.

MOULTON, William Fiddian, 1835-98, Wesleyan Methodist; biblical scholar; headmaster
In memoriam: William Fiddian Moulton, D.D., Head Master, Feb. 16th 1875 - Feb. 5th 1898. [A special issue of 'The Leys Fortnightly']. Cambridge: printed by Metcalfe, 1898. photo.port. (B&J)
-------. William F. Moulton: a memoir / by William Fiddian Moulton [Jun.] ... London: Isbister, 1899.

MOUNTAIN, Armine Simcoe Henry, 1797-1854, Adjutant-General in India
Memoirs and letters of the late Colonel Armine S. H. Mountain, C.B., Aide-de-Camp to the Queen, and Adjutant-General of Her Majesty's forces in India. Edited by his wife [A. S. H. Mountain]. London: Longman [etc.], 1857.

MUDIE, Charles Henry, 1850-79, family memoir of the son of the founder of Mudies
Circulating Library: philanthropist
Charles Henry Mudie: a memorial sketch. By one of his sisters [Mary Mudie]. Printed for private circulation. [London: R. Clay & Taylor], 1879. photo.port. (BL)

MUELLER, Friedrich Max-, 1823-1900, German-born orientalist & philologist
The life and letters of the Right Hon. Friedrich Max-Muller. Edited by his wife [Georgina Adelaide Muller]. London: Longmans, 1902. 2 volumes.

MUELLER, Georg, 1805-98, Bristol preacher and philanthropist
A brief account of the life and labours of George Muller (of Bristol) / by [Susannah Grace] Muller. London: J. Nisbet, 1883. 12mo; 2nd edition. 1887. (NC)
-------. George Muller of Bristol / by Arthur Tappan Pierson. London: J. Nisbet, 1899. (NC)
-------. Preaching tours and missionary labours of George Muller of Bristol / by Susannah Grace Muller. London: J. Nisbet, 1883. photo.port. (B&J); 2nd edition. 1889.
-------. Ten years after: a sequel to the *Autobiography* ... / compiled by George Frederick Bergin. London: J. Nisbet, [1909].
and other popular biographies

MUIR, Francis, 1797-1871, United Presbyterian Minister
Memorial volume in connection with the life and Ministry of the late Rev. Francis Muir, for forty-eight years Minister of Junction Street United Presbyterian Congregation, Leith. [Edited by James Waldie and others]. Printed for private circulation. [Leith?], 1873. photographic illustration.

MUIR, William, 1806-88, manufacturer of machine tools in Manchester; temperance worker
Brief memoir of William Muir, mechanical engineer, London and Manchester. Born 17th January 1806 - Died 15th June 1888. [By Robert Smiles]. London: printed by James Collins, 1888. 12mo. (B&J)

MULREADY, William, 1786-1863, Irish genre painter
Memorials of William Mulready / collected by Frederick George Stephens. London: Bell & Daldy, 1867. 4to. Photographically illustrated.

MUNRO, Christopher, 1816-85, Free Church Minister
Memorials of the late Rev. Christopher Munro, Free Church Minister of Strathy. [Edited by J. S. Munro]. Edinburgh: Macniven & Wallace, 1890. (B&J)

MUNRO, James, 1803-84, Free Church Minister
In memoriam: Rev. James Munro, Rutherglen. [Glasgow: printed by Aird & Coghill, c.1884]. (NC)

MURCHISON, Sir Roderick Impey, 1st Bart., 1792-1871, soldier; Director-General of the

Geological Survey
Life of Sir Roderick Impey Murchison / by Andrew Geikie. London: John Murray, 1875. 2 volumes; reprinted 1972.

MURKER, John, 1802-81, Scottish Congregational Minister
Rev. John Murker of Banff: a picture of religious life and character in the North / by James Stark. London: Hodder & Stoughton, 1887. (NLS)

MURPHY, George Mollett, 1823-87, working class member of London School Board; teetotaller
A friend of the people: the life of George M. Murphy, member of the London School Board ... / by Annie Taylor. London: Elliot Stock, 1886. photo.port.

MURRAY, Alasdair Heneage, d.1900, soldier killed in Boer War
Alasdair Murray, 1900: a few words and letters privately offered to those who, at Lochcarron and elsewhere, knew him well. [Edited by Charles Murray]. London: Spottiswoode, 1901.

MURRAY, Sir Charles Augustus, 1806-95, diplomat; author
The Honourable Sir Charles Augustus Murray, K.C.B.: a memoir / by Herbert Maxwell. Edinburgh: W. Blackwood, 1898.

MURRAY, Daniel, 1768-1852, Roman Catholic Archbishop of Dublin
Notices of the life and character of His Grace the Most Rev. Daniel Murray, the late Archbishop of Dublin ... / by William Meagher. Dublin: G. Bellew, 1853. (NUC)

MURRAY, David, 1807-79, Provost of Paisley & businessman there
Memoir of David Murray, late Provost of Paisley ... / by his son J. Clarke Murray. Paisley: Alexander Gardner, 1881. photo.port. (B&J)

MURRAY, James, n.d., religious boy
'I do love him', or the history of James Murray. By the author of 'Widow Goodwyn'. Birmingham: C. Caswell, 1864. 32mo. Pamphlet.

MURRAY, John, the third, 1808-92, publisher
A publisher and his friends: memoir and correspondence of the late John Murray ... / by Samuel Smiles. London: John Murray, 1891. 2 volumes; condensed & edited by Thomas Mackay. 1911.
-------. John Murray 111, 1808-1892: a brief memoir / by John Murray 1V. London: John Murray, 1919.

MURRAY, Peter, 1782-1864, doctor in Scarborough from 1826
'The beloved physician': a memoir of Peter Murray, M.D., of Bell Vue, Scarborough / by Robert Balgarnie. London: Simpkin Marshall, 1864. 12mo.

MURRISH, William, 1818-61, Cornish miner & Methodist
The miner of Perranzabuloe, or, simple records of a good man's life / by W. Davis Tyack. Leeds: H. W. Walker, 1866. (B&J)

MURSELL, James Philippo, 1799-1885, radical Baptist Minister
James Philippo Mursell, his life and work / by his son Arthur Mursell. London: James Clark, 1886. photo.port.

MUSPRATT, James Sheridan, 1821-71, chemical manufacturer
Biography of Dr. Sheridan Muspratt, F.R.S.E. [etc.], Professor of the College of Chemistry, Liverpool .... By a London barrister-at-law ... London: John Churchill, 1852. Pamphlet. (From 'The Lancet') (NLS)
-------. Biography of Samuel Muspratt / by William White. London, [1869]. (BL)

NAISH, Arthur, 1820-64, Bristol Quaker
A brief memoir of the life and character of Arthur Naish, of Bristol / by Joseph Storrs Fry. Bristol: W. Whereat, 1865. 12mo. Pamphlet. (NLS)

NANGLE, Edward, 1799-1883, Irish clergyman and printer
Edward Nangle, the Apostle of Achill: a memoir and a history/ by Henry Seddall. London: Hatchards, 1884. (BL)

NAPIER, Sir Charles, 1786-1860, Admiral
The life and correspondence of Admiral Sir Charles Napier, K.C.B., from personal recollections, letters and official documents / by Edward Hungerford Delavel Elders Napier. London: Hurst & Blackett, 1862. 2 volumes. (NLS)

NAPIER, Sir Charles James, 1782-1853, General; conqueror of Sind
The life and opinions of General Sir Charles James Napier, G.C.B. / by William Napier. London: John Murray, 1857. 4 volumes.
-------. Life of General Sir Charles James Napier, G.C.B. / by William Napier Bruce. London: John Murray, 1885.
-------. Sir Charles Napier / by William Francis Butler. London: Macmillan, 1894. (Engish Men of Action series)

NAPIER, Sir Joseph, 1st Bart., 1804-82, Lord Chancellor of Ireland
The life of Hon. Sir Joseph Napier, Bart., ex-Lord Chancellor of Ireland, from his private correspondence / by Alexander Charles Ewald. London: Longmans, 1887; revised edition. 1892.

NAPIER, Robert, 1791-1876, Govan shipbuilder
Life of Robert Napier, of West Shandon ..., President of the [Institution of] Mechanical Engineers / by James Napier. Edinburgh: W. Blackwood, 1904.

NAPIER, Sir William Francis Patrick, 1785-1860, General; historian of the Peninsular War
Life of General Sir William Napier, K.C.B., author of 'History of the War in the Peninsula', &c.. Edited by Henry Austin Bruce. London: John Murray, 1864. 2 volumes.

NASMITH, David, 1808-90, prison visitor in Glasgow; Secretary to the Bridewell Association
Memoirs of David Nasmith, his labours and travels in Great Britain, France, the United States and Canada / by John Campbell. London: John Snow, 1844.

NASMYTH, John, 1853-94, Church of Scotland Minister
Memoir of James Nasmyth, Minister of Ceres, 1878-1894. With selections from his writings. Arranged and edited by George Johnston. For private circulation. Edinburgh: R. & R. Clark, 1895. (NC)

NEALE, Edward Vansittart, 1810-92, Christian socialist; co-operator
Memorial of Edward Vansittart Neale, General Secretary of the Co-Operative Union, 1875-1891 ... / compiled by Henry Pitman. Manchester: Co-Operative Union, 1894.

NEALE, John Mason, 1818-66, Anglo-Catholic; liturgiologist
John Mason Neale, D.D.: a memoir / by Eleanor Ashworth Towle. London: Longmans, Green, 1906.

NEILD, John Camden, 1780-1852, inherited a fortune which he left to Queen Victoria
A short memoir of the late John Camden Neild, of Chelsea .../ by Henry Tattam. Privately printed. London, [1852]. (BL)

NEILSON, David, 1823-90, Free Church Minister
Memorials of the Rev. David Neilson, of Renfrew. Edited by James Moffat Scott.

Paisley: J. & R. Parlane, 1893.

NELSON, John, 1829-78, Free Church Minister
In memoriam: John Nelson, D.D.. Edinburgh: T. Nelson, 1878. 12mo.

NELSON, William, 1816-87, Scottish publisher
William Nelson: a memoir / by Daniel Wilson. Printed for private circulation. Edinburgh: T. Nelson, 1889.

NESBIT, Robert, 1803-55, Free Church missionary in Bombay
Memoir of the Rev Robert Nesbit, missionary of the Free Church of Scotland, Bombay/ by John Murray Mitchell. London: J. Nisbet, 1858.

NEW, Charles, 1840-75, Methodist missionary in East Africa; botanist
Memorials of Charles New, author of 'Life, wanderings and labours in Eastern Africa ... ' / by Samuel Saxon Barton. London: Methodist Free Churches Book Room, 1876; abbreviated version as: 'The life of Charles New, missionary to East Africa'. London: Andrew Crombie, [1889]. (NLS)

NEWCASTLE, Henry Pelham Fiennes Pelham-Clinton, 5th Duke of, 1811-64, Tory M.P.; Secretary of State for the Colonies
The life of Henry Pelham, fifth Duke of Newcastle, 1811-1864/ by John Martineau. London: John Murray, 1908.

NEWLAND, Henry Garrett, 1804-60, Tractarian clergyman
A memoir of the late Rev. Henry Garrett Newland, M.A., Vicar of Marychurch, Devon [etc.] (With extracts from his letters and papers) / by Reginald Neale Shutte. London: Joseph Masters, 1861. photo.port. (NLS)

NEWMAN, Edward, 1801-76, entomologist and writer
Memoir of the life and works of Edward Newman, F.L.S., F.Z.S. [etc.] / by his son [Thomas Prichard Newman]. London: John Van Voorst, 1876. photo.port. Pamphlet. (NLS)

NEWMAN, Francis William, 1805-97, freethinking brother of Cardinal Newman; passionate reformer
In memoriam: Emeritus Professor F. W. Newman: [obituary notices]. [1897] (BL)
-------. Memoir and letters of Francis W. Newman / by Isabel Giberne Sieveking. London: Kegan Paul, Trench, Trubner, 1909.

NEWMAN, John Henry, Cardinal, 1801-90, theologian & theological writer
Cardinal Newman / by Richard Holt Hutton. London: Methuen, 1891. (Leaders of Religion series)
-------. Cardinal Newman: reminiscences of fifty years since / by William Lockhart, one of his oldest living disciples. London: Burns & Oates, 1891. (NLS)
-------. Cardinal Newman, the story of his life / by Henry James Jennings. Birmingham: Houghton, 1882. photo.port. (B&J)
-------. The life of John Henry, Cardinal Newman, based on his private journals and correspondence / by Wilfrid Ward. London: Longmans, 1912. 2 volumes; reprinted Farnborough, Hants: Gregg, 1970.
--------. Newman / by William Barry. London: Hodder & Stoughton, 1904. (Literary Lives series)
-------. A short life of Cardinal Newman / by Joseph Smith Fletcher. London: Ward & Downey, 1890.
and other biographies

NEWTON, Robert, 1780-1854, Wesleyan Methodist
The life of the Rev. Robert Newton, D.D. / by Thomas Jackson. London: John Mason, 1855; another edition. London: Wesleyan Conference Office, 1874.

NICHOL, John, 1833-94, man of letters; friend of Swinburne
Memoir of John Nichol, Professor of English Literature in the University of Glasgow / by [William Angus] Knight. Glasgow: James Maclehose, 1896.

NICHOLLS, John Ashton, 1823-59, Manchester cotton manufacturer and pioneer of working-class education there
'Christian views of life and death': a sermon ... on the occasion of the death of John Ashton Nicholls, Esq., F.R.A.S.. With a sketch of his life [of 102 pages] / by William Gaskell. Manchester: Johnson & Rawson, 1859. (NLS)

NICHOLS, John Gough, 1806-73, printer and editor of the 'Gentleman's Magazine'
Memoir of the late John Gough Nichols, F.S.A. / by Robert Cradock Nicols. Westminster, June 1874. 4to. (B&J)

NICHOLSON, Cornelius, 1804-89, Westmorland businessman
A well-spent life: a memoir of Cornelius Nicholson, J.P. [etc.]. With a selection of his lectures and letters. [By Cornelia Nicholson]. Kendal: T. Wilson, 1890. (NLS)

NICHOLSON, John, 1821-57, Brigadier-General in India
The life of John Nicholson, soldier and administrator, based on private and hitherto unpublished documents / by Lionel James Trotter. London: John Murray, 1897.

NICHOLSON, Samuel, 1801-56, Baptist Minister in Plymouth
Memoir of the Rev. Samuel Nicolson. With selections from his correspondence, &c.. By a friend. Printed chiefly for private circulation. Plymouth: Alfred Davis, 1858. (NLS)

NICHOLSON, Samuel, 1811-87, Irish Methodist
Irish Methodist reminiscences, being mainly memorials of the life and labours of the Rev. S. Nicholson / by Edward Thomas. London: J. C. Watts, 1889. (NLS)

NICOLL, Harry, 1821-91, Aberdeenshire Minister
My father, an Aberdeenshire Minister, 1821-1891 / by William Robertson Nicoll. London: Hodder & Stoughton, 1908. 12mo.

NISBET, James, 1785-1854, religious publisher in London
Lessons from the life of the late James Nisbet, publisher, London: a study for young men / by John Aikman Wallace. Edinburgh: Johnstone, Hunter, 1867. (BL)

NIXON, John, 1815-99, Welsh mining engineer and mine owner
John Nixon, pioneer of the steam coal trade in South Wales: a memoir / by James Edmund Vincent. London: John Murray, 1900. (BL)

NOBLE, Robert Turlington, 1809-65, Anglican missionary in India
A memoir of the Rev. Robert Turlington Noble ... missionary to the Telugu People in South India ... / by John Noble. London: Seeely, Jackson & Halliday, 1867. (NLS)

NORTH, Brownlow, 1810-75, English evangelist in Scotland & Ulster; reformed debauchee
Brownlow North, B.A.: records and recollections / by Kenneth Moody-Stuart. London: Hodder & Stoughton, 1878. photo.port.

'NORTH, Christopher' see WILSON, John

NORTHCOTE, Sir Stafford Henry, 1st Earl of Iddesleigh see under IDDESLEIGH

NORTHUMBERLAND, Algernon Percy, 4th Duke of, 1792-1865, Admiral
In memoriam: obituary notices which were published on the death of the ... Duke of Northumberland ... Revised and reprinted for private distribution. Newcastle-upon-Tyne: Daily Journal Office, 1865. 4to. (B&J)

NOVELLO, Vincent, 1781-1861, music publisher; composer
The life and labours of Vincent Novello / by his daughter Mary Cowden Clarke. London: Novello, [1862].

NUNNERLEY, James I., n.d., soldier in the Charge of the Light Brigade
Short sketch of the life of Sergeant-Major J. I. Nunnerley, late of the Lancashire Hussars, and formerly Sergeant of the 'Death or Glory Boys' - 17th Lancers - and one of the 'Six Hundred'. Ormskirk: printed by P. Draper, 1890. (B&J)

OASTLER, Richard, 1789-1861, factory reformer; M.P.; newspaperman
Sketch of the life of the late Richard Oastler ... / by George Stringer Bull. Bradford: printed by Squire Auty, [1861]. (NUC)

O'BRIEN, James Thomas, 1792-1874, Church of Ireland Bishop of Ossery, Ferns and Leighlin
A memoir of the Right Rev. James Thomas O'Brien, late Lord Bishop of Ossory ... With a summary of his writings / by William George Carroll. Dublin: Robertson, 1875. (Reprinted from the 'Irish Times', etc.) (BL)

O'CONNOR, Paul James, [179-]-1878, Irish Catholic lay brother
The life of Brother Paul J. O'Connor. Dublin: M. H. Gill, 1887. photo.port. (NLS)

ODGER, George, 1820-77, shoemaker; trade unionist
The life and labours of George Odger. London, [1877]. (Reprinted from 'Saint Crispin, the Boot and Shoemakers' Journal') (BL)

O'DONOVAN, John, 1809-61, Irish historical writer
On the life and labours of John O'Donovan. London: T. Richardson, 1872. Pamphlet. (BL)

OGILVIE, John, 1797-1867, lexicographer
John Ogilvie, LL.D., and his first twenty-one classes. Privately printed. Aberdeen, 13th February, 1896.
-------. John Ogilvie, lexicographer, LL.D.: a biographical sketch ... / by Joseph Ogilvie. Aberdeen: John Rae Smith, 1902.

OGLE, John Furniss, 1823-65, Church of England missionary in Falkland Islands & North Africa
Life and missionary travels of the Rev. J. Furniss Ogle, M.A., from his letters. Selected by his sister [Jane Ogle] and edited by James Aitken Wylie. London: Longmans, Green, 1873. (B&J)

OLIPHANT, Laurence, 1829-88, writer; traveller; mystic
Laurence Oliphant: supplementary contributions to his biography / by Charles Newton Scott. London: Leadenhall Press, 1895. Pamphlet. (NLS)
-------. Memoir of the life of Laurence Oliphant, and of Alice Oliphant his wife / by Margaret Oliphant W. Oliphant. Edinburgh: W. Blackwood, 1891. 2 volumes; in one volume 1892.
-------. Personal reminiscences of Laurence Oliphant: a note of warning / by Louis Leisching. London: Marshall, [1892]. (NLS)

ORMEROD, Robert Moss, 1869-99, Methodist missionary in East Africa
Life of Robert Moss Ormerod, missionary to East Africa / by Joseph Kirsop. London:

Andrew Crombie, 1901. (BL)

ORPEN, Charles Edward Herbert, 1791-1856, Irishman; opened deaf and dumb school; clergyman
Life of Dr. Orpen, founder of the National Institution for the Education of the Deaf and Dumb at Claremont, near Dublin [etc.] / by Emma L. Le Fanu. London: Charles Westerton, 1860. (NLS)

OSBORN, Samuel, 1826-91, steelmaker; Mayor of Sheffield
Memoir of Samuel Osborn, J.P., Master Cutler, 1873-4, Mayor of Sheffield, 1890-1: a memorial sketch / by his brother-in-law William H. Tindall. Printed for private circulation. 1892. photo.port. (B&J)

OSBORNE, John, d.1865, racehorse trainer
Ashgill, or the life and times of John Osborne / written and compiled by J. B. Radcliffe ('Saxon'). London: Sands, 1900.

OSBORNE, Ralph Bernal see **BERNAL OSBORNE, Ralph**

O'SHAUGHNESSY, Arthur William Edgar, 1844-81, zoologist; writer
Arthur O'Shaughnessy: his life and his work, with selections from his poems / by Louise Chandler Moulton. London: Elkin Mathews & John Lane 1894. (NUC)

OSWELL, William Cotton, 1818-93, explorer in Africa; colleague of Livingstone
William Cotton Oswell, hunter and explorer: the story of his life ... / by his eldest son William Edward Oswell ... London: W. Heinemann, 1900. 2 volumes.

OUGHTON, Thomas, 1825-94, lawyer; administrator in Jamaica
In memoriam: Thomas Oughton, 1825-1894 / by Mary Abigail Oughton and others. London: J. M. Dent, 1895. (NUC)

OUSELEY, Sir Frederick Arthur Gore, 2nd Bart., 1825-89, clergyman; musician
The life of the Rev. Sir F. A. G. Ouseley, Bart., M.A., Mus.D. / by Frederick Wayland Joyce ... London: Methuen, 1896.
-------. Memorials of Frederick Arthur Gore Ouseley, Baronet, M.A., Doctor and Professor of Music in the University of Oxford / by Francis Tebbs Havergal. [Subscribers' Edition]. London: Ellis & Elvey, 1889. 4to.

OUTRAM, Sir James, 1st Bart., 1803-63, Lt.-General in Indian army
The Bayard of India: a life of General Sir James Outram, Bart, G.C.B., [etc.] / by Lionel James Trotter. Edinburgh: W. Blackwood, 1903.
-------. James Outram: a biography / by Frederic John Goldsmid. London: Smith, Elder, 1880. 2 volumes.
-------. A memoir of the public service rendered by Lieut. Colonel Outram, C.B.. Printed for private circulation. London: Smith, Elder, 1853. (NLS)

OWEN, Edward Roderic, 1856-96, soldier killed in Egyptian campaign
'Roddy Owen' (Brevet-Major, Lancashire Fusiliers, D.S.O.): a memoir / by his sister Mai Bovill & George Ranken Askwith. London: John Murray, 1897.

OWEN, Sir Hugh, 1804-81, Welsh educationalist & philanthropist
Sir Hugh Owen, his life and life-work / by William Edwards Davies ... [London]: National Eisteddfod Association, 1885.

OWEN, Sir Richard, 1804-92, surgeon; zoologist
The life of Richard Owen / by his grandson Richard Owen ... London: John Murray, 1894. 2 volumes.

PAGAN, James, 1811-70, editor of the 'Glasgow Herald'
In memoriam: Mr James Pagan, editor of the 'Glasgow Herald'. Born 18th October 1811 - Died 11th February 1870. Printed for private circulation. [Glasgow: printed by Robert Anderson, 1870]. photo.port.

[PAGET, Charles], 1799-1873, drowned nonconformist M.P. for Nottingham
In memoriam October 13 1873: [a collection of obituary notices of Charles Paget / arranged by F.P.]. [Mansfield: printed by T. W. Clarke, 1874]. (B&J)

PAGET, Sir James, 1st Bart., 1814-99, surgeon
In memoriam: Sir James Paget / by Howard Marsh. London: Smith, Elder, 1901. Pamphlet. (NLS)
-------. Memoirs and letters of Sir James Paget. Edited by Stephen Paget, one of his sons. London: Longmans, Green, 1900.

PALMER, Edward Henry, 1840-82, Professor of Arabic
The life and achivements of Edward Henry Palmer, late Lord Almoner's Professor of Arabic in the University of Cambridge, and Fellow of Saint John's College / by Walter Besant. 3rd edition. London: John Murray, 1883.

PALMER, Roundell see **SELBORNE, 1st Earl of**

PALMER, Samuel, 1805-81, landscape painter & etcher
The life and letters of Samuel Palmer, painter and etcher. Written and edited by Alfred Herbert Palmer. London: Seeley, 1892. (BL)
-------. Samuel Palmer: a memoir / by Alfred Herbert Palmer ... London: Fine Art Society, 1882. 4to. (NLS)

PALMER, William, 1824-56, 'The Rugeley Poisoner'
Illustrated life, career and trial of William Palmer of Rugeley ... London: Ward Lock, 1856.
-------. Illustrated and unabridged edition of 'The Times' Report of the trial of William Palmer for poisoning John Parsons Cook of Rugeley ... London: Ward Lock, 1856.
    and other similar popular productions

PALMER, William Frederick, n.d., cotton machine manufacturer
William Frederick Palmer: a souvenir. By a friend [i.e. Peter B. Allen?]. For private circulation. Southport: Robert Johnson, 1899. (B&J)

PALMERSTON, Henry John Temple, 3rd Viscount, 1784-1865, Whig Prime Minister
The life and correspondence of Henry John Temple, Viscount Palmerston / by Evelyn Ashley [but actually abridged by him from the two biographies below:]. London: R. Bentley, 1879. 2 volumes.
-------. The life of Henry John Temple, Viscount Palmerston. With selections from his diaries and correspondence / by Henry Lytton Bulwer. London: R. Bentley, 1870-74. 3 volumes. (Volume 3 edited by Evelyn Ashley). [Continued as:] 'The life of Henry John Temple, Viscount Palmerston, 1846-1865. With selections from his speeches and correspondence' / by Evelyn Ashley. London: R. Bentley, 1876. 2 volumes.
-------. Memoir of the Right Hon. Viscount Palmerston, K.G., G.C.B., etc. / by Edward Walford. London: Bradbury, Evans, 1865. 12mo. Pamphlet. (NLS)
-------. The story of the life of Lord Palmerston / by Karl Marx. Edited by his daughter Eleanor Marx Aveling. London: Swan Sonnenschein, 1899.
-------. Viscount Palmerston, K.G. / by John, Marquess of Lorne. London: Sampson Low, Marston, 1892. (Prime Ministers of Queen Victoria series)
    and other popular biographies

PANIZZI, Sir Anthony, 1797-1879, Chief Librarian of the British Museum
A biographical sketch Sir Anthony Panizzi, late Principal Librarian, British Museum / by Robert Cowtan. London: Asher, 1873.

-------. The life of Sir Anthony Panizzi, K.C.B., late Principal Librarian of the British Museum ... / by Louis Fagan. London: Remington, 1880. 2 volumes.

PARISH, Sir Woodbine, 1796-1882, British Minister at Buenos Aires
The life of Sir Woodbine Parish, K.C.H., F.R.S., 1796-1882 ... / by Nina Louisa Kay-Shuttleworth. London: Smith, Elder, 1910.

PARKE, William, 1797-1876, Wolverhampton bookseller
In memoriam W. Parke: a sketch / by James G.J.P. Brodhurst. Wolverhampton: A. Hinde, 1876. (BL)

PARKER, Sir William, 1st Bart., 1781-1866, Admiral of the Fleet; saw active service in China
The life of Admiral of the Fleet Sir William Parker, Bart. ... / by Augustus Phillimore. London: Harrison, 1876-80. 3 volumes; abridged as: 'The last of Nelson's captains: the life of Sir William Parker ...' London: Harrison, 1891.

PARKER, William Kitchen, 1823-90, anatomist
William Kitchen Parker, F.R.S., sometime Hunterian Professor of Anatomy and Physiology in the Royal College of Surgeons of England: a biographical sketch / by Thomas Jeffery Parker. London: Macmillan, 1893.

PARKES, Sir Harry Smith, 1828-85, diplomat in China in Japan
The life of Sir Harry Parkes, K.C.B., G.C.M.G., sometimes Her Majesty's Minister to China and Japan ... Volume 1: Consul in China / by Stanley Lane Poole. Volume 2: Minister Plenipotentiary to Japan / by Frederick Victor Dickins. London: Macmillan, 1894. 2 volumes. (BL)
-------. Sir Harry Parkes in China ... / by Stanley Lane Poole. London: Methuen, 1901. (NLS)

PARNELL, Charles Stuart, 1846-91, the 'uncrowned king' of Ireland; Irish leader in House of Commons
Charles Stuart Parnell: a memory / by Thomas Power O'Connor. London: Ward, Lock, Downey, 1891. 12mo. (BL)
-------. Charles Stuart Parnell, his love story and political life / by Katharine O'Shea (Mrs Charles Stuart Parnell). London: Cassell, 1914. 2 volumes.
-------. The life of Charles Stuart Parnell, M.P. ... / by Thomas Sherlock ... Dublin: T. D. Sullivan, 1887. (NLS).
-------. The life of Charles Stuart Parnell, 1846-1891 / by Richard Barry O'Brien. London: Smith, Elder, 1898. 2 volumes; in one volume 1910.
and other biographies

PARRY, Charles, 1833-68, naval officer
Memorials of Charles Parry, Commander, Royal Navy / by his brother Edward Parry. London: Strahan, 1870.

PARRY, Sir William Edward, 1790-1855, Rear-Admiral; Arctic explorer
Memoirs of Rear-Admiral Sir W. Edward Parry, Kt., F.R.S. [etc.], late Lieutenant-Governor of Greenwich Hospital / by his son Edward Parry. London: Longman [etc.], 1857.

PARSONS, Benjamin, 1797-1855, Congregational Minister in Gloucestershire
The earnest Minister: a record of the life, and selections from posthumous and other writings, of the Rev. Benjamin Parsons, of Ebley, Gloucestershire. Edited by Edwin Paxton Hood. London: John Snow, 1856. (NLS)

PASLEY, Sir Thomas Sabine, 2nd Bart., 1804-84, Admiral; friend of the Wordsworths
Memoir of Admiral Sir Thomas Sabine Pascoe / by his daughter Louise M. Sabine Pasley. London: E. Arnold, 1900.

PATER, Walter (Horatio), 1839-94, critic

The life of Walter Pater / by Thomas Wright. London: Everett, 1907. 2 volumes.

-------. Walter Pater / by Arthur Christopher Benson. London: Macmillan, 1906. (English Men of Letters series)

PATERSON, Alexander, 1790-1851, Free Church of Scotland home missionary

The missionary of Kilmany, being a memoir of Alexander Paterson. With notices of Robert Edie / by John Baillie. Edinburgh: T. Constable, 1853. (NC)

PATERSON, George, 1801-63, United Presbyterian Minister

Memorials of the Rev. George Paterson, East Linton. With a notice of his life. Edinburgh: William Oliphant, 1864. (NC)

PATERSON, Robert, 1795-1870, Church of Scotland Minister in Orkney

Memoir of Robert Paterson, D.D., Kirkwall / by his brother John Paterson. Edinburgh: Andrew Elliot, 1874. photo.port. (NC)

PATMORE, Coventry (Kersey Dighton), 1823-96, poet

Coventry Patmore / by Edmund Gosse. London: Hodder & Stoughton, 1905. (Literary Lives series)

-------. Memoirs and correspondence of Coventry Patmore / by Basil Champneys. London: G. Bell, 1900. 2 volumes.

PATON, Sir Joseph Noel, 1821-1901, H.M. Limner for Scotland

The life and work of Sir Joseph Noel Paton, R.S.A., LL.D., Her Majesty's Limner for Scotland ... / by H. T. Story. London, 1894. 4to. (B&J)

PATTERSON, Alexander Simpson, 1805-85, Church of Scotland Minister

Memoir of Alexander S. Patterson, D.D., Glasgow / by George Philip. With selections from his unpublished writings. Edinburgh: Andrew Elliot, 1886. photo.port. (NC)

PATTESON, Henry Staniforth, 1816-98, Norwich brewer; philanthropist

Henry Staniforth Patteson: a memoir / by Isabella Katharine Patteson. [Edited by Henry Oake]. Norwich: Agas H. Goose, 1899. (NLS)

PATTESON, John Coleridge, 1827-71, first missionary Bishop of Melanesia

Bishop Patteson, missionary bishop and martyr / by Edwin Palmer. London: S.P.C.K., [1871?]. 12mo. (NLS)

-------. Bishop Patteson, the martyr of Melanesia / by Jesse Page. 2nd edition. London: S. W. Partridge, [1891?].

-------. In memoriam: Bishop Patteson / by Charlotte Mary Yonge. London: William Skeffington, 1872. 12mo. (Reprinted with additions from the 'Literary Churchman') (NLS)

-------. Life of John Coleridge Paterson, missionary Bishop of the Melanesian Islands / by Charlotte Mary Yonge. London: Macmillan, 1874. 2 volumes. (NC); revised as: 'Sketches of the life of Bishop Patteson in Melanesia ...' London: S.P.C.K., 1873.

PATTISON, Mark, 1813-84, Rector of Lincoln College, Oxford

Recollections of Pattison / by Lionel Arthur Tollemache. Printed for private circulation. London: C. F. Hodgson, 1885. (Reprinted with additions from the 'Journal of Education')

PAUL, Robert, 1788-1866, Scottish religious bank manager

Memoir of Robert Paul, F.R.S.E., late Manager of the Commercial Bank of Scotland / by Benjamin Bell ... Edinburgh: John Maclaren, 1872.

PEACE, Charles Frederick, 1832-79, executed murderer

Life and examination of Charles Peace, charged with the Bannercross Murder. London: G. Parkess, [1878]. (Police News edition)

-------. The master criminal: the life story of Charles Peace. [1910]; reprinted London: C.A. Pearson, 1930; and other reprints. (BL)

PEACEFUL, William, 1810-77, Primitive Methodist Minister
Memorials of an earnest life, or records of the Rev. William Peaceful, Primitive Methodist Minister / by Isaac Dorricott. London: Elliot Stock, [1878]. 12mo. (NLS)

PEARCE, William, 1809-91, Methodist; chemical manufacturer
William Pearce, of Poplar: a chapter in the history of Methodism in East London / by Caesar Caine ... London: Charles H. Kelly, [1894]. (NLS)

PEARSE, Horatio, 1813-62, Wesleyan missionary in South Africa
The earnest missionary: a memoir of the Rev. Horatio Pearse, late General Superintendent of the Wesleyan Missions in the Port-Natal District, South-Eastern Africa / by Thornely Smith. London: Wesleyan Mission House, 1864. (NLS)

PEASE, Henry, 1807-81, Quaker; railway pioneer
Henry Pease: a short story of his life. [By Mary Henry Pease]. 2nd edition. London: Headley, 1898. photo.port.

PEASE, John Beaumont, d.1873 aged 70, Quaker philanthropist
In memoriam: John Beaumont Pease, who died November 12th 1873. Printed for private circulation. [1874?]. photo.port.

PEASE, Joseph, 1799-1872, Quaker; railway promoter; M.P.;
Joseph Pease: a memoir. Darlington: Harrison, Penney, [1872]. 4to. (Reprinted from the 'Northern Echo') (NLS)

PENGELLY, William, 1812-94, geologist
A memoir of William Pengelly, of Torquay, F.R.S., geologist. With a selection from his correspondence. Edited by his daughter Hester Pengelly ... London: John Murray, 1897.

PENNEFATHER, William, 1816-73, clergyman
The life and letters of the Rev. William Pennefather, B.A.. Edited by Robert Braithwaite. London: John F. Shaw, [1878].
-------. Recollections of the earlier years of our beloved friend William Pennefather / by S.W.C.. Kendal: printed by W. F. Robson, [1873]. 16mo. (B&J)

PERIGAL, Henry, 1801-98, astronomer; scientist
Henry Perigal, F.R.A.S., &c.: a short record of his life and works ... [By his brother Frederick Perigal]. London: Bowles, [1901].

PERRY, Stephen Joseph, 1833-89, Jesuit; astronomer
Father Perry, the Jesuit astronomer / by Aloysius Laurence Cortie. 2nd edition. London: Catholic Truth Society, 1890. (BL)

PETO, Sir Samuel Morton, 1st Bart., 1809-89, railway contractor; M.P.
Sir Morton Peto: a memorial sketch / by Henry Peto. Printed for private circulation. London: E. Stock, 1893. (B&J)

PETRIE, George, 1789-1866, archaelogist of Celtic Ireland
Eloge on the late George Petrie ... delivered at a Meeting of the Royal Irish Academy ... 1866 / by Charles Graves. Dublin: M.H. Gill, 1866. Pamphlet. (BL)
-------. The life and labours in art and archaeology of George Petrie, LL.D., M.R.I.A. ... / by William Stokes. London: Longmans, Green, 1868.

PETTIE, John, 1839-93, historical artist
John Pettie, R.A., H.R.S.A., / by Martin Hardie. London: A. & C. Black, 1908.

PETTY, John, d.1868, Primitive Methodist Minister
The life and labours of the Rev. John Pettie, late Minister of the Primitive Connection
... / by James Macpherson. London: George Lamb, 1870. (B&J)

PHELPS, Samuel, 1804-78, actor
The life and life-work of Samuel Phelps / by his nephew William May Phelps and John
Forbes-Robertson. London: Sampson Low [etc.], 1886. 2 volumes. (NLS)
-------. Memoirs of Samuel Phelps / by John Coleman [&] Edward Coleman. London:
Rivington, 1886.

PHELPS, William Whitmarsh, 1797-1867, Archdeacon of Carlisle
The life of the Reverend and Venerable William Whitmarsh Phelps, M.A. ..., late
Vicar of Appleby, Westmorland, and sometime Incumbent of Trinity Church, Reading / by
Charles Hole. Reading: Barcham & Beecroft, 1871-73. 2 volumes. (NLS)

PHILIP, John, 1775-1851, Scottish Congregational missionary in South Africa 'The
   Wilberforce of the Hottentots'
The Elijah of South Africa, or the character and spirit of the late John Philip, D.D.,
unveiled and vindicated / by Robert Philip. London: John Snow, 1851. 12mo. (NLS)

PHILLIPPO, James Mursell, 1798-1879, Baptist missionary in Jamaica
Life of James Mursell Phillippo, missionary in Jamaica / by Edward Bean Underhill.
London: Yates & Alexander, 1881. (NLS)

PHILLIPPS, Edward Thomas March, 1784-1859, Leicestershire clergyman
Records of the Ministry of the Rev. E. T. March Phillipps, M.A., for fifty years Rector
of Hathern in the County of Leicester [etc.]. [By Lucy F. March Phillipps]. London:
Longman [etc.], 1862. (NLS)

PHILLIPS, James Garland, 1828-60, missionary in Patagonia
The missionary martyr of Tierra del Fuego, being the memoir of Mr J. Garland
Phillips, late catechist of the Patagonian or South American Missionary Society / by his
brother G. W. Phillips. London: Wertheim, Macintosh and Hunt, 1861. (NLS) (BL - reads:
'The military martyr ...')

PHILLIPS, James Liddell, 1840-95, missionary in India
Dr J. L. Phillips, missionary to the children of India: a biographical sketch / by his
widow [Mary Sayles Phillips]. Completed and edited by W. J. Wintle. London: Sunday
School Union, [1898]; abridged as: 'The story of Dr. J. L. Phillips ...' 1900. (NUC)

PHILLIPS, Watts, 1825-74, dramatist; designer
Watts Phillips, artist and playwright / by Emma Watts Phillips. London: Cassell, 1891.

PHILLPOTTS, Henry, 1778-1869, Bishop of Exeter 1830-69
The life, times and writings of the Right Rev. Dr. Henry Phillpotts, Lord Bishop of
Exeter / by Reginald Neale Shutte. London: Saunders & Otley, 1863. Volume 1 (all
published).

PHIPPS, Pownoll, 1780-1858, soldier with East India Company
The life of Colonel Pownoll Phipps, K.C., H.E.I.C.S.. With family records / by
Pownoll W. Phipps. Printed for private circulation. London: R. Bentley, July 1894. (B&J)

PICTON, Sir James Allanson, 1805-89, Liverpool architect and benefactor
Sir James A. Picton: a biography / by his son James Allanson Picton. Liverpool: Gilbert
G. Walmsley, 1891.

PIGOTT, Richard, 1828?-99, Irish journalist; forger
   Recollections of Richard Pigott / by James O'Connor. Dublin: H. M. Gill, 1889. (BL)

PIKE, John (Deodatus) Gregory, 1784-1854, Baptist Minister
   A memoir and remains of the late Rev. John Gregory Pike, author of 'Persuasives to early piety', etc.. Edited by his sons John Baxter [Pike] and James Carey Pike. London: Jarrold, 1855.

PILKINGTON, George Lawrence, 1865-97, martyred Irish lay missionary in Uganda
   Pilkington of Uganda / by Charles Forbes Harford-Battersby ... London: Marshall, [1898].

PILKINGTON, Lionel Scott, 'Jack Hawley', 1828-75, eccentric; huntsman; buried in hunting costume among his cattle
   The life and eccentricities of Lionel Scott Pilkington, alias Jack Hawley of Hatfield, near Doncaster ... Doncaster: Edward Dale, [1876]. 12mo. (B&J)

PILLANS, James, 1778-1864, Rector of Edinburgh High School; Professor of Humanity and Laws, Edinburgh University
   Memoir of the late James Pillans, LL.D., Professor of Roman Literature in the University of Edinburgh. By an old student [A.R.]. Edinburgh: Maclachlan & Stewart, 1869. Pamphlet. (NLS)
   -------. Memoir of the late James Pillans, LL.D., Professor of Roman Literature in the University of Edinburgh / by James Gibson. [Edinburgh: Otto Schultz, 1904].

PILLANS, John, 1824-91, Congregationalist Minister
   John Pillans, his life and thought. Edited by James Stark. Huntley: William Simpson [etc.], 1891. (B&J)

PIRIE, William Robinson, 1804-85, Church of Scotland Minister; Principal of Aberdeen University; Moderator
   William Robinson Pirie: in memoriam. [By Penelope Pirie]. [Aberdeen: University Press, 1888]. photo.port. (NC)

PITMAN, Sir Isaac, 1813-97, inventor of phonography
   A biography of Isaac Pitman (inventor of phonography) / by Thomas Allen Reed. London: Griffith, Jones, Oakden & Welsh, [1890].
   -------. The life of Sir Isaac Pitman (inventor of phonography) / by Alfred Baker. London: Sir Isaac Pitman, 1908; 2nd edition. 1930.

PLACE, Francis, 1771-1854, radical reformer
   The life of Francis Place, 1771-1854 / by Graham Wallace. London: Longmans, Green, 1898; and many later reprints.

PLAYFAIR, Sir Hugh Lyon, 1786-1861, Indian army; Provost of St Andrews and conserver of the town
   Biographical sketch of the late Lieutenant-Colonel Sir Hugh Lyon Playfair, Provost of St Andrew's from 1842-1861 / by David Louden. St. Andrews, 1874. (NLS)
   -------. Memoirs of Sir Hugh Playfair, LL.D., J.P., &c., Lieutenant-Colonel Bengal Artillery, Provost of St Andrew's ... St. Andrew's: M. Fletcher, 1861.

PLAYFAIR, Sir Lyon, 1st Baron Playfair, 1818-98, scientific civil servant; M.P.
   Memoirs and correspondence of Lyon Playfair, first Lord Playfair of St. Andrews ... / by Thomas Wemyss Reid. London: Cassell, 1899; reprinted with introduction by Colin Armstrong. Jemimaville (Scotland): P.M. Pollak, 1976. (250 copies)

PLUNKET, William Conyngham, 1st Baron Plunket, 1764-1854, Irish M.P. and successor of Henry Grattan 'as champion of the Roman Catholic claims'; Lord Chancellor of Ireland

The life, letters and speeches of Lord Plunket / by his grandson David Plunket ... London: Smith, Elder, 1867. 2 volumes.

PLUNKET, William Conyngham, 4th Baron Plunket, 1828-97, Irish Anglican Archbishop of Dublin
William Conyngham Plunket, fourth Baron Plunket and sixty-first Archbishop of Dublin: a memoir / by Frederick Douglas How. London: Isbister, 1900.

POCOCK, Thomas, d.1891, worker for the blind
Pensions for the blind poor: memoir of Mr Thomas Pocock, late Hon. Secretary of the Royal Blind Pension Society. London: Office of the Society, [1891?]. 32mo. Pamphlet. (B&J)

POLLARD, Benjamin, 1792-1860, Methodist
The sucessful class leader exemplified in a memorial of Mr Benjamin Pollard / by Robert Plummer. London: Simpkin Marshall, 1861. (NLS)

POLLOCK, Sir George, 1st Bart., 1786-1872, Field-Marshal
The life and correspondence of Field Marshal Sir George Pollock, Bart. (Constable of the Tower [of London]) / by Charles Rathbone Low. London: W. H. Allen, 1873. photo.port.

POLLOCK, James Samuel, 1834-95, Anglo-Catholic priest
Father Pollock and his brother [Thomas Benson Pollock], mission priests of St Alban's, Birmingham. London: Longmans, Green, 1911. (B&J)

POLLOCK, Thomas Benson see **POLLOCK, James Samuel**

POMEROY-COLLEY, Sir George, 1835-81, Major-General in Africa
The life of Sir George Pomeroy-Colley, K.C.S.I., C.B., C.M.G., 1835-1881 ... / by William Francis Butler. London: John Murray, 1899.

POOL, Francis, n.d., religious biography
Francis Pool, a name which is written in heaven: memorials of a beloved father / by his daughter ... London: W. H. & L. Collingridge, [1890]. (B&J)

POOL, Robert, 1832-95, Scottish Congregational Minister
The life story of a village pastor (Robert Pool) / related by his son John J. Pool. London: James Clarke, 1897. (NLS)

POOLE, George, 1806-89, clergyman
Found ready: memorials of the Rev. George Poole, B.A., late Vicar of Burntwood / by his niece Sarah Mason. London: J. Nisbet, 1890.

POOLE, James, 1804-86, artist
James Poole. Born January 29th 1804 - Died March 14 1886: [a memoir]. Sheffield, 1886. (Reprinted from the 'Sheffield Independent') (BL)

POORE, John Legg, 1816-67, missionary in Australia
Ever working, never resting: a memoir of John Legg Poore / by John Corbin. London: Hodder & Stoughton, 1874. photo.port.

PORTREY, Richard Watson, 1849-69, religious student
The successful student early crowned: memorials of Richard Watson Portrey. [By Joseph Portrey]. London: Hamilton, Adams, 1869. (NUC)

POURIE, John, 1824-67, Free Church missionary in Calcutta
Memorials of the Rev. John Pourie, late Minister of the Free Church of Scotland in Calcutta. [By George Smith, LL.D.]. Published for the Congregation. Calcutta: W.

Newman, 1869. (NC)

POWELL, Walter, 1822-68, businessman
The thorough businessman: memoirs of Walter Powell, merchant, Melbourne and London / by Benjamin Gregory. London: Strahan, 1871.

PRATT, John, b.1756, centenarian; plant colletor
Notices of the life of John Pratt, now in his 106th year / by Thomas F. Tyerman. Oxford: Slatter & Rose, 1861. Pamphlet. (NLS)

PRESTWICH, Sir Joseph, 1812-96, geologist
Life and letters of Sir Joseph Prestwich, M.A., D.C.L., F.R.S., formerly Professor of Geology in the University of Oxford. Written and edited by his wife [Grace Anne Prestwich]. Edinburgh: W. Blackwood, 1899.

PRIMROSE, Hon. Edward Henry, 1848-85, soldier killed in Africa
In memory of Colonel the Honourable Edward Henry Primrose / by Catherine, Duchess of Cleveland. [1887?]. (BL)

PRINCE, John Critchley, 1808-66, dissipated Manchester poet
The life of John Critchley Prince / by Robert Alexander Douglas Lithgow. Manchester: Abel Heywood, 1880.

PRITCHARD, Charles, 1808-93, Professor of Astronomy, Oxford University
Charles Pritchard, D.D., F.R.S. [etc.], late Savilian Professor of Astronomy in the University of Oxford: memoirs of his life / compiled by his daughter Ada Pritchard ... London: Seeley, 1897.

PROUT, Samuel, 1783-1852, topographical water-colourist
Samuel Prout, artist / by J. Hine. [1880?]. Pamphlet. (Reprinted from the 'Transactions of the Plymouth Institution') (B&J)

PUGH, Philip, d.1871, Primitive Methodist Minister
Memoirs of the life, literary and itinerant labours of the Rev. Philip Pugh / by J. Pritchard. London: George Lamb, 1871. (B&J)

PUGIN, Augustus Welby Northmore, 1812-52, Gothic Architect
Recollections of A. N. Welby Pugin, and his father Augustus Pugin. With notices of their works / by Benjamin Ferrey. London: Edward Stanford, 1861.

PUMPHREY, Stanley, 1837-81, Quaker; ironmonger
Thr young man of God: memoirs of Stanley Pumphrey / by Henry Stanley Newman. Leominster: Orphans' Printing Press, [1882]. (NLS)

PUMPHREY, Thomas, 1802-62, Quaker schoolmaster
Memoir of Thomas Pumphrey, for twenty-seven years Superintendent of Ackworth School. Edited by John Ford. London: A. W. Bennett, 1864.

PUNSHON, William Morley, 1824-81, Wesleyan Methodist
The life of William Morley Punshon, LL.D. / by Frederick William Macdonald. London: Hodder & Stoughton, 1887.
-------. The Rev. W. M. Punshon, M.A.: a sketch of his life [etc.]. London: A. Osborne, 1871. photo.port. (NLS)
-------. William Morley Punshon, the orator of Methodism / by Joseph Dawson. London: C. Kelly, 1906. (Library of Methodist Biography)
-------. William Morley Punshon, preacher and orator, 1824-1881, being a biographical sketch of the late Dr. Punshon ... London: F. E. Longley, 1881. (NLS)

PURVES, David, 1808-83, Free Church Minister

A ministry in the South: memorials of the Rev. David Purves, Maxwellton Free Church. With a biographical sketch / by David Purves [Jun.]. Glasgow: David Bryce, 1884. photo.port.

PUSEY, Edward Bouverie, 1800-82, Tractarian leader; Professor of Hebrew, Oxford University

Dr Pusey / by George William Erskine Russell. London: Mowbray, 1905. (Leaders of the Church, 1800-1900 series)

-------. Life of Edward Bouverie Pusey, D.D. ..., Regius Professor of Hebrew in the University of Oxford / by Henry Parry Liddon. Edited by ... John Octavius Johnston and Robert James Wilson. London: Longmans, Green, 1893-97. 4 volumes.

-------. The story of Dr Pusey's life. [By Maria Trench]. London: Longmans Green, 1907.

PYER, John, 1790-1859, Congregational Minister

Memoirs of the late Rev. John Pyer / by Kate Pyer Russell. London: John Snow, 1865. (NLS)

QUARITCH, Bernard, 1819-99, bookseller

B.Q.: a biographical and bibliographical fragment / by Charles W[yman]. London: Ye Sette of Odd Volumes, 1880. 12mo.

QUICK, Robert Herbert, 1831-91, schoolmaster involved in teacher training

Life and remains of the Rev. R. H. Quick. Edited by Francis Storr. Cambridge: University Press, 1899.

RABAN, John, 1773-1851, Independent Minister; poet

The aged pilgrim and his songs, or memoir and poetical remains of the Rev. John Raban / by Thomas Ray. London: Ward, 1852. (NLS)

RADCLIFFE, Reginald, 1825-95; solicitor; evangelist in Canada, Russia & Denmark

Recollections of Reginald Radcliffe / by his wife [Jane Radcliffe]. London: Morgan & Scott, [1896].

RAFFLES, Thomas, 1788-1863, Liverpool Independent Minister

Memoirs of the life and ministry of the Rev. Thomas Raffles, D.D., LL.D. / by Thomas Stamford Raffles. London: Jackson, Walford & Hodder, 1864.

RAGLAND, Thomas Gajetan, 1815-58, Anglican missionary in India

A memoir of the Rev. Thomas Gajetan Ragland ..., itinerating missionary of the Church Missionary Society in North Tinnevelly, South India ... / by Thomas Thomason Perowne. London, 1861. (NUC)

-------. Memorial of the Rev. Thomas Gajetan Ragland / by H.V. [i.e. Henry Venn]. London: Seeley, Jackson & Halliday, 1859. Pamphlet. (Cambridge University Church Missionary Association, Occasional Papers, No. 2) (BL)

RAIKES, Henry Cecil, 1838-91, M.P.; Postmaster-General

The life and letters of Henry Cecil Raikes, late Her Majesty's Post-Master General / by Henry St John Raikes. London: Macmillan, 1898. (BL)

RALEIGH, Alexander, 1817-80, Congregational Minister; noted preacher; travel writer
Alexander Raleigh: records of his life. Edited by Mary Raleigh. Edinburgh: A. & C. Black, 1881.

RAMSAY, Sir Andrew Crombie, 1814-91, Scottish Director-General of the Geological Survey
Memoir of Sir Andrew Crombie Ramsay / by Archibald Geikie. London: Macmillan, 1893.

RAMSAY, Edward Bannerman (Burnett), 'Dean Ramsay', 1793-1872, Episcopalian Dean of Edinburgh
Memorials and recollections of the Very Rev. Edward Bannerman Ramsay, LL.D., F.R.S.E., Dean of Edinburgh / by Charles Rogers. London: Charles Griffin, 1873. (NLS)

RAPER, James Hayes, 1820-97, temperance worker
A brief memoir of James Hayes Raper, temperance reformer, 1820-1897 / by J. Deane Hilton. London: Ideal Publishing Union, 1898.

RATTENBURY, John, 1806-79, Wesleyan Minister
The Rev. John Rattenbury: memorial sketch / by Gervase Smith. And memorial sermon / by William Morley Punshon. London: Wesleyan Conference Office, 1880.
--------. The Rev. John Rattenbury: memorials. Edited by his son H. Owen Rattenbury. 2nd revised and enlarged edition. London: T. Woolner, 1884.

RAWLE, Richard, 1812-89, Anglican Bishop of Trinidad and West Indies 1872-88
Bishop Rawle: a memoir / by his executors George Mather and Charles John Blagg. London: Kegan Paul, Trench, Trubner, 1890.

RAWLINSON, Sir Henry Creswicke, 1st Bart., 1810-95, Assyriologist; Major-General
A memoir of Major-General Sir Henry Creswicke Rawlinson, Bart., K.C.B., F.R.S. [etc.] / by George Rawlinson ... London: Longmans, Green, 1898.

READE, Charles, 1814-84, novelist and dramatist
Charles Reade as I knew him / by John Coleman. London: Traherne, 1903.
-------. Charles Reade, dramatist, novelist, journalist: a memoir / compiled chiefly from his literary remains by Charles L. Reade and Compton Reade. London: Chapman & Hall, 1887. 2 volumes.

REED, Andrew, 1787-1862, philanthropist working with orphans, incurables and the mentally ill; Independent Minister
Memoirs of the life and philanthropic labours of Andrew Reed, D.D.. With selections from his journals. Edited by his sons Andrew and Charles (James) Reed. London: Strachan, 1863.

REED, Sir Charles, 1819-81, Chairman of London School Board
Memoir of Sir Charles Reed / by his son Charles Edward Baines Reed. London: Macmillan, 1883.

REED, William, 1800-58, Bible Christian Minister
Memoir of William Reed, Bible Christian Minister / by James Thorne. Shebbear: J. Thorne, 1869.

[REES, Arthur Augustus], 1815-84, naval officer; religious writer & pastor
Memoirs of Arthur Augustus Rees, Minister of the Gospel at Sunderland / by William Brockie. Sunderland: Hills, 1884. (NLS)
-------. The midshipman and the minister, the quarter-deck and the pulpit. [By James

Everett]. London: Hamilton, Adams, 1867. 12mo. (B&J)

REES, Henry, 1798-1869, Welsh Calvinist Methodist leader
Life and letters of Henry Rees / compiled and translated by his grand-daughter Annie Mary Davies, from his memoirs published in Welsh by Owen Thomas. For private circulation only. Bangor: Jarvis and Foster, 1905. (Welsh memoir published in 1890)

REEVE, Henry, 1813-95, editor of 'Edinburgh Review' 1855-95
Memoirs of the life and correspondence of Henry Reeve, C.B., D.C.L. / by John Knox Laughton. London: Longmans, Green, 1898. 2 volumes.

REEVES, (John) Sims, 1818-1900, tenor singer
The life and artistic career of Sim Reeves / by Sutherland Edwards. London: Tinsley, [1881]. photo.port. (NLS)

REEVES, William, 1779-1852, Lambeth Methodist layman
Father Reeves, the Methodist class leader: a brief account of Mr William Reeves, thirty-four years a class leader in the Wesleyan Methodist Society, Lambeth / by Edward Corderoy. London: Hamilton, Adams, 1853. 12mo.

REEVES, William, 1815-92, Irish Anglican Bishop; President of Royal Irish Academy
Life of the Right Rev. William Reeves, D.D., Lord Bishop of Down, Connor and Dromore ... / by Mary Catharine Ferguson. Dublin: Hodges, Figgis, 1893.

REID, James, 1832-?94, Glasgow locomotive manufacturer; on Glasgow Town Council
In memoriam: James Reid, of 10 Woodside Terrace, Glasgow, and of Auchterarder, Perthshire. [Glasgow: University Press, 1894]. (B&J)

REID, (Thomas) Mayne, 1818-83, novelist
Captain Mayne Reid: his life and adventures / by Elizabeth Reid, his widow. Assisted by Charles H. Coe. London: Greening, 1900. (NLS)

REITH, Archibald, 1810-94, schoolmaster in Aberdeen
Dr Archibald Reith: biography and selections from his writings / by George M. Reith. Aberdeen: William Jolly, 1898. (NC)

RENTON, Henry, 1804-77, United Presbyterian Minister
Memorials of the Rev. Henry Renton, M.A., being funeral sermons, biographical notices, pulpit and press tributes, &c.. Kelso: J. & J.H. Rutherfurd, 1877. 12mo. (NC)

REYNOLDS, Henry, d.1869, clergyman; at Oxford University
A memoir of the Rev. Henry Reynolds, B.D., formerly Fellow and Tutor of Jesus College, Oxford. [By Charles Williams]. Oxford: printed by E. Baxter, 1870. Pamphlet. (B&J)

REYNOLDS, Henry Robert, 1825-96, Congregational Minister; editor
Henry Robert Reynolds, D.D.: his life and letters. Edited by his sisters. London: Hodder & Stoughton, 1898.

REYNOLDS, Sir John Russell, 1st Bart., 1828-96, doctor
In memoriam: Sir J. Russell Reynolds, Bart., M.D., F.R.S. [etc.], President of the British Medical Association ... 1896. Pamphlet. (B&J)

RHIND, Alexander Henry, 1833-63, Scottish historian; founded the Rhind Lectures
Memoir of Alexander Henry Rhind, of Sibster / by John Stuart. Edinburgh: printed by Neill, 1864. (NC)

RHODES, James, d.1873 aged 68, domestic biography of Yorkshire businessman and worthy

In affectionate remembrance of James Rhodes, timber merchant, Bradford and West Hartlepool, who passed to his rest Feb. 13th 1873, in the 69th year of his age. [1873]. 12mo. photo.port. (B&J)

RHODES, William, 1792-1856, Baptist Minister
Power in weakness: memorials of the Rev. William Rhodes, of Damerham / by Charles Stanford. London: Jackson & Walford, 1858. (NC)

RICE, Benjamin, 1814-88, missionary in India
Benjamin Rice, or fifty years in the Master's service / by his son Edward Peter Rice. London: Religious Tract Society, [1889]. (NLS)

RICHARD, Henry, 1812-88, Welsh pacifist M.P.; 'the leading Nonconformist of the 1860s'
Henry Richard, M.P.: a biography / by Charles Septimus Miall. London: Cassell, 1889.
-------. Memoirs of Henry Richard, the apostle of peace / by Lewis Appleton. London: Trubner, 1889.

RICHARDSON, Charles, 1791-1864, Wesleyan local preacher
The peasant preacher: memorials of Mr Charles Richardson, a Wesleyan evangelist, commonly known as the 'Lincolnshire Thrasher' ... / by John E. Coulson. 2nd edition. London: Hamilton, Adams, 1866. (NLS)

RICHARDSON, Sir John, 1787-1865, naturalist; arctic explorer
The life of Sir John Richardson, C.B., LL.D. [etc.], Inspector of Naval Hospitals and Fleets / by John McIlraith. London: Longmans, Green, 1868. (NUC)

RICHMOND, Sir Charles Gordon Lennox, 5th Duke of, 1791-1860, soldier; racehorse owner
Memoir of Charles Gordon Lennox, fifth Duke of Richmond. [By William Pitt Lennox]. London: Chapman & Hall, 1862.

RICKMAN, George, n.d., temperance worker
George Rickman: a biographical sketch / by William White. Reading: George Lovejoy, [1875]. Pamphlet. (B&J)

[RIDDELL, William Easton], d.1883, religious footballer
A bright sunset, or recollections of the last days of a young football player. [By Mrs Charles Riddell]. 2nd edition. London: Hodder & Stoughton, 1885. photo.port.; and later editions. (NC)

RIDGWAY, John, 1786-1860, Methodist; manufacturer in Potteries
A prince in Israel, or sketches of the life of John Ridgway, Esq. / by James Stacey. London: Hamilton, Adams, 1862. (NLS)

RIPLEY, John, 1822-92, temperance worker and reformer
Teetotaller and traveller: the life and journeyings of the late John Ripley. Edited by Mary Anna Paull Ripley. London: National Temperance Publication Depot, 1893.

RITCHIE, James, 1834-89, Wesleyan Minister & temperance worker
A brief record of the life of the Rev. James Ritchie / by Edward Davidson. London: C. H. Kelley, [1892]. 16mo. Pamphlet. (NLS)

ROBERTS, David, 1796-1864, Scottish artist
The life of David Roberts, R.A. / compiled from his journals and other sources ... by James Ballantine. Edinburgh: A. & C. Black, 1866. 4to. (BL)

ROBERTS, Frederick Charles, 1862-94, Welsh medical missionary in China

Frederick C. Roberts, of Tientsin, or for Christ and China / by [Mary I.] Bryson ... London: H. R. Allenson, 1895.

ROBERTS, Robert Wilson, d.1857 aged 38, in Royal Navy; religious
The service and the reward: a memoir of the late Robert Wilson Roberts, R.N. / by George John Cayley. London: Daniel F. Oakey, 1858. 12mo. (NLS)

ROBERTSON, Frederick William, 1816-53, clergyman
A lecture on Frederick W. Robertson, M.A. ... / by F.A. Noble. Bath: R. E. Peach, 1872. (NLS)
-------. Life and letters of Frederick W. Robertson, M.A., Incumbent of Trinity Chapel, Brighton, 1847-53. Edited by Stopford Augustus Brooke. London: Smith, Elder, 1865. 2 volumes. photo.port.; Library Edition. London: C. Kegan Paul, 1882.
-------. Robertson of Brighton. With some notices of his times and contemporaries / by Frederick Arnold. London: Ward & Downey, 1886.

ROBERTSON, James, 1803-60, Church of Scotland Minister; theologian
Life of the Rev. James Robertson, D.D., F.R.S.E., Professor of Divinity and Ecclesiastical History in the University of Edinburgh / by Archibald Hamilton Charteris. Edinburgh: W. Blackwood, 1863; abridged as: 'A faithful Churchman: memoir of John Robertson, D.D., F.R.S.E., Professor of Church History in the University of Edinburgh' [etc.] / by Archibald Hamilton Charteris. Edinburgh: R. & R. Clark, 1897. (NC)

ROBERTSON, James, 1816-97, United Presbyterian Minister
James Robertson, of Newington: a memorial of his life and work. [By M.H.M.] ... Edinburgh: Andrew Elliot, 1887.

ROBERTSON, John, 1821-75, surgeon; layman
The rest attained: in memoriam John Robertson, M.D., Kelso / by I. Walker. Edinburgh: Maclaren & Macniven, 1877.

ROBERTSON, Thomas William, 1829-71, actor & dramatist
The life and writings of T. W. Robertson / by Thomas Edgar Pemberton. 2nd edition. London: R. Bentley, 1893.

ROBERTSON, William Bruce, 1820-86, United Presbyterian Minister, 'outstanding preacher' & poet
Life of William B. Robertson, D.D., Irvine. With extracts from his letters and poems / by James Brown, *D.D.*. Glasgow: James Maclehose, 1888.
-------. Robertson of Irvine, poet-preacher / by Arthur Guthrie. Ardrossan: Arthur Guthrie, 1889.

ROBINSON, Charles Burt, d.186-, Sunday School worker in Leicester
A tribute to the memory of the late C. B. Robinson, Esq., of Leicester / by James Phillippo Mursell. London: E. Marlborough, 1862.

ROBINSON, William, b.1817, Primitive Methodist missionary in Africa
Life on the ocean, or Captain William Robinson, one of the pioneers of Primitive Methodism in Fernando Po ... / by John Hall. London: F. H. Hurd, 1874. 12mo. (B&J)

ROBSON, (Thomas) Frederick [i.e. **Thomas Robson BROWNHILL**], 1822-64, actor
Robson: a sketch / by George Augustus Sala. London: J. C. Hotten, 1864. (NLS)

RODBARD, Alfred, 'Roddie', 1892-1900, 'wee boy'
Leaves from a little life . By 'Auntie Katie'. London: Marshall, 1900. 16mo. Pamphlet. (NLS)

ROE, Bryan, 1859-96, missionary in West Central Africa
Byran Roe, a soldier of the Cross: missionary travels and adventures in West Central

Africa / by Charles R. Johnson ... London: Charles H. Kelly, 1896. (NUC)

ROEBUCK, Francis Algernon Disney, 1819-85, soldier and actor
   Biography and memorial sketch of Francis Algernon Disney Roebuck, late Capt., 23rd Royal Welch Fusiliers. [By Vane Bennett]. Cape Town, 1885.

ROEBUCK, John Arthur, 1801-79, barrister; radical M.P.
   Life and letters of John Arthur Roebuck, P.C., Q.C., M.P.. With chapters of autobiography. Edited by Robert Eadon Leader. London: E. Arnold, 1897.
   -------. The Right Hon. John Arthur Roebuck, M.P., Q.C.. [By T.F.]. [London: Womens' Printing Society, 1880. Pamphlet. (NLS)

ROGERS, Henry, n.d., child
   The folded lamb, or memorial of an infant son ... / by his mother ... 3rd edition. London: Wertheim & Macintosh, 1857. 12mo. (B&J)

ROGERS, Samuel, 1763-1855, banker; poet; an ugly man
   The early life of Samuel Rogers / by Peter William Clayden. London: Smith, Elder, 1887.
   -------. Samuel Rogers and his circle / by Richard Ellis Roberts. London: Methuen, 1910.
   -------. Samuel Rogers and his contemporaries / by Peter William Clayden. London: Smith, Elder, 1889. 2 volumes. (NLS)

ROGERS, William, 1819-96, clergyman; educational reformer
   Reminiscences of William Rogers, Rector of St Botolph's, Bishopsgate / compiled by Robert Henry Hadden. London: Kegan Paul, Trench, 1888.

ROGERS, William, 1846-86, Irish Presbyterian Minister
   Memoir of the Rev. William Rogers, M.A., LL.D., Minister of Whiteabbey Presbyterian Church, Ireland / by Robert Barron. Belfast: Religious Tract & Book Depot, 1898.

ROMANES, George John, 1848-94, scientist
   The life and letters of George John Romanes, M.A., LL.D., F.R.S., late Honorary Fellow of Gonville and Caius College, Cambridge. Written and edited by his wife [Ethel Romanes]. London: Longmans, Green, 1896.

ROSCOE, Edward, 1864-85, dead Oxford undergraduate; writer of promise
   In memoriam: Edmund Roscoe. Born June 6 1864 - Died Jan. 2 1885. [Oxford, 1885]. Pamphlet. (B&J)

ROSE, Sir George, 1782-1873, Master in Chancery
   In remembrance of the Honourable Sir George Rose ... / by G.W.B[ell]. Printed for private circulation. London, [1877]. (BL)

ROSE, Hugh, c.1807-91, Edinburgh merchant and philanthropist
   Hugh Rose: a sketch of his life. Written for her own children / by one of his daughters. Printed by request for private circulation. [Edinburgh?], 1893. (NLS)

ROSIE, Thomas, 1825-60, Scottish Coast Mission worker
   Coast missions: a memoir of the Rev. Thomas Rosie / by James Dodds. London: J. Nisbet, 1862. (NLS)

ROSS, Alexander Johnstone, 1819-87, Presbyterian Minister then clergyman; critic; friend of Lady Byron
   Memoir of Alexander J. Ross, D.D., Rector of Snelston, Derbyshire ... [By Adelaide Ross]. London: William Isbister, 1888. photo.port. (NLS)

ROSS, Bruno Stewart, d.1882 aged 2 years, little boy

From the valley of the shadow: in memoriam Bruno Stewart Ross, died 19th November 1882, aged two years and five weeks. By Saladin [i.e. William Stewart Ross]. [1882]. Pamphlet. (NLS)

ROSS, Robert, 1840-81, Free Church Minister & temperance advocate
Memorials of the Rev. Robert Ross, East Free Church, Forfar / by John Ross. Edinburgh: Macniven & Wallace, [1882]. (NC)

ROSS, William, 1836-96, Free Church Minister & temperance advocate
In memory of the Rev. William Ross, Cowcaddens. [Edited by A.R.]. Glasgow: printed by Aird & Coghill, [1905]. (NC)
-------. William Ross, of Cowcaddens: a memoir / by his son John Murdoch Ebenezer Ross. London: Hodder & Stoughton, 1905. (NC)

ROSSETTI, Dante Gabriel, 1828-82, Pre-Raphaelite artist & poet
Dante Gabriel Rossetti: a record and a study / by William Sharp. London: Macmillan, 1882. (English Men of Letters series)
-------. Life of Dante Gabriel Rossetti / by Joseph Knight. London: Walter Scott Publishing, 1887. (Great Writers series)
-------. Recollections of Dante Gabriel Rossetti / by Thomas Hall Caine. London: Elliot Stock, 1882. photo.port.

ROUND, Joseph, n.d, Staffordshire collier & Wesleyan
'The Good Master', or light in a dark place, being some particulars of the faithful life of Joseph Round, a Staffordshire collier. With extracts from his letters. By E.A.. London: Morgan & Chase, [1865]. 16mo. (BL)

ROWAN, Arthur Blennerhassett, 1800-61, Archdeacon of Ardfert
Memorial pages to Archdeacon Rowan. Dublin: George Herbert, 1862. 12mo. Pamphlet. (NLS)

ROWLAND, James, d.1892 aged 68, clergyman
Memorials of the Rev. James Rowland, of Henley-on-Thames. By his three daughters ... Reading: Barcham & Beecroft, 1874. photo.port. (B&J)

ROWNTREE, Joseph, 1801-59, Quaker educationalist
Memoir of Joseph Rowntree. Edited by Joseph Stephenson Rowntree. Privately printed. 1859.

ROXBURGH, John, 1806-80, Free Church Minister
Memorials of John Roxburgh, D.D., Minister of St John's Free Church, Glasgow. Edited by George Gordon Cameron. Glasgow: D. Bryce, 1881. photo. port. (NC)

RUDMAN, George, 1832-51, religious biography
The miracle and movement, or the dead raised, the lost found, Hell defeated and grace triumphantly displayed in a brief memoir of George Rudman (of Cheltenham), who fell sweetly asleep in Jesus on Lord's Day, May 11 1851, in the 19th year of his age / by Joseph F. Rudman. London: Houlston & Stoneman, 1852. Pamphlet. (NLS)

RUSKIN, John, 1819-1900, art critic; painter; conservationist; writer; social reformer
John Ruskin / by Frederic Harrison. London: Macmillan, 1902. (English Men of Letters series)
-------. John Ruskin: a sketch of his life, his work and his opinions. With personal reminiscences ... / by Marion Harry Spielmann. London: Cassell, 1900. (NLS)
-------. The life and work of John Ruskin / by William Gershom Collingwood. London: Methuen, 1893. 2 volumes.
-------. The life of John Ruskin / by Edward Tyas Cook. London: G. Allen, 1911. 2 volumes.
-------. Ruskin and his circle / by Ada Earland. London: Hutchinson, 1910. 12mo.

and many other studies of his work and teachings

RUSSEL, Alexander, 1814-76, editor of 'The Scotsman'
Alexander Russel: [a collection of obituary notices]. Printed for private circulation. Edinburgh, 1876.

RUSSELL, Alfred, d.1899 aged 23 years, religious biography
A conquest of grace: an account of the conversion and the Lord's gracious dealings with Alfred Russell, of Wimbledon, who died June 24 1899 aged 23 years ... / by his mother [E. F. Russell]. London: E. Wilsmhurst, [1899]. 12mo. (B&J)

RUSSELL, Julian Watts- see **WATTS-RUSSELL, Giulio**

RUSSELL, Lord John, 1st Earl Russell, 1792-1878, Prime Minister
The life of Lord John Russell / by Spencer Walpole. London: Longmans, Green, 1889. 2 volumes.
-------. Lord John Russell / by Stuart J. Reid. London: Sampson Low, Marston, 1895. (The Prime Ministers of Queen Victoria series)

RUSSELL, John, 1795-1883, Devonshire clergyman; 'The Sporting Parson'
A memoir of the Rev. John Russell and his out-of-door life. [By Edward W. L. Davies]. London: R. Bentley, 1878; new edition as: 'The out-of-door life of ...' 1883.

RUSSELL, Neil Muir, 1825-50, Free Church theological student
The life and remains of Neil Russell, student, Kilmarnock. [Edited by Thomas Main]. Kilmarnock: James Mathie, 1852. (NLS)

RUSSELL & CHENIES, Lord Wriothesley, 1804-86, aristocratic clergyman; temperance worker
Personal recollections of Lord Wriothesley Russell and Chenies / by Francis William Bradney Dunne. London: Elliot Stock, 1888. photo.port. (B&J)

RUSSELL OF KILLOWEN, Sir Charles Arthur Russell, 1st Baron, 1832-1900, Lord Chief Justice
The life of Lord Russell of Killowen / by Richard Barry O'Brien. London: Smith, Elder, 1901.

RUTH, William, d.1864 aged 19 years, religious private soldier in 76th Regiment
A comrade's voice, being a short account of William Ruth, Private in H.M. 76th Regiment of Foot, who fell asleep in Jesus, November 19th 1864, aged 19 years and 4 months. London: S. W. Partridge, 1865. 12mo. (NLS)

RYAN, Vincent William, 1816-86, Irish Anglican Bishop of Mauritius
Bishop Ryan: a memorial sketch / by William Morley Egglestone. Stanhope by Darlington: W. M. Egglestone, 1889. (B&J)

RYDER, Thomas, n.d., Baptist Pastor in Nottingham
Memorials of Thomas Ryder, Pastor of the Baptist Church, Storey Street, Nottingham/ compiled by Robert Dawson. Nottingham: printed by J. Derry, 1875. (B&J)

RYLANDS, John, 1801-88, merchant; founder of the John Rylands Library, Manchester
In memoriam: John Rylands. Born February 7 1801 - Died December 11 1888. [By S.R. Green]. Printed for private circulation. Manchester, 1889. 4to. (B&J)

RYLANDS, Thomas Glazebrook, 1818-1900, wire mill owner
A memoir of Thomas Glazebrook Rylands, of Highfields, Thelwall, Cheshire / compiled by R. D. Radcliffe. Privately printed. 1901. (NLS)

SACHS, Marcus, 1812-69, Free Church Professor of Hebrew and a former German Jew
Marcus Sachs: in memoriam. [By William D. Geddes]. Aberdeen: [printed by Arthur King], 1872. (NC)

SADLER, Thomas, 1822-91, Unitarian; edited Crabbe Robinson's 'Diaries'
Memoir of Thomas Sadler, Ph.D. / by Henry Morley. Address at the funeral, and memorial sermon / by James Drummond. [Privately printed]. [1891]. (B&J)

SAKER, Alfred, 1814-80, African explorer & Baptist missionary
Alfred Saker, missionary to Africa: a biography / by Edward Bean Underhill. London: Baptist Missionary Society, 1884. photo.port.

SALT, Sir Titus, 1st Bart., 1803-76, Yorkshire woollen manufacturer; builder of Saltaire model town
Sir Titus Salt, Baronet: his life and its lessons / by Robert Balgarnie. London: Hodder & Stoughton, 1877. photographic portrait & illustrations.

SANDEMAN, David, 1826-58, Scottish missionary in China
Memoir of the life and brief Ministry of the Rev. David Sandeman, missionary to China / by Andrew Alexander Bonar. London: J. Nisbet, 1861. (NC)

SANDEMAN, Sir Robert Groves, 1835-92, soldier and administrator in India
Colonel Sir Robert Sandeman, his life and work on our Indian frontier: a memoir. With selections from his correspondence and official writings / by Thomas Henry Thornton. London: John Murray, 1895.

SANDERSON, W., n.d., West Yorkshire Primitive Methodist Minister
Life of the Rev. W. Sanderson, Primitive Methodist / by Charles Kendall. London: C. Lamb, 1873. (B&J)

SANDERSON, William, n.d., Liverpool Independent Methodist
Life and labours of William Sanderson, of Liverpool. Wigan: Independent Methodist Bookroom, 1899. (B&J)

SANDWITH, Humphry, 1822-81, army doctor in Middle East
Humphry Sandwith: a memoir / compiled from autobiographical notes by his nephew Thomas Humphry Ward. London: Cassell, 1884.

SAPHIR, Adolph, 1831-91, Hungarian-born Jewish convert to Presbyterianism
'Mighty in the Scriptures': a memoir of Adolph Saphir, D.D./ by Gavin Carlyle. London: John F. Shaw, 1893.

SAVILLE, Jonathan, n.d., Yorkshire Methodist
Memoirs of Jonathan Saville, of Halifax; including his autobiography. [Edited] by Francis Athon West. 4th edition. London: Wesleyan Conference Office, [1857]. 16mo. (B&J)

SAYERS, Tom, 1826-65, boxer
Memoirs of Tom Sayers, Champion of England ... London: William Wright, 1858. 16mo. (NLS)
-------. Tom Sayers, sometime Champion of England, his life and pugilistic career ... Edited by the author of 'Pugilistica' [Henry Downes Miles]. London: S.O. Beeton, 1866. 12mo. (NLS)

SCHETKY, John Christian, 1778-1874, Marine Painter to Queen Victoria
Ninety years of work and play: sketches from the public and private career of John Christian Schetky, late Marine Painter in Ordinary to her Majesty / by his daughter [S.F. L. Schetky]. Edinburgh: W. Blackwood, 1877. (NLS)

SCHOFIELD, Robert Harold Ainsworth, 1851-83, medical missionary in China 1873-83
Memorials of R. Harold A. Schofield, M.A., M.B. (late of China Inland Mission), first medical missionary to Shan-Si, China / chiefly compiled from his letters and diaries by his brother Alfred Taylor Schofield. London: Hodder & Stoughton, 1885. photo.port; new edition. 1898. (NC)

SCHOFIELD, William, n.d., Yorkshire Methodist
William Schofield, an earnest Yorkshire Methodist: his life, his character, its lessons ... / by John Sykes. Huddersfield: Parkin, 1882. (B&J)

SCHOLEFIELD, James, 1789-1853, Greek scholar
Memoirs of the late Rev. James Scholefield, M.A., late Fellow of Trinity College Cambridge, Regius Professor of Greek in the University of Cambridge ... / by his widow [Harriet Scholefield]. With notices of his literary career / by William Selwyn. London: Seeley, Jackson & Halliday, 1855.

SCORESBY, William, 1789-1857, clergyman; scientist; Arctic explorer
The life of William Scoresby / by his nephew Robert Edward Scoresby-Jackson. London: T. Nelson, 1861. (BL)

SCOTT, James, 1796-1860, sheepfarmer
Life of James Scott, of Allanshaw, and pastoral farmer, Ross-shire / by John Thomson. Kelso: J. & J.H. Rutherfurd, 1879.

SCOTT, James, b.1846, Scottish evangelist
James Scott, a labourer for God / by Andrew Alexander Bonar. London: Morgan & Scott, [1885].

SCOTT, Lord John, d.1860, Scottish aristocrat
Memorial of Lord John Scott, who died Jan. 3 1860. [1860]. (NLS)

SCOTT, William, 1813-72, tractarian clergyman
In memoriam: William Scott. [1872]. Pamphlet. (Reprinted from the 'Guardian'). (B&J)

SCOTT, William, d.1869, domestic biography of a Leicester worthy
A loving tribute to the memory of Mr William Scott, of 7, Market Street, Leicester, died Sept. 21st 1869. Printed for private distribution. Northampton, 1870. 12mo. (B&J)

SCOTT, William Affleck, 1862-95, Church of Scotland Missionary in East Africa
A hero of the Dark Continent: memoir of Rev. Wm Affleck Scott, M.A., M.B., C.M., Church of Scotland missionary at Blantyre, British Central Africa / by William Henry Rankine. Edinburgh: W. Blackwood, 1896. (NC)

SEAFIELD, Ian Charles Ogilvie-Grant, 8th Earl of, 1851-84, clan chief
In memoriam Ian Charles, eighth Earl of Seafield, twenty-seventh Chief of the Clan Grant. Born 7th October 1851 - Died 31st March 1884. Inverness: 'Northern Chronicle' Office, [1884].

SEARS, Septimus, 1819-77, religious editor
Memoir of the life and labours of the late Septimus Sears, who was for thirty-five years Minister of the Gospel of Christ at Clifton, Bedfordshire ... London: Houlston, 1880. (NLS)

SEATON, Sir John Colborne, 1st Baron, 1778-1863, Field-Marshal; Governor-General of Canada
The life of John Colborne, Field-Marshal Lord Seaton, G.C.B., G.C.H., [etc.] / compiled from his letters, records of his conversations and other sources by George Charles Moore Smith. London: John Murray, 1903.

SEDDON, Thomas, 1821-56, landscape-painter, especially of Egypt
Memoirs and letters of the late Thomas Seddon, artist / by his brother [John Pollard Seddon]. London: J. Nisbet, 1858. 12mo.

SEDGWICK, Adam, 1785-1873, geologist and opponent of Darwin; Cambridge University
The life and letters of the Reverend Adam Sedgwick, LL.D., D.C.L., F.R.S. [etc.] / by John Willis Clark and Thomas McKenny Hughes. Cambridge: University Press, 1890. 2 volumes: reprinted Farnborough: Gregg, 1970.

SEDGWICK, Joseph, 1797-1853, Brighton Pastor
A memoir of Mr Joseph Sedgwick, late Pastor of the Church assembling in Ebenezer Chapel, Brighton ... [By Samuel Milner]. Brighton: C. A. Johnson, 1853. (B&J)

SEEBOHM, Benjamin, 1798-1871, Quaker
Private memoirs of B[enjamin] and E[sther] Seebohm. Edited by their sons. London: Provost, 1873.

SELLARS, Samuel, 1811-73, Methodist Minister
The quaint preacher, or the life and sayings of Samuel Sellars / by his son [Samuel Sellars]. 2nd edition. London: Andrew Crombie, 1892. (B&J)
-------. Samuel Sellars: memories and remains. [By William Motley Hunter]. London: T. Newton, 1875. (NLS)

SELWYN, George Augustus, 1809-78, Anglican Bishop of New Zealand, then of Lichfield
Bishop Selwyn of New Zealand and Lichfield: a sketch of his life and work. With some gleanings from his letters, sermons and speeches / by George Herbert Curteis. London: Kegan Paul, Trench, 1889.
-------. In memoriam: a sketch of the life of the Right Rev. George Augustus Selwyn, late Bishop of Lichfield ... / by E. A. Curtis. Newcastle: printed by C. Hickson, 1874. (B&J)
-------. Memoir of the life and episcopate of George Augustus Selwyn, D.D., Bishop of New Zealand, 1841-1867: Bishop of Lichfield, 1867-1878 / by Henry William Tucker. London: William Wells Gardner, 1879. 2 volumes. photo. ports.

SELWYN, John Richardson, 1844-98, Anglican Bishop in Melanesia
Bishop John Selwyn: a memoir / by Frederick Douglas How. London: Isbister, 1900.

SETON, Alexander, 1814-52, soldier in Australia; mathematician
A short memoir of the late Lieut.-Col. Alexander Seton, of Mounie, Aberdeenshire. [Printed for private use]. Edinburgh: John Hughes, 1854. (B&J)

SEVERN, Joseph, 1793-1879, painter; with Keats when he died
The life and letters of Joseph Severn / by William Sharp. London: Sampson Low, Marston, 1892.

SEYMOUR, Sir Michael, 3rd Bart., 1802-87, Admiral; M.P.
Memoir of Rear-Admiral Sir Michael Seymour, Bart., K.C.G.. [By Richard Seymour]. Not published. London: printed by Spottiswoode, 1878.

SHAFTESBURY, Anthony Ashley Cooper, 7th Earl of, 1801-85, the foremost philanthropist of the age
The life and work of the seventh Earl of Shaftesbury, K.G. / by Edwin Hodder. London: Cassell, 1887. 3 volumes; one volume edition 1887; reprinted Shannon: Irish University Press, 1971.
-------. A memoir of the Right Hon. Earl of Shaftesbury, K.G. / compiled from original sources under the direction of the editor of the 'Record'. London: 'Record' Newspaper Office, 1885. (BL)
and other popular biographies

SHAIRP, John Campbell, 1819-85, classicist; poet; Principal of St Andrew's University

from 1868-84
Principal Shairp and his friends / by William Angus Knight. London: John Murray, 1888. (NLS)

SHARP, Isaac, 1806-97, Quaker missionary
Isaac Sharp, an apostle of the nineteenth century / by Frances Anne Budge ... London: Headley, 1898.

SHARP, John, 1812-52, Quaker; schoolmaster
Memoir of John Sharp, late Superintendent of Croydon School. [By S. H.]. London: W. & F. G. Cash, 1857. (NLS)

SHARPE, Samuel, 1799-1881, banker; egyptologist
Samuel Sharpe, Egyptologist and translator of the Bible / by Peter William Clayden. London: Kegan Paul, Trench, 1883.

SHARPLES, James, 1825-93, Lancashire blacksmith and artist
James Sharples, blacksmith and artist / by Joseph Baron. Manchester: John Heywood, [1894]. Pamphlet. (NLS)

SHAW, Barnabas, 1788-1857, Wesleyan missionary in South Africa
Barnabas Shaw: the story of his life and missionary labours in Southern Africa ... / by William Moister. London: Wesleyan Conference Office, 1877. (NLS)

SHAW, James, 1826-96, Scottish rural schoolmaster
A country schoolmaster: James Shaw, Tynron, Dumfriessshire. Edited by Robert Wallace. Edinburgh: Oliver & Boyd, 1899. (NLS)

SHAW, John, 1814-79, Yorkshire Methodist
John Shaw, of Pudsey, a man 'mighty in the Scriptures', and 'greatly beloved' / by Alfred Colbeck. London: J.C. Watts, 1890. (NLS)

SHAW, William, 1798-1872, Wesleyan missionary in South-East Africa
Memoir of the Rev. William Shaw, late General Superintendent of the Wesleyan Missions in South-Eastern Africa. Edited by his oldest surviving friend [i.e. William Binnington Boyce]. London: William Nichols, 1874.

SHEE, Sir Martin Archer, 1769-1850, portrait painter; President of the Royal Academy
The life of Sir Martin Archer Shee, President of the Royal Academy, F.R.S., D.C.L. / by his son Martin Archer Shee. London: Longmans [etc.], 1860. 2 volumes.

SHEIL, Richard Lalor, 1791-1851, Irish M.P. and dramatist
Memoirs of the Right Hon. Richard Lalor Sheil / by William Thomas McCullagh Torrens. London: Hurst & Blackett, 1855. 2 volumes.

SHEPPARD, George Edmund, 1841-88, Anglican priest in South Africa
Memorials of a Cowley Father: a short account of the life and work of George Edmund Sheppard, who died at Cape Town, South Africa, on April 28 1888, from the effects of fever contracted while on mission work. London: J. T. Hayes, 1889. Pamphlet. (NLS)

SHERBROOKE, Robert Lowe, 1st Viscount, 1811-92, statesman; Governor-General of Canada
Life and letters of the Right Hon. Robert Lowe, Viscount Sherbrooke. With a memoir of Sir John Cope Sherbrooke [1764-1830], sometime Governor-General of Canada / by Arthur Patchett Martin. London: Longmans, Green, 1893. 2 volumes.
-------. Robert Lowe, Viscount Sherbrooke: [a biography] / by James Francis Hogan. London: Ward & Downey, 1893. (NLS)

SHERMAN, James, 1796-1862, Independent Minister; temperance worker

Memoir of the Rev. James Sherman; including an unfinished autobiography. [Edited] by Henry Allon. London: J. Nisbet, 1863. (NC)

SHEWELL, John Talwin, d.1866 aged 84, poet; Italian traveller; Quaker
Memoir of the late John Talwin Shewell. To which is appended notes of his Italian journey and fugitive poems. [By Elizabeth Shewell]. Printed for private circulation. Ipswich: printed by William Hunt, 1870. 4to. (B&J)

SHREWSBURY, William James, 1795-1866, Methodist missionary in West Indies and South Africa; temperance worker
Memorials of the Rev. William J. Shrewsbury / by his son John Victor Brainerd Shrewsbury. London: Hamiton, Adams, [1867].

SHUTTLEWORTH, Henry Cary, 1850-1900, work with boys' clubs; clergyman
Henry Cary Shuttleworth: a memoir / by George William Erskine Russell. London: Chapman and Hall, 1903.

SIBTHORP, Richard Waldo, 1792-1879, Anglican, then Catholic, then Anglican then Catholic priest
Richard Waldo Sibthorp: a biography told chiefly in his own correspondence ... / by John Fowler. London: W. Skeffinton, 1880. photo. port.

SIDEBOTHAM, Joseph, 1824-85, Manchester botanist; calico manufacturer
Joseph Sidebotham: a memoir / by Leopold Hartley Grindon. Printed for private circulation. Manchester: Palmer & Howe, 1886. photographic portrait & other illustrations.

SIDGWICK, Henry, 1838-1900, educationalist; philosopher
Henry Sidgwick: a memoir. [By Arthur and Eleanor Mildred Sidgwick]. London: Macmillan, 1906.

SIEMENS, Sir (Charles) William, 1823-83, manufacturing electrical engineer
The life of Sir William Siemens, F.R.S., D.C.L., LL.D. [etc.] / by William Pole. London: John Murray, 1888; reprinted Telford: Ironbridge Museum Library, 1986.

SILWOOD, George, 1839-87, soldier; religious biography
George Silwood, of Keswick: a brief memoir and letters of one who was perfected through suffering. London: Hodder & Stoughton, 1888. (NLS)

SIM, Arthur Fraser, 1861-95, African missionary
The life and letters of Arthur Fraser Sim, priest in the Universities' Mission to Central Africa. Preface by George Body. London: U.M.C.A., 1896. (NC)

SIMPSON, David, 1795-1864, Free Church Minister
Memoirs and remains of the Rev. David Simpson, A.M., Minister of Trinity Free Church, Aberdeen / by W. Kinnaird Mitchell. Aberdeen: A. & R. Milne, 1865. photo.port. (NLS)

[SIMPSON, Edward], 1815-80, forger of antiquities
Flint Jack: a short history of a notorious forger of antiquities / by Joseph Stevens ... Reading: printed at the Blagrave Street Steam Printing works, 1894. Pamphlet. (B&J)

SIMPSON, Sir James Young, 1st Bart., 1811-70, doctor who introduced chloroform into regular use; Free Churchman
Memoir of Sir James Y. Simpson, Bart., M.D. [etc.], one of Her Majesty's Physicians for Scotland, Professor of Midwifery in the University of Edinburgh [etc.] / by John Duns. Edinburgh: Edmonston & Douglas, 1873. photo. port.
-------. Memoir of Sir James Y. Simpson, M.D., D.C.L. etc., etc.. With an account of the funeral and funeral sermons. Edinburgh, 1870. Pamphlet. (Reprinted from the 'Daily

Review')

-------. Sir James Y. Simpson / by Eve Blantyre Simpson. Edinburgh: Anderson & Ferrier, 1896. (Famous Scots series)

-------. Sir James Young Simpson and chloroform (1811-1870) / by Henry Laing Gordon. London: Unwin, 1897. (Masters of Medicine series)

SIMPSON, William Overend, 1831-81, Methodist missionary in India
    W. O. Simpson, Methodist Minister and missionary. Early life and life in the home work / by Samuel Wray. Mission life / by Robert Stephenson. Edited by Joseph Bush. London: T. Woolmer, [1886].

SIMPSON, William Sparrow, 1827-97, clergyman
    Memoir of Sparrow Simpson, D.D., Rector of St Vedast's and Sub-Dean of St Paul's Cathedral. Compiled and edited by William John Sparrow Simpson. London: Longmans, Green, 1899.

SINCLAIR, <u>Sir</u> George, <u>2nd Bart.</u>, 1790-1868, M.P; writer; reformer; friend of Byron
    Biographical sketch of the late Sir George Sinclair, of Ulbster, Baronet. [By his brother Alexander Sinclair]. [1868]. Pamphlet. (B&J)

-------. Memoirs of Sir George Sinclair, Bart., of Ulbster / by James Grant. London: Tinsley, 1870. (NLS)

SKINNER, James, 1818-81, clergyman; organised the English Church Union
    James Skinner: a memoir. [By Catherine M. Marsh]. London: Kegan Paul, Trench, 1883.

SLADE, James, 1783-1860, clergyman; educationalist
    Memoir of the Rev. Canon Slade ... / by James Augustus Atkinson. Bolton: Daily Chronicle, 1893. (BL)

SMART, Henry Thomas, 1813-79, organist; composer
    Henry Smart, his life and works / by William Spark. London: William Reeves, 1881. photo.port.

SMEE, Alfred, 1818-77, surgeon; metallurgist; inventor of 'Smee's Battery'
    Memoir of the late Alfred Smee, F.R.S. / by his daughter [Elizabeth Mary Olding]. With a selection from his miscellaneous writings. London: G. Bell, 1878.

SMETHAM, James, 1821-89, unsuccessful painter and essayist
    James Smetham, painter, poet, essayist / by William George Beardmore. London: Charles H. Kelley, [1906]. 12mo. (Library of Methodist Biography)

SMILEY, William, 1830-86, Irish Methodist Minister
    The life and letters of the Rev. William Smiley, LL.D., of the Irish Methodist Conference / by Mary H. H. Smiley. Edited with an introduction by Thomas McCullagh. London: T. Woolmer, 1888.

SMITH, Alexander, 1829-67, Scottish poet & essayist
    The early years of Alexander Smith, poet and essayist: a study for young men, chiefly reminiscences of ten years companionship / by Thomas Brisbane. London: Hodder & Stoughton, 1869. (NC)

SMITH, Atkinson, 1800-52, Primitive Methodist Minister
    The Christian Minister in earnest, or the life of Atkinson Smith / by Charles Kendall. London: Ward, 1854. 12mo. (NLS)

SMITH, Coverdale, n.d., evangelist
    The successful evangelist: memoirs of Mr Coverdale Smith, late of Eston, Yorkshire / by John Stocks. London: Hamilton, Adams, 1870.

SMITH, George, 1824-1901, publisher

George Smith: a memoir. With some pages of autobiography. [Edited by Elizabeth Smith]. For private circulation. London, 1902. (B&J)

SMITH, George, b.1825, Scottish born hermit in the Lake District

The Skiddaw hermit. [By George Middleton]. Ambleside: George Middleton, 1891. Pamphlet. (NLS)

SMITH, George, 1831-95, worker with canal boatmen; manufacturer

George Smith (of Coalville): a chapter in philanthropy. London: Haughton, 1881. (BL)
-------. George Smith of Coalville: the story of an enthusiast / by Edwin Hodder. London: J. Nisbet, 1896. (BL)

SMITH, Gervase, d.1882, Wesleyan Methodist Minister

The Rev. Gervase Smith, D.D.: a memorial volume. Edited by his son Alfred Owen Smith. London: T. Woolmer, 1882.

SMITH, Henry John Stephen, 1826-83, mathematician

Biographical sketches and recollections (with early letters) of Henry John Stephen Smith, M.A., F.R.S.. [By Charles Henry Pearson]. For private circulation. Oxford: Horace Hart, 1894. 4to. (B&J)

SMITH, James, b.18--, Baptist Minister

A narrative of the life and labours of the late Rev. James Smith (Baptist Minister), of Tunbridge Wells / by T. T. Ball ... Ely: Shelton & Tibbitts, 1897. (B&J)

SMITH, James Elimalet, 'Shepherd Smith', 1801-57, universalist; socialist

'Shepherd' Smith the universalist: the story of a mind, being a life of the Rev. James E. Smith, M.A. ... / by William Anderson Smith. London: Sampson Low, Marston, 1892.

SMITH, John, 1823-93, saintly teacher at Harrow School

Recollections and impressions of the Rev. John Smith, M.A., for twenty-five years assistant master at Harrow School / by Edward Davy & Gerald Henry Rendall. London: Smith, Elder, 1913.

SMITH, John Pye-, 1774-1851, Congregational Minister; writer; temperance worker

Memoirs of the life and writings of John Pye Smith, D.D., LL.D. [etc.], late theological tutor of the Old College, Homerton / by John Medway. London: Jackson & Walford, 1853. (NLS)

SMITH, Joseph, b.1765, domestic biography

Brief notices of Joseph and Sarah Smith (with other papers), written and selected for their grandchildren and descendants. London: printed by Richard Barrett, 1854. 4to.

SMITH, Joseph, b.1823, Yorkshire Wesleyan diarist & local preacher

Memoir of Joseph Smith of South Holme, late of Huggate and Riseborough, Wesleyan local preacher. With records from his diary, together with sermons and speeches, from 1823 to 1898. Malton: R. J. Smithson, 1900. (B&J)

SMITH, Malcolm, 1860-91, United Prebyterian Minister, drowned while bathing

In memoriam: Malcolm Smith, B.D., late Minister of Wilton United Presbyterian Church, Hawick, drowned while bathing at Spittal, near Berwick on Friday 21st August 1891. Hawick: W. Henderson, 1891.

SMITH, Reginald Southwell, 1809-95, clergyman in Dorset

Brief memorials of Reginald Southwell Smith, Canon of Salisbury, and for sixty years Rector of West Stafford, Dorset. Born at Sydling St Nicholas, August 18th 1809 - Died at Stafford Rectory, December 28th 1895. Dorchester: 'Dorset County Chronicle', 1896.

SMITH, Richard Baird, 1818-61, engineer in India

Richard Baird Smith, the leader of the Delhi heroes in 1857: private correspondence [with connecting narrative] of the commanding engineer during the Siege ... / by Henry Meredith Vibart. Westminster: A. Constable, 1897. (NLS)

SMITH, Sir Robert Murdoch, 1835-1900, Royal Engineer Major-General; diplomat; archaeologist

The life of Major-General Sir Robert Murdoch Smith, K.C.M.G.. Royal Engineers / by his son-in-law William Kirk Dickson. Edinburgh: W. Dickson, 1901.

SMITH, Southwood see **SMITH (Thomas) Southwood**

SMITH, Thomas Assheton, 1776-1858, sportsman; M.P.

Reminiscences of the late Thomas Assheton Smith, Esq., or the pursuits of an English country gentleman / by John Eardley-Wilmot. London: John Murray, 1860.

SMITH, (Thomas) Southwood, 1788-1861, doctor; sanitary reformer; Unitarian

Dr Southwood Smith: a retrospect / by his grand-daughter Gertrude Lewes. Edinburgh: W. Blackwood, 1898.

SMITH, William, 1816-96, life assurance company manager in Edinburgh; translated Fichte

Memoir of William Smith / by Helen Hardie Smith. Edinburgh: printed by S. Armour, 1912.

SMITH, William (Henry), 1808-72, scholar; critic; author; poet

The story of William and Lucy Smith. Edited by George Spring Merriam. Edinburgh: W. Blackwood, 1889.

SMITH, William Henry, 1825-91, wholesale newsagent; M.P.; First Lord of the Treasury

Life and times of the Right Hon. William Henry Smith, M.P. / by Herbert Maxwell. Edinburgh: W. Blackwood, 1893. 2 volumes; one volume edition as 'Life of ...' 1894.

SMITH, William Lepard, d.1869 aged 74, Baptist layman

Memorials of William Lepard Smith. [Edited by M. E. Smith]. Printed for private circulation. London: printed by Pardon, [1871]. (B&J)

SMITH, William Robertson, 1846-94, dismissed Free Church theologian

The life of William Robertson Smith / by John Sutherland Black and George Chrystal. London: A. & C. Black, 1912.

SMITHIES, Thomas Bywater, 1816-83, editor

T. B. Smithies (Editor of 'The British Workman'): a memoir / by George Stringer Rowe. London: S. W. Partridge, 1884. photo.port.

SMYTHIES, Charles Alan, 1844-94, missionary Bishop of Zanzibar

The life of Charles Alan Smythies, Bishop of the Universities' Mission to Central Africa / by G. W. [i.e. Gertrude Ward]. Edited by Edward Francis Russell. London: U.M.C.A., 1898.

SNEPP, Charles Busbridge, d.1880, clergyman

Scriptural remembrances of a faithful pastor: Reverend Charles B. Snepp, LL.M.. [Edited by Julia A. Snepp]. London: J. Nisbet, 1881. 12mo. photo. port. (NLS)

SOMERSET, Boscawen Thomas George Henry, b. c.1834, clergyman in Wales

A brief memorial of the life and labours of the Rev. Boscawen T.G.H. Somerset, M.A., late Rector of Crickhowel. Bristol: printed by J. Arrowsmith, [189-]. 12mo. (B&J)

SOMERVILLE, Alexander Neil, 1813-89, Free Church missionary in Spain, India & Australia
A modern apostle: Alexander N. Somerville, D.D., 1813-1889 ... / by George Smith. London: John Murray, 1890.

SOPWITH, Thomas, 1803-79, Newcastle mining engineer
A souvenir of Mr Thomas Sopwith ... on his retirement from professional occupations in 1871. By the Editor of the Hexham Courant. [1871]. (BL)
-------. Thomas Sopwith, M.A., C.E., F.R.S. ... With excerpts from his diary of fifty-seven years / by Benjamin Ward Richardson. London: Longmans, Green, 1891. (NLS)

SORTAIN, Joseph, 1809-60, Church of Ireland clergyman
Memorials of the Rev. Joseph Sortain, B.A., of Trinity College, Dublin / by Bridget Margaret Sortain. London: J. Nisbet, 1861. (NLS)
-------. Sortain of Brighton: a review of his life and ministry / by Benjamin Samuel Hollis. London: S.W. Partridge, 1861. (NLS)

SOTHERN, Edward Askew, 1826-81, comedian
A memoir of Edward Askew Sothern / by Thomas Edgar Pemberton. London: R. Bentley, 1889.

SOUTH, John Flint, 1797-1882, surgeon
Memorials of John Flint South, twice President of the Royal College of Surgeons, and Surgeon to St Thomas's Hospital (1841-63) / collected by Charles Lett Feltoe. London: John Murray, 1884. (NLS)

SOUTHEY, <u>Sir</u> Richard, 1808-1901, Governor in South-West Africa
The life and times of Sir Richard Southey, K.C.M.G., etc., formerly Colonial Secretary to the Cape Colony and Lieut.-Governor of the Cape Colony of Griqualand West / by Alexander Wilmot. London: Sampson Low [etc.], 1904.

SOWERBY, Francis, 1803-86, Lincolnshire farmer and Methodist
Memorial sketch of Mr Francis Sowerby, of Aylesby, Grimsby. [London: printed by Hayman & Lilly, c.1886]. 12mo. photo. port. (B&J)

SOYER, Alexis Benoit, 1809-58, the most famous chef of his day
Memoirs of Alexis Soyer ... Compiled and edited by F. Volant and J. R. Warren. London: W. Kent, 1859. (NUC)

SPARLING, John, 1815-90, Lancashire clergyman
Pages from the life of John Sparling, of Petton. Edited by his daughter Emma Florence Cunliffe ... Edinburgh: printed by The Riverside Press, 1904. (NLS)

SPEARS, Robert, 1825-99, Ulster Unitarian
Memorials of Robert Spears, 1825-1899. [By Robert Collyer]. Belfast: Ulster Unitarian Christian Association, 1903.

SPENCER, <u>Hon</u>. George (Ignatius), 1799-1864, aristocratic convert priest
Life of Father Ignatius of St Paul, Passionist (The Hon. and Rev. George Spencer) / compiled chiefly from his autobiography, journal and letters [by Pius Devine]. Dublin: James Duffy, 1866.

SPOOR, Joseph, n.d., Pastor
The earnest preacher: memoirs of the Rev. Joseph Spoor / by E. Hall. 4th edition. London: Joseph Toulmin, [c.1870]. (B&J)

SPROTT, John, 1780-1869, Relief Church Minister; in Canada
Memorial of the Rev John Sprott. Edited by his son George Washington Sprott. Edinburgh: G. A. Morton, 1906. (NC)

SPROULE, Nathaniel, 1830-62, Irish religious biography
A sermon from the grave: memoir of Nathaniel Sproule, who slept in Jesus May 28 1862. [By James R. Dill]. London: William Freeman, 1862. 12mo. Pamphlet. (NLS)

SPURGEON, Charles Haddon, 1834-92, Baptist leader & eminent preacher
From the pulpit to the palm-branch: a memorial of C. H. Spurgeon. Sequel to the sketch of his life entitled 'From the usher's desk to the Tabernacle pulpit ...' London: Passmore & Alabaster, 1893.
-------. From the usher's desk to the Tabernacle puplit: the life and labours of Pastor C. H. Spurgeon / by Robert Shindler. Authorised edition. London: Passmore & Alabaster, 1892.
-------. The life and work of Charles Haddon Spurgeon / by Godfrey Holden Pike. Subscribers Edition. London: Cassell, [1892-3]. 4 volumes. 4to.
-------. The life of the late Charles Hadden Spurgeon / by Charles Ray. London: Isbister [etc.], 1903. (NC)
-------. Pastor C. H. Spurgeon, his life and work to his forty-third birthday / by George John Stevenson. London: Passmore & Alabaster, 1877.
-------. Personal reminiscences of Charles Haddon Spurgeon / by William Williams. London: Religious Tract Society, 1895.
-------. The Rev. C. H. Spurgeon: twelve realistic sketches, taken at home and on the road. By a travelling companion. London: James Clarke, 1877. photo. port. Pamphlet. (NLS)
and other titles

SPURGEON, James Archer, b.1837, brother of C.H. Spurgeon & co-pastor
James Archer Spurgeon, D.D., LL.D., preacher, philanthropist and co-pastor with C. H. Spurgeon at the Metropolitan Tabernacle / by Godfrey Holden Pike ... London: Alexander & Shepheard, 1894.

STACEY, James, 1818-91, Methodist Minister with literary interests
James Stacey, D.D.: reminiscences and memorials / by William John Townsend. London: Hodder & Stoughton, 1891. (NUC)

STAFFORD (born O'BRIEN), Augustus Stafford O'Brien, 1811-57, Irish M.P.
A sketch of character [of A. S. O'B. Stafford]. [By Mayow Wynell Mayow]. London, Dec. 1857. Pamphlet. (B&J)

STANFORD, Charles, 1823-86, Baptist leader
Charles Stanford, memories and letters. Edited by his wife [Jane Stanford]. London: Hodder & Stoughton, 1889.

STANLEY, Arthur Penrhyn, 1815-81, Dean of Westminster
Arthur Penrhyn Stanley, his life, work and teachings / by Grace Atkinson Oliver. 3rd edition. London: Sampson Low [etc.], 1885. (NC)
-------. The life and correspondence of Arthur Penrhyn Stanley, D.D., late Dean of Westminster / by Rowland Edmund Protheroe & George Granville Bradley. London: John Murray, 1893. 2 volumes. *Spine reads: 'Life and letters ...'
-------. Recollections of Arthur Penrhyn Stanley, late Dean of Westminster: three lectures delivered in Edinburgh ... / by George Granville Bradley. London: John Murray, 1883.

STANLEY, Robert Swan, n.d., tax inspector
Memoirs of Robert Swan Stanley, late Collector of Inland Revenue, Liverpool ... [By Thomas Stanley]. London: printed by C. Green, 1875. (B&J)

STARK, Alexander, 1786-1881, Free Church Minister
In memoriam: the Rev. Alexander Stark, M.A., Minister of the Free Church of Scotland. Born 2nd February 1786 - Died 12th August 1881. Printed for private circulation. Glasgow: Gillespie, 1882. (NC)

STARK, Joseph, 1798-1877, Free Church Minister
In memoriam: the Rev. Joseph Stark, M.A., Minister of the Free Church of Scotland. Born 16th January 1798 - Died 24th August 1877. [1877]. (NC)

STARLEY, James, 1830-81, 'father of the cycle industry'
The life and inventions of James Starley, father of the cycle industry. Coventry: William Starley, [1902]. Pamphlet. (NLS)

STAUNTON, Sir George Thomas, 1st Bart., 1781-1859, diplomat; M.P., writer on China
Memorials of the chief incidents of the public life of Sir George Thomas Staunton, Bart. [etc.], one of the King's Commissioners to the Court of Pekin, and afterwards for some time Member of Parliament for South Hampshire, and for the Borough of Portsmouth. Printed for private circulation. London: printed by L. Booth, 1856. (NUC)

STEERE, Edward, 1828-82, Anglican missionary Bishop in Central Africa
A memoir of Edward Steere, D.D., LL.D., third missionary Bishop in Central Africa / by Robert Marshall Heanley. 1888; 2nd revised edition. London: G. Bell, 1890.

STEPHEN, Sir James Fitzjames, 1st Bart., 1829-94, judge and jurist
The life of Sir James Fitzjames Stephen, Bart., K.C.S.I., a Judge of the High Court of Justice / by his brother Leslie Stephen. London: Smith, Elder, 1895.

STEPHEN, John, 1800-81, Free Church Minister
Memorials of a faithful pastor, being a sketch of the life, and a selection from the discourses, of the late Rev. John Stephen, A.M., Free John Knox Church, Aberdeen / by William Selbie. Aberdeen: R. Walker, 1882. photo. port.

STEPHENS, Edward see **JORDAN, Joseph**

STEPHENS, Joseph Rayner, 1805-79, Manchester Chartist and agitator
Life of Joseph Rayner Stephens, preacher and political orator / by George Jacob Holyoake ... London: Williams & Norgate, [1881].

STEPHENS, Prescot William, d.1882, naval officer in China, Africa & South America
Memoir of Captain Prescot William Stephens, R.N., late of H.M.S. 'Thetis' / by Benjamin Arthur Heywood. London: J. Nisbet, 1884. (NLS)

STEPHENSON, Robert, 1803-59, railway & civil engineer
The life of Robert Stephenson, F.R.S., engineer ... / by John Cordy Jeaffreson. London: Longman [etc], 1864. 2 volumes.

STERLING, William, 1811-83, United Presbyterian Minister
Memorials of the Rev. William Sterling, United Presbyterian Church, Coatbridge. Edinburgh: Oliphant, Anderson & Ferrier, 1883. (NC)

STEVEN, David, 1789?-1869, Free Church layman 'who was distinguished from his youth by superior mental endowments'
Memorial of David Steven / by Alexander Auld. Wick: W. Rae, 1874. 12mo. photo.port. (NLS)

STEVENSON, John Frederick, 1833-91, Baptist Minister; in Canada
Memorials of the Rev. John Frederick Stevenson, B.A., LL.B., D.D. / by his wife [M. B. Stevenson]. London: James Clarke, 1891.

STEVENSON, Robert Louis (Balfour), 1850-94, author and traveller
The life of Robert Louis Stevenson / by Graham Balfour. London: Methuen, 1901. 2 volumes; later editions in one volume.
Robert Louis Stevenson / by Margaret Moyes Black. Edinburgh: Oliphant, Anderson & Ferrier, [1898]. (Famous Scots series)

-------. Stevensoniana: an anecdotal life and appreciation of Robert Louis Stevenson ... [Edited] by John Alexander Hammerton. Edinburgh: John Grant, 1907.
and other titles

STEVENSON, William Fleming, 1832-86, Irish Presbyterian Minister
Life and letters of William Fleming Stevenson, D.D., Minister of Christ Church, Rathgar, Dublin / by his wife [Elizabeth Montgomery Stevenson]. London: T. Nelson, 1888.

STEWART, Sir Donald Martin, 1st Bart., 1824-1900, Field-Marshal; Commander-in-Chief 1881-5
Field-Marshal Sir Donald Stewart, G.C.B., [etc.]: an account of his life, mainly in his own words. Edited by George Robert Elsmie. London: John Murray, 1903.

STEWART, James Haldane, 1766-1854, clergyman
Memoir of the life of the Rev. James Haldane Stewart, M.A., late Rector of Limpsfield, Surrey / by his son David Dale Stewart. London: Thomas Hatchard, 1856; 2nd revised edition, 1857.

STEWART, Robert, n.d., missionaries in China
Robert and Louisa Stewart in life and in death ... / by Mary E. Watson (sister of Mrs Stewart) ... London: Marshall Brothers, 1895. (NLS)

STEWART, Sir Robert Prescott, 1825-94, Irish musician and composer
Memoir of Sir Robert P. Stewart, Kt., Mus.Doc., Professor of Music in the University of Dublin (1862-94) / by Olinthus John Vignoles. London: Simpkin, Marshall [etc.], [1898].

STICKLAND, Jasper, d.1867 aged 34 years, Wesleyan; in the glove trade
Christian heroism in death: the experiences of Jasper Stickland, of Milborne Port, who entered into rest June 5th 1867, aged 34 years. For private circulation. London: printed by Hayman Brothers, 1867. 12mo.

STIRLING, James, 1777-1856, temperance worker
The gloaming of life: a memoir of James Stirling / by Alexander Wallace. Glasgow: Scottish Temperance League, [1857]. 12mo; Centenary Edition 1876.

STIRLING, William, 1811-83, United Presbyterian Minister
Memorials of the Rev. William Stirling, United Presbyterian Church, Coatbridge. Edinburgh: Oliphant, Anderson & Ferrier, 1883. (NC)

STOCK, John, 1817-84, Baptist pastor in Huddersfield
Memorial sketch of John Stock, LL.D., Minister of Salendine Nook Chapel, Huddersfield / by Alexander M. Stalker. London: Baptist Tract & Book Society, 1885. (NLS)

STOKES, William, 1804-78, Irish surgeon and medical writer
William Stokes, his life and work (1804-1878) / by his son (Sir) William Stokes. London: T. Fisher Unwin, 1898. (Masters of Medicine Series)

STORY, Robert, 1790-1859, Church of Scotland Minister
Memoir of the life of the Rev. Robert Story, late Minister of Rosneath, Dunbartonshire ... / by Robert Herbert Story. Cambridge: Macmillan, 1862.

STOTT, George, 1835-89, missionary in China
In memoriam: George Stott, of the China Inland Mission. London: Morgan & Scott, [1894]. Pamphlet. (NLS)

STOUGHTON, John, 1807-97, Congregationalist; church historian
A short record of a long life [of John Stoughton] / by his daughter [Georgina King

Lewis]. London: Hodder & Stoughton, 1898.

STOW, David, 1793-1864, Scottish educationalist
Memoir of the life of David Stow, founder of the training system of education / by William Fraser. London: J. Nisbet, 1868. (B&J)

STOWELL, Hugh, 1799-1865, evangelical clergyman in Salford
Hugh Stowell, a life and its lessons / by Charles Bullock. London: 'Home Words' Publishing Office, [1882]. (BL)
-------. Memoirs of the life and labours of the Rev. Hugh Stowell, M.A., Rector of Christ Church, Salford ... / by John Buxton Marsden. London: Hamilton, Adams [etc.], 1868.

STRATFORD DE REDCLIFFE, Stratford Canning, 1st Viscount, 1786-1880, Ambassador to the Ottoman Empire
The life of Lord Stratford / by W. R. Richmond. London: Collins, [190-]. (Collins Wide World Library)
-------. The life of the Right Hon. Stratford Canning, Viscount Stratford de Redcliffe, K.G., G.C.B., D.C.L., LL.D., from his memoirs and private and official papers / by Stanley Lane-Poole. London: Longmans, Green, 1888. 2 volumes; new edition 1890; abridged as: 'Lord Stratford de Redcliffe: a sketch' / by A. L. Lee ... London: J. Nisbet, 1897.

STREADER, William Tolladay, [d.189-], life-saver; customs officer
'To the rescue', being the life of William T. Streader of Her Majesty's Customs, who has probably saved more lives from drowning than any man now living ... / by S. Horton ... London: Thomas Mitchell, [1898]. (B&J)

STREATFIELD, William, d.1860, clergyman
Memoir of the Rev. W. Streatfield, M.A., Vicar of East Ham, Essex, and late Fellow of Trinity College, Oxford / by his daughters [Emily and Henrietta Sophia Streatfield]. Printed for private circulation only. London: printed by Benjamin Pardon, 1869. photo.port. (B&J)

STREET, George Edmund, 1824-81, architect, especially of churches
Memoir of George Edmund Street, R.A., 1824-1881 / by his son Arthur Edmund Street. London: John Murray, 1888. photo.ports.

STUART, Alexander Moody, 1790-1859, Free Church Minister
Alexander Moody Stuart, D.D.: a memoir, partly autobiographical / by his son Kenneth Moody Stuart. London: Hodder & Stoughton, 1899.

[STUNT, George], d.188-, religious soldier killed at Battle of Ingogo, Natal
The life and letters of a soldier / by Eva Travers Evered Poole. 3rd enlarged edition. London: J. Nisbet, 1883. 12mo.

STURGE, Joseph, 1793-1859, Quaker; M.P.; philanthropist
A brief account of the professional life of Joseph Sturge / by his brother Walter Sturge. 1906.
-------. Life of Joseph Sturge / by Alexandrina Peckover. London: Swan Sonnenschein, 1890.
-------. Memoirs of Joseph Sturge / by Henry Richard. London: S. W. Partridge, 1864. photo.port.

STURT, Charles, 1795-1869, soldier; Australian explorer
Life of Charles Sturt, sometime Capt. 39th Regt., and Australian explorer / by Mrs Napier George Sturt. London: Smith, Elder, 1899.

SUCKLING, Robert Alfred, 1818?-51, clergyman
A short memoir of the Rev. Robert Alfred Suckling, M.A., late Perpetual Curate of

Bussage / by Isaac Williams. London: J. Masters, 1852.

SUGDEN, Jonas, d.1857, Yorkshire woollen manufacturer; Methodist
Commerce and Christianity: memorials of Jonas Sugden, of Oakworth House / by Robert Spence Hardy. London: Hamilton, Adams [etc.], 1858.

SULIVAN, Sir Bartholomew James, 1810-90, Admiral; hydrographer
Life and letters of the late Admiral Sir Bartholomew Sulivan, K.C.B., 1810-1890. Edited by his son Henry Norton Sulivan ... London: John Murray, 1896.

SULLIVAN, Alexander Martin, 1830-84, Irish nationalist politician
A. M. Sullivan: a memorial / by Timothy Daniel Sullivan. Dublin: T. D. Sullivan, 1885. Pamphlet. (NLS)

SULLIVAN, Sir Arthur Seymour, 1842-1900, composer; collaborator with Gilbert
Sir Arthur Sullivan: his life and music / by Benjamin William Findon. London: J. Nisbet, 1904.
-------. Sir Arthur Sullivan: life-story, letters and reminiscences / by Arthur Lawrence ... London: James Bowden, 1899.
-------. Souvenir of Sir Arthur Sullivan, M.V.O.: a brief sketch of his life and works / by Walter J. Wells. London: George Newnes, 1901. 4to.

SULLIVAN, Barry, 1821-91, actor
Barry Sullivan and his contemporaries: a histrionic record / by Robert M. Sillard. London: T. Fisher Unwin, 1901. 2 volumes.

SUMMERS, Charles, 1827-78, sculptor
A hero of the workshop and a Somersetshire worthy: Charles Summers, sculptor - the story of his struggles and triumph / by Margaret Thomas. London: Hamilton, Adams [etc.], [1879].

SUMNER, Charles Richard, 1790-1874, Bishop of Winchester
Life of Charles Richard Sumner, D.D., Bishop of Winchester ... during a forty years' episcopate / by George Henry Sumner. London: John Murray, 1876.

SUTCLIFFE, William, n.d, Methodist businessman from Bacup
The closer walk: a memoir of the late William Sutcliffe, Esq., late of Hempsteads, Bacup / by William Lonsdale Watkinson. London: Wesleyan Conference Office, 1876. photo.port. (B&J)

SWAN, William, 1818-94, Professor of Natural Philosophy, St Andrew's University
The Emeritus-Professor: a sketch of the last years of William Swan, LL.D., for some time Professor of Natural Philosophy in the University of St Andrew's / by J.L.G.. Printed for private circulation. Selkirk: G. Lewis, [1901]. (NC)
-------. A Scotch Professor of the old school: a sketch of the life of William Swan, LL.D., Professor of Natural Philosophy in the University of St Andrew's from 1859 to 1890. Glasgow: James Maclehose, 1910. (B&J)

SWANWICK, Frederick, n.d., engineer
Frederick Swanwick: a sketch / by John Frederick Smith. Printed for private circulation. Edinburgh: printed by Morrison & Gibb, 1888.

SYME, James, 1799-1870, 'the greatest living authority in surgery'
Memorials of the life of James Syme, Professor of Clinical Surgery in the University of Edinburgh, Vice-President of the Royal College of Surgeons, Edinburgh [etc.]. [By Robert Paterson]. Edinburgh: Edmonston & Douglas, 1874.

[SYMINGTON, John Macalister], d.1893?, religious boy
A memory [of John Macalister Symington]. London: Marshall, [1893]. 32mo.

Pamphlet. (NLS)

SYMONDS, John Addington, 1840-93, writer; critic; homosexual
John Addington Symonds: a biography compiled from his papers and correspondence / by Horatio Robert Forbes Brown. London: John C. Nimmo, 1895. 2 volumes; in one volume 1903.

[T., Allan Knight], 1877-93, religious boy killed on his bicycle
'I never expected such happiness': the last days of a young cyclist / by Lucy Ann Bennett. London: Marshall, [1897]. 16mo. Pamphlet. (NLS)

TAIT, Archibald Campbell, 1811-82, Archbishop of Canterbury
Archibald Campbell Tait: a sketch of the public life of the late Archbishop of Canterbury / by Augustus Charles Bickley. London: J. Nisbet, 1882.
-------. Life of Archibald Campbell Tait, Archbishop of Canterbury / by Randall Thomas Davidson & William Benham. London: Macmillan, 1891. 2 volumes.
-------. A sketch of the life and work of the Most Rev. Archibald Campbell Tait, Archibshop of Canterbury. London: F. E. Longley, [1882]. Pamphlet. (NLS)

TAIT, Craufurd, d.1878, clergyman son of Archbishop of Canterbury
Catherine and Craufurd Tait, wife and son of the Archbishop of Canterbury. Edited ... by William Benham. London: Macmillan, 1879.

TAIT, Frederick Guthrie, 1870-1900, golfer; killed in Boer War
F. G. Tait: a record, being his life, letters and golfing diary / by John Laing Low. London: J. Nisbet, 1900. (NC)

TAIT, Lawson, 1845-[99?], surgeon; gynaecologist
Lawson Tait: a summary of the life-work of a great surgeon. Compiled by a Birmingham journalist, and carefully revised by a Birmingham surgeon. Birmingham: Holland, [1899]. Pamphlet. (NLS)

TAIT, Peter Guthrie, 1831-1901, physicist
Life and scientific work of Peter Guthrie Tait ... / by Cargill Gilston Knott. Cambridge: University Press, 1911. 4to.

TALBERT, James, d.1893 aged 84, Dundee temperance advocate; bedridden for 64 years
James Talbert, Dundee: recollections of his saintly life and patient sufferings / by J. C. Smith. 2nd edition. Dundee: printed by James P. Mathew, 1895. (NC)

TALBOT, Theodore Mansell, 1839-76, 'one of the most beautiful and saint-like characters of this generation'
Recollections of Theodore Mansell Talbot and his times / by Baldwyn Leighton. Privately printed. London: [printed by Strangeways], 1889. 12mo. (NLS)

TALFOURD, Sir Thomas Noon, 1795-1854, judge and author
A memoir of Mr Justice Talfourd. By a member of the Oxford Circuit. London: Butterworths, 1854. Pamphlet. (Reprinted from the 'Law Magazine') (NLS)

TANNER, Joseph, 1808-67, Minister in Cirencester
The life, diary and letters of the late Joseph Tanner, for twenty-one years Minister of the Gospel at Cirencester. With an obituary / by his widow [Mary Tanner]. Oxford: J. C. Pembrey, 1870. photo.port. (NUC)

TANNER, William, 1815-66, Quaker; in Norway

Memoir of William Tanner / compiled chiefly from autobiographical memoranda. Edited by John Ford. York: William Sessions, 1868. photo.port.

-------. William Tanner / by Matilda Sturge. London: Samuel Harris, [1888]. (Reprinted from the 'Friends' Quarterly Examiner'). Pamphlet. (NLS)

TASKER, James, d.1881, religious boy

In memoriam James Tasker. [By Archibald Hamilton Charteris]. Printed for private circulation. Glasgow: printed by Aird & Coghill, 1882. photo. port. (NC)

TASKER, William, 1811-79, Free Church Minister

Memorials of the Rev. William Tasker, Minister of the West Port Church, Edinburgh. Edinburgh: John Maclaren, 1880. 12mo. photo.port. (NC)

TATHAM, Benjamin, n.d., Baptist (?) Pastor

A brief memoir of Benjamin Tatham, late Minister of the Gospel at Eastbourne. To which is added a selection of letters. And an account of Mrs S. Prodger. London: printed by W. H. Collingridge, [1866]. 12mo. (NLS)

TATHAM, Richard Ecroyd, 1838-61, Quaker Sunday School teacher

The Sabbath School teacher: a memoir of Richard E. Tatham / by John Ford. 2nd edition. York: Thomas Brady, 1861. photo. port. (NLS)

TAYLOR, Reynell George, 1822-86, General in India

Reynell Taylor, C.B., C.S.I.: a biography / by Ernest Cambier Parry. London: Kegan Paul, Trench, 1888.

TAYLOR, Thomas Ebenezer, d.1863 aged 21 years, Lake District poet

A memoir of Thomas Ebenezer Taylor, who died aged 21 years / by his father. With selections from his literary remains. Edited by George Gilfillan. London: H. J. Tresidder, 1864. photo.port. (NLS)

TAYLOR, William (John), 1834-92, navvy with the Evangelization Society

A marvel of Grace: the late Wiliam Taylor, 'The Navvy' (evangelist for 25 years ...). With an introduction / by the late William E. Smith ... 2nd revised edition. Strathaven: printed by N.W. Bryson, 1895. (B&J)

-------. The life and work of the late William Taylor the navvy ... With an introduction / by William E. Smith. Glasgow: printed by John J. Rae, 1892.

TAYNTON, William, ?1805-91, clergyman

Memorials of the Rev. William Taynton, B.A., Caius College, Cambridge, sometime Incumbent of Barton St. David, Somerset / by George Hewitt. Brighton: A. N. Robertson, 1892. (B&J)

TEBAY, Thomas George, n.d., Preston infirmary and workhouse doctor

Memorials of Thomas George Tebay, M.D. / by Charlotte Tebay ... Privately printed. 1893. (B&J)

TELFER, Edward Armstrong, 1822-93, Wesleyan Minister

The successful soul-winner. Incidents in the life of the Rev. Edward Armstrong Telfer, Wesleyan Minister: a memorial and a tribute / by his widow [Annie E. Telfer] ... London: Elliot Stock, 1894. (NLS)

TEMPLETON, John, 1802-86, tenor singer

Templeton and Malibran: reminiscences of those renowned singers. With original letters and anecdotes. Edited by W.H.H.. London: William Reeves, [1880?]. photo.ports.

TENNYSON, Alfred, 1st Baron Tennyson, 1809-92, Poet-Laureate

Alfred Lord Tennyson: a memoir / by his son [Hallam Tennyson]. London: Macmillan,

1898. 2 volumes.

-------. Lord Tennyson: a biographical sketch / by Henry James Jennings. London: Chatto & Windus, 1884. photo.port.

-------. Memoirs of Tennyson / by Henry Drummond Rawnsley. Glasgow: J. Maclehose, 1900.

-------. Notes and marginalia illustrative of the public life and works of Alfred Tennyson, Poet Laureate / by Joseph Huband Smith. London: James Blackwood, [1873]. (B&J)

-------. Tennyson and his friends. Edited by Hallam Tennyson. London: Macmillan, 1911.

TERRELL, Henry, 1807-71, 'Dartmoor philosopher'; 'one of the most amusing of men'
     Harry Terrell, a Dartmoor philosopher: a memoir / by William Frederick Collier. Plymouth: William Brendon, 1896. (NLS)

TERRISS, William [i.e. William Charles James LEWIN], 1847-97, actor
     The life of William Terriss, actor ... / by Arthur J. Smythe. Westminister: A. Constable, 1898. (NLS)

TERROT, Charles Hughes, 1790-1872, Episcopal Bishop of Edinburgh
     Memoir of the late Bishop Terrot / by Edward Bannerman Ramsay. [1872]. 4to. (BL)

THACKERAY, William Makepeace, 1811-63, novelist
     A brief memoir of the late Mr Thackeray / by James Hannay. Edinburgh: Oliver & Boyd, 1864. Pamphlet. (B&J)

-------. Life of William Makepeace Thackerary / by Herman Charles Merivale & Frank Thomas Marzials. London: Walter Scott Publishing, 1891. (Great Writers Series)

-------. Thackeray, the humourist and the man of letters: the story of his life ... / by Theodore Taylor ... London: J. C. Hotten, 1864. photo. port.

-------. William Makepeace Thackeray: a biography ... / by Lewis Melville London: Hutchinson, 1910. 2 volumes.
     and other biographies

THOMAS, David, 1811-75, Congregational Minister
     Memorials of the Rev. David Thomas, B.A., of Bristol. Edited by his son Henry Arnold Thomas. London: Hodder & Stoughton, 1876. (NLS)

THOMAS, John, d.1867 aged 75, Methodist missionary to the Friendly Isles
     A pioneer: a memoir of the Rev. John Thomas, missionary to the Friendly Isles / by George Stringer Rowe. London: T. Woolmer, 1885. (NLS)

THOMAS, Sidney Gilchrist, 1850-85, inventor and metallurgist
     Memoir and letters of Sidney Gilchrist Thomas, inventor. Edited by Robert William Burnie. London: John Murray, 1891.

THOMAS, Thomas, 'Thomas of Carnarvon', 1804-77, Canon of Bangor
     Father and son: memoirs of Thomas Thomas, Canon of Bangor, Vicar of Carnarvon [etc.], and of (Thomas) Llewelyn Thomas, Fellow and Vice-Principal of Jesus College, Oxford ... Edited by Harriet Thomas ... London: Henry Frowde, 1898.

THOMAS, Thomas, 1805-81, Welsh Baptist
     In memory of the Rev. Thomas Thomas, D.D., formerly President of the Baptist College, Pontypool ... Born January 12th 1805 - Died at Cardiff December 7th 1881. Cardiff: printed by William Jones, 1882. 12mo. Pamphlet. (B&J)

THOMAS, (Thomas) Llewelyn, 1840-97 see THOMAS, Thomas 1804-77

THOMAS, Urijah Rees, 1839-1901, Congregational Minister
     Urijah Rees Thomas, his life and work / by David Morgan Thomas. London: Hodder & Stoughton, 1902.

THOMASON, James, 1804-53, Governor in North Western Provinces, India 1843-53
James Thomason / by Richard Temple. Oxford: Clarendon Press, 1893. (Rulers of India series)

THOMPSON, Jacob, 1806-79, landscape painter
The life and works of Jacob Thompson / by Llewellynn Jewitt. Published for the author. London: J. S. Virtue, 1882. 4to.

THOMPSON, William, 'Bendigo', 1811-89, boxer; later a Minister
The story of 'Bendigo', the champion prize fighter of England / by Thomas M. Winter. London: Morgan & Scott, [190-?]. Pamphlet. (B&J)

THOMSON, Adam, 1779-1861, Church of Scotland Minister
Life and ministry of the Rev. Adam Thomson, D.D., Coldstream, and his labours for free and cheap Bible printing / by his son-in-law P. Landreth. Edinburgh: A. Elliot, 1869. (NC)

THOMSON, Alexander, 1798-1868, advocate; vigorous social reformer
Memoir of Alexander Thomson, of Banchory / by George Smeaton. Edinburgh: Edmonston & Douglas, 1869.

THOMSON, David, 1817-80, Professor of Natural Philosophy, Aberdeen University
David Thomas, M.A., Professor of Natural Philosophy in the University of Aberdeen: a sketch of his character and career / by William Leslie Low. Aberdeen: D. Wyllie, 1894.

THOMSON, George, 1819-78, missionary in Africa
Memoir of George Thomson, Cameroon Mountains, West Africa. By one of his nephews. Edinburgh: Andrew Elliot, 1881. (NLS)

THOMSON, James, 1834-82, poet; 'the laureate of pessimism'
The laureate of pessimism: a sketch of the life and character of James Thomson ('B.V.'), author of 'The City of Dreadful Night' / by Bertram Dobell. London: The author, 1910. Pamphlet.
-------. The life James Thomson ('B.V.'). With a selection from his letters and a study of his writings / by Henry Stephens Salt. London: Reeves & Turner, 1899.

THOMSON, Joseph, 1858-95, African explorer
James Thomson, African explorer: a biography / by his brother John Baird Thomson. With contributions by friends. London: Sampson Low, Marston, 1896; new edition. 1898.

THOMSON, Peter, 1851-80, Free Church Minister
A Scotch student: memorials of Peter Thomson, M.A., Minister of the Free Church, St Fergus / by George Steven. Edinburgh: Macniven & Wallace, 1881. (NC)

THOMSON, Thomas, 1768-1852, advocate; legal antiquary
Memoir of Thomas Thomson, advocate. [By Cosmo Innes]. Edinburgh: printed by T. Constable, 1854. (Bannatyne Club). (c.100 copies printed)

THOMSON, Thomas Smith, 1843-84, medical missionary in India
Memoirs of Thomas Smith Thomson, L.R.C.P., L.R.C.S., medical missionary at Neyoor, Travancore, South India / by J. H. Hacker. London: Religious Tract Society, 1887. (NLS)

THOMSON, William, 1819-90, Archbishop of York
The people's Archbishop: the late Most Reverend William Thomson / by Charles Bullock. London: Home Words, [1891]. (NLS)

THOMSON, William Burns, 1821-93, Scottish medical missionary in Arabia & Madagascar

W. Burns Thomson, F.R.C.S.E., F.R.S.E.: reminiscences of medical missionary work. With biographical chapters / by J.C.D. ... London: Hodder & Stoughton, 1895. (NLS)

[THORBURN, William David], 1846-88, advocate; philanthropist
In memoriam [William David Thorburn]: 1846-1888. [By John Hay Thorburn]. Printed for private circulation. Leith: William Nimmo, [1888]. 4to. (NC)

THORNE, James, 1795-1872, Bible Christian preacher and editor
James Thorne, of Shearbear: a memoir / compiled from his diaries and letters by his son [John Thorne]. London: Bible Christian Book Room, 1873.

THORNE, Samuel, 1798-1873, Bodmin printer for the Bible Christian church
Samuel Thorne, printer: memorials / by Samuel Ley Thorne. Plymouth: printed by G. P. Friend, 1874; 2nd edition. London: Elliot Stock, 1875. 16mo. (NLS)

THORNE, Samuel Thomas, d.1891, Bible Christian Missionary in China
Samuel Thomas Thorne, Minister of the Gospel ... and missionary to Yun-Nan in South-Western China / by Thomas Ruddle. London: Bible Christian Missionary Committee, 1893. (NLS)

THORNEYCROFT, George Benjamin, 1791-1851, foundry owner; M.P.
Diligent in business, fervent in spirit: a memoir of the late G. B. Thorneycroft, Esq., of Wolverhampton / by Joseph Butterworth Owen. London: Hamilton, Adams, 1856.

THOROLD, Anthony Wilson, 1825-95, Bishop of Rochester, then Winchester
The life and work of Bishop Thorold: Rochester 1877-91; [then of] Winchester 1891-95 ... / by Charles Hare Simpkinson. London: Isbister, 1896.

THRING, Edward, 1821-87, headmaster of Uppingham School
Edward Thring, headmaster of Uppingham School: life, diary and letters by George Robert Parkin. London: Macmillan, 1898. 2 volumes; abridged edition. 1900.
-------. Edward Thring, teacher and poet / by Henry Drummond Rawnsley. London: T. Fisher Unwin, 1889.
-------. A memory of Edward Thring / by John Huntley Skrine. London: Macmillan, 1889.

TIDMAN, Arthur, 1792-1868, Foreign Secretary of the London Missionary Society
In loving remembrance of the Rev. Arthur Tidman, D.D., for twenty-seven years Foreign Secretary of the London Missionary Society. Born November 14th 1792 - Died March 8th 1868. London: printed by Yates and Alexander, [c.1868].

TIPTAFT, William, b.1803, clergyman, then Baptist Minister
Memoir of the late William Tiptaft, Minister of the Gospel, Abingdon, Berks ... With a selection from his letters / by Joseph Charles Philpot. 2nd edition. London: J. Gadsby, 1867.

TITCOMB, Jonathan Holt, 1819-87, first Bishop of Rangoon, then of Northern and Central Europe
A consecrated life: memoir of the Right Rev. Bishop Titcomb, D.D. ... / by Allen Thomas Edwards. London: Robert Banks, 1887. 12mo. photo.port.

TODHUNTER, Isaac, 1820-84, mathematician at Cambridge University
In memoriam: Isaac Todhunter. Cambridge: Macmillan & Bowes, 1884. Pamphlet. (Reprinted from the 'Cambridge Review')

TOMBS, Sir Henry, *V.C*, 1824-74, Major-General in India
Memoir of Major-General Sir Henry Tombs, V.C., K.C.B., R.A.. Woolwich: Royal Artillery Institution, 1913.

TOMLINSON, Charles, 1808-97, scientific writer

The life of Charles Tomlinson, F.R.S., F.C.S. [etc.] / by his niece Mary Tomlinson. London: Elliot Stock, 1900.

TOWNLEY, Charles Gostling, d.1856, evangelical clergyman especially in Ireland
The sceptic saved, and saving others, or memorials of Charles Gostling Townley, LL.D. / by Samuel Martin. London: T. Nelson, 1857. (NC)

TOYE, Thomas, 1810-79, Belfast Minister
Brief memorials of the late Rev. Thomas Toye, Belfast / by his widow [Jane Toye]. Belfast: S.E. M'Cormick, 1873. photo.port. (NLS)

TOYNBEE, Arnold, 1852-83, social philosopher; economist
Arnold Toynbee: a reminiscence / by Alfred Milner. London: E. Arnold, 1895. (NLS)
<u>see also</u> **TOYNBEE, Joseph**

TOYNBEE, Joseph, 1815-66, surgeon; father of Arnold Toynbee
Reminiscences and letters of Joseph and Arnold Toynbee. Edited by Gertrude Toynbee. London: Henry J. Glaisher, [1910]. (NLS)

TOZER, William George, 1829-99, Anglican Bishop in Africa
Bishop Tozer. By a worker in the Universities' Mission to Central Africa. London: S.P.C.K., 1900. (Mission Heroes series) (NLS)

TRAIN, Joseph, 1779-1852, 'The antiquary of Galloway'; correspondent of Sir Walter Scott
Memoir of Joseph Train, F.S.A. Scot., the antiquarian correspondent of Sir Walter Scott / by John Patterson. Glasgow: Thomas Menzies, 1857. (B&J)

TREGELLES, Edwin Octavius, 1806-86, civil engineer & Quaker Minister
Edwin Octavius Tregelles, civil engineer and Minister of the Gospel. [Extracted from his papers and diaries]. Edited by his daughter Sarah E. Fox [and her husband J. Hingston Fox]. London: Hodder & Stoughton, 1892. photo.port.

TRELAWNY, Edward John, 1792-1881, author; adventurer; intimate of Shelley
Edward Trelawny: a biographical sketch / by Richard [John Frederick] Edgcumbe. Plymouth: W.H. Luke, 1882. (BL)

TRENCH, James, 1808-55, Superintendent of Edinburgh City Mission
Memoir and remains of the Rev. James Trench, late Superintendent of the Edinburgh City Mission / by Andrew Thomson. Edinburgh: Johnstone & Hunter, 1855. (NC)

TRENCH, Richard Chenevix, 1807-86, Anglican Archbishop of Dublin; poet; philologist
Archbishop Trench, poet and divine. London: S.P.C.K., [1891]. Pamphlet. (NLS)
-------. Richard Chenevix Trench, Archbishop: letters and memorials. Edited by [Maria C. Trench]. London: Kegan Paul, Trench, 1888. 2 volumes.

TROTTER, Coutts, 1837-87, Vice-Master of Trinity College, Cambridge
Coutts Trotter: in memoriam / by Michael Foster, John Willis Clark, and Sedley Taylor. Cambridge: Macmillan & Bowes, 1888. Pamphlet. (NLS)

TROUP, George, 1821-79, journalist; sanitary reformer
Life of George Troup, journalist / by George Emslie Troup. Edinburgh: Macniven & Wallace, 1881.

TROUP, James, 1829-97, Scottish Congregational Minister
Memoirs of Rev. James Troup, M.A., Minister of Helensburgh Congregational Church / by James Stark. Helensburgh: J. Lindsay, 1897. (NC)

TROYTE, Arthur Acland-, d.1857, tractarian

A layman's life in the days of the Tractarian movement. In memoriam Arthur Acland-Troyte / by his son John Edward Acland. Oxford: James Parker, 1904. (NC)

TRUSCOTT, Thomas, 1848-88, Free Methodist missionary in Sierra Leone
The life of Thomas Truscott, missionary to Sierra Leone / by Joseph Kirsop. London: A. Crombie, [1890]. (NLS)

TRYON, Sir George, 1823-93, Vice-Admiral; Commander-in-Chief Mediterranean
Life of Vice-Admiral Sir George Tryon, K.C.B. / by Charles Cooper Penrose Fitzgerald. Edinburgh: W. Blackwood, 1897; cheap edition. 1898. (NLS)

TUCKER, Henry St. George, 1771-1851, Chairman of East India Company
The life and correspondence of Henry St. George Tucker, late Accountant-General of Bengal and Chairman of the East India Company / by John William Kaye. London: R. Bentley, 1854.

TUCKER, John Thomas, 1818-66, missionary in India
Sowing and reaping: the life of the Rev. J. T. Tucker, missionary of the Church Missionary Society in Tinnevelly / by George Pettitt. London: J. Nisbet, 1872. (NLS)

TUFNELL, William, 1780-1855, clergyman, then Pastor
Love's tribute to the memory of the blessed, being gleanings from the life and letters of the late excellent (in Jesus) Mr William Tufnell. By Josiah. [sic]. [For private circulation]. London: W. H. Collingridge, 1856. (B&J)

TUKE, James Hack, 1819-96, Quaker banker; philanthropist, especially in Ireland
James Hack Tuke: a memoir / compiled by Edward Fry. London: Macmillan, 1899.

TUKE, Samuel, 1784-1857, Quaker; York philanthropist concerned with the treatment of the insane
Samuel Tuke, his life, work and thoughts. Edited by Charles Tylor. London: Headley Brothers, 1900.

TULLOCH, John, 1823-86, theologian; Principal of St Andrew's University
A memoir the life of John Tulloch, D.D., LL.D., Principal and Primarius Professor of St Mary's College, St Andrew's ... / by Margaret Oliphant. Edinburgh: W. Blackwood, 1888.

TUNNICLIFFE, Jabez, 1809-65, Baptist; founder of the Band of Hope in 1847
The life and labours of the Rev. Jabez Tunnicliffe, Minister of the Gospel at Call Lane Chapel, Leeds, and founder of the Band of Hope in England ... Collected and arranged by Henry Marles. London: William Tweedie, 1865.

TURNBULL, Henry James Thomson, 1846-77, United Presbyterian Minister
Memoir of the Rev. Henry J. T. Turnbull, junior Minister, United Presbyterian Church, Nairn / by his brother William Wilson Turnbull. Printed for private circulation. Glasgow: William W. Turnbull, 1878. photo.port. (NLS)

TURNER, James, 1818-55? Aberdeenshire evangelist
James Turner, or how to reach the masses / by Elizabeth McHardie. Aberdeen: A. Brown, 1875; 3rd edition. London: T. Woolmer, 1889.

TURNER, Joseph Mallord William, 1775-1851, water-colourist; landscape painter
The life of J. M. W. Turner, R.A., founded on letters and papers furnished by his friends and fellow academicians / by Walter Thornbury. London: Hurst & Blackett, 1862. 2 volumes; 2nd edition. 1877. Reprinted London: Ward Lock, 1970.

TURNER, Samuel, 1778-1854, Minister in Sunderland
Brief account of the life, call to the Ministry and death of Samuel Turner, forty-five

years Minister of Cornmarket Chapel, Sunderland ... Saffron Walden: R. Heffer, 1882. Pamphlet. (B&J)

TURNER, Thomas, n.d., Yorkshire Methodist
The happpy and useful Christian, or the life of Thomas Turner, late of Farsley, near Leeds / by J. Meyers. London: Jarrold, [1857?]. 16mo. (B&J)

TURNER, Thomas, 1773-1865, surgeon
Memoir of Thomas Turner, Esq., F.R.C.S., F.L.S., Member of the Council of the Royal College of Surgeons of England, etc.. By a relative. London: Simpkin, Marshall [etc.], 1875. photo.port.

TWEEDIE, William King, 1803-63, Free Church Minister
Tribute to the memory of the late W. K. Tweedie, D.D., of Free Tolbooth Church, Edinburgh: [an address / by William Brown, F.R.C.S.E.]. [Edinburgh, 1863]. Pamphlet. (NLS)

TWELLS, Henry, 1823-1900, clergyman; headmaster; writer
A memoir of the Rev. Henry Twells, M.A., Honorary Canon of Peterborough / by William Clavell Ingram. London: Wells Gardner, Darton, [1901]. (B&J)

TYRRELL, William, 1807-79, Anglican Bishop in Australia
The life and labours of the Right Rev. William Tyrrell, D.D., first Bishop of Newcastle, New South Wales / by Richard George Boodle. London: Wells, Gardner, Darton, [1881].

ULLATHORNE, William Bernard, 1806-89, Roman Catholic Archbishop of Birmingham; friend of Newman
Life of Archbishop Ullathorne. [1889]. photo.ports. (Reprinted from the 'Oscottian')

URWICK, William, 1791-1868, Irish Congregationalist; temperance worker
The life and letters of William Urwick, D.D., of Dublin. Edited by his son [William Urwick]. London: Hodder & Stoughton, 1890.

UZIELLI, Matthew, 1805-60, railway director
Matthew Uzielli: [obituary notices]. [London, 1861]. (B&J)

VANDELEUR, Arthur, n.d., religious soldier
The life of Arthur Vandeleur, Major, Royal Artillery. [By Catherine M. Marsh]. London: J.Nisbet, 1879.

VANDELEUR, (Cecil Foster) Seymour, 1869-1901, died in South African War
Seymour Vandeleur, Lieutenant-Colonel, Scots Guards & Irish Guards ... / by Frederick Ivor Maxse. London: William Heinemann, 1906. 4to.
-------. Seymour Vandeleur, the story of a British officer, being a memoir of Brevet-Lieutenant-Colonel Vandeleur ... / by Frederick Ivor Maxse. London: National Review Office, 1905. (BL)

VASEY, Thomas, 1814-71, Yorkshire Wesleyan Minister
The late Rev. Thomas Vasey. [By Josiah Pearson]. For private circulation only. Harrogate: printed by G. Exelby, 1871. Pamphlet. (B&J)
-------. The life of Thomas Vasey / by his widow [Mary Jane Vasey]. 2nd edition. London: Elliot Stock, 1874. (NLS)

VAUGHAN, James, d.1889 aged 83, clergyman
In loving and sacred memory of the Rev. James Vaughan, Prebendary of Chichester, entered into rest May 7th 1889 in his eighty-fourth year. London: Hatchards, [1890]. (Reprinted from the 'Watchword') Pamphlet. (NLS)

VAUGHAN, Robert, 1795-1868, Congregational theologian and writer
Robert Vaughan, D.D.: a memorial. London: James Clarke, 1869. photo. port. (B&J)

VAUGHAN, Robert Alfred, 1823-57, Congregationalist; poet
Memoir of Robert Alfred Vaughan, author of 'Hours with the mystics', &c. / by Robert Vaughan. 2nd revised edition. London: Macmillan, 1864.

VEITCH, John, 1829-94, Scottish philosopher & man of letters
Memoir of John Veitch, Professor of Logic and Rhetoric, University of Glasgow / by Mary R. L. Bryce. Edinburgh: W. Blackwood, 1896.

VENABLES, Addington Robert Peel, 1827-76, Anglican Bishop of the West Indies
Addington Venables, Bishop of Nassau: a sketch of his life and labours for the Church of God / by William Francis Henry King. London: Wells, Gardner, 1877. photo.port. (NLS)

VENN, Henry, 1796-1873, clergyman; Hon. Secretary Church Missionary Society
Memoir of Henry Venn, B.D., Prebendary of St Paul's, and Honorary Secretary of the Church Missionary Society / by William Knight. New edition. London: Seeley, Jackson and Halliday, 1882.

VICARS, Hedley Shafto Johnstone, 1826-55, religious soldier in the Crimea
Memorials of Captain Hedley Vicars, Ninety-Seventh Regiment. [By Catherine M. Marsh]. London: J. Nisbet, [1856].

VIGNOLES, Charles Blacker, 1793-1875, civil & railway engineer
Life of Charles Blacker Vignoles, F.R.S. [etc.], soldier and civil engineer ...: a reminiscence of early railway history / by his son Olinthus John Vignoles. London: Longmans, Green, 1889.

VINCENT, Henry, 1813-78, Chartist
Henry Vincent: a biographical sketch / by William Dorling. London: James Clarke, 1879. photo.port.

WADDY, Samuel Dousland, 1804-76, Methodist Minister
The life of the Rev. Samuel D. Waddy, D.D. / by his youngest daughter [Adeline Waddy]. London: Wesleyan Conference Office, 1878. photo.port.

WAGNER, George, 1818-57, clergyman
Memoir of the Rev. George Wagner, M.A., late Incumbent of St. Stephen's Church, Brighton / by John Nassau Simpkinson. Cambridge: Macmillan, 1858.

WAKEFIELD, Thomas, 1836-1901, missionary in East Africa
Thomas Wakefield, missionary and geographical pioneer in East Equatorial Africa / by E. S. Wakefield. London: Religious Tract Society, 1904.

WAKELEY, Thomas Stanley, 1832-99, Kent pastor & religious newspaper editor
Gathered fragments: a memorial of Thomas Stanley Wakeley, late Pastor of Providence Chapel, Rainham, Kent, and editor of the 'Gospel Banner'. Also a brief memoir of his wife [Mary Anne Wakeley]. Edited by his brother R. M. Wakeley. Oxford: J.C. Pembrey, 1902.

WAKLEY, Thomas, 1795-1862, surgeon; editor of 'The Lancet'; M.P.

The life and times of Thomas Wakley, founder and first editor of 'The Lancet', Member of Parliament for Finsbury, and Coroner for West Middlesex / by Samuel Sprigge. London: Longmans [etc.], 1897. (BL)

WALKER, Frederick, 1840-75, artist; prolific book illustrator

Frederick Walker and his works / by Claude Phillips. London: Seeley, 1897.

-------. The life and letters of Frederick Walker, A.R.A. / by John George Marks. London: Macmillan, 1896.

WALKER, George Washington, 1800-59, Quaker misisonary; in Australia and South Africa

The life and labours of George Washington Walker, of Hobart Town, Tasmania / by James Backhouse and Charles Taylor. London: A. W. Bennett, 1862.

-------. A short notice of the conversion and life of George Washington Walker. York: printed by William Sessions, 1868. Pamphlet.

WALKER, Henry Wootton, n.d., religious boy

The lamb sheltered: a memoir / by I. Walker. Edinburgh: John Maclaren, 1872. 16mo. (B&J)

WALKER, William, n.d, missionary in Ceylon

Pioneers of Ceylon: a brief record of the life of William Walker. Bedford: Bedford Publishing Company, 1897. (B&J)

WALLACE, Robert, 1831-99, Scottish Minister, then editor of the 'Scotsman', lawyer and radical M.P.

Reminiscences of the late Robert Wallace, Esq., M.P. / by Roderick Lawson. Paisley: J. & R. Parlane, 1899. Pamphlet. (B&J)

WALMSLEY, Sir Joshua, 1794-1871, M.P.; Mayor of Liverpool; businessman & philanthropist

The life of Sir Joshua Walmsley / by his son Hugh Mulleneux Walmsley. London: Chapman and Hall, 1879. photo.port.

WALSHE, John William, n.d., artist

The life and letters of John William Walshe, F.S.A.. Edited with an introduction by Montgomery Carmichael. London: Burns & Oates, [1901].

WANTAGE, Robert James Loyd-Lindsay, *V.C.*, 1st Baron, 1832-1901, soldier; M.P.; Red Cross pioneer; Financial Secretary at the War Office

In memory of Robert James, Baron Wantage, V.C., K.C.B.. Born April 17 1832 - Died at Locking June 10 1901. [Wantage: printed by Nichols, 1901]. Pamphlet. (B&J)

-------. Lord Wantage, V.C., K.C.B.: a memoir / by his wife [Harriet Sarah Loyd-Wantage]. London: Smith, Elder, 1907.

WARBURTON, John, d.1857, Baptist Pastor in Trowbridge

A testimony to ... a Covenant God, as displayed in the last illness and blessed death of the late John Warburton, Minister of the Gospel, and for 42 years Pastor ... at Zion Chapel, Trowbridge. 3rd edition. London: John Gadsby, 1858. (B&J)

WARBURTON, John, 1815-92, Baptist Minister

Memorials of the late John Warburton, of Southill. Edited by C. Hemington. London: F. Kirby, 1892. (B&J)

WARD, Thomas, b. c.1831, religious railway workman

A light for the line, or the story of Thomas Ward, a railway workman. [By Catherine M. Marsh]. London: J. Nisbet, 1858. 16mo. (NLS)

WARDLAW, Ralph, 1779-1853, Scottish Congregational Minister & miscellaneous writer
Memoirs of the life and writings of Ralph Wardlaw, D.D. / by William Lindsay Alexander. Edinburgh: A. & C. Black, 1856.

WARE (afterwards HIBBERT-WARE), Samuel Hibbert, n.d., doctor
The life and correspondence of the late Samuel Hibbert Ware, M.D., F.R.S.E. [etc.] / by Mary Clementina Hibbert-Ware. Manchester: J. E. Cornish, 1882. (250 copies only) (BL)

WARREN, George, n.d., Derbyshire Primitive Methodist ploughman
Piety behind the plough, or observations founded on the life and character of Mr George Warren, of Weston Underwood, Derbyshire / by John Barfoot. London: Richard Davies, [1864?]. 12mo. (NLS)

WATERHOUSE, Theodore, 1839-91, architect
Theodore Waterhouse, 1838-1891: notes of his life, and extracts from his letters and papers. [By Edward Fry]. For private circulation. London: Chiswick Press, 1894.

WATERTON, Charles, 1782-1865, naturalist; traveller; Catholic; eccentric
Charles Waterton, his home, habits and handiwork: reminiscences of an intimate and most confiding personal association for nearly thirty years / by Richard Hobson. London: Simpkin, Marshall [etc.], 1866.

WATSON, Edward, b.1814, artist; work with Y.M.C.A.
Edward Watson, his life and work: a biographical sketch / by George Leonard Leigh. Birmingham: Clarendon Art Fellowship, 1899. photo. port. Pamphlet. (NLS)

WATSON, James, 1799-1874, radical publisher; Chartist; Owenite
James Watson: a memoir of the days of the fight for a free press in England, and of the agitation for the People's Charter / by William James Linton. Manchester: Abel Heywood, [1879]: reprinted Woburn Press, 1971.

WATSON, Joshua, 1771-1855, London wine merchant; philanthropist; co-founder of King's College, London
Memoir of Joshua Watson. Edited by Edward Churton. Oxford: J.H. & J. Parker, 1861. 2 volumes; 2nd edition. 1863.

WATSON, W. W., n.d., music critic for the 'Dundee Advertiser'
W. W. Watson: a sketch. By one of his sons. Dundee: printed by John Leng, 1887. (B&J)

WATTS, Alaric Alexander, 1797-1864, editor of several newspapers; poet
Alaric Watts: a narrative of his life / by his son Alaric Alfred Watts. London: R. Bentley, 1884. 2 volumes.

WATTS-RUSSELL, Giulio, d.1867 aged 17, killed fighting for the Holy See
Giulio Watts-Russell, pontifical zouave / by Valerian Cordella ... Leamington: Art & Book Co., [1895]. 12mo. (NLS) [Consists of 2 parts: (Part 1: a reissue of:) 'A biography of Giulio Watts-Russell, pontifical zouave: a biography' / by ... Valerian Cardella ... London: St. Joseph's Retreat, [1868]. (Part 2: a new part) 'Giulio Watts-Russell, twenty-seven years after his death: a sequel to his biography' / by Claud R. Lindsay].

WAUCHOP, Andrew Gilbert, 1846-99, Major-General
General Wauchop / by William Baird. Edinburgh: Oliphant, Anderson & Ferrier, 1900. (NLS)
-------. The life of Major-General Wauchop, C.B., C.M.G., LL.D. / by George B. S. Douglas. Edinburgh: Oliphant, Anderson [etc.], 1900.

WEAVER, Richard, 1827-61, miner, then evangelist
The life of Richard Weaver, the converted collier / by Richard Cope Morgan. London:

Morgan & Chase, [1861].

WEBB, Sidney Roberts, 1867-96, medical missionary in Congo
A young Congo missionary: memorials of Sidney Roberts Webb, M.D. / by William Brock. London: H. R. Allenson, 1897.

WEBSTER, George, 1830?-90, Irish Catholic; anti-abstainer
George Webster, D.D.: a memoir / by Alfred George Dann ... Dublin: William McGee, 1892. photo.port. (NLS)

WEDDERBURN, Sir David, 3rd Bart., 1835-82, Scottish M.P. and advocate
Life of Sir David Wedderburn, Bart., M.P. / compiled from his journals and writings by his sister [Louisa Jane Percival]. London: Kegan Paul, Trench, 1884.

WEDGWOOD, John, 1788-1869, Primitive Methodist
Memoir of the life and labours of Mr John Wedgwood, one of the first and most successful of the home missionaries of the Primitive Methodist Society. By a layman. London: George Lamb, 1870. 12mo. (NC)

WELD, Sir Frederick Aloysius, 1823-91, colonial administrator in Australia & New Zealand; Catholic
The life of Sir Frederick Weld, G.C.M.G., a pioneer of Empire / by Alice Fraser, Lady Lovat. London: John Murray, 1914.

WELLESLEY, Thomas see PIGOTT, Emily Jessie

WELLINGTON, Arthur Wellesley, 1st Duke of Wellington, 1769-1852, Field-Marshal; Tory Prime Minister
History of the life of Arthur, Duke of Wellington. [By Alexis Henry Brialmont]. Translated from the French with emendations and additions / by George Robert Gleig. London: Longman [etc.], 1858-60. 4 volumes.
-------. Life and campaigns of Arthur, Duke of Wellington, K.G. ... / by George Newenham Wright. London: Fisher, 1841. 4 volumes.
-------. On the life and character of the Duke of Wellington / by Francis, 5th Earl of Ellesmere. 2nd edition. London: John Murray, 1852. (Murray's Railway Reading series)
-------. Memoir of the Duke of Wellington. London: Longman [etc.], 1852. (Reprinted from 'The Times')
-------. Notes of conversations with the Duke of Wellington, 1831-1851 / by Philip Hemnry, 5th Earl of Stanhope. Printed for private circulation. [1886]; London: John Murray, 1888.
-------. Personal reminiscences of the first Duke of Wellington. With sketches of his guests and contemporaries / by George Robert Gleig. Edited by his daughter Mary E. Gleig. Edinburgh: W. Blackwood, 1904.
-------. Three years with the Duke, or Wellington in private life. By an ex-Aide-de-Camp [i.e. Lord William Pitt Lennox]. London: Saunders & Otley, 1853.
and other biographies and very many funeral sermons

WENGER, John, 1811-80, Baptist missionary in India
The life of the Rev. John Wenger, missionary to India, and the translator of the Scriptures into Bengali and Sanscrit / by Edward Bean Underhill. London: Baptist Missionary Society, 1886. photo.port. (NC)

WEST, Daniel, 1815-57, Wesleyan missionary in West Africa
The life and journals of David West, Wesleyan Minister, and deputation to the Wesleyan Mission Stations on the Gold Coast, West Africa / by Thomas West. London: Hamilton, Adams, 1857. (NLS)

WEST, Richard Temple, 1827-93, Anglo-Catholic clergyman
Richard Temple West: a record of life and work / by Thomas Thellusson Carter.

London: John Masters, 1895. (NLS)

WESTBURY, Richard Bethell, 1st Baron, 1800-73, Lord Chancellor
The life of Richard Bethell, Lord Westbury, formerly Lord High Chancellor. With selections from his correspondence / by Thomas Arthur Nash. London: R. Bentley, 1888. 2 volumes.

WESTCOTT, Brooke Foss, 1825-1901, Bishop of Durham; theologian
Bishop Westcott / by Joseph Clayton. London: A.W. Mowbray, 1906. (Leaders of the Church, 1800-1900 series) (NLS)
-------. Life and letters of Brooke Foss Westcott, D.D., D.C.L., sometime Bishop of Durham / by his son Arthur Westcott. London: Macmillan, 1903. 2 volumes.

WESTROPE, Richard, 1855-96, Congregational Minister in Leeds
Pledged to the people: a brief account of the Rev. Richard Westrope and Belgrave Chapel, Leeds. London: John Whitehead, 1896. Pamphlet. (NLS)

WESTON, Samuel, 1795-1856, Independent Minister
Sketch of the life of the late Samuel Weston, Minister of the Independent Church, Wooburn, Buckinghamshire / by John Hayden. High Wycombe: John Lane, 1857. Pamphlet. (NLS)

WHATELY, Richard, 1787-1863, Archbishop of Dublin; philosopher
Life and correspondence of Richard Whately, D.D., late Archbishop of Dublin. Edited by Elizabeth Jane Whately. London: Longmans, Green, 1866. 2 volumes; in one volume 1868.
-------. Memoirs of Richard Whately, Archbishop of Dublin. With a glance at his contemporaries and times / by William John Fitzpatrick. London: R. Bentley, 1864. 2 volumes.

WHELER, Stephen Glyn, 1802-1865, religious general in India
Memoir of Colonel Wheler (afterwards Major-General) E.I.C.S. / by Henry Mascall Conran ... London: Morgan & Chase, [1867]. (NLS)

WHERRY, Robert, 1808-73, Wisbech worthy and J.P.; Baptist
Work here, rest beyond: a sketch of the life of Robert Wherry, Esq., J.P., of Wisbech / by Edward Carey Pike. London: Simpkin, Marshall, 1873. photo.port. (NLS)

WHEWELL, William, 1794-1866, philosopher; mathematician; Master of Trinity College, Cambridge
The life, and selections from the correspondence of William Whewell, D.D., late Master of Trinity College, Cambridge / by Janet Mary Douglas. London: C. Kegan Paul, 1881.

WHITE, Edward, 1819-99, Free Church Minister in London
Edward White, his life and work / by Frederick Ash Freer. London: Elliot Stock, 1902.

WHITE, Harry [i.e. William Henry], 1865-97, missionary to the Congo
Harry White, missionary to the Congo / by John Edward Roberts. London: Alexander & Shepheard, 1901. (NLS)

WHITE, John, 1833-95, with W.H. Smith for 42 years; Y.M.C.A. Bible class leader
John White: a memoir / compiled by Mrs Edward Smith. London: Hodder & Stoughton, 1896. (NLS)

WHITE, Luke, d.1856, murder victim
A brief memoir of the life and character of Mr Luke White (late of Bolton-upon-Dearne) who, with Elizabeth his wife, were cruelly murdered in their house on the 4th December 1856 by John Harrop. London: Judd & Glass, 1857. Pamphlet. (B&J)

WHITE, William, 1820-1900, Quaker; printer; alderman
William White, a brother of men / by Oliver Morland. Birmingham: Morland, 1903. (B&J)

WHITE, Sir William Arthur, 1824-91, diplomat
Sir William White, K.C.B., K.C.M.G., for six years Ambassador at Constantinople: his life and correspondence / by Henry Sutherland Edwards. London: John Murray, 1902.

WHITEHEAD, Charles, 1804-62, novelist, poet, dramatist
A forgotten genius: Charles Whitehead. A critical monograph / by Henry Thomas Mackenzie Bell. London: Elliot Stock, 1884; new edition. as: 'Charles Whitehead, a forgotten genius. With extracts from his works and a new Preface' / by Henry Thomas Mackenzie Bell. London: Ward, Lock & Bowden, 1894.

WHITEHEAD, Henry, 1825-96, clergyman; writer
Henry Whitehead, 1825-1896: a memorial sketch / by Hardwicke Drummond Rawnsley. Glasgow: James Maclehose, 1898.

WHITWELL, Thomas, 1837-78, Quaker; Cleveland ironmaster
Thomas Whitwell: a biographical sketch, with appendices. Edited by William Thomlinson. Middlesborough: The 'Gazette' Steam Printing & Publishing Office, [1878]. (B&J)

WIFFEN, Benjamin Barrow, 1794-1867, biographer; reformer
The Brothers Wiffen [i.e. Benjamin Barrow and Jeremiah Holmes]: memoirs and miscellanies. Edited by Samuel Rowles Pattison. London: Hodder & Stoughton, 1880. (B&J)

WIGHT, Henry, 1801-61, advocate, then Congregational Minister
Memoir of the Rev. Henry Wight / by his son [Ninian Wight]. Edinburgh: Edmonston & Douglas, 1862.

WILBERFORCE, Samuel, 1805-73, Bishop of Oxford then of Winchester
Bishop Wilberforce / by George William Daniell. London: Methuen, 1891. (Leaders of Religion series)
-------. Bishop Wilberforce / by Reginald Garton Wilberforce. London: A. W. Mowbray, 1905. (Leaders of the Church, 1800-1900 series)
-------. Life of the Right Rev. Samuel Wilberforce, D.D., Lord Bishop of Oxford and afterwards of Winchester. With selections from his diary and correspondence / by Arthur Rawson Ashwell and [for Volumes 2 & 3] Reginald Garton Wilberforce]. London: John Murray, 1880-82. 3 volumes; revised and abridged in one volume. London: Kegan Paul, 1888.

WILDMAN, Robert, n.d., bank manager; Wesleyan; temperance worker
Robert Wildman, the story of an active life / by A. B. Smith. Colne: W. Croasdale, [1887?]. Pamphlet. (B&J)

WILKINS, George, 1830-86, founder of the Theatre Gospel Hall, Derby
An earnest life, being memorials of George Wilkins, of Derby, printer, preacher & painter / by his widow [Mary Wilkins] ... Derby: Wilkins & Ellis, 1887. Pamphlet. (NLS)

WILKINSON, James John Garth, 1812-99, Swedenborgian; homeopathic doctor
James John Garth Wilkinson: a memoir of his life. With a selection from his letters / by Clement John Wilkinson. London: Kegan Paul, Trench, Trubner, 1911.
-------. James John Garth Wilkinson: an introduction / by Frederick H. Evans. 1912. Pamphlet. (Reprinted from 'The Homeopathic World')

WILKINSON, Johnson, 1822-97, twin infantry Generals
The memoirs of the Gemini Generals [i.e. Johnson Wilkinson & Osborn Wilkinson] / by

Osborn Wilkinson & Johnson Wilkinson. 2nd edition. London: A. D. Innes, 1896. (B&J)

WILLIAMS, John, 1796-1852, Welsh missionary martyr in Polynesia
John Williams, the missionary martyr of Polynesia / by James Joseph Ellis. London: S. W. Partridge, [1890]. (BL)
-------. Memoirs of the life of the Rev. John Williams, missionary to Polynesia / by Ebenezer Prout. London: John Shaw, 1843.
-------. Missionary heroes: the Rev. John Williams, martyr of Erromanga / by Alexander Williamson. Edinburgh: Crawford & M'Cabe, 1884. Pamphlet. (NLS)

WILLIAMS, Montagu Stephen, 1835-92, 'the poor man's magistrate'
A chequered career: the life of Montagu Williams, Q.C., schoolmaster, soldier, actor, dramatist, journalist, barrister and police magistrate / by James Peddie. London: Alfred Boot, [189-]. Pamphlet. (B&J)

WILLIAMS, Richard, 1817-51, surgeon, then missionary in Patagonia
A memoir of Richard Williams, surgeon, catechist to the Patgonian Missionary Society in Tierra del Fuego / by James Hamilton. London: J. Nisbet, 1853; new edition. 1857.

WILLIAMS, Rowland, 1817-70, liberal Anglican; Vice-Principal of Lampeter College
The life and letters of Rowland Williams, D.D.. With extracts from his note books. Edited by his wife [Ellen Williams]. London: Henry S. King, 1874. 2 volumes. photo.port.

WILLIAMSON, Thomas, 1796-1855, Minister in the Associate Presbytery
Memorials of the late Rev. Thomas Williamson, Melrose. [Edited with a memoir by Alexander Lowrie]. Edinburgh: William Oliphant, 1856. 12mo. (NLS)

WILLS, Thomas, 1850-99, chemist
The life of Thomas Wills, F.C.S., demonstrator of chemistry, Royal Naval College, Greenwich / by his mother Mary Wills Phillips and her friend J. Luke. London: J. Nisbet, 1880. (NC)

WILLS, William Gorman, 1828-91, dramatist & painter
W. G. Wills, dramatist and painter / by Freeman Wills. London: Longmans, Green, 1898.

[WILMSHURST, John Ebenezer], b.1875, Baptist; in Tasmania
Taken home: a brief record of a beloved son [J. E. Wilmshurst]. [By Jonathan and Elizabeth Wilmshurst]. 3rd edition. London: E. Wilmshurst, [1894]. 12mo. (B&J)

WILSON, Daniel, 1778-1858, Anglican Bishop of Calcutta
The life of the Right Rev. Daniel Wilson, D.D., late Lord Bishop of Calcutta, and Metropolitan of India. With extracts from his journals and correspondence / by Josiah Bateman. London: John Murray, 1860. 2 volumes.

WILSON, David Hamilton, 1799-1853, Newcastle worthy
A tribute to departed worth, being a memoir of David Hamilton Wilson, late Senior Secretary of the Newcastle-upon-Tyne Sunday School Union, who died June 18th 1853 / by E. Ridley. Newcastle-upon-Tyne: printed by Mcliver & Bradley, [1853]. Pamphlet. (B&J)

WILSON, Edward James, 1787-1854, architect
A brief memoir of Edward James Wilson, F.S.A. ... / by John Britton. London: Nichols, 1855. 16mo. (Reprinted from 'The Builder')

WILSON, Effingham, 1783-1868, publisher
In memory of Effingham Wilson: [obituary notices]. Printed for private circulation. London: printed by Effingham Wilson, 1868. 12mo. photo.port. (B&J)

WILSON, George, 1818-59, Professor of Technology Edinburgh University; Director of the Industrial Museum of Scotland; religious writer

Memoir of George Wilson, M.D., F.R.S.E., Regius Professor of Technology in the University of Edinburgh and Director of the Industrial Museum of Scotland / by his sister Jessie Aitken Wilson. London: Macmillan, 1862.

WILSON, James, 1795-1856, Scottish naturalist and zoologist

Memoirs of the life of James Wilson, Esq., F.R.S.E., M.W.S., of Woodville / by James Hamilton. London: Nisbet, 1859.

WILSON, James, 1805-60, M.P.; political economist; founder of 'The Economist'

Memoir of the Right Hon. James Wilson / by his son-in-law Walter Bagehot. London: H. Bale, 1861. (Reprinted from 'The Economist')

WILSON, John, 'Christopher North', 1785-1854, Scottish writer; academic; critic

'Christopher North': a memoir of John Wilson ... / compiled from family papers, etc. by his daughter Mary Gordon. Edinburgh: Edmonston & Douglas, 1862. 2 volumes; new edition. Edinburgh: Thomas C. Jack, 1879.

-------. Professor Wilson: a memorial and estimate. By one of his students. Edinburgh: 'Edinburgh Guardian', 1854. (NC)

WILSON, John, 1804-75, Free Scottish Presbyterian Minister & educationalist in India

The life of John Wilson, D.D., F.R.S., for fifty years philanthropist and scholar in the East / by George Smith. London: John Murray, 1878; 2nd abridged edition. 1879.

WILSON, Thomas, 1811-94, Admiral

Admiral Thomas Wilson, C.B.: [a memoir]. Privately printed. Edinburgh, 1897. (NLS)

WINGATE, William, 1808-99, Scot with the Hungarian Protestant Church

Life and work of the Rev. William Wingate, missionary to the Jews / by Gavin Carlyle. London: A. Holness, [190-]. (B&J)

WINSLOW, John Whitmore, 1835-56, Irish undergraduate

Hidden life: memorials of John Whitmore Winslow, undergraduate of Trinity College, Dublin / by his father Octavius Winslow. 3rd edition. London: John H. Shaw, 1859. (NC)

WISEMAN, Nicholas (Patrick Stephen), Cardinal, 1802-65, Archbishop of Westminster

The last illness of His Eminence Cardinal Wiseman / by John Morris. 3rd edition. London: Burns, Lambert & Oates, 1865.

-------. The life and times of Cardinal Wiseman / by Wilfrid Ward. London: Longmans, Green, 1897. 2 volumes; one volume edition 1898.

WOOD, Alexander, 1817-84, Edinburgh doctor, sanitary and social reformer; introduced the hypodermic syringe into use

Alexander Wood, M.D.: a sketch of his life and work / by his brother-in-law Thomas Brown, *F.R.S.E.*. Edinburgh: Macniven & Wallace, 1886. (NC)

WOOD, Isaac, 1794-1865, clergyman

Memoir of the Venerable Isaac Wood, M.A., Archdeacon of Chester and, forty-five years, Vicar of Middlewich ... / by Richard William Dibdin. London: J. Nisbet, 1866. photo.port. (B&J)

WOOD, James, b.1836, Gloucester eccentric

Life and anecdotes of Jemmy Wood, the eccentric banker, merchant and draper of Gloucester ... [By Charles H. Savory]. London: Kent [etc.], [1882]. Pamphlet. (B&J)

WOOD, James, 1844-99, Liverpool businessman; Southport Methodist & worthy

Memorials of James Wood, LL.D., J.P., of Grove House, Southport / by Eliza A. Wood ... London: Charles H. Kelly, 1902.

WOOD, John George, 1827-89, clergyman; natural history writer; editor of the 'Boys' Own Paper'
The Rev. J. G. Wood, his life and work / by Theodore Wood. London: Cassell, 1890.

WOOD, Joseph, 1797-1869, Wesleyan Minister
The life of the Rev. Joseph Wood. With extracts from his diary / by Henry W. Williams. London: Wesleyan Conference Office, 1871.

WOOD, Joseph, 1801-90, artist
Joseph Wood (1801-1890): a short biography. With some account of his artistic career in England and America / by his son [Joseph D. Wood]. London: printed by William Reeves, [1890]. (B&J)

WOODFORD, Sir John George, 1785-1879, Major-General; in Peninsula War
A brief memoir of Major-General Sir John George Woodford, K.C.B., K.C.H.: a paper read to the Keswick Literary and Scientific Society ... / by John Fisher Crosthwaite. Keswick: M. Bailey & T. Mayson, 1881. photo. port. (NC)

WOODHOUSE, Alfred John, 1822-80, clergyman
In memoriam: Rev. A. J. Woodhouse, Vicar of Ide Hill, 1863-1880. London: printed by Cassell, Petter & Galpin, [1880]. (NLS)

WOODWARD, Bernard Bolingbroke, 1816-69, Royal Librarian; miscellaneous writer
A brief memoir of Bernard Bolingbroke Woodward, B.A., F.S.A., Librarian in Ordinary to the Queen and Keeper of the Prints and Drawings at Windsor Castle. [By Frederick Bolingbroke Ribbans]. London: Longman [etc.], 1873. photo. port. (B&J)

WORDSWORTH, Christopher, 1807-85, Bishop of Lincoln
Christopher Wordsworth, Bishop of Lincoln, 1807-1885 / by John Henry Overton and Elizabeth Wordsworth. London: Rivingtons, 1888.

WORSNOP, Thomas, 1779-1869, temperance advocate
The life and sayings of Thomas Worsnop, the great apostle of total abstinence in the North of England, who died April 25th 1869 / by Francis Butterfield. Bingley: printed by Thomas Harrison, [1870]. 12mo. (B&J)

WRIGHT, Edward, 'Ned', b.1836, evangelist
Incidents in the life of Edward Wright / by Edward Leach. London: Hodder & Stoughton, 1870. (NLS)
-------. Ned Wright: the story of his life. London: Hodder & Stoughton, 1874. 12mo. (NLS)

WRIGHT, George, 1789-1873, Baptist Minister
Memorials of George Wright, for forty-eight years Pastor of the Baptist Church of Beccles / compiled by Samuel King Bland. London: Elliot Stock, 1875. photo. port. (NLS)

WRIGHT, John, 1821-65, religious Hull riverman
Religion and the river, or observations founded on the life and character of Captain John Wright, riverman / by W. Woodward. [Hull: printed by William Adams, 1865?] 12mo. (NLS)

WRIGHT, John Skirrow, 1822-80, Liberal M.P.; button manufacturer; Baptist
John Skirrow Wright, M.P.: a memorial tribute / by Eliezar Edwards. Printed for the compiler. Birmingham: E. Edwards, 1880. (BL)

WRIGHT, Thomas, 1789-1875, Manchester prison visitor
The life of Thomas Wright, of Manchester, the prison philanthropist. [By Thomas Wright McDermid] ... Manchester: John Heywood, [1876]. 12mo. photo.port.

WYNNE, Frederick Richards, 1827-96, Irish Anglican bishop
    The life of Frederick Richards Wynne, D.D., Bishop of Killaloe ... / by James Owen Hannay. London: Hodder & Stoughton, 1897.

YARRELL, William, 1784-1856, naturalist and natural history writer
    Memoir of William Yarrell / by Leonard Blomefield. Privately printed. Bath, 1888. 12mo. Pamphlet. (BL)

YOUNG, Charles Mayne, 1777-1856, actor
    A memoir of Charles Mayne Young, tragedian. With extracts from his son's journal / by Julian Charles Young. London: Macmillan, 1871.

YOUNG, Henry, d.1869, Irish Roman Catholic priest
    A sketch of the life of the late Father Henry Young, of Dublin / by Georgiana Fullerton. London: Burns & Oates, 1874. (NLS)

YULE, Sir Henry, 1820-89, geographer and Royal Engineer in India
    A memoir of Colonel Sir Henry Yule, R.E. [etc]. With a bibliography of his writings / by his daughter Amy Frances Rule. For private circulation. London: John Murray, 1903. (Reprinted from the 3rd edition of his 'Marco Polo')

ZOUCHE, Robert Curzon, <u>14th Baron</u>, 1810-73, M.P.; eastern traveller; bibliophile
    Notice of Lord Zouche. [By Richard Monckton Milnes]. Privately printed. London: Chiswick Press for Philobiblion Society, [c.1873]. Pamphlet. (c.50 copies printed) (B&J)

PART 2

BIOGRAPHIES OF VICTORIAN WOMEN

ABERCROMBIE, Barbara, 1811-91, Treasurer of Edinburgh Medical Mission
In memoriam: Barbara Abercrombie. Born 7th January 1811 - Died 1st March 1891. Edinburgh: T. and A. Constable, 1891.

ACLAND, Lady Sarah, 1815-78, wife of Sir Henry Wentworth Acland, Professor of Medicine, University of Oxford
A sketch of the life and character of Sarah Acland. Written for the nurses of the 'Sarah Acland Memorial Home,' Oxford. Edited by Isambard Brunel. London: Seeley, 1894.

ADA, 1857-61, precociously religious child
Story of Ada. By her mother. London: W. H. Broom, [c.1862]. 16mo. (B&J)

ADAMS, Catherine, d.1891, servant <u>see</u> **M'LAREN, Catharine Ann**

ADCOCK, Matilda, n.d., religious biography
A brief memorial of Matilda Adcock, late of Oakham, Rutland, gathered chiefly from her lip or pen. By a friend and member of the Church. Oxford: J. C. Pembrey, 1877. Pamphlet.

AGAR, Anne (Rawson) 1799-1870, Methodist in York
Memoir of Mrs Benjamin Agar, of York. With extracts from her diary and correspondence / by Luke H. Wiseman. London: Wesleyan Conference Office, 1872.

AIKENHEAD, Mary, 1787-1858, Irish nun; founder of the Order of the Irish Sisters of Charity
Mary Aikenhead, her life, her work and her friends ... / by S[arah] A[tkinson]. Dublin: M. H. Gill, 1879. photo.port. (NLS)

AILSA, Evelyn Kennedy (Stuart), Marchioness of, 1848-88, Scottish religious aristocrat and philanthropist
In memoriam: Evelyn, Marchioness of Ailsa. [By Catherine M. Marsh]. Edinburgh: Andrew Stevenson, [c.1888]. 32mo. (NLS)

AINSWORTH, Sophia Magdalen (Hanmer), 1819-92, Catholic nun
Mrs Sophia Ainsworth ... : a commemorative tribute of affection / by her elder brother Anthony John Hanmer: [a biographical sketch]. Printed for private distribution. London, 1894; 2nd issue with corrections and additions as: 'A commemorative tribute of affection to Mrs Sophia Ainsworth, in religion Sister Mary Anne Liguori of Jesus Crucified' / by her brother Anthony John Hanmer. Printed for private circulation only. Edinburgh: printed by Neill, 1899.

AITKEN, Agnes, 1808-79, Scottish Free Presbyterian
Memorials of the late Miss Agnes Aitken. With Preface by George Smeaton. Edinburgh: James Taylor, 1882. (NLS)

ALEXANDER, Sophia, 1806-65, Quaker
Memorials of William H. Alexander and Sophia Alexander, of Ipswich. London: F. B. Kitto, 1867. (BL)

ALICE MAUD MARY, Princess, Grand Duchess of Hesse-Darmstadt, 1843-78, second daughter of Queen Victoria; liberal intellectual
Alice, Grand Duchess of Hesse, Princess of Great Britain and Ireland: biographical sketch and letters. [Edited by her sister Helena, Princess Christian]. London: John Murray, 1884. Reisued as: 'Alice, Grand Duchess of Hesse: letters to Her Majesty the Queen'. New and popular edition. With a memoir / by [Helena] Princess Christian. London: John Murray, 1885.
-------. Footprints of a life: in memory of the beloved Princess Alice of Great Britain and Ireland, Grand Duchess of Hesse-Darmstadt / by Isabella K. Goode. London: Hatchards, 1879.

ALLEN, Hannah Hunton Stafford, 1814-80, Norwich Quaker
A beloved mother: life of Hannah S. Allen / by her daughter [J. B.]. London: Samuel Harris, 1884. photo.port.

ALLEN, Maria, 1790-1871, Staffordshire Wesleyan
Memoir of Mrs Allen, of Woodhead Hall, Staffordshire. [By her son William Shepherd Allen]. Newcastle-under-Lyme: D. Dilworth, 1871; 2nd edition. Manchester, 1872. (NLS)

'A.L.O.E' see **TUCKER, Charlotte Maria**

ALSOP, Christine (Majolier), 1805-79, French Quaker in Britain
Memorials of Christine Majolier Alsop / compiled by Martha Braithwaite. London: Samuel Harris, 1881.

ANDERSON, Louisa (Peterswald), d.1882, missionary in the West Indies
William and Louisa Anderson: a record of their life and work in Jamaica and Old Calabar / by William Marwick. Edinburgh: Andrew Elliot, 1897.

ARMOUR, Mary Susan, 1782-1855, Scottish religious governess
Recollections of Miss Mary S[usan] Armour. [By David Dickson]. Printed for private circulation. Edinburgh: [printed by H. Armour], 1858. (NLS)

ARMSTRONG, Elizabeth (Hall), 1820-1900, managed a farm herself for 50 years
In affectionate remembrance of Mrs Elizabeth Armstrong, of Sorbietrees / by James Shadden. [1900]. 16mo. (NLS)

AUSTIN, Sarah (Taylor), 1793-1867, translator; historian
Three generations of Englishwomen: memoirs and correspondence of Mrs John Taylor, Mrs S[arah] Austin, and Lady Duff-Gordon / by Janet Ann Ross. London: John Murray, 1888. 2 volumes; revised & enlarged edition. London: T. Fisher Unwin, 1892.

AYCKBOWM, Emily Harriet Elizabeth, 1836-1900, Anglican nun; work with underprivileged children
Emily H. E. Ayckbowm, Mother Foundress of the Community of the Church. London: Church Extension Association, 1914.

AYR, Agnes Templeton, n.d., Scottish
Brief memorials of Agnes Templeton Ayr. [By M.K.]. Glasgow, [1883]. 16mo.

BAILLIE, Lady Grisell, 1822-91, aristocrat & the first Scottish Presbyterian lady deaconess
Lady Grisell Baillie: a sketch of her life / by Katherine Charlotte, Countess of Ashburnham. With a selection of her addresses ... Edinburgh: printed by R. & R. Clark, 1893. (NLS)

BAIRSTOW, Hannah (Watt), 1816-62, Huddersfield Methodist
Walking in the light: a memoir of Mrs Hannah Bairstow, of Huddersfield, Yorkshire / by Thornley Smith. London: William Tegg, 1868. 12mo.

BALFOUR, Lady Blanche Mary Harriet Gascoigne (Cecil), 1825-72, mother of A.J. Balfour, Prime Minister
Lady Blanche Balfour: a reminiscence / by James Robertson, *of Whittingehame*. Edinburgh: Oliphant, Anderson & Ferrier, [1897].

BALL, Frances (Mary Teresa), 1794-1861, Irish nun
The life of Mother Frances Mary Teresa Ball, foundress in Ireland of the Institute of the Blessed Virgin Mary / by Henry James Coleridge. London: Burns & Oates, 1881. (*Quarterly Series*, Vol. 33)

-------. Mrs Ball, foundress of the Institute of the Blessed Virgin Mary in Ireland and the British Colonies ... : a biography / by William Hutch. Dublin: James Duffy, 1879.

BANNERMAN, Lady Margaret (Gordon), 1789-1878, inspired a serious romance in Thomas Carlyle
Carlyle's first love - Margaret Gordon, Lady Bannerman: an account of her life, ancestry and homes, her family and friends / by Raymond Clare Archibald. London: Bodley Head, 1910.

BARBER, Michael Fairless, 'Michael Fairless', 1869-1901, writer
Michael Fairless, her life and writings / by William Scott Palmer (Margaret Emily Dawson) and A. M. Haggard. London: Duckworth, 1913. 12mo.

BARROW, Elizabeth Browning, 1828-98, Baptist
Memoir of Elizabeth Browning Barrow (Mrs Samuel Barrow), 1828-1898. London: printed by Riddle and Couchman, 1899. (B&J)

BARTLETT, Lavinia Strickland, 1806-75, Baptist Sunday school teacher
Mrs Lavinia Strickland Bartlett and her class at the Metropolitan Tabernacle, being a brief account of the life and labours of Mrs Lavinia Strickland Bartlett ... / by her son Edward H. Bartlett. London: Passmore & Alabaster, 1877. photo.port.

BASS, Matilda, 1832-?80, spiritual biography; poet
She walked with God, and was not, for God took her: memorials of Mrs Bass / by her sister J. V. B[ishop]. London: William Mack, [1882]. photo. port. (NLS)

BATH, Elizabeth, 1772-1856, shopkeeper & religious biographer
'The light of the village': a sketch of Elizabeth Bath. By a pastor's wife. London: Ward, 1867. Pamphlet. (NLS)

BAYER (or BAUER), Karoline, d.1877, kept mistress of Leopold of Belgium; imprisoned in a London house
Memoirs of Karoline Bauer. London: Remington, 1884-85. 4 volumes. (Volumes 1 & 2 are titled: 'Posthumous memoirs ... ')

BAYLEY, Elizabeth, 1749-1854, religious centenarian
Piety and usefulness a hundred years old: a memoir of Mrs Elizabeth Bayley, of Birmingham, who after a life of holiness and benevolence, died at the advanced age of a hundred and five years. With an introduction and reflection by John Angell James. Birmingham: J. W. Shovell, Hudson [etc.], 1856. 12mo. (NLS)

BAYLY, Ellen Ada <u>see</u> 'LYALL, Edna'

BEAMISH, Esther Matilda Grace, d.1882, missionary worker especially in Algiers
'A voice that is still': memorials of Esther Beamish / by F[rances] L. M. B[eamish] ... London: J. F. Shaw, [1886]. photo.port. (NLS)

BEATTY, Fanny, d.1892, missionary in India
A broken journey: memoir of Mrs Beatty, wife of the Rev. William Beatty, Indian missionary, lost in the 'S.S. Roumania', October 1892. [By Sara Rea]. London: J. Nisbet, 1894.

[BEITH, Julia], d.1866, Scottish Free Church Minister's wife
Sorrowing yet rejoicing, or a narrative of successive bereavements in a Minister's family. With an account of the mother's illness and death / by Alexander Beith. Enlarged edition London: T. Nelson, 1878. 12mo. (NC)

BENDLE, Mrs., d.1880, Bible Christian

Memoir of Mrs Bendle / by James Bendle. London: Bible Christian Book Room, [c.1880].

BENNETT, Sarah, 1797-1861, governess
The Christian governess: a memoir and a selection from the correspondence of Miss Sarah Bennett / by George Bright Bennett ... London: J. Nisbet, 1862. (NLS)

BENSON, Edmunda, 1851-73, religious young woman
A short account of the life and death of Edmunda Benson / written by her father [William Benson]. London: Houlston, [1874]. 12mo. Pamphlet. (Reprinted from 'The Little Gleaner')

BERGER, Charlotte Sophia Steigen, 1791-1861, Methodist
Memoir of Charlotte Sophia Steigen Berger, of Saffron-Walden / by John Holland Brown. London: S. Marlborough, 1879. photo.port. (NLS)

BICKERSTETH (later BIRKS), Elizabeth S., d.185-, spiritual biography
Doing and suffering: memorials of Elizabeth and Frances, daughters of the late Rev. E. Bickersteth / by their sister [Charlotte Ward] ... London: Seeley, Jackson and Halliday, 1860. (NLS)

BICKERSTETH, Frances, d.1854 <u>see</u> BICKERSTETH, Elizabeth S.

BOORNE, Mary, d.187-?, Reading religious woman
Mary Boorne: in memoriam. [By her husband?] James Boorne. Reading: Barham and Beecroft, [1876]. 4to.

BOOTH, Catherine (Mumford), 1829-90, co-founder and 'Mother of the Salvation Army'
The life of Catherine Booth, the mother of the Salvation Army / by Frederick St. George de Latour Booth-Tucker. London: Salvation Army Book Department, 1892. 2 volumes; abridged as 'The short life of Catherine Booth ... '. London: Salvation Army Publishing House, 1893.
-------. Mrs Booth of the Salvation Army / by William Thomas Stead. London: J. Nisbet, 1900.

BOWDEN, Mary Ann, d.1860, graphic religious biography
The lost one found: a brief memorial of Mary Ann Bowden. [By A.E.S.]. London: J. Mason, [1862]. 24mo. (NLS)

BOYD, Charlotte (McNaughten), 1847-89, Irish-born religious wife in Oldham
Devoted, or working for God: some reminiscences of Mrs Thomas Boyd (nee Chassie McNaughten) / by her husband [Thomas Boyd]. London: J. Nisbet, 1889. (NLS)

BRAITHWAITE, Anna (Lloyd), 1788-1859, Quaker; travels in America
Memoirs of Anna Braithwaite, being a sketch of her early life and ministry, and extracts from her private memoranda, 1830-59 / by her son Joseph Bevan Braithwaite. London: Headley Bros, 1905.

BRAITHWAITE, Martha, 1823-95, Quaker
Loving service: a record of the life of Martha Braithwaite / by her daughter Elizabeth Braithwaite Emmott. London: Headley Bros, 1896.

BROADLEY, Maria Charlotte, d. c.1882, Anglican nun
Mother Charlotte (Mrs Broadley of Carnmenellis): a sketch / by Louisa Herbert. Truro: Mrs John, 1882. Pamphlet. (NLS)

BRONTE (later NICHOLLS), Charlotte, 1816-55, novelist
Charlotte Bronte: a monograph / by Wemyss Reid. London: Macmillan, 1877.
-------. Charlotte Bronte and her circle / by Clement King Shorter. London: Hodder &

Stoughton, 1896.

-------. Life of Charlotte Bronte / by Augustine Birrell. London: Walter Scott Publishing, 1887. (Great Writers Series)

-------. The life of Charlotte Bronte ... / by Mrs [Elizabeth Cleghorn] Gaskell. London: Smith, Elder, 1857. 3 volumes; new edition. with an introduction by Clement King Shorter. London: Smith, Elder, 1909; and numerous later editions.

BROOKFIELD, Jane Octavia, 1821-96, novelist
    Mrs Brookfield and her circle / by Charles and Frances Brookfield. London: Sir Isaac Pitman, 1905. 2 volumes; revised edition 1906.

BROOKS, Elizabeth, n.d., 'excellent Christian female' from Manchester
    Memoirs of Mrs Elizabeth Brooks, of Manchester. Hanley: printed by Allbut, [1883?].

BROWN, Isabella Cranston see **BROWN, John**, 1810-82

BROWNING, Elizabeth (Barrett), 1806-61, major poet
    Elizabeth Barrett Browning / by John Henry Ingram. London: W. H. Allen, 1888. (Eminent Women Series)

BULWER (afterwards BULWER-LYTTON), Rosina (Doyle), Baroness Lytton, 1804-82,
    half-mad wife of Bulwer Lytton; minor writer and novelist
    A blighted life. By the Right. Hon. Lady Lytton. London: London Publishing Office, 1880. *Cambridge Bibliography of English Literature* says 'Not by Lady Lytton', so note the following rejoinder: 'Refutations of an audacious forgery of the Dowager Lady Lytton's name to a book, the publication of which she was totally ignorant'. Privately printed, 1880. Pamphlet.

-------. Life of Rosina, Lady Lytton. With numerous extracts from her ms autobiography, and other original documents, published in vindication of her memory / by Louisa Devey. London: Swan Sonnenschein, 1887.

BUNDY, Mrs., d.1851, 'aged Christian' from Brighton
    Short memorials of Widow Bundy, an aged Christian in humble life, who died April 8th 1851 at Brighton / by E. Jenyns. Brighton: Henry S. King, 1853. (NLS)

BUNSEN, Frances von, Baroness Bunsen, 1791-1876, Welsh heiress married to the
    German Ambassador in London
    The life and letters of Frances, Baroness Bunsen / by Augustus John Cuthbert Hare. London: Daldy, Isbister, 1879. 2 volumes.

BURNS (later BEGG), Isobel, 1771-1858, surviving sister of Robert Burns
    Isobel Burns (Mrs Begg): a memoir / by her grandson [Robert Burns Begg]. Privately printed for family circulation. Edinburgh: printed by George Waterson, 1891: reissued Paisley: Alexander Gardner, 1894. (NLS)

BURTON, Lady Isabel (Arundell), 1831-96, Catholic; wife of Sir Richard Burton;
    traveller
    The romance of Isabel, Lady Burton: the story of her life / told in part by herself, and in part by William Henry Wilkins. London: Hutchinson, 1897. 2 volumes; and later editions.

BUSS, Frances Mary, 1827-94, outstanding pioneer of higher education for girls, and
    founder of North London Collegiate School; leading feminist
    North London Collegiate School for Girls. In memoriam - Frances Mary Buss: obiit Christmas Eve, 1894. [1895]. 4to.

BUTCHER, Agnes Annie, 1868-85, religious girl
    'Gone before': a brief memorial of Agnes Annie Butcher. [By W.H. Summers]. London: Elliot Stock, 1886. 16mo. Pamphlet.

C., Mary Elizabeth, n.d., religious biography
'Leaning on her beloved': a memorial of M.E.C.. London: J. Nisbet, 1857.

CAMERON, Jane, n.d., Scottish female convict
Memoirs of Jane Cameron, female convict. By a prison matron [i.e. Frederick W. Robinson]. London: Hurst and Blackett, 1864. 2 volumes; new edition. London: Richard Edward King, [1864]. (but could be fiction?)

[CAMPBELL, Jessie], n.d., religious girl
Sacred recollections of a beloved daughter who 'is not dead but sleepeth'. With a brief memoir of the closing part of a life that was 'met with Christ in God'. [By Henrietta Ann Campbell]. Printed for private circulation. Liverpool: printed by George Smith Watts, 1854.

CANNING, Charlotte (Stuart), <u>Countess Canning</u>, 1817-61, Lady-in-Waiting to Queen Victoria; wife of the Viceroy of India
The story of two noble lives; being memorials of Charlotte, Countess Canning, and Louisa, Marchioness of Waterford / by Augustus John Cuthbert Hare. London: G. Allen, 1893. 3 volumes.

CARLILE, Ann Jane, 1775-1866, Irish temperance advocate
Ann Jane Carlile: a temperance pioneer / by Frederick Sherlock. London: Frederick Sherlock, 1897.

CARPENTER, Mary, d.1877 aged 90 years, scientific instrument maker?
In memory of Mary Carpenter, of 24 Regent Street, London, who died Oct. 30 1877, aged 90 years. Privately printed. Bristol: J.W. Arrowsmith, [1878]. photographically illustrated. (B&J)

CARPENTER, Mary, 1807-77, worker among homeless children, especially in Bristol; phrenologist
The life and work of Mary Carpenter / by Joseph Estlin Carpenter London: Macmillan, 1879; 2nd edition. 1881.

CHALECRAFT, Elizabeth, n.d., Bible Christian
A mother in Israel ...: memoir of Mrs Elizabeth Chalecraft / by F. W. Bourne. London: Bible Christian Book Room, 1874.

CHATELAIN, Henrietta Marie, 1823-97, French-born nun in London and in the Crimea
Sister Chatelain, or forty years' work in Westminster. Edited by Amabel Kerr. London: Catholic Truth Society, 1900.

CHATTERTON (later DERING), <u>Lady</u> Henrietta Georgiana Marcia Lascelles (Iremonger), 1806-76, Catholic miscellaneous writer; literary society; diary 1837-59
Memoirs of Georgiana, Lady Chatterton. With some passages from her diary / by the late Edward Heneage Dering. London: Hurst and Blackett, 1878; 2nd edition. 1901.

CHEALES, Edith Bellingham, 1859-81, religious girl; poetess
Memorials of a beloved child / by her mother [Edith B. Cheales]. 2nd edition. London: Alfred Holmes, [1888].

CHISHOLM, Caroline (Jones), 1808-77, founder of the Female Emigrant Society, especially to Australia
Memoirs of Mrs Caroline Chisholm, and sketches of her philanthropic labours in India, Australia and England / by Eneas Mackenzie. London: Webb, Millington, 1852. 12mo.
-------. Story of the life of Mrs Caroline Chisholm, the emigrants' friend, and her adventures in Australia. London: Trelawny Saunders, [1852]. 24mo.

CLARKE, Mary Anne (Thompson), 1776-1852, Regency adventuress; mistress to various people, including Frederick Duke of York, using her influence to obtain army promotions

The authentic and impartial life of Mrs Mary Anne Clarke .../ by Elizabeth Taylor. London: T. Tegg, 1809. ('Well embroidered')

-------. Biographical memoirs and anecdotes of the celebrated Mary Anne Clarke / by J. Herbert and W. Wilson. London: W. Wilson, [1809]. 12mo.

-------. Memoirs of Mrs Anne Clarke ... London: C. Chappel, 1809.

CLOUGH, Anna Jemima, 1820-92, first Principal of Newnham College, Cambridge
A memoir of Anna Jemima Clough / by her niece Blanche Athena Clough. London: Edward Arnold, 1897.

COLERIDGE, Sara, 1802-52, daughter of Samuel Taylor Coleridge and editor of his works; children's writer; poetess
Memoir and letters of Sara Coleridge. Edited by her daughter [Edith Coleridge]. London: Henry S. King, 1873. 2 volumes; 4th edition. 1874.

COLMAN, Helen Caroline, 1831-95, Methodist, writer
In memoriam: Caroline Colman / by her daughter Laura Elizabeth Stuart. Printed for private circulation. Norwich: printed by Fletcher, 1896.

COLQUHOUN, Henrietta Maria, n.d., Scottish
Memorials of H.M.C. (Henrietta Maria Colquhoun) / by John Campbell Colquhoun. Edited by his sons. London: Hatchards, 1870. (BL)

COMSTOCK, Elizabeth L. (Rous), 1815-1891, Quaker; in America
Life and letters of Elizabeth L. Comstock / compiled by her sister Mrs C. Hare. London: Headley Brothers, 1895.

COOK, Annie Elizabeth, d.1880, daughter of Thomas Cook, travel agent; temperance worker; accidentally gassed in the bath
A father's tribute and memorial, with a Minister's testimony, elicited by the sudden and distressing death of Annie Elizabeth Cook, which occured at Thorncroft, Stoneygate, Leicester, on November 6th 1880 ... [By Thomas Cook]. Printed for private circulation. Leicester: printed by S. Barker, [1880]. photo.port. (B&J)

COOKE, Sophia, 1814-95, missionary in Singapore
Sophia Cooke, or forty-two years' work in Singapore / by Eliza Ann Walker. London: Elliot Stock, 1899. (NLS)

COOPER, Emma see **COOPER, Mary Ann**

COOPER, Mary Ann (Thompson), d.1854, Baptist
The root and the branches: memoirs of Mrs Mary Ann Cooper and her two grandchildren, Emma and Sarah Ann Cooper / by John Cooper. London: Houlston & Stoneman, 1854. Pamphlet. (NLS) *Could be the same as below?*

COOPER, Mary Anna, n.d., Baptist
Memorials of a beloved mother, being a sketch of the life of Mrs Cooper. [By Charlotte Bickersteth Wheeler] ... London: Wertheim and Macintosh, 1853. 12mo; 2nd edition with appendix. 1862.

COOPER, Sarah Ann see **COOPER, Mary Ann**

[COOTER, Eliza], 1841-60, religious 'blind deaf mute' from Sussex
Light in darkness: a short account of a blind deaf-mute. [By Sarah Robinson]. London: J. Nisbet, 1859. (NLS)

-------. The darkness past: a sequel to 'Light in darkness': a short account of a blind deaf mute. [By Sarah Robinson]. London: J. Nisbet, 1861. photo.port. (NLS)

CRAVEN, Pauline Marie Armande Aglae (La Ferronnays), 1808-91, French writer; diarist
A memoir of Mrs Augustus Craven (Pauline de la Ferronnays) ... With extracts from her diaries and correspondence / by Maria Catherine Bishop. London: R. Bentley, 1894. 2 volumes; 3rd edition. 1896.
------- . Mrs Craven, nee La Ferronnays / by Viscont Le Meaux. Translated by Lady Martin. 2nd edition. London, [1891]. Pamphlet. (NLS)

CRIPPS, Julia see **CRIPPS, Henry William**

CROAD, Rebecca Caroline Hayman, n.d., Swindon religious poetess
A service of suffering, or leaves from the biography of Mrs Croad, of Swindon. With extracts from her writings ... [Edited by J. G. Westlake]. London: W. Mack, [1885?]. 12mo.

CROSS, Mary Ann see **'ELIOT, George'**

CRUDELIUS, Mary (M'Lean), 1839-77, founder of Edinburgh Ladies' Educational Association
A memoir of Mary Crudelius. Edited by Katherine Burton. Printed for private circulation. [Edinburgh], 1879.

D., Emily B., b.1841, Irish religious poetess
I am so happy: a memoir of Emily B. D.. Edited by C. M. Fleury. Dublin: William Carson, 1854. 12mo. (NLS)

DALHOUSIE, Ida Ramsay (Bennet), Countess of, 1857-87, she and her husband died of food poisoning on board ship returning from New York
Biographical sketch of the life of the Earl and Countess of Dalhousie. With an account of the funeral tributes to their memory, etc. / compiled by Samuel Hay. Dunoon: S. Martin, 1888. photo.ports. (NC)

DANIELL, Georgiana Fanny Shipley, 1834/5-94, social and philanthropic work among soldiers
A soldier's daughter: a short memorial of Miss [Georgiana] Daniell, of Aldershot. London: J. Nisbet, 1894.

DANIELL, Louisa (Drake), d.1871, army missioner and welfare worker
Aldershot: a record of Mrs [Louisa] Daniell's work amongst soldiers, and its sequel / by her daughter [Georgiana F. S. Daniell]. London: Hodder & Stoughton, 1879.

DARLING, Isabella Bunyan, d.1875, religious young Scottish woman
Joy in Jesus: brief memorials of Bella Darling / by Samuel MacNaughton ... Edinburgh: Andrew Elliot, 1876. 12mo. photo.port.

[DAVIE, Mary Ann], n.d., religious biography of a Cornish widow
Told for a memorial: the story of Mary Ann ... 3rd edition. London: J. Nisbet, 1891.

DAVIS, Jane Bailey, n.d., tract distributor
Early sunset, or memorials of the late Miss Jane Bailey Davis, of Hill Top / by Gervase Smith. [Privately printed]. London: printed by Hayman Brothers, 1865.

[DAWSON, Rosie], n.d., religious girl
A noble girl: a Christian endeavour story / by Lucy Hill. Stoke-on-Trent: Vyse & Hill, 1896. Pamphlet. (NLS)

[DE LA MARE, Rose], n.d., dead child
Rose: some of mother's memories. [By A. de la Mare]. London: Charles H. Kelly,

DE LISLE, Eleanora Maria, 1811-96, Catholic aristocrat
Laura de Lisle, wife and widow of Ambrose Phillipps de Lisle, of Garendon Park and Gracedieu Manor: a sketch of her life and character / by Alexander P. F. Cruikshank. Leamington: Art Book Company, 1897.

DENING, Emma Geraldine Henrietta Hamilton (Hooper), 1841-72, preached 4500 sermons in the West of England
'She spake of Him', being recollections of the loving labours and early death of the late Mrs Henry Dening / by her friend Fanny E. Guinness. Bristol: W. Mack, [1872]. photo.port.

DENISON, Charlotte, d.1859 aged 83, widow of John Denison, M.P.
Memoir of Mrs Denison. [1859]. (B&J)

DE ROS, Georgiana (Lennox), <u>Baroness de Ros</u>, 1795-1891, wife of 23rd Baron; social life; present at the Jubilees of George 111 and Victoria
A sketch of the life of Georgiana, Lady de Ros. With some reminiscence of her family and friends, including the Duke of Wellington / by her daughter [Blanche H. G. Swinton]. London: John Murray, 1893.

'DORA, <u>Sister</u>' <u>see</u> **PATTISON, Dorothy Wyndlow**

DOUBLEDAY, Mary, n.d., Leicestershire worthy
Memoir of Mrs Doubleday, of Long-Clawson, Leicestershire / by John Newton, London: J. Mason [etc.], 1856. 12mo. (B&J)

DOWDLE, <u>Mrs</u> <u>see</u> DOWDLE, James

DRAKEFORD, Martha, d.1859, aged 10, religious girl
Brief memoir of Martha Drakeford, of Leicester, who died in the Lord, January 31 1859, aged 10 years and 3 months. Written by her father. London: W. H. Collingridge, 1860. (NLS)

DRANE, Augusta Theodosia ('Mother Francis Raphael'), 1823-94, Catholic nun; historical and devotional writer
A memoir of Mother Francis Raphael, O.S.D. (Augusta Theodosia Drane), sometime Provincial of the Congregation of Dominican Sisters of Catherine of Sienna. Edited by Bertrand Wilberforce. London: Longmans, Green, 1895.

DRIFFIELD, <u>Mrs</u>. (Crawford), 1769-1851, Methodist
A Christian at fourscore: a memorial of Mrs Driffield / by E. Drewett. Kidsgrove: Thomas Wardle, 1864. 12mo. (NLS)

DRUMMOND, Maria (Kinnaird), d.1891 aged 80, literary and social reminiscences
Maria Drummond: a sketch. [By Charles Kegan Paul]. London: Kegan Paul, Trench, Trubner, 1891. 12mo.

DRURY, <u>Mrs</u>., 1823-64, domestic biography
Brief memorials of the late Mrs Drury. Born at Kidderminster, Sept. 28 1823 - Died at Newcastle-upon-Tyne Sept. 20 1864. Privately printed. Newcastle-upon-Tyne: printed by A. Reid, [1864]. photo.port.

DRYSDALE, Helen, d.1891, Scottish religious girl
A Scotch jewel newly set: a brief memorial of Nellie Drysdale / by M. C. Lees ... Edinburgh: Oliphant, Anderson and Ferrier, 1891.

DUFF-GORDON, <u>Lady</u> Lucie (or Lucy) Christiana (Austin), 1821-69 <u>see</u> **AUSTIN Sarah**

DUNCAN, Margaret (Wilson), 1784-1874, Edinburgh schoolmistress; ran the National School Mistresses Training College at Salisbury for 22 years
In memoriam: Mrs Duncan (Margaret Wilson). [By William Alexander]. Aberdeen, 1892. 4to. (NLS)

DYER, Mary (Atkins), 1851-87, wife of Methodist Minister
Christhood as seen in the life work of Mary Dyer / by her husband George Dyer ... London: T. Woolmer, [1889]. (NLS)

EDWARD, Catherine (Grant), 1813-61, Scottish missionary to Jews
Missionary life among the Jews in Moldavia, Galicia and Silesia: memoir and letters of Mrs Edward. With preface by Alexander Moody Stuart. London: Hamilton, Adams, 1867.

ELDER, Mrs., d.1896, Scottish Free Church Minister's wife
Memorials of the late Rev. J. R. and Mrs Elder of Arrochar / by Patrick Wood Minto [and others]. Edinburgh: Oliphant, Anderson & Ferrier, 1900.

'ELIOT, George' (i.e. Mary Ann or Marian EVANS, later CROSS), 1819-80, major novelist
George Eliot / by Mathilde Blind. London: W. H. Allen, 1883. (Eminent Women Series)
------- . Life of George Eliot / by Oscar Browning. London: Walter Scott, 1890. (Great Writers series)

ELLING, Anne, n.d., Wiltshire centenarian
The Wiltshire centenarian, her wonderful life and happy death at the age of one hundred and two years ... / by William Jeffery. 9th edition. Westbury: W. Michael, [1872]. 16mo. (B&J)

ELLIOTT, Charlotte (Babington), 1789-1871, poet and hymn writer
'The King in his beauty': a tribute to the memory of Miss Charlotte Elliott / by Octavius Winslow. London, [1872]. 16mo. (BL)
-------. Memoir of Charlotte Elliott ... / by her sister E. B[abington] ... [1875]. 12mo. (BL)

ELLIOTT, Eleanor (Weatherell), 1813-82, Manx poet and religious writer
Manx recollections: memorials of Eleanor Elliott / by Katherine A. Forrest. London: J. Nisbet, 1894.

ELLIS, Sarah (Stickney), 1812-72, lapsed Quaker; writer on temperance and education
The home life and letters of Mrs Ellis. Compiled by her nieces. London: J. Nisbet, [1893].

EVANS, Mary Anne see **'ELIOT, George'**

[EWING, Elisabeth Constance Lindsay Orr], 1862-78, Scottish religious girl
In memoriam: Ella. Printed for private circulation. Edinburgh, 1879. photo.port. (NC)

EWING, Juliana Horatia (Gatty), 1841-85, children's writer of 'good straightforward stories' and of verse
Juliana Horatia Ewing and her books / by Horatia Katharine Frances Eden (born Gatty). London: S.P.C.K., [1896].

FAIRLESS, Michael see **BARBER, Michael Fairless**

FALLON, Jane, 1832-88, Irish Catholic nun

A nun, her friends and her Order, being a sketch of the life of Mother Mary Xaveria Fallon, sometime Superior-General of the Institute of the Blessed Virgin in Ireland, and its dependencies / by Katherine Tynan. London: Kegan Paul, Trench, Trubner, 1891.

FARRAND, Eliza <u>see</u> **FARRAND, Rebecca**

FARRAND, Rebecca, 1821-56, Quaker; visitor to New York State

A sister's memorial, or a little account of Rebecca Farrand. Also, drawn up by her, a brief sketch of an elder sister [Eliza Farrand]. [By Sarah Ann Farrand]. London: W. & F. G. Cash, 1857.

FAUCIT, Helen(a) (the stage name of **Helena Saville, <u>Lady</u> Martin),** 1817- 1898, actress

Helena Faucit (Lady Martin) / by Theodore Martin. Edinburgh: William Blackwood, 1900.

FEILDING, <u>Lady</u> Clare Mary Henrietta, n.d., Catholic

A sketch of the life of Lady Clare Feilding, a Child of Mary in the world. Printed for private circulation. Leamington, 1900. (B&J)

FERGUSON Margaret Duncan (Low), d.1887, Free Church Minister's wife

In memoriam: Margaret Duncan, daughter of Matthew Low, Esq., flax spinner, Keathbank, Blairgowrie, and wife of the Rev. Archibald Ferguson ... Died on the 19th February 1887, at the Free Church Manse, Alyth ... [Alyth: printed by T. M' Murray, 1887]. Pamphlet. (NLS)

FERNIE, Jessie Kerr, n.d., religious girl

In memoriam: Jessie Kerr Fernie. [By B. Fernie]. [Liverpool: D. Marples, c.1893].

FERRIER, Mary (Lewis), 1796-1857, Welsh-born Methodist

A memoir of Mrs M. Ferrier. Including sketches of her brother-in-law and sister [Emma, d.1843]. By a member of the family. London: J. Mason, 1858. 16mo. (NLS)

FERRIER, Susan (Edmonstone), 1782-1854, Scottish novelist

Memoir and correspondence of Susan Ferrier, 1782-1854, based on her private correspondence. Edited by John A. Doyle. London: John Murray, 1898; reissued London: John Murray, 1929. (Edition of 300 copies)

FLETCHER, Eliza, b.1831, Scottish religious poet; reformer

A woman's work, being memorials of Eliza Fletcher. Edited with a sketch of her life by Charles Adamson Salmond. Glasgow: J. N. Mackinlay, 1884; illustrated edition. 1887; and other editions.

FREEMAN, Sarah Ann (Bottomley), d.1868 aged 30 years, Birmingham Quaker

In affectionate remembrance of Sarah Ann Freeman, wife of Henry Freeman, of Harborne, near Birmingham ..., who died the 13th of 9th Month 1868, aged 30 years. Birmingham: White & Pike, [1868]. 16mo.

FRY, <u>Lady</u> Sophia (Pease), 1837-97, philanthropist in Darlington; Liberal M.P.'s wife

Lady Fry, of Darlington / by Eliza Orme. London: Hodder & Stoughton, 1898.

FULLERTON, <u>Lady</u> Georgiana Charlotte, 1812-85, Catholic; novelist; philanthropist

Life of Lady Georgiana Fullerton. From the French of [Pauline] Craven / by Henry James Coleridge. London: R. Bentley, 1888.

GARDEN, Margaret (Maitland), 1807-85, teacher; advocate's wife; philanthropist in Aberdeen

Mrs Garden: a memorial sketch. [By William Alexander, of Aberdeen Free Press]. Printed for private circulation. 1887. 4to. (NLS)

GARFIT, Louisa Emily (de Bunsen), 1849-87, religious biography
In memoriam Lisa Garfit. April 22nd 1887. [By Alice M. Bethune]. London: Hatchards, 1887. 12mo. (NLS)

GEORGE, Elizabeth, 1831-56, religious worker
Memoir of Elizabeth George / by Henry J. Piggott. London: John Mason, 1858.

GIBSON, Helen Lockhart, 1836-88, Scottish temperance worker; tract distributor
'Not weary in well-doing', or the life and work of Mrs Helen Lockhart Gibson / by her husband [W. Gibson] ... Edinburgh: John Menzies, 1888. (NLS)

GILBERT, Elizabeth Margaretta Maria, 1826-85, blind; pioneer of work for other blind people
Elizabeth Gilbert and her work for the blind / by Frances Martin. London: Macmillan, 1887.

GILCHRIST, Anne, 1828-85, author, friend of Rossetti
Anne Gilchrist, her life and writings. Edited by Herbert Harlakenden Gilchrist ... London: T. Fisher Unwin, 1887. (NLS)

GILL, Hannah, n.d., religious woman in the West Midlands
'A more than consequence': some memoirs of Hannah Gill / by her son Thomas Howard Gill. For private circulation. London: printed by Saunders, 1872. photo.port.(B&J)

GILPIN, Henrietta <u>see</u> **GILPIN, Bernard**

GLADSTONE, Alice Jane <u>see</u> **GLADSTONE, Jane May**

GLADSTONE, Catherine (Glynne), 1812-1900, wife of W. E. Gladstone; worked with him for the reclamation of prostitutes; philanthropist
Catherine Gladstone: life, good works and political efforts / by Edwin A. Pratt. London: Sampson Low, Marston, 1898.

GLADSTONE, Jane May, n.d., wife of a clergyman
In memoriam: Jane May Gladstone and her children, Alice Jane Gladstone, John Tilt Gladstone. [By John Hall Gladstone]. With a sermon ... / by James Hamilton. 2nd enlarged edition. Printed for private circulation only. [London: Unwin Brothers], 1866.

GORDON, Barbara Sophia, 1841-60, spiritual biography
Dawn and sunrise: brief notices of the life and early death of Barbara Sophia Gordon / by C[harlotte] B[ickersteth] ... London: Seeley, Jackson and Halliday, 1860. 12mo. (NLS)

GORDON, Elisabeth, <u>Duchess of Gordon</u> (Brodie), 1794-1864, wife of the 5th Duke, Scottish Free Presbyterian; renounced the world
Life and letters of Elisabeth, last Duchess of Gordon / by Alexander Moody Stuart. London: J. Nisbet, 1865.

GOSSE, Emily, 1806-57, wife of Philip Gosse; social worker in East End of London
'Tell Jesus': recollections of Emily Gosse / by Anna Shipton. 1863. 12mo; enlarged edition. London: Morgan and Chase, [1911]. 16mo.

GRAEME, Eliza Helen Marriott, n.d., religious girl
The bud of promise: a memoir of Eliza H. M. Graeme / by David Pitcairn. London: John Henry Jackson, [etc.], 1854. (NLS)

[GRANT, Emily Frederica], d.1851 aged 16, religious poet and writer
'Looking unto Jesus': a narrative of the brief race of a young disciple [Emily Frederica Grant] / by her mother [J. T. Grant]. Bath: Binns and Godwin, [etc.], [1852].

GREEN, Henrietta, n.d., Quaker
Henrietta Green: a memoir. Printed for private circulation. Ashford: printed by H. D. and A. B. Headley, [1881]. photo.port. (B&J)

GREENAWAY, Kate, 1846-1901, illustrator of children's books
Kate Greenaway / by Marion Harry Spielman and George Somes Layard. London: A. & C. Black, 1905; reprinted Bracken Books, 1986.

GREENWAY, Hannah (Angel), 1807-74, religious biography
Memorial of the Lord's goodness to the late Hannah Greenway, of London / by her brother [Benjamin Angel]. Oxford: J. C. Pembrey, 1874.

GREENWELL, Dorothy ('Dora'), 1821-82, poet and essayist
Memoirs of Dora Greenwell / by William Dorling. London: James Clarke, [1885].

GREY, Mary, n.d., daughter of Hon. John Grey
Brief sketches of the early history, conversion and closing period of the life of Mary, second daughter of the Hon. John Gray ... / by H[enry Cavendish] G[rey]. London, [1855]. 12mo.

GROTE, Harriet, 1792-1878, 'Queen of the radicals'; biographer
Mrs Grote: a sketch / by Elizabeth Eastlake. London: John Murray, 1880.

GURNEY, Priscilla, b.1809, Quaker reformer on the Isle of Wight and in East Anglia
Memoir of Priscilla Gurney. Edited by Susannah Corder. London: W. & F.G. Cash, 1856. 12mo.

H., Maria E., 1823-50, religious girl died in Italy
The bow in the cloud: a memoir of M.E.H. / by her sister [H. Greene], the author of 'Ellen Mordaunt'. London: T. Hatchard, 1857. 12mo. (NLS)

HALL, Mary, 1816-78, domestic biography
Mary Hall of Thorpe Underwood, 1816-1878: a record of impressions. With extracts from her note books and journals / by Joseph Truman. Bristol: W. C. Hemmons, 1908. (Only 25 copies printed) (B&J)

HALLAHAN, Mother Margaret Mary, 1803-68, founder of an order of nuns
Life of Mother Margaret Mary Hallahan, foundress of the English Congregation of St. Catherine of Sienna ... [Edited by Augusta Theodosia Drane]. London: Longmans, Green, Reader and Dyer, 1869.

[HAMILTON, Mary C.], [d.c.1867], Scottish servant girl; religious diarist
Only a servant, or a brief memorial of Mary H---. By an Elder of the Church [i.e. John B. Bishop] ... Edinburgh: Andrew Elliot, 1870. 12mo; 3rd edition. 1873 (NLS)

HANIE, n.d., servant; Plymouth Brethren?
Faithful Hanie, or disinterested service: memoirs of a Ninevite servant / by Henry Groves. London: J. Nisbet, [etc.], 1866. 12mo.

HARE, Maria (Leycester), 1798-1870, mother of A. J. C. Hare
Memorials of a quiet life [i.e. of Maria Hare] / by Augustus John Cuthbert Hare. London: G. Allen, 1872. 2 volumes; Supplementary Volume. [1876].

HARFORD-BATTERSBY, Eleanor Dundas, 1818-84, religious aristocrat
In memoriam: Eleanor D. Harford-Battersby, obiit April 15 1884. Brief memorials of

her life and work. Newport & Market Drayton: Horne & Bennison, 1884. photo. port. Pamphlet. (NLS)

HARLEY, Sukey, d.1853 aged 70, Shropshire peasant
Memoir of Sukey Harley, of the parish of Pulverbach, near Shrewsbury / by the late rector's daughter [Jane Gilpin]. [New edition.] London: William Wileman, 1881. 12mo.

HARRIS, Eliza Ann, b.1834, spiritual biography
The broad road and the narrow way: a brief memoir of Eliza Ann Harris. By the author of 'The Female Jesuit' [i.e. Jemima Thompson]. London: J. Nisbet, 1859. (NLS)

HARRISON, Ann, b.1800, Sheffield infants schools; tract distributor
Memoranda of the late Ann Harrison, of Weston. With introductory remarks / by T. Best. [Printed for private circulation. Sheffield, 1859]; new edition. London: Wertheim, Macintosh & Hunt, 1860.

HART, Mary, n.d., missionary in Hankow, China
Mary Hart, memories and letters. Printed for private circulation. Frome: Butler, Tanner, [1896].

HAVERGAL SISTERS - three religious sisters
The sisters: reminiscences and records of active work and patient suffering: Frances Ridley Havergal - Maria V. G. Havergal / by Charles Bullock. London: 'Home Words' Publishing Office, [1890].
　　see also **SHAW, Ellen P. (born HAVERGAL)**

HAVERGAL, Frances Ridley, 1836-79, hymn writer; poet
Frances Ridley Havergal: the last week [of her life]. [By Maria V. G. Havergal.] London: J. Nisbet, [1879]. 16mo.
------ . Memorials of Frances Ridley Havergal / by her sister Maria Vernon Graham Havergal. London: J. Nisbet, [1880]; and many later editions.
------- . 'Within the Palace gate': a tribute to the memory of Frances Ridley Havergal / by Charles Bullock. New edition. London: 'Hand and Heart', [1879].

HAY, Sarah Sands, 1845-?64, 'quiet usefulness'; religious philanthropy in Preston cotton famine
The youthful sufferer glorified: a memorial of Sarah Sands Hay, daughter of the Rev. David Hay. London: Wesleyan Conference Office, [186-]. 12mo. (NLS)

HAYES (later BUSHNELL) Catherine, 1825-61, Irish singer of international status
Memoir of Miss Catherine Hayes, 'The Swan of Erin'. By a contributor to the Dublin University Magazine. London: Cramer, [1852?]

HEATH, Caroline, 1835-87, actress
Miss Heath: a biographical sketch. By Dramaticus. Leicester: E. Lamb, 1879.

HEBBRON, Elizabeth, 1803-60, Primitive Methodist in Hexham
The Christian living and dying: memoirs of the late Mrs Elizabeth Hebbron / by her brother Errington Ridley. 2nd edition. Newcastle-upon-Tyne: 'Home Piety' Office, 1864.

[HENDERSON, Rachel], n.d., religious girl
Rachel: a life sketch / by Isabel Mary Jones. [Oxford: printed by Mowbray, 1895]. Pamphlet. (NLS)

HERDMAN, Emma, 1844-?97, Irish worker with North Africa Mission
A biographical sketch relative to the missionary labours of Emma Herdman in the Empire of Morocco / by Albert Augustus Isaacs. London: S. W. Partridge, 1900. (NLS)

HERSCHELL, Helen S., d.1854, Irvingite

'Far above rubies': memoirs of Helen S. Herschell / by her daughter Ridley Haim Herschell. London: Walton and Maberley, 1854.

HESSEL, Eliza, 1829-?55, religious biography

True womanhood: memorials of Eliza Hessel / by Joshua Priestley. Leeds: printed by H. W. Walker, 1859. (NLS)

HILL, Mary Ann (Bobbett), 1839-74, Methodist

A modern Phoebe, being a memorial sketch of the late Mrs Sydney Hill / by William Shaw Caldecott. Printed for private circulation. London: Elliot Stock, 1875. 12mo.

HILTON, Marie, 1821-96, introduced the creche system into Stepney

Marie Hilton, her life and work, 1821-1896 / by her son J. Deane Hilton. London: Isbister, 1897.

HINCKSMAN, Dorothy, 1802-59, missionary in Antigua; shipwrecked in West Indies

Memoir of Mrs Hincksman, late of Lytham, Lancashire / by John Hannah. London: John Mason, 1861. (NLS)

------- . The story of the wreck of the 'Maria' mail boat. With a memoir of Mrs Hincksman, the only survivor / by John Hannah. London: C. H. Kelly, [186-]. (*Possibly a version of the above?*)

HOBSON, Catharine Leslie, 1823-?86, nurse in the Crimea

Catharine Leslie Hobson, lady-nurse, Crimean War, and her life / by William Fraser Hobson. London: Parker, 1888. photographic portrait & illustrations. (NLS)

HODGSON, Mary Bell, 1840-62, religious girl from York

Mary Bell Hodgson: a memorial / by Joseph Bush. Bolton: William Parkhouse, 1865. 16mo. (NLS)

HOLY, Lucy Maria, 1843-71, religious biography

Memorials of Lucy Maria Holy. London: S.W. Partridge, 1872. photo.port. (NLS)

[HOPPUS, Martha], d.1853, domestic biography

Memorials for a wife. Dedicated by her husband [John Hoppus] to their children. London: Judd & Glass, 1856. 12mo. photo.port. (NLS)

HOUGHTON, Mrs. see **HOUGHTON, John**

HOYLE, Elizabeth, n.d., Manchester domestic biography

Memorial of Mrs Isaac Hoyle, of Priory Gate, Sale / by William W. Stamp. Printed for prviate circulation. [London: printed by Hayman Bros & Lilly, 187-]. 16mo. photo.port. (B&J)

HURD, Mary Fanny Bickford, 1849-81, Methodist; in the West Indies

Fanny Hurd, or the story of a West Indian missionary's daughter. Edited by Nehemiah Curnock ... London: T. Woolmer, 1886. 12mo.

INGELOW, Jean, 1820-97, poet; novelist

Some recollections of Jean Ingelow and her early friends. London: Wells Gardner, Darton, 1901.

INGLIS, Christina A. see **INGLIS, Andrew**

ISHAM, Lady Emily, d.189-, widow of Sir Charles Isham; spiritualist; vegetarian
Emily: [letters and condolences]. [Edited by C. E. Isham]. Horsham: printed by J. R. Tydeman, 1899. (B&J)

JAMESON, Anna Brownell (Murphy), 1794-1860, Irish art historian; writer; women's rights campaigner
Memoirs of the life of Anna Jameson, author of 'Sacred and Legendary Art', etc. / by her niece Geraldine Macpherson. London: Longmans, Green, 1879.

JARRETT, Rebecca, d. c.1885, reformed prostitute
Rebecca Jarrett / by Josephine Elizabeth Butler. London: Morgan & Scott, [1885]. (NLS)

JEFFREY, Mary (Whitehead), d.1862, young Minister's wife; died in childbed
In memoriam: a tribute of affection to the memory of a beloved wife / by Robert T. Jeffrey. Printed for private circulation. Edinburgh, 1862. photo. port. (NLS)

JOHNSON, Lucy S. see **JOHNSON, William Thomas**

JOHNSTON, Alice, 1816-?60, Scottish religious woman
Submission and its reward: a memoir of Alice Johnston ... / by James Gailey. London: J. Nisbet, 1863.

JONES, Agnes Elizabeth, 1832-68, Nightingale nurse; pioneer of workhouse nursing
Agnes Jones, or she hath done what she could / by Julia Ann Elizabeth Roundell. London: Bickers, 1896. (B&J)
------- . Memorials of Agnes Elizabeth Jones / by her sister [J. Jones] ... London: Strahan, 1871.

JONES (afterwards LEWIS), Mary, *of Llanfihangel-y-Pennant,* 1784-1866, Welsh religious woman
From the beginning, or the story of Mary Jones and her Bible. Collected from the best materials and retold / by M. E. R[opes]. London: Religious Tract Society, 1876; reissued: London: British and Foreign Bible Society, [1883]; another edition as 'The story of Mary Jones and her Bible'. 1904.
------- . Mary Jones of Ty'nyddol ... / by Robert Oliver Rees. London: Hatchards, 1887. 16mo. (NLS)
and other titles in Welsh

K., I. N. (later Mrs T--), 1825-?57, Scottish clergy wife
Inheriting the promises: a memorial of a brief but blessed life / by John Renton. London: J. Nisbet, 1861. (NLS)

KEARY, Annie, 1825-79, traveller; novelist; children's writer
Memoir of Annie Keary / by her sister [Eliza Keary]. London: Macmillan, 1882. photo. port.; 2nd edition. 1883.

KEELEY, Mary Ann (Goward), 1806-79, actress
The Keeley's on the stage and at home / by Walter Goodman. London: R. Bentley, 1895.

KELL, Elizabeth (Dunkin), d.1873, Unitarian Minister's wife
Memorials of Rev. Edmund Kell, M.A., F.S.A., and Mrs Kell, of Southampton. [By

Joanna Dunkin]. London: Williams & Norgate, 1875. (NLS)

KENNEDY, Margaret Stephen, 1814-91, missionary in northern India
Memoir of Margaret Stephen Kennedy / by her husband James Kennedy, late missionary in Northern India. London: J. Nisbet, 1892. (NLS)

KERR, Mother Henrietta Mary Emma, 1842-84, aristocratic Catholic nun
The life of Mother Henrietta Kerr, religious of the Sacred Heart. Edited by John Morris. Roehampton: printed by James Stanley, 1886; 3rd edition. 1892. photo.port.

KIDD, Margaret (Burnett), 1789-1857, religious woman from Hull
Christ in his disciple: a brief sketch of the history, character and dying experience of the late Mrs Margaret Kidd, of Kingston-upon-Hull / compiled by R. A. Redford. Hull: J. W. King, [1857]. Pamphlet. (NLS)

KINNAIRD, Mary Jane Kinnaird (Hoare), Baroness, 1816-88, Scottish joint founder of the Y.W.C.A.; wife of 10th Baron Kinnaird
Mary Jane Kinnaird / by Donald Fraser. London: J. Nisbet, 1890.

KNAPP, Susanna, 1770-1856, Methodist
Fruits of righteousness in the life of Susanna Knapp, of The White House, Lowesmore, Worcester / by Edith Rowley. London: Hamilton, Adams, 1866. 12mo. (NLS)

KNIGHT, Ada M., n.d., Training College founder
Memoir of Mrs Athro Knight, founder and Principal of Knightsville College ... / by Emmie S. Oram. Brockley: Knightsville College, 1901. (B&J)

LAMBERT, Ester Ann, 'Hetty', 1872-93, in the Methodist New Connection
Strength perfected in weakness, being memorials of Hetty Lambert / by William John Townsend. London: S. W. Partridge, [1893]. (NLS)

LAURIE, Catherine Ann, d. 1895, Scottish domestic biography
In memory of Catherine Ann Laurie, Nairne Lodge, Duddingston, Midlothian, who departed this life on the 31 July 1895. Edited by her husband [S. S. Laurie]. Privately printed. Edinburgh: printed by T. & A. Constable, 1896.

LEAKEY, Caroline Woolmer, 1827-81, religious writer; lived in Tasmania
Clear, shining light: a memoir of Caroline W. Leakey, the author of 'God's tenth', 'Lip sins', etc. / by her sister Emily [P. Leakey]. New edition. London: John F. Shaw, [1882?].

[LEGGE, Mary], 1802-79, religious biography; Independent
A life of consecration: memorials of Mrs Mary Legge. By one of her sons [Alfred Owen Legge]. London: J. Nisbet, 1883. photographic portrait & illustrations. (NLS)

LESLIE, Eleanor (Atlee), 1800-92, Catholic convert boarding at a convent in Edinburgh
Eleanor Leslie: a memoir / by Jean Mary Stone. Leamington: Art and Book Company, 1898.

LINTON, Eliza Lynn, 1822-98, novelist; anti-feminist; first woman employed as a newspaper feature writer
Mrs Lynn Linton: her life, letters and opinions / by George Soames Layard. London: Methuen, 1901.

LITTLEBOY, Sarah, d.1870 aged 75, Great Berkhampstead Quaker, poet and diarist

Memoranda relating to the late Sarah Littleboy, of Boxwells, Great Berkhampstead. With selections from her poetry and manuscripts. For private circulation only. London: printed by R. Barrett, 1873. photo.port. 4to.

'LIZZIE', d.1886, Baptist girl
A short memoir entitled 'A lamb of the flock' / by Joseph Rigby. Malton: printed by George Barnby Russell, [1888]. 16mo. Pamphlet. (NLS)

LLOYD, Bessy (Wilks), 1830-71, Primitive Methodist in the Black Country
A bright light in a dark place, or eminent piety in the Black Country as exemplified in the life of Mrs Philip Lloyd, of Bilston / by Frederick R. Andrews. London: G. Lamb, 1873.

LOWDELL, Mary Caroline (Joplin), d.1882, religious wife of Brighton doctor
Loving and beloved: a memorial sketch of Mary Caroline Lowdell / compiled by Emma Holland. Brighton: D. B. Friend, 1883. 12mo. (NLS)

LUCAS, Margaret (Bright), 1818-90, temperance worker and suffrage; sister of John Bright, M.P.
Margaret Bright Lucas: the life story of a 'British woman', being a memoir ... / by Henry J. B. Heath. London: for the author, 1890.
------- . Memoir of Margaret Bright Lucas, President of the British Women's Temperance Association. [By Louisa Stewart and Jessie A. Fowler]. London: The Association, [n.d.]. (B&J)

'LYALL, Edna' [i.e. Ellen Ada BAYLY], 1857-1903, minor novelist; feminist
Edna Lyall: an appreciation. With biographical and critical notes / by George A. Payne. Manchester: John Heywood, [1903].
------- . The life of Edna Lyall (Ada Ellen Bayly) / by J. M. Escreet. London: Longmans, Green, 1904.

LYALL, Isabella D., d.1891, Scottish United Presbyterian missionary in West Africa
Nwan Ima, the woman of love: memorial sketch of Isabella D. Lyall, missionary, Old Calabar / by Jessie Hood. Edinburgh: Robert R. Sutherland, 1892. 12mo. (NLS)

[LYON, Jane Joanna], 1843-54, religious girl
Early grace with early glory: a brief memorial of a beloved daughter [Jane Joanna Lyon] / by William P. Lyon. London: Eard, [1855]. 12mo. (NLS)

LYTTON, Lady Rosina Bulwer see BULWER-LYTTON, Lady Rosina

M., Ada S.], d.1878, religious girl
Ada, or the memoir of a consecrated young life / by W.J.M.. 4th edition. London: Walter G. Wheeler, 1891. 32mo. Pamphlet. (NLS)

McDOUGALL, Harriette (Bunyon), 1818-86, missionary and bishop's wife in Sarawak in 1850s
An early Victorian heroine: the story of Harriette McDougall / by Mary Bramston. London: National Society's Depository, 1911.

MACKENZIE, Anne, d.1877 aged 64, missionary in East Africa
An elder sister: a short sketch of Anne Mackenzie and her brother [Frederick Charles Mackenzie] the missionary bishop / by Frances Awdry. London: Bemrose, 1878. photo.port. (NLS); 3rd edition. 1904.

M'LAREN, Catharine Ann, 1823-93, Secretary of the Dean Bank Institution for the

training of neglected and destitute children, Edinburgh

Memories: Catherine Ann M'Laren. Printed for private circulation. Edinburgh: A. Elliot, 1894. (NLS)

*Includes a brief memoir of Catherine Adams, d.1891 aged 'above eighty', servant.

McLEAN, Jean, d.1897, missionary in China and Japan

God my exceeding joy: a sketch of the trials, labours & triumphs of the late Miss Jean Mclean / by her twin sister Margaret [McLean]. 2nd edition. London: Passmore and Alabaster, [etc.], 1899. (NLS)

McNEILL, Lady Elizabeth (Wilson) see McNEILL, Sir John

MACPHERSON, Isabella, 1842-88, Scottish religious slum worker

Isabella Macpherson: a devoted life / by John Macpherson. London: Morgan and Scott, [1889]. (NLS)

MARCHANT, Naomi, d.1857 aged 12, religious girl

A Sussex lamb safely folded away, or some account of the Lord's dealings with Naomi Marchant, of Rotherfield, Sussex, who departed this life on her birthday, March 11th 1857, aged 12 years / by Benjamin Tatham. London: W. H. Collingridge, [1857]. Pamphlet. (NLS)

MARSHALL, Emma (Martin), 1830-99, popular children's writer

Emma Marshall: a biographical sketch / by Beatrice Marshall. London: Seeley, 1900.

MARSHALL, Lydia, n.d., religious woman

Memoir of Lydia Marshall / by S. M. Benson. [Hertford: printed by Stephen Austin, 187-]. (B&J)

MARTIN, Emma, 1812-51, Owenite socialist; freethinker

The last days of Mrs Emma Martin, advocate of free thought / by George Jacob Holyoake. London: J. Watson, 1851.

MARTIN, Helena, Lady see FAUCIT, Helena

MARTINEAU, Harriet, 1802-76, writer; 'deaf bluestocking'; atheist; essayist; historian; political economist

Harriet Martineau / by Florence Fenwick Miller. London: W. H. Allen, 1884. (Eminent Women Series)

MARTYN, Caroline Eliza Derecourt, 1867-96, Christian socialist

Life and letters of Caroline Martyn / by Lena Wallis. London: Labour Leader Publishing Department, 1898.

MARY FRANCIS, Mother, n.d., Catholic nun

In memoriam: Mother Mary Francis of the Five Wounds, O.S.F., foundress and first Abbess of St. Mary's, Mill Hill / by George Carter. Printed for private circulation. [188-]. (B&J)

[MENTEITH, Margaret], [d.188-], social reminiscences

'Farewell to thee!' or 'Margaret, a sketch' / by Mrs Nelson. Newbury: Thomas Hawkins, 1889. 12mo. (B&J)

MEREDITH, Susanna, 1823-1901, pioneer of the rehabilitation of women prisoners

Susanna Meredith: a record of a vigorous life / by Mary Anne Lloyd. London: Hodder & Stoughton, 1903.

METHUEN, Mary Matilda Cecilia, 1823-53, religious biography

'The fountain sealed': a memoir of Mary M. C. Methuen, author of 'The morning of life' / by her mother [Louisa Mary Methuen]. Bath: Binns and Goodwin, [1857]. (NLS)

MEURICOFFRE, Harriet (Butler), d.1900, religious and social work in Italy
In memoriam: Harriet Meuricoffre / by her sister Josephine Butler. London: Marshall, [1901]. (NLS)

MILLER, Elizabeth, 1841-58, autobiography; Baptist; religious poetess
The loving-kindness of the Lord illustrated, or a memoir of Elizabeth Miller, of Wycombe Marsh, Bucks. [Edited by her father J.P. Miller]. Wycombe: printed by W. Butler, 1858. 16mo. Pamphlet. (NLS)

MILNES, Elizabeth, 1820-?65, Secretary of the Sabbath Alliance of Scotland
Lizzie Milnes: a memoir of a beloved wife. With selections from her letters, poetry and scripture thoughts / by John Roberts ... Edinburgh: MacLaren and MacNiven, 1876.

MINET, Emily, 1835-92, nurse in Warwickshire
A short memoir of Emily Minet, for twenty years Lady Superintendent of the Nursing Home, Stratford-upon-Avon. Edited by Charles Granville Gepp. London: Rivington & Percival, 1894. (NLS)

MITCHELL, Jane Stuart, d.1878 aged 81, Free Church wife
The strong faith of a good woman: memoir of the late Jane Stuart Mitchell, of Aberdeen, containing some account of her labours of love for Glenlivet, her birthplace. Aberdeen: D. Wyllie, 1893. Pamphlet. (NLS)

MOFFAT, Mary (Clarke), 1793-1883, Scottish missionary wife
The lives of Robert and Mary Moffat / by their son John Smith Moffat. London: T. Fisher Unwin, 1885. photo.port.

MOHL, Mary Elizabeth (Clarke), 1793-1883, intellectual living mainly in Paris and running an influential salon for forty years
Madame Mohl, her salon and her friends: a study of social life in Paris / by Kathleen O'Meara. London: R. Bentley, 1885.

MONSELL, Hon. Harriet, 1812-83, Anglican nun at the Community of St. John the Baptist, Clewer, Windsor
Harriet Monsell: a memoir / by Thomas Thellusson Carter. London: J. Masters, 1884; 3rd edition. 1890.

MONTEFIORE, Lady Judith (Cohen), d.1862, Jewish philanthropist <u>see</u> **MONTEFIORE, Sir Moses**

MORGAN, Mrs. (Roberts), 1797-1852, devoted Welsh clergy wife
The clergyman's wife: a memoir of the late Mrs Morgan, of Syston / by her husband Edward Morgan. Carnarvon: printed by G. Parry, 1854. (NLS)

MORGAN, Lady Sydney (Owenson), 1776-1859, Irish novelist
The friends, foes and adventures of Lady Morgan / by William John Fitzpatrick. Dublin: W. B. Kelly, 1859. (Reprinted from the *Irish Quarterly Review*) (BL)
------- . Lady Morgan: her career, literary and personal. With a glimpse of her friends, and a word to her calumniators / by William John Fitzpatrick. London: Charles J. Skeet, 1860.

MORTIMER, Favell Lee (Bevan), 1802-78, religious writer
The author of 'The Peep of Day', being the life story of Mrs Mortimer / by her niece Louisa Clara Meyer ... London: Religious Tract Society, [1901].

MOSELEY, Elizabeth Kenworthy, 1839-57, religious girl
A wreath for an early grave, or a brief memorial of Elizabeth Kenworthy Moseley / by

John Skidmore. London: J. Mason, [185-?]. 12mo. (NLS)

MOULDING, Sarah, d.1871, St Alban's workhouse Christian
A brief sketch of the life of Mrs Moulding, an aged Christian in St Alban's Union Workhouse, chiefly derived from her own letters / by ... Henry Smith [*Incumbent of Christ Church, St Albans*]. London: William Hunt, 1872. 16mo. (NLS)

MOULE, Mary, 1801-73, Dorset clergyman's wife
The memory of the just is blessed: a brief memorial of Mrs Moule, of Fordington. Dorchester: printed by Henry Ling, 1877. photo.port.

MURRAY, Eliza, b.1829, Peterborough religious woman
Memoir of the late Eliza Murray, of Peterborough. Peterborough: E. B. Sergeant, 1866. (NLS)

NADEN, Constance Caroline Woodhill, 1858-99, poet, scientist
Constance Naden: a memoir / by William Richard Hughes. London: Bickers [etc.], 1890.

[NEWLAND (later POULSON), Sarah], b.1814, religious biography
My mother's memoir: a record of the Providence of God / by her son Edward Poulson. London: Houlston, 1888. Pamphlet. (NLS)

NEWTON, Adelaide Leaper, 1824-54, religious biography
A memoir of Adelaide Leaper Newton / by John Baillie. London: J. Nisbet, 1856; and many other editions.

NEWTON, Elizabeth, 1779-1865, wife of a Wesleyan minister
Memorials of the life of Mrs Newton / by her daughter. 2nd edition. London: Wesleyan Conference Office, 1868. 12mo.

NICHOLSON, Nancy (Jackson), 1788-1854, a disgusting and filthy woman - albeit a clergy wife - who died 'unrespected and unlamented'. A truly extraordinary narrative
The life of Mrs Nancy Nicholson, of Drax [Yorkshire], who died at Asselby, August 6 1854. Howden: printed by William Small, 1855. (NLS)

NONY, *Little*, 1868-79, child
God is love, or memorials of Little Nony. By her mother. Preface by Miss [Frances Ridley] Havergal. London: J. Nisbet, 1880. (NLS)

O., M. A., n.d., religious biography
'They shall be Mine, saith the Lord': a simple memorial of M.A.O.. A sequel to 'First fruits unto the Lord: a memorial of E.R. [q.v.].' / by Henry Smith [*Incumbent of Christ Church, St. Albans*]. London, [1870]. 16mo. (BL)

O'BRIEN, Attic, d.1883, Irish Catholic diarist and religious poet
Glimpses of a hidden life: memories of Attie O'Brien / gathered by Mary Anne O'Connell. Dublin: M.H. Gill, 1887. (NLS)

O'BRYAN, Mary, n.d., Bible Christian

The maiden preacher, wife and mother: life of Mary O'Bryan / by Samuel L. Thorne. London: Partridge, 1889. (BL)

OGILVY, Hon. Olivia Barbara (Kinnaird), d.1871, Scottish domestic biography

In memoriam: the Hon. Mrs Ogilvy. Printed for private circulation. Dundee, 1871. 12mo. (NLS)

O'HAGAN, Mary, n.d., Irish Catholic abbess

In memoriam. Mary O'Hagan, abbess and foundress of the Convent of Poor Clares, Kenmare. [By Mary Frances Cusack]. London: Burns, 1876.

OLIPHANT, Alice see OLIPHANT, Laurence

OLIVER, Mary (Chin), 1802-64, Baptist; kept a diary in 1851 and a boarding school for
young girls

Unobtrusive piety, being a memoir of Mrs Mary Oliver. With extracts from her diary and letters / by her husband [Edward James Oliver]. London: printed by J. Briscoe, 1865. 12mo.

OPIE, Amelia (Alderson), 1769-1853, Norfolk novelist and poet; Quaker

Memoir of Amelia Opie / by Cecilia Lucy Brightwell. London: Religious Tract Society, 1855.

P., Nannie, d.1856 aged 8 years, religious girl

Nannie P., or recollections of a good little girl. By her aunt. London Book Society, 1857. 12mo.

PACKWOOD, Alice (Wildsmith), c.1800-53, clergy wife

A Christian life and its close: a memorial of Alice, the wife of the Rev. J. Packwood, Curate of Sutton Coldfield, Warwickshire. [By J. Packwood]. Birmingham: Benjamin Hall, 1852. (NLS)

PALMERSTON, Emily Mary Temple (Lamb), Viscountess (later Countess Cowper, 1787-
1869, wife of the Prime Minister; political and society hostess

Lady Palmerston: a biographical sketch. [By Abraham Hayward]. London, 1872. (Reprinted from 'The Times')

PARRY, Lady Catharine Edwards, 1808-96, wife of the Arctic navigator

Catharine Edwards Parry: a record of her life, told chiefly in letters / compiled by her daughter [Louisa Hamond]. Printed for private circulation. Norwich: printed by Fletcher, [1899]. (B&J)

PATCHELL, Adelaide Maria (Stuart), d.1899, academically promising Irish religious
girl; drowned

By love serve one another: a memoir of Adelaide Maria Patchell, M.A. / by Margaret Black & Irene H. Barnes. London: Marshall Bros, 1901. (NLS)

PATTISON, Dorothy Wyndlow ('Sister Dora'), 1832-78, nursing sister and reformer;
sister of Mark Pattison

'Inasmuchas ...' the story of Sister Dora of Walsall (D. W. Pattison) / by Millicent Price. London: S.P.C.K., 1952.
------- . Sister Dora: a biography / by Margaret Lonsdale. London: C. Kegan Paul, 1880; 2nd edition. 1887.
-------- . Sister Dora: personal reminiscences of her later years. With some of her letters.

[Edited] by Ellen H. M. Ridsdale. Walsall: J. & W. Griffin, 1880.

PEARSON, Emma, d.187-?, religious biography
The hidden jewel: brief memorials of Emma, the beloved daughter of the Rev. Josiah Pearson. London: S.W. Partridge, [1877]. (B&J)

PEASE, Martha Lucy (Aggs), 1824-53, Quaker wife
A memoir of Martha Lucy Pease / by Mary Aggs. Printed for private circulation. 1859. 4to.

PEEL, Henrietta Maria, n.d., Yorkshire Moravian
Memorials of Henrietta Maria Peel, Crag Cottage, Windhill, Bradford. [For private circulation]. Bradford: printed by John Dale, 1864. 12mo. photo.port. (B&J)

PERFECT, Harriet, d.1875, disabled religious woman and religious writer
The message from the throne: a brief memoir of Harriet Perfect ... / by Anna Shipton. London: Morgan and Scott, [1876]. 12mo. photo.port. (NLS)

PETRE, Hon. Laura Maria (Stafford-Jerningham), n.d., nun
Life of the Hon. Mrs Edward Petre (Laura Stafford-Jerningham), in religion Sister Mary of St. Francis ... / by A. Mason Clarke. Leamington: Art and Book Company, 1899.

PETRIE, Irene Eleanor Verita, 1864-97, missionary in India with Church Missionary Society
Irene Petrie, missionary to Kashmir / by Mary Louisa Georgina Carus-Wilson. 2nd edition. London: Hodder and Stoughton, 1900.

PHILLIMORE, Lady Charlotte, 1813-92, aristocrat
In memoriam: Charlotte, Lady Phillimore. Born Dec. 4 1813 - Died Jan. 19 1892. Privately printed. [London: Church Printing Company, 1892].

PICKERING (afterwards STIRLING), Anna Maria Diana Wilhelmina (Spencer-Stanhope), 1824-1901, country life & society
Memoirs of Anna Maria Wilhelmina Pickering. Edited by her son [Percival] Spencer Pickering ... Privately printed. 1902. 2 volumes; London: Hodder & Stoughton, 1903.

PIGOTT, Emily Jessie (Kemp), 1851-1900, martyred missionary in China
Steadfast unto death, or martyred for China: memorials of Thomas Wellesley and Jessie Pigott / by C. A. Pigott. London: Religious Tract Society, 1903. (NLS)

PIGOTT, Emma, n.d., domestic reminiscences
Recollections of our mother Emma Pigott. Edited by her daughter Blanche Anne Frances Pigott. Privately printed. London: J. Nisbet, 1890.

PITT, Priscilla, n.d., Quaker
Memoir of Priscilla Pitt, the beloved wife of George Pitt, of Berkeley House, Mitcham, Surrey ... / compiled by her son. Printed for private circulation only. Croydon: printed by Jesse W. Ward, 1899. 16mo. (B&J)

[POCOCK, Sophia Elizabeth], n.d., religious girl
Sophie Elizabeth: in memoriam / by her father [William Willmer Pocock]. [Privately printed]. Guildford, [1868]. 16mo.

POOCK, Elizabeth, 1789-1858, Norfolk Baptist Pastor's wife
The doubter delivered, being a memoir of the late Mrs Elizabeth Poock. [By Thomas Poock]. London: Houlston & Wright, 1858. Pamphlet. (NLS)

POTTER, Sarah Elizabeth, n.d., religious biography
A brief memorial of Sarah Elizabeth Potter. [1860?] (B&J)

POULSON, Sarah, n.d., religious biography

My mother's memoir: a record of the Providence of God / by her son Edward Poulson. London: R. Banks, 1884.

POULSON, Sophy, n.d., girl

The life of Sophy Poulson: a true love story of a good and beautiful girl / by Edward Poulson. London: Reeves & Turner, [1887].

PRATTEN, Catherina Josepha, d.1895 aged 74 years, composer and guitarist

Reminiscences of Madame Sidney Pratten, guitariste [sic] and composer / by Frank Mott Harrison. Bournemouth: Barnes & Mullins, 1890. 12mo. (NLS)

PRIESTLEY, Mary Anne, d.187-, Wesleyan Minister's wife

A mother in Israel: memorials of Mary Anne Priestley, wife of the Rev. Joshua Priestley / by her husband [Joshua Priestley]. London: Wesleyan Conference Office, [1879]. 12mo.

PRODGER, Mrs. Samuel, d.1864 in childbed aged 26 years

A brief memoir of Benjamin Tatham, late Minister of the Gospel at Eastbourne. To which is added a selection of letters. And an account of Mrs S. Prodger. London: printed by W. H. Collingridge, [1866]. 12mo. (NLS)

PRUST, Mary Ann (Randall), 1804-66, infant and Sunday School worker

Memorials of the life of Mrs Edmund T[hornton] Prust, of Northampton / by her husband [Edmund Thornton Prust]. Printed for private circulation. London: printed by the Gresham Steam Press, [1866]. (NLS)

R., E., d.186-, religious woman from St Albans

First-fruits unto the Lord: a memorial of E. R., a Bible-woman of St. Albans / by Henry Smith [*Incumbent of Chirst Church, St Albans*]. London: William Hunt, 1866. 12mo. photo. port. (NLS) <u>see also</u> **O., N.A.**

'RACHEL' <u>see</u> **[HENDERSON, Rachel]**

RATCLIFFE, Jane Elizabeth, d.1864 aged 12 years, child

Our only child, or the life of Jane Elizabeth Ratcliffe / by her father Thomas Ratcliffe, Primitive Methodist Minister. London: William Lister, 1865. 16mo. (NLS)

RENTON, Agnes, 1781-1852, domestic biography

A brief memorial of the late Mrs Renton, of Tilstock Parsonage, Shropshire, especially in her declining day ... / by W[illiam] R[enton]. London: Wertheim & Macintosh, 1852. 16mo. (NLS)
------- . Memorial of Mrs Agnes Renton. [By A. R[enton]]. For the private use of the family. [Kelso: printed by J. & J. H. Rutherford, 1866]. (NC)

RICHARDS, Mary (David) 1832-78, Welsh Methodist Minister's wife; invalid

Strength perfected in weakness: memorials of Mary Richards. Edited by E. A. H. [i.e. Elizabeth Anna Gordon] ... London: Partridge, [1881]. (NLS)

RICHARDSON, Anna Deborah, n.d., autobiography; literary; travel

Memoir of Anna Deborah Richardson. With extracts from her letters. For private circulation only. Newcastle-upon-Tyne: printed by J. M. Carr, 1877. (B&J)

RIGG, Caroline, 1824-99, Guernsey woman

In memoriam: Caroline Rigg. Born May 14th 1824 - Died December 17th 1889. [By C.

Edith Rigg]. Printed for private circulation. London: Hazell, Watson and Viney, 1892. (B&J)

ROBERTS, <u>Mrs</u>. Joseph, n.d., Wesleyan Minister's wife
Youthful records of Mrs Roberts, wife of the Rev. Joseph Roberts, Wesleyan Minister. [By Martha Hill]. London: Wesleyan Book Society, 1864.

ROBERTSON, <u>Mrs</u>., d.1873, Church of England clergy wife
In memoriam. [Mrs Robertson, wife of the Rev. D. Robertson ...] By T. G. Horton ... [Wolverhampton: J. McD. Roebuck, 1873]. 16mo. Pamphlet. (B&J)

ROBSON, Elizabeth J. J. (Kirbell), d.1859, Quaker of Saffron Walden, Essex
A memoir of Elizabeth J. J. Robson, who died 15th of 10th Month 1859. London: A. W. Bennett, 1860.

ROBSON, Emma (Hodge), 1837-69, Primitive Methodist Minister's wife
Sunset at noonday: memorials of Mrs J. T. Robson, of Hull / by Joseph Wood. London: G. Lamb, [etc.], 1871. (NLS)

ROGERS, Mary, d.1853, religious biography
Mary Rogers, or a short and simple annal of the poor / by Thomas Harding. Printed for the author. Cross-Hill, Craven: printed by Robert Smith, 1859. 32mo. (NLS)

[ROSS, Margaret], 1796-1888, reformed Irish drinker
Old Margaret, or a saint at last / by J. Elder Cumming. London: Mr. Scott, [1890]. 12mo. (NLS)

ROSSETTI, Christina Georgina, 1830-94, poet; Tractarian
An appreciation of the late Christina Georgina Rossetti / by Brooke Foss Westcott ... London: S.P.C.K., 1899. Pamphlet. (NLS)
------- . A brief memoir of Christina G. Rossetti / by Ellen A. Proctor. With a preface / by William Michael Rossetti. London: S.P.C.K., 1895. 16mo.
------- . Christina Rossetti: a biographical and critical study / by Mackenzie Bell. London: Thomas Burleigh, 1898.

ROW, Hepzibah, 1839-64, religious girl
A brief memoir of Hepzibah Row / by her father [John Row]. Tunbridge: J. Row, 1864. 12mo. (NLS)

ROW, Susanna, n.d., domestic biography
Memoir of the late Miss Susanna Row, of Cardington, Bedfordshire ... / by Sarah Smith Jones. Hexham [Frome printed], [1867].

RUSSELL, <u>Lady</u> Elizabeth Anne (Rawdon), 1793-1874, French wife of Lord William Russell; traveller
Memoir of Lady William Russell / by Annie Jane Harvey. Privately printed. London: Chiswick Press, 1876.

RUSSELL, Frances Anna Maria (Elliot), <u>Countess Russell</u>, 1815-98, second wife of the Prime Minister Lord John Russell
Lady John Russell: a memoir. With selections from her diaries and correspondence. Edited by Desmond MacCarthy and Agatha Russell. London: Methuen, 1910.

RUTHQUIST, Alexina Mackay, 1848-92, Scottish Zenana missionary in India
A. Mackay Ruthquist, or singing the Gospel among Hindus and Gonds. [By Mrs J. W. Harrison]. London: Hodder and Stoughton, 1893. (NLS)

RYDER, Sophia, n.d., nun
A daughter of the Venerable Mother Pelletier, Sister Mary of the Sacred Heart [i.e.

Sophia Ryder]. For private circulation only. East Finchley: Convent of the Good Shepherd, 1902.

SANDEMAN, Margaret (Stewart), c.1802-83, Scottish landowner's wife and Free Churchwoman
Memoir of Mrs Stewart Sandeman, of Bonskeid and Springland / by her daughter [Margaret Fraser Barbour]. London: J. Nisbet, 1883. (NLS)

SCHIMMELPENNINCK, Mary Anne (Galton), 1778-1856, miscellaneous writer; Wesleyan, then Quaker, finally a Moravian
Life of Mary Anne Schimmelpenninck, author of 'Select Memoirs of Port Royal', and other works. Edited by her relation Christiana C. Hankin. London: Longman, [etc.], 1858. 2 volumes; 2nd edition. 1858.

SCOTT, Alicia Anne (Spottiswood), Lady John Douglas Scott, 1809-1900, song writer & traditionalist
The burial of Lady John Scott, authoress of 'Annie Laurie', 16 March 1900. Glasgow, [1900]. (NLS)

SCOTT, Mary, n.d., daughter(?) of a clergyman
Memoir of Mary Scott / by Thomas Scott, of Aston Sandford. Birmingham, [1855?]. 32mo.

SCOTT-MONCRIEFF, Mary, 1811-86, Scottish domestic biography
Mary Scott-Moncrieff. Born June 9th 1811 - Died August 27th 1886. [Privately printed]. [Portobello: printed by T. Adams, c.1886]. (NLS)

SEEBOHM, Esther (Wheeler), d.1864 aged 66, Quaker; in North America
Private memoirs of B[enjamin] and E[sther] Seebohm. Edited by their sons. London: Provost, 1873.

SEELEY, Elizabeth Phebe, 1844-?83, missionary in Syria
In the light: brief memorials of Elizabeth Phebe Seeley / by her sister ... London: British Syrian Schools and Bible Mission, 1884. (NLS)

SEWELL, Mary (Wright), 1797-1884, writer of moral tales for children; Quaker
The life and letters of Mrs Sewell / by Mary Bayly. London: J. Nisbet, 1889.

SHAW, Elizabeth (Flamank), 1773-1872 aged 99, Wesleyan Methodist
'Long life and peace': memorials of Mrs Elizabeth Shaw, for eighty-seven years a member of the Wesleyan Methodist Church / by Robert C. Barratt. London: Wesleyan Conference Office, 1875. (NLS)

SHAW, Ellen Prestage, 1823-86, religious biography
Outlines of a gentle life: a memorial sketch of Ellen P. Shaw. Edited by her sister Maria Vernon Graham Havergal. London: J. Nisbet [etc.], 1887. (NLS)
    see also **HAVERGAL SISTERS**

SHEPHERD, Annette, 1798-1876 religious woman; anti-slaver; Staffordshire
Memoir of Miss Shepherd, of Cheadle, Staffordshire / by Buckley Yates. Manchester: Tubbs and Brook, 1876. (NLS)

SHIRREFF, Emily Anne Eliza, 1814-97, educationalist, especially of Froebel and kindergartens